Management in Education
Reader 1

The Open University
Faculty of Educational Studies

Management in Education (E321)
Course Team

Carolyn Baxter
Oliver Boyd-Barrett
Lydia Campbell
Sheila Dale
Digby Davies
Lance Dobson
Tony Gear (chairman)
Philip Healy
Donald Holms
Vincent Houghton (deputy chairman)
Christine King
Royston McHugh
Reg Melton
John Miller
Edward Milner
Colin Morgan
Robert Nicodemus
Gerald Normie
Gwynn Pritchard
Adam Westoby

Management in Education Reader 1

The Management of Organizations and Individuals

Edited by
Vincent Houghton, Royston McHugh and
Colin Morgan for the Management in Education
Course Team at The Open University

Ward Lock Educational
in association with
The Open University Press

ISBN 0 7062 3469 3 paperback
      0 7062 3468 5 hardback

First published 1975
Reprinted 1976

Set in 10 on 11 point Plantin and printed by
Willmer Brothers Limited, Birkenhead
for Ward Lock Educational
116 Baker Street, London W1M 2BB
Made in England

Contents

Acknowledgments

The Open University and publishers would like to thank the following for permission to reproduce copyright material. All possible care has been taken to trace ownership of the selections included and to make full acknowledgment for their use.

Administrative Science Quarterly for "The management of interdepartmental conflict: a model and review" by Richard E. Walton and John M. Dutton; Allyn and Bacon for "The individual and organization: some problems of mutual adjustment" by Chris Argyris from *Education Administration and the Behavioral Sciences: A Systems Perspective* by M. M. Milstein and J. A. Belasco (eds) 1973; *American Education* for "Organization development in schools" by Terry Newell; Athlone Press for "Theory about organization: a new perspective and its implications for schools" by T. Barr Greenfield from the forthcoming title *Administering Education: International Challenge* by Meredydd Hughes (ed) and for "Role theory and educational administration" by Peter S. Burnham from *Education Administration and the Social Sciences* by G. Baron and W. Taylor (eds) 1969; *Berkeley Journal of Sociology* for "The three types of legitimate rule" by Max Weber, translated by Hans Gerth; *Education Administration Quarterly* for "Decisional participation and teacher satisfaction" by James A. Belasco and Joseph A. Alutto; *Educational Research* for "Office and expertise in the secondary school" by Leonard E. Watson; reprinted from *Higher Education* (1972) no. 2 pp. 207–19, with permission of Elsevier Scientific Publishing Company, Amsterdam, "Decision type, structure and process evaluation: a contingency model" by Marvin W. Peterson; Eric Hoyle for "The study of schools as organizations"; *Industrial Training International* for "Managing organizational change" by W. J. Reddin; *Intellect: The National Review of Professional Thought* for "The demise of administrative mystique" by Cameron Fincher; *International Review of Administrative Sciences*, IIAS, Brussels for "The nature and contents of management" by Carlos Paramés; reproduced by special permission from *The Journal of Applied Behavioral Science* vol. 6 no. 1 pp. 3–19, 1970, NTL Institute, "Leadership style, confidence in management and job satisfaction" by Philip J. Sadler; this article first appeared in *New Society*, London, the weekly review of the social sciences: "Industry in a new age" by Tom Burns; copyright The Open University for "Exchange and conflict in the school" by Harry L. Gray, "The management of educational change: towards a conceptual framework" by Ray Bolam, "Organizational analysis in education: an empirical study of a school" by Joyce Oldham, and

University of Leeds Institute of Education (June 1956), Researches and Studies 14, with a postcript by the author (1974), "Some aspects of the 'headmaster tradition' " by George Baron; *Organizational Behaviour and Human Performance* for "Toward a behavioral theory of leadership" by Gary Yukl; by permission of the Oxford University Press, Oxford, *Sociology* vol. 7 1973, "Decision making on the school curriculum: a conflict model" by John Eggleston © Oxford University Press 1973; *Moral Education* for "The school as a social system" by B. Sugarman; *Public Administration* (London) for "On decisions and decision making" by P. H. Levin; *Public Administration Review* for "The dissimilarity of educational administration" by John Walton, and for "Models of man and adminstrative theory" by Alberto Guerreiro Ramos; Routledge and Kegan Paul Ltd for "The professional-as-administrator: the case of the secondary school head" by Meredydd G. Hughes from the forthcoming title *The Role of the Head* by R. S. Peters (ed); Teachers College Press for "Administrative theory and change in organizations" by Daniel E. Griffiths from *Innovation in Education* by M. B. Miles (ed) 1964; University of London Institute of Education, *London Education Review* summer 1974 vol. 3 no. 2, "Professionality, professionalism and control in teaching" by Eric Hoyle.

General Introduction

This book of readings, with its companion volume, has been prepared by members of a Course Team at the Open University as an integral part of the third-level course, *Management in Education*, offered by the Faculty of Educational Studies. It has been difficult to choose a representative selection of articles for this subject area, as there is a considerable amount of material available which is directly relevant and of similar standing, and even more material which is peripherally relevant. It is also difficult to achieve a degree of coherence among the articles which have been selected, because the whole area of studies in the management of education lacks the coherent structure which would be available in longer-established discipline areas. Indeed, it must be a clear duty of the editors to reflect the state of current knowledge, with its conflicts and confusions, rather than impose an order which, however neat and convenient, bears little relation to reality.

We are also conscious that management studies, together with other social sciences, may well be in a "watershed" situation. Some of the articles chosen reflect a sense of unease about the state of existing explanation, and some authors focus upon areas which they claim need increasing attention if progress is to be made. Despite the fluidity of the present situation there is a need to bring together ideas and statements germane to educational management, because the scale of investment in education and the debate about greater participation in educational decision-making, both by the professionals and by the community at large, reflect an increasing concern for greater managerial efficiency and accountability.

Allied to this, we would argue for a commitment from all concerned to work for the improvement of management approaches and techniques in order to facilitate learning and development opportunities for others. However, we do not advocate the improvement of techniques alone but would wish to see them located within a coherent ideology and value system.

The division of our material into two Readers is to some extent an arbitrary process, but the general emphasis in Reader 1 is on management as related to organizations and individuals, whilst Reader 2 is concerned more with the systematic application of tools and techniques, drawn from the management sciences and economics, to educational situations.

This Reader therefore focuses on people behaving within organizations, stressing the social context of management and the need to take into account relevant factors which may be within the organization itself,

1

in the local community, or which emanate from a national or international source.

The Reader is divided into four parts, of which the first—"Management and Educational Administration"—is a scene-setting for the whole Reader. The second section is entitled "Aspects of Organizational Theory". As there is such a flood of articles in this area, it is inevitable that any choice should seem invidious; we do hope, nevertheless, that ours is reasonably representative. As well as the theoretical aspects, we have included the kind of case material which can give life to such theory. It is the third section, "Individuals and Organizations", which represents most clearly the view of man, organizational man, which we suggest is most appropriate to this Reader. We are concerned with responsibilities and hierarchies; genetic endowment and personal liberty or development have to find their place elsewhere in the course. The final section is entitled "Theory and Practice" and is very strongly school oriented. In examining current practice and the research which has been made on that practice, it is important to try to place the *mores* of the time within some kind of ethical framework. It is never enough to accept an improved *status quo* (with a more important place for oneself) as the main objective, any more than it would be enough to keep up with or anticipate whatever would be fashionable.

The editors of both Reader 1 and Reader 2 would like to express their gratitude and appreciation to Rhiannon Davies for her unstinting efforts during the editing of the manuscripts.

1 Management and Educational Administration

INTRODUCTION
In the first article, "The Demise of Administrative Mystique", Dr Fincher's argument is concerned with the fact that the mounting costs of public higher education have produced a pattern which "is sufficiently discontinuous to merit description as a revolution". He continues: "successful administrators now must hold their positions in accordance with the forces that shape administrative decisions". He concludes by cautioning us against "specious forms of expertise" and against the indiscriminate use of impressive-sounding jargon. The Reader commences, without apology, with a salutary warning.

This is followed by a short article by Paramés which attempts a definition of management. Then comes one by Walton who is interested, very correctly and importantly, in the differences between educational administration and administration in general. He suggests that the pursuit of leisure is one objective which may be in the realm of educational administration but can hardly be found in general administration. He concludes with the Aristotelian notion that the life of the intellect may bring no rewards beyond itself.

The article by Levin is concerned with the establishment of a model of decision making and decision makers. It is a deceptive article in that, if it is thought to be easily understood, it is probably not understood at all. Perhaps the nodal sentence of the whole article is the following: "the key ... lies in the fact that in forming a resolve upon action decision makers become bound by their resolve". This refers to the importance of commitment, whether it is a personal commitment, a philosophical or political one, or one which arises as a result of the rejection of the commitment of others which is being forced upon one. We can only advise that this article be read extremely carefully; the argument has been succinctly worked out and it would be a gross impertinence to try to summarize it briefly in this introduction. The paper by Peterson is more concerned with the taxonomic questions which arise in decision making. It is followed by the final article in the section, by Ramos, which stresses the importance of the image of man and looks closely at the traditional models. He refers in some detail to the work of Presthus and adds a third model, that of "parenthetical man", to the two types suggested by that author. Ramos's article is regarded as especially important by the three editors and represents a point of view with which they have much sympathy. This conclusion to the section will be regarded by some as sounding a note of optimism, qualified or otherwise; but for others it may suggest a counsel of despair.

1.1   The Demise of Administrative Mystique

Cameron Fincher

In their well-received book, *The Managerial Revolution in Higher Education* (1966), Francis E. Rourke and Glenn E. Brooks contended that the mounting costs of public higher education have provoked an emerging pattern of managerial and fiscal restrictions by state agencies. They believe that the pattern is sufficiently discontinuous to merit description as a revolution.

Their survey disclosed an increasing concern with the varying costs of educational programs and the effective uses of campus facilities. The management of universities was becoming increasingly rationalized through conscious efforts to plan the future development of institutions, to relate educational means to educational ends, and to gain a maximum return from resource use. Bureaucracy was not as extensive as first thought, but they did find evidence of "new styles in university management" in which the general conduct of university affairs was more public, and decision-making less intuitive.

The major implication of the managerial revolution is the pervasive belief that management methods are so highly rationalized that they can be dissociated from their origins and transferred from one organizational setting to another. More accurately, there is the growing belief that managerial concepts are unitary and trans-organizational.

Since 1966, the managerial revolution has continued with no signs of slackening. There are numerous implications of the revolution, however, that have not been drawn carefully and that are not understood fully by either those in administrative positions or those who are affected directly by administrative decisions. It is not the interchangeability of administrative functions that constitutes the major implications but rather the changing nature of administrative process. The similarities of industrial, commercial, financial, military, and other public organizations are often obvious, but the truly interchangeable executive may remain more myth than fact. Rourke and Brooks did not find evidence that "new techniques of management would bring a new type of machine-tooled decision-maker into positions of leadership in university administration", but they

Source: *Intellect* (Summer 1973) Vol. 101, Part 2350, pp. 499–501.

did find that top-level administrators were more interested in creating and using specialized staff services.

There is no doubt that the changing functions of academic administration are producing a demand for more explicit and rigorous decision-making on the part of college and university administrators. The traditional model of the academic man who meets his administrative responsibilities with broad experience, mature judgment, and good grace no longer is regarded as viable for the organizational complexities of the modern university. Charisma, if such a concept is still meaningful, is no longer a compelling factor in either the selection or appraisal of administrators. Personal charm, influence, and persuasion remain as residual variables or extraneous factors, but they are not the predominant force that they once were.

The major outcome of the managerial revolution, therefore, is the demise of what may be regarded as administrative mystique. The demise is not due to any serendipitous disclosure that the administrator indeed does don his trousers one leg at a time. Nor is it merely the intense pressures of student protest, faculty restiveness, legislative hostility, or campus disruption that make the administrator more nearly human. It is the changing nature of academic administration itself that removes from the individual sufficient opportunity to maintain any semblance of special knowledge or unique method that could be regarded as mystique.

In the past, the source of mystique in administration has been the fortuitous role of subjective opinion and intuitive judgment in decision-making. When decisions proved in consequence to be highly effective, the mystique was enhanced. When decisions did not prove effective, they readily could be rationalized, because the decision-making steps could not be retraced. This was in keeping with romanticized or mythological notions of leadership, and helped to create an image of uncommon talent or special gifts—when the administrator was right.

Bureaucracy, with its reliance on fixed jurisdiction, sought to eliminate mystique and to substitute experience as a basis for decision. The location of a decision at its lowest hierarchical level and the rule of exception served the need for logic and consistency. It also provided a rationale for developing administrative sophistication through the accumulative experience that could be gained by time-in-grade and up-through-the-ranks promotion. This produced a conception of professional experience that, in due time, generated its own mystique.

The current demise of mystique is caused by a strong shift from a reliance and emphasis on professional experience to a demand for explicit technique. The shift began with notions of administrative theory that provided explanatory concepts for administrative behavior. It is intensified by the development of analytic skills that diminish radically the role of subjective opinion, intuitive judgment, and previous experience. The continuing abolition of mystique means that there is, for the moment, no special lure or attraction for administrative positions, and that, once positioned, the administrator can make no pretense of a special calling. Successful administrators now must hold their positions in accordance with the forces that shape administrative decisions, their understanding of issues and problems that are inherent in the administrative process, and their command of a host of managerial techniques and procedures. For the latter, it will be their understanding of limitations, as well as promises, that determine their command.

The dominance of technique over experience has been accelerated by the development of accounting systems that permit a more meaningful fiscal control of resources and expenditures; the ascent of behavioristic concepts and methods in dealing with the human aspects of organizational life; the popularity of schema-graphic methods that permit better visualization of decision processes; and the expansiveness of mathematical-computer methods that facilitate ready access to quantified information about operations and procedures.

The development of sophisticated fiscal and budgetary systems reflects the increasing use of budgets as an execution of administrative policy. Budgets no longer are perceived as an encumbrance to administrative action, but as a highly suitable vehicle for bringing organizational goals into reality. With the increasing interplay of behavioral science in management, there has been an intensified awareness of the importance of organizational theory and a receptivity to such movements as organization development in which the resistance to change is reduced through behavioristic concepts and methods.

The use of schema-graphic methods began with the organization chart as a means of showing the relationships and line of authority among personnel within the organization. Gantt bars have been followed by flow charts and the sophistication of network analysis. PERT and Critical Path Method are indicative of the readiness with which the use of schematic methods clarify operational procedure and depict operational structure.

The rapid expansion of computer technology has made vast strides in the areas of operations research, institutional research, and computer models based on corporate-planning concepts. Simulation has proven quite adaptable to the analytical processes involved in program-budgeting and resource allocation management. Indeed, it is the technological progress in the processing of information and the development of management information systems in industry and business that would seem to cast the most serious doubt on the traditional role of academic administrators.

The two major forces involved in the changing nature of administrative decision-making may be identified as quantitative analysis and behaviorism. Combined in a somewhat synergistic manner, they have moved decision-making an appreciable distance from former notions of professional experience and mature judgment. Computer technology has permitted an increasingly sophisticated analysis of quantified variables, while behaviorism as a conceptual vantage point has increased the concern with specific, concrete events.

The interaction of quantitative analysis and behavioral concepts has produced an interesting assortment of management concepts that now have been introduced into academic administration. A matrix of these concepts would show management information systems, planning-programming-budgeting systems, and cost-benefit analysis as being quite high in the quantitative dimension. Administrative theory, organization development, and management-by-objectives would not require intensive quantitative analysis, but would rank quite high in the behavioral dimension. Operations research, corporate-planning models, and simulation would have both quantitative and behavioral components that are quite strong. The major thrust within the matrix of management concepts, nonetheless, is decision by technique, as opposed to decision by experience. It is this shifting emphasis that denotes the importance of management science for academic administration.

In the shifting emphasis from experience to technique, there is a change in the conceptualization of the administrator's role. This change is from a role of ideational and collegial leadership to a rapidly expanding concern with resource management and executive decision-making. Also implied is a difference not only in how the decision is made, but what it is made about. The shift is from a concern with course contents, curricula requirements, and faculty relations to an ends-orientation in which the assessment of results, the allocation of fiscal and physical resources, a monitoring function, and continuous planning cycles are predominant.

Implicit in the changing role of the administrator is a centralization of decision-making responsibility and authority. Since management techniques have extensive informational and procedural requirements, the locus of decision cannot be distributed broadly. Inherent in the technique is a required diversity of expertise that necessitates some form of group decision, involving either an administrative team or a presidential cabinet.

It should be evident that information is an essential component of the techniques involved. Decisions are made on the basis of more specific information about the factors involved, but there is no direct implication that such decisions will produce a more significant change in organizational function. In other words, the procedures permit administrative decision-making on a more technical basis, but with little assurance that the decisions are about more important academic matters. Gains have been made in the degree of formalization, specificity, and rigorousness, but not necessarily in importance.

The advent of managerial thinking in academic administration, therefore, is not without disadvantages. There are benefits from any efforts to make administrative decisions more explicit, systematic, and effective. There is even better reason to remove from the administrator any cloak of mystery as to how he functions, what purposes he serves, and how he arrives at decisions, policies, and plans. Yet, the transfer of managerial techniques from other organizations may prove disadvantageous in many respects.

Management concepts, as presently propagated in business and industry, have been influenced greatly by the U. S. Department of Defense and other governmental agencies, posing some difficulty in the reconciliation of goals and objectives. Academic administration long has been torn between models of public administration and business management, but whether academic administration should be developed along the lines of business management or public administration never has been decided adequately. Most institutions of higher education probably are administered by an uncritical mixture of concepts and techniques borrowed from both fields. The usefulness of each model undoubtedly changes from problem to problem and in terms of certain institutional traditions, as well as administrator preferences. It is not uncommon, therefore, to find rigid adherence to one model in juxtaposition with slavish imitation of the other. That academic administrators need not choose between the two should be obvious. That they have been able to borrow and merge the best of two worlds is highly doubtful.

When the managerial practices of business or industrial organizations are borrowed by academic administrators, they involve a certain burden of proving equivalency, equipotentiality, or transferability. The same burden is placed on academic administrators who would plead the special or unique status of educational institutions. They must demonstrate satisfactorily that management practices and concepts are not applicable to the demands of administration in higher education. Even modifications or refurbishments must be examined with the same criticalness.

One of the more serious implications of the changing situation in administration, however, is the exact locus of the decision itself. It is well to emphasize that administrators cannot relinquish administrative responsibility for decisions. Yet, the expanding use of management support staffs implies that technique well may exercise an undesirable dominance over knowledge and experience. Group problem-solving approaches to a decision may conceal the actual source of the decision in ways unsuspected by participants. Given a choice between intuitive grasps of certain situations and highly specific information that may or may not be relevant, there is no way of knowing which way the decision will tip. Numerous problems remain to be worked out concerning the best use of technical or management support personnel in administrative decision-making.

Systems analysts are quick to emphasize that judgment and intuition still must play a part in decision-making, and virtually all organizational theorists agree that decision-making responsibility must be vested in persons and not in procedure. Yet, the exact nature and function of decisions remain elusive. Despite the advances that have been made in information sciences, there are no adequate standards for the utility of

9

information in the decision-making process. Management sciences can provide an abundance of detailed information, but they cannot provide all the information that might be desired, and they consistently may fail to provide the information most relevant to the decision at hand.

For these reasons, the limitations, as well as the advantages, of management concepts and practices must be recognized by academic administrators. We must protect ourselves not merely against the jargon, but also against the specious forms of expertise that provide much in the way of procedure and little in the way of substance for decision-making. An adequate administrative theory that would be relevant for academic leadership is yet to be developed. There is much to learn from a critical examination of theory and practice in other organizational settings, and rapid progress has been made in the development of management science as such. There is a need, nonetheless, for academic administrators to examine their own professional roles and to articulate in a more meaningful fashion their own purposes and functions.

REFERENCE

ROURKE, F. E. and BROOKS, G. E. (1966) *The Managerial Revolution in Higher Education*, Johns Hopkins University Press.

1.2 The Nature and Contents of Management

Carlos Paramés

"Management" has many meanings, even in English, and can be used in a very broad sense. Though this is to be expected with a word expressing all-inclusive concern for the modern rationalization, some attempt to define it is required, particularly as Burnham's Theory and more recent observations stimulate wider discussion. For instance, some consider that development is a question of organizing ability rather than of means, and maintain that management is the most significant instrument of progress in the United States. At all events management science and technology are taught in all the larger universities there and study and research in them are very intensive, in the field of public administration as well as of business management. The formal and in-service training of the principal Federal officials is centred on management. The movement is gradually spreading to other countries owing to the world-wide interest in ensuring better management and appropriate organization.

The literature on the subject gives various indications as to what management is. It may be deduced from the French *Traité de science administrative* that management includes administrative management and the related technical problems, research as applied to the objectives of an organization, the promotion of trade and market studies, financial and personnel administration, and methods of action. According to other sources more closely connected with United States tendencies, management implies direction, planning, programming, regulating, financial, personnel, and equipment management, output and time control, the conduct of meetings, and upward as well as downward communications. In the United Kingdom, the Fulton Report considers managers "responsible for organization, directing staff, planning the progress of work, setting standards of attainment and measuring results, reviewing procedures and quantifying different courses of action". Apart from some slight differences the ideas are very similar. Two positions have recently been adopted in Spain. One describes management activity as an aggregate of functions and techniques of management, and the other

Source: *International Review of Administrative Sciences* (1971) Vol. 37 (English Summary of Spanish paper).

stresses the fact that management is a cross-roads for heterogeneous knowledge, science, and technology of a pragmatic nature, available for those who have to make decisions and solve problems, and that any more precise definition is hazardous.

A few lessons and conclusions may be drawn from the above:

Management concerns the activities of the principal and the exercise of his responsibilities.

It is a profession and not a discipline and can be used in all human activities.

Management places administrative work in a new setting in which it is judged solely on results.

It is less a matter of doing things than of getting them done, and thus calls for teamwork.

It is practised in specialized units and specially in task units.

In considering the contents of management, there is first a series of quantitative analysis techniques for the preparation and the control of policies. Recent work carried out by the Committee on Administrative Practices of ILAS distinguishes nineteen techniques divided into three categories: budgetary programming techniques (budget-cost analysis, cost-effectiveness analysis, cost-unity analysis, value analysis, performance budgeting, budgetary control, PPBS), quantitative management techniques based on mathematics (systems analysis, management by objectives, project evaluation, PERT and CPM, operational research), and various accounting techniques.

This leads to an examination of the role of management in the training of civil servants. In 1968, those mainly responsible for civil service training in Europe met at the Higher School of Public Administration at Caserta, Italy, to consider the question, which was again discussed the following year at Alcala de Henares. From the discussions, a clear tendency emerged to include various subjects related to management in the wider sense—quantitative analysis techniques, planning and programming, O & M, operational research, and information processing—in the programmes of training seminars.

However, the controversial question arises whether modern management methods can be applied in public administration. Nevertheless, judging from the conclusions of the United Nations Interregional Seminar on the Use of Modern Management Techniques in the Public Administration of Developing Countries held at Washington from 27 October to 6 November 1970, four sectors seem to claim special attention: data and other information processing systems, planning and budgeting, operational research, and human relations. This confirms the work of other organizations, apart from variations in the detailed lists of techniques. If variations of approach are also disregarded, a list can be made of what is generally recognized to be essential: analysis of results, systems analysis, data processing, operational research, O & M, PPBS, and the utilization of mathematical or econometric models. Recourse should at the same time be had to psychosociology and futurology in order to mitigate the inhuman coldness of the techniques.

1.3 The Dissimilarity of Educational Administration

John Walton

ABSTRACT

Educational administration is conceived as a public form of general administration. Its dissimilarity consists of the fact that to some extent its responsibilities do not extend to the products of the educational institutions. Rather, they end at the point where they maintain satisfactory conditions for leisure activities. In this respect educational administration may serve as a model for the governance of an increasing number of organizations, both public and private.

How does educational administration differ from administration in general? This question has been often raised, and it is particularly relevant when proposals arise to establish a graduate college devoted to the art and science of administration. The discussion that follows attempts to answer it by showing how educational administration differs in one important aspect from administration in general. However, it may well be that this distinction will not long continue, not because educational administration will lose this characteristic feature, but because other kinds of administration will be compelled to adopt it. Therefore, the unique aspect of educational administration may serve as a predictor of the future of administration in general.

Readers who are familiar with my earlier attempts to make some sense out of educational administration (Walton, 1959) may make a surprised guess that I have had second thoughts about the notion that "administration is everywhere the same". It is true that I have had second thoughts, but they have not changed my original conception of the administrative phenomenon; at one level of abstraction it is possible to conceive of administration as the same activity in all organizations. Moreover, it is important to do so. There are advantages in a *formal* sense, and it is a less parochial way of viewing administration than if we looked at it first and only through its relationships with substantive activities of educational organizations.

However, at another level of consideration, we may think of adminis-

---

Source: *Public Administration Review* (Jan.–Feb. 1970), pp. 56–9.

tration as varying with the purposes and substantive activities of organizations. This distinction is no mere sophistry. An analogue may be found in the ways we discuss "the role of the school". At one level we can view the role of the school as invariant, for example, the purpose of formal education, under all circumstances, is to transmit the cultural heritage. But we may also talk about the school as changing its role; for example, a school system that abolishes its vocational programs and becomes entirely college preparatory can be said to have changed its role. Similarly, educational administration can be analyzed at one level to include such general administrative functions as the discernment of organizational purposes, staffing, coordinating, and public relations; or it may be defined in less formal and more specific language: recruiting instructors in business education, scheduling an overcrowded urban high school on two shifts, electioneering for the passage of a bond issue, or raising money for an independent college. Both approaches to the study of administration are useful, the first in a more general, theoretical sense, and the second in a more operational sense.

It is in the latter sense that educational administration is discussed below.

ALLEGED DIFFERENCES

First, two frequently alleged differences between educational and other kinds of administration should be examined carefully to determine whether or not they have been exaggerated. It has been argued perceptively and persuasively, if not precisely, that educational administration, having joined "the cult of efficiency", brought into educational organizations certain inappropriate characteristics of business and military administration (Callahan, 1962). The imitation hypothesis is certainly plausible, and one that is well-nigh irresistible in attempting to account for some general administrative phenomena that are considered inappropriate in educational organizations. But we are compelled to invoke other hypotheses. Perhaps, for example, bureaucracy in educational organizations came about because of the same conditions in these organizations that made it necessary in the army and in business. And the phrase "cult of efficiency" reflects a strange and curious bias. Efficiency can hardly be called a cult; it is rather one of the most fundamental concepts in Western Society (see Tawney, 1926). Moreover, it is a very versatile concept and can be applied to all kinds of organizations without violating any of the other values that are held in higher rank than those attached to it. Efficiency simply means that we attempt to accomplish the objectives we want with as little expenditure of resources as possible, not that we conserve resources by sacrificing our goals.

A second alleged difference between educational and other kinds of administration is that the former is responsible for the accomplishment of intangible and remote results; other kinds of administration can measure their degree of success. The school administrator, for example, cannot tell how successful his schools have been in preventing crime, unemployment, and other forms of negative utility; whereas, the industrial manager can usually measure his product and his profit. This is patently not always so. Educational administrators can know in a gross kind of a way how successful their schools are, and in industry in modern technological society the number of criteria of success has increased, including some that are not readily measurable; for example, modern industry's gesture toward attempting to improve the urban situation. But even if this difference were as great as it is alleged to be, it would not make any theoretical difference; educational administration has as one principal criterion of success the achievement of purposes that are external to the organizational activities. That the accomplishment of these purposes cannot be precisely evaluated is a cause of frustration, not of ideological differences.

Now for one way in which educational administration differs from administration in general, let us look first at one aspect of the rational, bureaucratic pattern of administration which prevails in all organizations. It is an assumed causal nexus between means and ends, and an assumption that the ends, purposes, or goals of administration are ultimately external to the means. Making a profit, producing elegant motor cars, forcing the enemy to surrender, eradicating poverty, or curing cancer are all goals or purposes that have been adopted by gigantic organizations and their administrators. It is assumed also, but not dogmatically, that all the "workers" in these organizations are doing what they do in order to achieve these goals, although it is now admitted that subjectively these workers may be motivated by a variety of incentives: money, the possibility of fame, belief in the morality of work, association with other workers, and intrinsic interest in the work. This conception of administration fits what we know about educational administration up to a point; for example, a school superintendent may give high priority to a kind of education (the means) that may reasonably be expected to equip inner-city youth with salable skills (the end). But this is not a completely accurate description of educational administration. It does not apply, for instance, to a great deal of college and university administration. Wherein lies the difference? We shall attempt a detailed explanation.

If we take the phrase "education for leisure time" as one of the purposes or goals of educational organizations we are still adhering to the "rational" pattern of administration. The inference is that through some means we can and should provide people with the knowledge, attitudes, and skills that will enable them to make pleasant and profitable use of their leisure time; and it is our parenthetical observation here that gives the first intimation of the fallacy of this kind of reasoning—the leisure time in turn is to be "utilized" for some purposes extrinsic to it. I say fallacy because the classical definition of leisure is time spent on activities for their own sake. Moreover, it is just as appropriate to speak of education as leisure as it is to speak of it as a means of preparing for leisure.

"It is clear then," writes Aristotle in *Politics*,

> that these are branches of learning and education which we must study merely with a view to leisure spent in intellectual activity, and these are to be valued for their own sake; whereas those kinds of knowledge which are useful in business are to be deemed necessary, and exist for the sake of other things.

Etymologically, the word "school" derives from σχολη meaning leisure. Ancient and classical philosophers recognized very early that much of education is leisure, i.e. pursued for its own intrinsic value. And in modern society the problem of the nature of leisure is extremely acute. It must be obvious to all scholars in education that the expansion of formal education is, to some degree at least, due to the modern necessity for providing, not education for leisure, but education *as* leisure. And this is true notwithstanding the pressure to conceive of formal education solely as a productive institution "to shape the human resources of the nation so as to 'fit' the economic and military requirements of the United States."[1]

What are the implications of this theory of education for administration of educational institutions? Simply these: educational administration must formulate its goals in terms of both the product of the schools, colleges, and universities—e.g. the reading ability of their graduates, the level of vocational and professional competence, or the quality of research produced—and the provision of conditions for intellectual leisure, that is, the pursuit of intrinsically valuable teaching, learning, and research.[2] These activities are not to be construed as having only negative utility, e.g. keeping youth off the labor market and rescuing old age from boredom, but as a positive good. Consequently, education in the ghettos and in developing countries as well as in modern, affluent societies should provide for intrinsically valuable experiences. Education as leisure is a human right.

Now, if we look again at educational administration, we observe that at one level educational administration still fits into the pattern of administration in general: it consists of selecting and maintaining organizational means for the accomplishment of desired objectives. These objectives consist of both "products" of the educational organization, e.g. literate citizens, skilled workmen, *et al.*, and "working" conditions for leisure that is intrinsically valuable. The difference between these two kinds of objectives will bear further analysis, particularly with respect to the relationship between non-administrative means and ends; here we can consider them both as ends accomplished in part by administrative means.

Obviously, this administrative model does not coincide with one of the most currently popular organizational models, that of "inputs" and "outputs", since in an organization devoted to leisure there are no outputs. This illustrates how administrative theory can correct organizational theory, and it also shows how educational administration may both differ from and give direction to other kinds of administration.

Business, public, and military administration rarely adopt the conditions effective for the pursuit of leisure as a positive goal. Public administration may support parks, stadia, marinas, concerts, libraries, and other enterprises wherein leisure activities are encouraged, but it usually justifies these activities by subsequent effects; for example, the improvement of health and morality, better informed citizens, or by the negative utilitarian criterion that they keep people out of mischief—the bread and circuses theory. However, it may not be long before almost all organizations will incorporate into their purposes and goals conditions for the pursuit of activities for leisure; and they will be compelled to evaluate their results by how pleasurable, satisfying, meaningful, and intrinsically valuable these activities are.

At this point it might be well to point out that educational administration, because of the relative acceptability of the pursuit of the intellectual life for its own sake, is in an excellent position to lead the way. It is important, however, that we develop intelligible methods of discourse about the intrinsically valuable. The existentialists, the contemplatives, and the mystics have made a start, but usually not in language that "sound" administrators will want to employ.

PROFESSIONAL EDUCATION

Since the purpose of this discourse is to indicate how this, or any other, alleged dissimilarity of educational administration will affect the curriculum for the art and science of administration, I shall close by indicating in outline what I think the professional education of educational administrators should be.

Primarily, I think it should be modern management; public management, perhaps, but management. It is nothing short of quaint to assume that any one man can comprehend and control the complexities of professional organizations[3] (more and more of them are becoming professional), and, in any event, the administrator's energies are consumed by organizational demands. Moreover, there appears to be nothing in the dissimilarity of educational administration to make management training inappropriate. Certainly an administrator should understand the ethos of the substantive system within the organization he administers, and this he may have to acquire through some participation in it at some level, but he certainly does not have to have two careers, one in teaching and/or research, and one in administration.

Second, the curriculum for prospective administrators should include a thorough training in administrative theory from Weber to modern systems theory.

Third, there should be adequate education in practical theory in guiding organizations, in public relations, coordination, managing conflict, and the intelligent use of all types of information systems, including high-speed electronic computers.

Fourth, the curriculum should include the classical literature on the uses of power, the responsibilities of leadership, and the sources and nature of educational policy.

Fifth, it should include continuous and rigorous training in the arts and skills of personal communication.

And finally, to return to the main thesis, prospective educational administrators should learn to be comfortable with one of the realities of human experience and one that Aristotle recognized; it is that one of their responsibilities is to provide optimum conditions for the intellectual life, which may have no purpose beyond itself.

NOTES

1 Green (1968): an excellent analysis of the relations among labor, work, leisure, jobs, and education.
2 Clive Beck has done an excellent paper entitled "The Intrinsically Valuable in Education", which to my knowledge has not been published.
3 See Bennis (1968).

REFERENCES

ARISTOTLE, *Politics*, Book VIII.
BENNIS, W. G. (1968) "Future of the Social Sciences", *The Antioch Review*, Summer 1968, pp. 227–55.
CALLAHAN, R. (1962) *Education and the Cult of Efficiency*, University of Chicago Press.
GREEN, T. F. (1968) *Work, Leisure, and the American Schools*, Random House, p. 164.
TAWNEY, R. H. (1926) *Religion and the Rise of Capitalism*, Harcourt, Brace.
WALTON, J. (1959) *Administration and Policy-Making in Education*, The Johns Hopkins University Press (revised edition, 1969).

1.4 On Decisions and Decision Making

P. H. Levin

This paper originated in work done on a study of town expansion schemes, supported by a grant from the Social Science Research Council to Professor D. V. Donnison. The writer is grateful to the SSRC for their support and deeply indebted to Professor Donnison for his continuing help and encouragement.

INTRODUCTION

To judge by the frequency with which the term "decision" is employed, it is a useful one. In domestic life, we talk of deciding what clothes to put on in the morning, or whether to buy a new car. We talk of commercial organizations making decisions—to shut down a factory, or to introduce a new product. We talk of the Government's decision to raise the standard rate of income tax, or of a local authority's decision to install a parking meter scheme.

Used in this way, the concept of "decision" is evidently a trivial one: a decision is merely something which comes before an action. So limited a concept does not do justice to the complexity of the processes by which governments and organizations make decisions. It does not, for example, afford us any means of describing what goes on during the often lengthy period separating the first awareness of a need for a decision and the decision itself, and the further lengthy period separating decision and action. If we are to understand how decisions are made, and how actions come about, we need to develop a model of the decision-making process, with concepts and a language which will enable us to describe the relationship between "first awareness of need" and decision, and between decision and action. The purpose of this paper is to develop such a model.

Any model that is put forward must pass certain tests. It must provide some way of identifying a decision which does not depend on the decision having been implemented. The difficulty of perceiving when a decision is made, and by whom, has been attested to by numerous observers:[1] our

---

Source: *Public Administration* (Spring 1972) Vol. 50, pp. 19–43 (edited extracts).

model must enable this difficulty to be surmounted or avoided. It must enable us to "explain" a wide range of empirical observations. Why are some decisions irrevocable and others not? In what way are certain decisions "crucial"? What is the particular significance of a "formal" decision? What is the distinguishing feature of a "decision in principle"?

The first step in developing a model that will enable these questions to be answered is to elaborate a definition of the term "decision", one that will enable observations about the activities that go into the making of a decision, and about the relationship between decision and action, to be integrated with observations about the act of decision making itself. [. . .]

WHAT IS A DECISION?

Certain events [. . .] are manifestations of a resolve upon action being—or having been—deliberately formed. Such a resolve may form slowly in an individual's mind, or it may form as the result of a mental act at some moment in time. A collective resolve may be formed by a group of people, sometimes emerging in the course of communication within the group, sometimes generated by the casting of votes. Where a resolve upon action is formed as the result of a deliberate individual or collective act, we shall term that act a "decision". Those who participate in that act we shall term "decision makers".

Decisions, then, are about actions. Necessarily they are about envisaged, particular actions. It follows that decision makers are able to distinguish between those envisaged actions and others. Hence the envisaged, resolved-upon actions must possess at least a certain level of what we shall term "specificity". Specificity is simply the property by virtue of which one course of action may be distinguished from another. The higher the specificity of an envisaged action, the more closely will that action be specified, and the closer will the specification be to a single blueprint for action. It should be noted that specificity is not only a function of the level of detail of an envisaged action. If a decision is made to reject 90 out of 100 fully detailed blueprints for action, there is still further deciding to do before it is clear what action is to be taken, i.e. before the point of maximum specificity is reached. Specificity, then, is basically a function of the range of options for action which a specification leaves open.

A decision, if it comes to fruition as intended, will be manifested by the action that it specifies. [. . .] These manifestations may be described, for the obvious reason, as ultimate ones. But decisions [. . .] also have immediate manifestations, in that the decision act itself will be manifest to those who take part in it or are in attendance, while public announcements will subsequently manifest the decision to a wider audience. What is the nature of the relationship between the decision act and its subsequent and ultimate manifestations?

The key to this relationship lies in the fact that in forming a resolve upon action decision makers become *bound* by their resolve: they incur what will be termed "commitment" towards the intended subsequent and ultimate manifestations. Commitment towards an intended course of action may be defined as the state of mind arising from the expectation, whether conscious or not, that a penalty—for a decision maker personally or for the group to which he belongs—will follow from the abandonment of the intention. Commitment is a relative quantity, and its strength will be measured by the penalty which is perceived to be associated with substituting another action (or no action at all) for the one intended, before it is implemented. (Once it is implemented, commitment to it will be complete, since no change will be possible.) Commitment thus constitutes a perceived incentive to a decision maker to persist in his intention. The stronger the commitment, i.e. the greater the penalty perceived to be attached to a change, the greater the incentive to persist. But strong commitment is no guarantee that no change will be made: it will sometimes be considered worth paying the penalty. We shall use the term "committed" to describe someone who has incurred commitment: it is obviously not to be construed as "irrevocably committed".

It appears that commitment to the ultimate manifestation of a decision will be generated not only by the decision act and its immediate manifestation—which in the case of collective decision making is always inseparable from the decision itself—but also by subsequent manifestations, and that its strength will be influenced by the manner and pervasiveness of these manifestations. An individual who communicates a private resolve to one other person who is bound to secrecy can amend his decision probably without suffering any great penalty. On the other hand, once his intention is made known to others, he is likely to feel that to alter it without the excuse of new information or a change in external circumstances will lower his standing in the eyes of his colleagues and associates: what guarantee will they have that his intention will not change yet again? The members of a decision-making group are likely to feel the same way regarding the standing of the group. Eckstein (1956) is remarking on the same phenomenon when he observes that "decision makers who are fully and publicly accountable acquire political and psychological stakes in their own decisions and develop a justificatory rather than a critical attitude towards them". In other words, they incur commitment.

The essential implications of an act of forming a resolve appear to be capable of being described in terms of the two factors commitment and specificity, and this enables us to restate our definition of the term "decision" as follows: a decision is a deliberate act that generates commitment on the part of the decision maker towards an envisaged course of action of some specificity. The term may be used equally validly of an individual privately resolving upon an action and of a group of people going through a formal procedure to the same effect.

A decision maker, then, envisages an action being carried out. Once his resolve has formed, he envisages a penalty to be attached to a change. [. . .] Decision making is a purposive act, intended to achieve a desired outcome, and this too is necessarily envisaged by the decision maker. It follows that also envisaged by him, whether implicitly or explicitly, will be relationships between action and outcome. All these conceptions that the decision maker has in his mind will evidently be seen in juxtaposition: they will be the components of a mental picture, a picture that we shall refer to as an "action schema".

The concept of the schema has been found to be a useful one in explaining phenomena of visual perception and in understanding how past experience predisposes an organism to behave in certain ways rather than others (Abercrombie, 1960). A schema has been defined as "an active organization of past reactions or of past experiences which must always be supposed to be operating in any well-adapted organic response" (Bartlett, 1932). The schema that someone uses when faced with a new situation provides him with preconceptions and expectations: it determines what features of the new situation register with him, and what interpretations he puts on what he registers. Often a person sees only what fits his schema, as when he fails to notice slight misprints in newspapers. If what he sees is incontrovertibly inconsistent with his schema and he cannot reject what he sees, then he modifies the schema. Thus new experience and old are fitted together, and provide him with a new schema, an active and self-consistent organization of old and new information.

In a situation that calls for a course of action to be chosen, a person's schema will possess certain characteristics. It will contain elements that motivate him towards action, elements which—in the context of his personal set of "values"—constitute perceived "desirable outcomes". It will also contain elements which reflect the resources seen as being available to him, and constitute perceived "scope for action". It is the perceived desirable outcomes and scope for action which will largely determine the information that he takes in concerning his situation. A man looking at a tree will register one set of "facts" if he carries an axe and wishes to heat his home and a very different set if he carries a rope and wants a grandstand view of a nearby football match. His schema is focused on what he perceives as the need and scope for action—hence the term "action schema".

The components of an action schema may be classified under three headings—"action", "outcome", and "action/outcome relationships". Under the heading of "action" will fall all perceived courses of action, including actions specifically called for by certain outcomes, and all perceived restrictions and limitations on action. (Some of these will result in some of the perceived courses of action being labelled "forbidden" and others "permitted"; other restrictions will have the effect of "tying" two or more actions together so that one cannot be undertaken—or can only be undertaken—without the other.) Under the heading of "outcome" will fall postulated desired outcomes (goals), all outcomes expected to follow from specific actions, and all perceived restrictions and limitations on outcomes. (Some of these will take the form of limits of toleration, others will have the effect of "tying" two or more outcomes together so that one will not be tolerated—or will only be tolerated—in the absence of the other, yet others will take the form of requirements that the outcome should be an optimum.) Finally, under the heading of "action/ outcome relationships" will fall relationships implicitly identified (e.g. expressed in statements of the form "if this action, then that outcome") or explicitly (e.g. "the number of people initially accommodated in this housing estate will be determined by the number of bed spaces"). Action/outcome relationships may be seen as probabilistic or as conditional, and may accordingly subsume assumptions about the influence of independent variables, reflecting such factors as the behaviour of the economic climate or of other people not susceptible to the decision maker's control. By using the action/outcome relationships, a specification of the action called for to achieve a particular desired outcome can be derived from the specification of that outcome, and a specification of the outcome following from a given action can be derived from the specification of that action.

An analogous classification is presented by March and Simon (1958) in a discussion of the content of the human memory. "The memory content includes: (a) values or goods: criteria that are applied to determine which courses of action are preferred among those considered; (b) relations between actions and their outcomes; i.e. beliefs, perceptions, and expectations as to the consequences that will follow from one course of action or another; and (c) alternatives: possible courses of action." There is evidently a close similarity between this classification and that presented in the previous paragraph of the contents of an action schema, which is perhaps the more complete of the two.

We can now take our definition of "decision" a step further. *A decision is a deliberate act that generates commitment on the part of the decision maker towards an envisaged course of action of some specificity, and is moreover an act that is made in the light of—and is consistent with some at least of the elements of—an action schema, the components of which are classifiable under the headings of action, outcome, and action/ outcome relationships.*

In adopting this definition we are taking it as axiomatic that there is consistency between the decision and some at least of the elements of the action schema. Hence we are making a restricted assertion about the "rationality" of the decision. But the validity of our definition does not depend either on the elements of the schema being mutually consistent or on the schema being an accurate reflection of reality. Thus the schema may contain desired outcomes which are inherently irreconcilable but not recognized to be so, or a permitted course of action which is in reality physically incapable of being implemented, but a decision based on that schema will be no less a decision for that.

How well does our definition relate to others that have been put forward? According to Frankel (1963), "by decision making is understood an act of determining in one's own mind a course of action, following a more or less deliberate consideration of alternatives; and by decision is understood that which is thus determined". This definition raises the question of *what* is determined by a decision. [. . .] Thus Frankel's definition, unlike ours, is applicable only to the relationship between a decision and the acts that immediately manifest it, and not to the relationship between decision and ultimate action.

A similar point can be made about the definition put forward by Elliott Jaques (1966), a definition to which our present formulation in fact owes a great deal. To Jaques, a decision is a psychological event characterized by (1) the exercise of discretion, e.g. in selecting a course of action; (2) prescribed non-discretionary limits, it being possible to exercise discretion only within these limits; (3) a goal, towards which the decision maker is aiming; and (4) committal, by which is meant that an external, observable event would result from a decision, a wrong decision causing waste or harm in some form. Clearly the exercise of discretion corresponds to our deliberate act. Clearly too the prescribed non-discretionary limits and goal constitute elements of an "action schema", if we are to understand them to refer to what the decision maker perceives. (If they are meant to refer to a "real" situation, then they will give rise to rather than directly constitute such elements.) And one would expect Jaques to agree that relationships linking goal and action would be present in a decision maker's mind. Committal, however, would seem to correspond not to commitment but to the immediate manifestation, the observable act that marks—and may be said to be determined by—a decision. Hence Jaques' definition, like Frankel's, does not embrace the relationship between decision and ultimate action.

Another definition of the term "decision" has been supplied by Etzioni (1968): "by decision we mean a conscious choice between two or more alternatives". The implication that alternatives have been distinguished takes care of the specificity element in our own definition, while deliberate acts are clearly conscious ones and thus comply with Etzioni's definition on that account. Although his definition makes no specific reference to commitment, he does elaborate on that definition by stating that 'it is mainly through the decision-making processes that vague and abstract societal commitments, whose directions are indicated by the values and goals to which the actor subscribes, are translated into specific commitments to one or more specific courses of action". In total, therefore, Etzioni's view of decision making accords well with our own definition of "decision".

THE PROCESS OF DECISION MAKING

It was pointed out above that certain decisions had immediate, subsequent and ultimate manifestations. We shall use the term "decision-making process" to denote the sequence of activities lying between the immediate manifestation (or even the initial formation of a purely private resolve) and the ultimate manifestation, the actual occurrence of the action resolved upon. The aim now is to formulate a classification of the activities that constitute the decision-making process, with particular reference to those processes that culminate (or are intended, but fail to culminate) in a deliberate change in the physical environment.

It is necessary first to note the distinction that is to be made between two types of action. [. . .] Some actions, like building a housing estate or airport, impinge directly on the "real world", on the population at large; others, like setting up a commission of inquiry or submitting a proposal to a committee, impinge directly only on those who are actively concerned in some way with bringing about (or preventing) the development.

Correspondingly the outcomes that result from actions of the first kind take the form of changes in the activities of sections of the population, e.g. changes in travel patterns and habits, and changes in the domicile of those displaced or accommodated by the constructions; the most significant outcomes that result from actions of the second kind take the form of changes in the perceptions of those who participate in the process of bringing into being the new development.

The distinction between two types of action and outcome reflects the distinction that may be made between the "real-world system" and the "institutional system" (a distinction that finds a parallel in that made by Friend and Jessop (1969) between what they term the "community system" and the "governmental system"). We shall define each of these as a system of inter-related activities. The real-world system will embrace all those activities engaged in by the population at large—working, dwelling, shopping, receiving a service such as education or medical care, leisure activities, travelling, etc. The institutional system will embrace all activities directed towards formulating or influencing the action taken by government to support, regulate; or change more fundamentally the patterns of activities that constitute the real-world system. The implementation of a physical development is one of the actions that brings about fundamental change in the sense that it involves altering the "structure" of the real-world system, the relatively fixed framework within which the various activities take place. The making of such an alteration we shall term an "intervention" in the real-world system.

Actions of the two types that we have identified—actions within the institutional system, hereafter referred to as institutional actions, and interventions in the real-world system—obviously relate in different ways to the decision-making processes with which we are concerned. An intervention in the real-world system comes at the end of the process, while there will typically occur a succession of institutional actions actually in the course of the process. Now, an envisaged institutional action will be the focus of an "institutional schema" and an envisaged intervention will be the focus of an "intervention schema". In the course of the decision-making process the schemata of each type in the minds of those who are concerned undergo changes. An intervention schema develops as new information and judgements relating to the need and scope for intervention are added to it and incorporated into it. The schema becomes more extensive as new variables are linked into it; it becomes clearer, as the implications of action/outcome relationships are explored and as conflicts between incompatible goals or incompatible actions are made evident; it becomes more consistent as these conflicts are resolved by eliminating certain goals or actions from consideration; and the remaining possible courses of action become more fully specified as more and more outcomes and direct constraints on action are taken into account. [. . .]

In part, an institutional schema develops in a broadly similar way. But—and it is an important but—instead of being focused on a single action throughout the decision-making process (in the way that an intervention schema is focused on a single—albeit complex—intervention) it is focused at successive points in time on one of a succession of envisaged institutional actions. Thus in the case of the local authority which wishes to build a housing estate part of the sequence of decisions might be: — local authority decides to invite tenders; builders decide to submit tenders; authority decides tentatively to accept one tender; authority decides to apply for loan sanction; Ministry decides to give loan sanction. Each decision, once fully manifested, helps to structure the action schema for the next decision—which indeed is its purpose—by making it possible for that decision to be taken and also by limiting the scope for that decision. Evidently what the decision maker perceives is a continually unfolding institutional schema, each successive state of which is conditioned by the decision (whether his own or not) that leads up to it.

We may usefully make one further distinction between ways in which a schema develops, and that is according to whether or not it does so independently of the schema of another individual or body. Independent development of an intervention schema takes place when new information and judgements, for example, are incorporated into it without reference to anyone else's views of the need and scope for intervention. Independent development of an institutional schema takes place when, for example, formal steps are taken by a planning agency: although the subject matter of the step (e.g. of an application for loan sanction) may have been influenced by other people, no one else can be involved in the actual taking of the step.

A schema may, however, develop through interaction with that of another individual or group. "Interactive" development of an intervention schema takes place when, for example, one group persuades another to share its view that its "facts" are wrong, or that insufficient importance is being attached to certain of the envisaged outcomes of an intervention. Interactive development of an institutional schema takes place when, for example, one group succeeds in changing the pattern of perceived institutional goals and commitments embodied in the institutional schema of another. This may come about as the result of persuasion, or through bargaining, which has the effect—if carried to a successful conclusion—that the two sides both acquire a new commitment, namely to honour the bargain. It is in practice unusual for interactive development of one type of schema to take place without interactive development of the other. Once preferences have formed for a particular specification or range of specifications for intervention, then there almost certainly exists commitment, and the pattern of preferences cannot be significantly changed without changing the pattern of commitment.

We have, then, identified three distinct processes through which schemata may develop: processes made up of (i) decisions and actions leading to the independent development of an intervention schema only; (ii) decisions and actions leading to the independent development of an institutional schema only; and (iii) decisions and actions leading to the interactive development of schemata of both types. We may broaden each category to include decisions and actions *intended* to lead to the development of a schema as well as those that actually do have that result. There now appears to be a good correspondence between these three categories of process and, respectively, technical, administrative and political processes as familiarly described.

Each of these three types of process is conventionally characterized in less abstract terms. Thus the purpose of the technical process is to enable an intervention to be specified, the purpose of the administrative process is to enable—by complying with logical necessity and prescribed procedural rules—an intervention actually to be made, and the purpose of the political process is to mobilize support for it. These purposes are evidently those that the proponents of a proposal would have in mind, but we should not overlook the fact that opponents (or semi-opponents) of the proposal may undertake processes falling into each of our three categories with the aim of halting or deflecting it. Henceforth the terms technical, administrative, and political will be used to denote the three processes through which a schema may develop, and accordingly will include anti-intervention as well as pro-intervention processes, although we shall primarily be concerned with the latter.

Now, the point has already been made that immediate and subsequent manifestations of a decision result in the decision makers incurring commitment to the specified action that is intended to constitute the ultimate manifestation. We can say further that many of the decisions and actions which comprise technical, administrative and political processes will themselves constitute subsequent manifestations of the initial act of resolve. Their purposes as listed in the previous paragraph are evidence of this. Hence we may expect these decisions and actions to generate commitment to the proposed ultimate action. We may also expect, from our definition of the technical process, that an increase will invariably take place in the specificity of the envisaged action which commands the commitment. [...]

A MODEL OF THE DECISION-MAKING PROCESS

The elements of our model of the decision-making process have been put forward [in the previous section]. We have suggested that the decisions and actions that together comprise an overall decision-making process may be divided into technical, administrative and political categories, and have defined the collection of decisions and actions falling into each category as constituting a technical, administrative and political process respectively. We have suggested also that in the course of the decision-making process as a whole the decision makers become increasingly committed to an increasingly specific ultimate course of action. [...] The final step in the analysis is to attempt to distinguish what the separate contributions of the three "sub-processes" to the growth of specificity and commitment would be if each in turn were allowed to dominate. Before doing that, it will be helpful to consider the views that other writers have formed of the three sub-processes.

The administrative process has been examined by Donnison and Chapman (1965). Their definition of the term is less narrow than our own, and may include elements which we would regard as technical or political. Nevertheless, their comments are of interest.

> At the start of the story the participants can select from among all the choices practicable at that time. Each decision that is made thereafter reduces the number of alternatives still available, until the last act is reached which determines the final outcome of the story in question. At certain stages in this process decisions are taken which select one route and exclude many others potentially available up to that point. These major junctions in the map across which the administrator travels are the crucial stages in his progress.

We infer that one junction has to be reached before the next can be attained: this reflects the enabling aspect of the administrative process. The successive reduction in the number of (presumably ultimate) alternative actions [...] clearly amounts to a rise in the specificity of the envisaged ultimate action. The decisions which exclude certain of the alternatives hitherto available generate commitment to those that remain: the fact that no retracing of steps would seem to be possible implies that there is a hundred per cent commitment to the remaining alternatives.

The technical process involves the generation and incorporation into an intervention schema of information and judgements about the real-world system. These often come about through what R. G. S. Brown (1970) describes as "search activity" [...].

The search may be intensive or it may be superficial. The more it is extended, the more complete will be the decision maker's model of the situation, and the closer will his actual decision approximate to a theoretically ideal one (always assuming that he structures his material logically when he has it, since there is a point beyond which additional information does not assist effective decision making but is merely confusing) [p. 145].

Brown's "model of the situation" more or less corresponds to our action schema, and his "logical structuring of material" to the development of a self-consistent action schema. However, our model of the decision-making process enables us to offer an explanation, which Brown does not do, of his assertion that there is a point beyond which additional information is merely confusing. As information comes to hand, one integrates it into a self-consistent action schema. If this goes well, and a course of action with no apparent drawbacks appears, one acquires confidence that it is the right course, i.e. one becomes psychologically committed to it. If one then receives a piece of information seriously at variance with the schema, then either one's commitment is destroyed, which is when confidence is liable to be replaced by confusion, or—as has been known—the new information may be suppressed and the level of commitment maintained.

"Politics", which we may take as being synonymous with political processes, has been defined by Meyerson and Banfield (1955) as "the activity by which an issue is agitated or settled"—a definition that has much in common with that of Klein (1967), in whose view "politics are essentially about the reconciliation of conflicting interests". Thus the essence of the political process is interaction between groups of people, and the essence of its outcome is that (a) some form of alignment between schemata is reached, a general description which will cover a state in which conflicting interests have become reconciled; and (b) there is a commitment towards upholding the settlement or carrying out the action agreed upon. It would appear, moreover, that political activity cannot exist independently of an issue; furthermore it would seem that an issue can exist only when some individual or group has already acquired a commitment towards a course of action of some specificity.

These illustrations of what is meant by administrative, technical and political processes give us some clue to the form that decision-making processes would ideally take. In a process that was perfect from the administrative point of view, there would be no going back, no re-opening of decisions or annulment of actions once they were taken. A critical path programme which is designed to maximize the "efficiency" of an administrative procedure also has the effect of maximizing the disincentive to a retracing of steps. [. . .] The implication is that in an administratively perfect process there would be 100 per cent commitment to each action as it was taken, notably to those actions that marked an increase in specificity of the envisaged proposal. [. . .]

A decision-making process that was perfect from the technical point of view would look very different. No commitment would be generated in the course of the searching and learning part of the technical process. Only when all possible interventions and their implications had been explored would preferences be formed and commitment thereby generated. [. . .] Ideally a single preferred proposal would emerge and, to the commitment generated by the forming of the preference and the staking of judgement on it, would be added commitment generated by the administrative and political processes as the project moved towards implementation. This commitment would be to a single course of action of maximum specificity, which subsumes other courses of action of lower specificity. [. . .]

A process that is perfect from the political point of view [. . .] must begin with some commitment to a proposal of at least some specificity, but the commitment will not be so high as to inhibit political activity—bargaining, say, or mediation. As the area of conflict is progressively reduced—as agreement on certain "sub-issues" is reached, for example—commitment and specificity will increase hand in hand. [. . .]

We have now taken our model of the decision-making process a step further by identifying three distinct modes in which commitment and specificity may together develop. Each of the three modes would appear to correspond to optimal progress of one of the three sub-processes. In practice many decision-making processes [. . .] will proceed by different modes at different times. [. . .] When it happens that a single mode is particularly strongly in evidence, one would expect to find that the mode is dictated by the conditions under which the process is taking place, and it is possible to formulate hypotheses as to the different conditions under which this would occur. Thus, where power lies with a single group the administrative mode might be expected to predominate. Where the problems are highly complex and their solution depends on finding solutions to nth order problems, the technical mode might be predominant. Where the cooperation of several groups is essential for the implementation of the ultimate action, the political mode might be most in evidence.

CONCLUSIONS

In this paper we have developed a definition of the term "decision", making use of the concepts of specificity, commitment and action schema. Using this definition, and the distinction we have drawn between institutional and real-world systems, we have been able to derive a model of the decision-making process, a model which resolves the process into three elements: administrative, technical and political.

Any new framework for analysis such as is presented here ought to earn its keep in two ways. First, it ought to enable us to explain and relate past observations of decision-making behaviour, and to suggest testable hypotheses—to serve as a tool of political science. In this paper the framework presented has been put to a limited test in this respect.

Second, such a framework ought to have practical applications. It ought to enable us to ask old questions in a new and more cogent form, and to pose new questions about the form of decision-making processes.

It is appropriate, therefore, to end this paper with some of the questions that have been left in the writer's mind. Experts of one kind or another frequently use the label "administrative" or "technical" to demarcate areas of interest within which they claim the right to make or influence decisions: are we and they sufficiently aware that administrative and technical processes may, besides *enabling* actions to be specified and to be implemented, generate a great deal of commitment to such actions, thereby tending to make it inevitable that these actions *will* be implemented and leaving little scope for political activity? Do administrative processes in Britain today *require* administrators to incur too much commitment? If less commitment were generated by administrative processes, would political processes founder for lack of momentum? Is it feasible for the public to participate at a point sufficiently early in decision-making processes for commitment on the part of administrators and others to be relatively low? These are some of the questions which deeper and more rigorous study of governmental decision-making processes should enable us to answer.

NOTE

1 See, for example, Mackenzie (1967) p. 234 and Brown (1970) p. 147.

REFERENCES

ABERCROMBIE, M. L. JOHNSON (1960) *The Anatomy of Judgement*, Hutchinson, p. 30 (and Penguin, 1969, p. 30).
BARTLETT, F. C. (1932) *Remembering*, Cambridge University Press (cited by Abercrombie 1960).
BROWN, R. G. S. (1970) *The Administrative Process in Britain*, Methuen.
DONNISON, D. V. and CHAPMAN, V. (1965) *Social Policy and Administration*, Allen and Unwin, pp. 34–5.
ECKSTEIN, H. (1956) "Planning: a Case Study", *Political Studies*, Vol. IV, No. 1, pp. 46–60 (reprinted as "Planning: the National Health Service" in Rose, R. (ed.) (1969) *Policy-Making in Britain*, Macmillan, pp. 221–37.
ETZIONI, A. (1968) *The Active Society*, Free Press, pp. 249–51.
FRANKEL, J. (1963) *The Making of Foreign Policy*, Oxford University Press, p. 1.
FRIEND, J. K. and JESSOP, W. N. (1969) *Local Government and Strategic Choice*, Tavistock Publications, p. 101.
JAQUES, E. (1966) *The Nature of Decision Making*, a paper presented at a meeting of the Operational Research Society, 15 Feb. 1966.

KLEIN, R. (1967) in a review of Nicholson, M., *The System*, in the *Observer*, 24 Sept. 1967 (cited in Hill, D. M. (1970) *Participating in Local Affairs*, Penguin, p. 196).

MACKENZIE, W. J. M. (1967) *Politics and Social Science*, Penguin.

MARCH, J. G. and SIMON, H. A. (1958) *Organizations*, Wiley, p. 11.

MEYERSON, M. and BANFIELD, E. C. (1955) *Politics, Planning and the Public Interest*, Free Press, p. 304.

For further development of the ideas presented in this paper, see the author's *Government and the Planning Process*, to be published by Allen and Unwin, spring 1976.

1.5 Decision Type, Structure and Process Evaluation: A Contingency Model

Marvin W. Peterson

ABSTRACT

Governance proposals for higher education in the United States are often promulgated on the basis of some utopian goal or on the assumption that a given proposal is the panacea for multifaceted problems or that it is equally applicable to diverse institutional settings. This paper, rather than promulgating a single proposal, takes a more analytic approach and develops a contingency model for identifying appropriate decision-making structures. First, emergent conditions in American higher education's external environment, in the internal social environment of its colleges and universities, and in the development of higher education management systems are analyzed to establish some long-range criteria for evaluating decision-making effectiveness. Second, a typology of institutional decisions categorized as policy, managerial, and operating decisions is presented. An analysis of the nature and content of each major type of decision suggests divergent patterns of formal and informal decision-making structures and patterns, and differing content and functions for the supporting management information technology which might be appropriate to each of the decision types or categories. Finally, the analysis relates the contingency notions of decision structure and type to the criteria for evaluating the decision-making process and suggests how they are compatible or might be modified to be more compatible. The model is a general conceptual one which the author suggests can be used on either an institution-wide basis or with particular subunits of a college or university.

Decision-making in colleges and universities in the United States and, I assume, numerous other countries is in a state of despair. It is simultaneously labeled as bureaucratic and authoritarian *or* overly democratic and permissive; as a collegial community *or* a divisive political entity; as a tool of the establishment *or* a weapon of the student radicals. New forms and proposals exist in droves and are under constant discussion. The topic is either a tirade or tiresome; middle grounds are seldom struck.

Source: *Higher Education* (May 1972) Vol. 1, No. 2, pp. 207–19.

The purpose of this paper is an attempt to strike a middle ground in its suggestion that appropriate decision structures may be contingent upon the type of decision being made—in its assumption that governance problems are not easily resolved by notions of shared authority, university senates, faculty unions, increased authority, decentralization or the other myriad of bromides, but that it may be a complex combination. The title also suggests that decisions might be evaluated, i.e. determined to be effective. Unfortunately, effectiveness implies that the decisions have a goal against which decisions can be judged. No doubt, there are often many goals for a given decision; for example, open admissions may serve a different purpose for different institutions or even be justified for different reasons by faculty groups within the same institution. More helpful, if one is to attempt to evaluate the longer-range effectiveness of a college or university as an organized entity, is to assess its decision-making pattern or process, and not merely its decisions. Unfortunately, evaluating the decision-making process is not just a matter of assessing whether the processes are responsive (decisions get made), are viewed as legitimate, or produce good decisions. Decision processes exist in different organizational environments to which they must relate; i.e. effectiveness of decision-making processes is also contingent on environmental conditions. Evaluation at this level is carried on in other organizations but seldom in higher education. Finally, the paper recognizes the pervasiveness of informal, as well as formal, structures, although this may not be crucial.[1] Most persons are aware that the informal patterns in colleges and universities are often more important than the formal ones, that the informal ones have a way of being formalized over time, and that they are in practice often inseparable. It would therefore seem more important to know their source and how they influence decision making than to assume that one or the other is more appropriate.

In light of these comments the central focus of this paper might be entitled, "How Do Emergent Conditions in the Decision-Making Environment of Colleges and Universities Affect the Establishment of More Effective Decision-Making Processes?" A threefold response to this question is provided. First, an attempt will be made to highlight some critical emergent conditions or contingencies, both inside and outside of institutions of higher education in the United States, that affect the informal and formal structures and, more importantly, that suggest criteria for evaluating the decision-making processes. Second, an analysis of certain categories of decisions suggests some guidelines for the structure of the decision process and the information technology that might be utilized. Finally, the structures suggested in the second part will be reviewed against the criteria identified in the discussion of emergent conditions. The aim is more to establish a pattern for evaluating the effectiveness of decision-making processes than to identify the *most appropriate* structures.

Some critical emerging conditions in higher education in the United States today suggest potentially conflicting criteria for effective decision-making processes in higher education: (1) the growth of external forces demanding greater control of resources, improved accountability for them, and use of legal guidelines or restrictions in some activities; (2) the expansion within the larger higher education system and at the institutional level of management science-based tools and techniques; and (3) the pressure within institutions for greater participation, decentralization and democratization.

External forces
The external forces affect colleges and universities primarily through two major mechanisms: control of financial and physical resources and control of legal documents, statutes or rulings.

After a period of rapid growth and expanding financial support from state and federal governments, from alumni and private sources, and from student tuition and financial aid in the '50's and '60's, the current financial stringency resulting from a limited tax base, other competing demands for government resources and the economic recession, have introduced increased state legislative and federal agency demands for efficient use of funds and tighter controls on expenditures. State coordination, which grew rapidly in the same period and which has reduced institutional autonomy in some areas, is facing increased legislative pressures to further tighten financial controls within the institution rather than to focus on the more creative planning and coordination activities that many had hoped would be assumed (Berdahl, 1970; Palola et al., 1970). A final force tightening the grip on financial controls has resulted from the federal government's tendency to shift from grants-in-aid, directly distributed to students and faculty members, to institutional grants and, more recently, grants to state and regional agencies, consortia and other compacts.

Three other external forces have had strong impacts on legal rulings affecting higher education. The period of student activism in the last half of the 1960's has hastened the development of state and federal legislative riders to appropriations bills as well as more direct legislative efforts to control student conduct. At the same time courts have been expanding the notion of due process as it relates to student discipline. Also, the recent developments in the passage of public employee bargaining laws in many states have hastened the trend toward faculty unionization in many institutions and increasingly brought the institution—faculty member relationship under the purview of the law (O'Neill, 1971).

The net effect of these external forces seems quite obvious. Increasingly, decisions in the areas of student discipline and faculty—employee relationships are stipulated by law or must follow legal guidelines. In the financial area greater demands for responsibility and accountability of persons in specific positions are accompanied by increasingly stringent guidelines. Both the financial and legal restrictions tend to induce not only more formal decision structures but also clearer lines of *authority* and centralization of *authority* in college and university administrative positions whose incumbents can then be held responsible.

Internal forces

The conflict of internal and external forces is highlighted by the internal forces' press toward lesser emphasis on authority and centralization. The size of some of our American institutions has led to a consensus that they are either too large or too unmanageable in their present rambling, specialized form in which large numbers of department chairmen may report to one dean, or numerous deans, center and institute directors, etc. may report to one vice president. Student and faculty demands for settings in which they can have improved learning—teaching relationships, demands for more participatory or responsive decision-making, and suspicion or mistrust of persons in administrative positions all contribute to the resistance to authority and centralization. These demands are partially weakened by indications that faculty, while desiring extensive influence, are unwilling to spend substantial amounts of time in governance activities (Dykes, 1968). The emerging practice in the academic area, to rotate or review administrators at fixed periods of time, also suggests a tendency to limit the authority of persons in those positions.

The tendency of these internal forces is thus in the direction of greater decentralization of authority, and toward basing decision-making not on authority in formally established positions but on more informally-based patterns of influence derived from information or expertise, an appeal to common values, or the accepted social norms of the group. The reality, of course, is that students and faculty are often subdivided into interest groups more closely resembling a political interest group system.

The development of management systems

The final development which is spurred by the financial stringency of the times is the growth and development of managerial science techniques to assist college and university decision-making efforts. While Veblen raised tirades against the "captains of erudition" over fifty years ago, the development of techniques of financial and budget analysis, program-planning and budgeting systems, computer-based management information systems, simulation and forecasting models and the like are all relatively recent arrivals on the higher education scene. They have been spurred in the past five years by consulting firms, by efforts of individuals such as Judy and Levine in their development of the CAMPUS simulation at Toronto, by Ford Foundation grants to Yale, Stanford, Toronto, and other institutions, and most recently, by the USOE through the

WICHE Planning and Management Systems program (now National Center for Higher Education Management Statistics). At the institutional level the developments are reflected by the emergence and proliferation of offices of financial analysis, institutional research, directors of administrative data systems and most recently, planning officers at the vice presidential level. The concern, however, is not to raise Veblen's tirade but rather to ensure that this emerging information technology is used in support of the academic decision-making structure which is primarily concerned with the university's major productive activities of teaching, learning and service. Our formal and informal academic decision-making structures must not be made subservient to this information technology. Rourke and Brooks in their study, *The Managerial Revolution,* have found that centralization of authority is associated with the development of computer-based management systems, thus indicating some reason for concern.

This brief discussion of the three force fields has suggested direct implications for decision-making processes in the areas of financial resource accountability, student rights and discipline, and faculty institution relations. More important, however, are the criteria that it suggests for an overall assessment of a college or university's decision-making pattern. First it suggests the desirability for a decision structure which has an authority system that can be responsive to, and account for, resources and legal requirements of external groups. Second, a participation pattern that ensures students and faculty members an opportunity to be influential seems needed. The need to make these two mutually supportive rather than in constant conflict is a corollary criterion. Third, it must be ensured that the information system is integrated into the decision-making structure rather than becoming subservient to it. Finally, the structure probably should provide for decentralization (but with accountability), which is widely in demand, and promises some relief from problems of size, diversity of interests, and teaching—learning needs of faculty and students.

A TYPOLOGY OF DECISIONS

In analyzing a college or university's decision-making system, it is helpful to look at structural and informational requirements which seem to be appropriate for different categories of decisions. Such an analysis is suggested by Herbert Simon (1965) in a discussion in which he holds that all decisions are essentially composed of both a "value" component—an "imperative quality" or "ethical" content—and a "factual" component— "statements about the observable world and the way in which it operates." This view of decisions suggests that information technology and the expertise to deal with the factual component of the decision are extremely useful, providing they do not override the "value" component of the decision. This distinction will thus be utilized to relate the role of information technology to different types of higher education decisions.

The decision typology suggested for this analysis, however, is not one which classifies decisions in the usual higher education categories of financial, academic, personnel, student, facilities and the like, but rather is one which cuts across these more traditional categories and applies to all of them. The three categories to be discussed are policy, managerial, and operating, or control, decisions (Anthony, 1965). The usefulness of these categories lies in the different levels of abstraction which they imply and the differing implications which they suggest for decision-making structure and informational technology. While the discussion of them assumes a university-wide perspective, they apply equally at the college or departmental level, and their implications at those levels will be discussed in the final section.

Policy, managerial and operating decisions can be distinguished along four dimensions in addition to the Simon "fact-value" distinction: the time range over which they apply, the range of individuals or organizational units directly affected, their content, and their means-ends relationships. Each category will be discussed with reference to these dimensions, to the implications for structural and informational technology requirements, and to the examples of structures that most nearly fit the requirements.

Policy decisions
Policy decisions are those which are concerned with a university's major goals and priorities, its general program strategies for achieving them, and its strategies for obtaining the resources needed to achieve them. In this sense policy decisions are long term, affect all individuals or units and are primarily concerned with obtaining agreement on desired ends for the institution. Since there is bound to be disagreement on these ends, based more on value concerns than on factual ones, the most appropriate structure is probably one which ensures that all points of view are considered, and all possible implications explored, so that compromise or agreement necessary to commitment can be reached. The role of information in policy decisions, while limited, still implies the need for doing comparative studies of other similar institutions; forecasting to assess trends affecting higher education demand and its resource sources; undertaking periodic long-term review of institutional goal achievement and resource utilization; and reevaluation of institutional goals and assessments of overall structure and functions. It would appear that, with few exceptions, colleges and universities engage in little or no overt decision-making or research at the policy level, our current U.S. surplus of Ph.Ds being a most pregnant example.

While it is possible that a highly respected administrative group could effectively operate as a policy team, its decisions would probably be highly suspect in today's university where student and faculty trust of administration is low. The new university senate model, which includes students, faculty, administration and perhaps trustees or other constituents, offers a promising structure in terms of the demands for participation and the structural requirements for dealing with policy level issues. While these bodies are still at an embryonic stage of development, preliminary studies suggest that they are viewed as representative and do gain substantial commitment and involvement from their student and faculty members. They provide not only a group to assess policy issues but a legitimate sounding board which is readily accessible in crisis situations, such as the necessity of calling in civil authorities. Their problems seem to result from their inability to initiate action—a role which could be filled by the president or other top administrative officers—their lack of adequate administrative staff, and the necessity to deal with detail issues which float to the top (Dill, 1971).

Managerial decisions

Managerial decisions focus on issues related to allocation of resources among programs (college level units in a university setting), the coordination of their efforts insofar as they are interdependent, and the mediation of conflicts between and among them. In this sense managerial decisions have a shorter time perspective and may affect fewer units than policy decisions. They also are concerned with development of programs as means of achieving policy. It is at this level that efforts in the fast-expanding information technology to build simulation models for assessing the resource requirements of various program alternatives, program-budgeting systems, cost-benefit analysis techniques and other measurements of program productivity and effectiveness are most useful and, perhaps, most complex. At this level there is generally agreement about priorities (ends), if a policy group exists, but there are still disagreements about which programs (means) will best achieve the ends. The value aspect of the decisions is decreased, and fact content increased compared to policy decisions. While the role of information in assessing the alternatives may increase in policy decisions, the role of judgment in interpreting the factual implications will remain nevertheless substantial.

This analysis identifies a decision structure in which there is greater analytic effort required, suggesting the need for an academic administrator who understands the information technology and is not dominated by it. The assumed commitment to policy level priority suggests a decision structure in which substantial agreement exists. However, the difficult analysis and interpretations of the many program alternatives which could be generated suggests that substantial time commitments are required. Further, the wide range of judgment still implies the usefulness of including the many varied perspectives of representatives of different constituencies, although perhaps they are not as numerous as at the policy level. The structure that seems appropriate is that of the executive committee or the working committees related to the policy body in which compromises and workable solutions can be reached.

It should be noted that the faculty bargaining unit or union concerns itself primarily with this level of decision making and the operating level to be discussed next. Although having indirect impact on policy, once a faculty group enters a bargaining arrangement, its primary concerns are usually below the institutional policy level. However, in institutions where faculty have no existing direct influence in policy decisions and little at the program or operating level, a bargaining unit may actually enhance faculty's role in governance as well as provide improved working conditions and financial benefits. The difficulty with the bargaining model, vis-à-vis our initial criteria, is that it fails to provide an effective formal opportunity for students to directly influence decisions at the policy or managerial level.

Operating decisions
Operating decisions are concerned with the way in which program activities are carried out (decisions on whom to admit, schedules of courses, whom to hire or promote, how to spend funds allocated to the program for travel, etc.). The information requirements of such decisions are satisfied by straightforward reports on enrollments, class size, budget statements and the like, which indicate whether resources and activities are being utilized appropriately. The value content of the decision if related to policy guidelines is low, and the factual content high. These decisions can be handled efficiently by routine administrative procedure with occasional review by appropriate policy groups. Yet a cursory review of faculty committee structures and activities suggests that these are often the types of decisions on which they spend the most time. This appears to be an inefficient use of faculty time and an expensive way to accomplish the task at hand. Faculty themselves while desiring to be influential, resist spending more time on the decision-making process (Dykes, 1968). Most appropriately these are matters which might be handled by administrative personnel; their use at college and even at departmental levels as administrative assistants is growing in larger universities and has been received favorably once faculty realize they themselves still have substantial influence over policy and are not giving up control of one more of their prerogatives.

AN OVERVIEW: RELATED ISSUES
This general analysis of decision structures and information technology by decision category has suggested some appropriate ways in which they may be related to satisfy the criterion of integrating the information system within the decision structure. Viewing this set of decision categories at the college or department level suggests the need for training either deans or department chairmen in the use of that technology or for assigning them assistants with such expertise as to assure its inte-

gration at the respective levels. A further highlight is the need to keep program structure and the information technology subservient to policy. If effective policy bodies are not established, new programs concerned with their own survival and supported by the rigidities of the information technology's program classification structure may become just as rigid as our old academic units (for a discussion of the dynamic in government, see Moynihan, 1970).

This analysis of decision categories also provides some notion of the structures which seem to meet the internally generated criterion of providing ample student, faculty, and other constituency participation which allows them substantial influence without requiring extensive involvement on all matters. The distinction of the fact and value content of decisions suggests another mode of enhancing faculty involvement and making it more effective. Too often in university decision groups, faculty members have to spend their own expensive, and grudgingly given time on the drudgery of data collection and analysis which could be accomplished by more administrative support. Or more likely, they ignore the "factual" side of the decision issue.

The concern for the externally generated criterion of maintaining positions of authority which can be responsive to the external demands for accountability is not apparent in the analysis. However, several suggestions are implicit. One possible mechanism to ensure identification of administrative leaders who can deal with the external demands and yet be sensitive to internal needs is a joint selection committee of higher level administrators with student or faculty constituents. This may provide for better selection of persons, performed by those who are realistically aware of both internal and external forces, than would direct appointment by a higher administrator or selection of nominees by a faculty group. Further, some period of training or concern for administrative development may enhance the growth and development of academic administrators caught in the authority-influence system vise and the growing management technology.

While the notion that rotation of administrators could limit the authority of the person in that position has already been suggested, a procedure calling for the appointment of administrators for a limited period of time, with subsequent review rather than strict rotation, may provide a better possibility of attracting and retaining competent personnel. The practice of reviewing administrators is rare, although instances such as that of President Brewster last year at Yale may set an example.

Finally an increased concern for administrative style may allow administrators to retain their influence while in an authority position. The potential initiating role in policy structure deliberations has already been noted. In smaller units, such as departments, there is strong evidence that a supportive leadership style can enhance the chairman's influence with, and trust by, his faculty even if he merely consults rather than directly involves them (Peterson, 1970). The problem of maintaining the balance of influence and authority, however, is probably as much a matter of educating students and faculty members to, and keeping them aware of, the forces requiring an authoritative response through their involvement on crucial or policy issues as it is a matter of administrative selection, training or definition of the positions of authority.

The final criterion that this analysis has not yet directly considered is the potential for decentralization found in the decision-making structures discussed. The notion that experts in information technology should be placed in major academic units or colleges (even departments), as well as in the central administrative staff, has been mentioned as a device to protect against the centralizing tendencies of development. Additionally, the three categories of decisions inherently provide the potential for decentralization if one recalls that the same decision categories can apply at the school or department as well as the university level. Since managerial and operating decisions flow from policy decisions, the question is merely how much policy autonomy to give to the college and the department. If policy is not decentralized, managerial decisions still can be. The truly centralized institution is one in which even operating level decisions are centralized. The university senate model mentioned in our policy discussion has the potential for decentralization if similar units are established at the school and college level. As a matter of fact, it appears that in some institutions which have formed a university senate, it has been necessary to create analogous structures at lower levels merely to keep the university-wide body from becoming inundated with questions which were really only of concern to a particular college. This suggests that as a strategy for developing policy level decision-making structures which are both effective and decentralized, one might wish to begin first at the department or college level or at least consider their development simultaneously with that of the university level.

One of the paradoxes of current organizational dynamics in universities is that students and faculty who demand participation in only top-level decision-making bodies may find that they have created a highly centralized structure which either reduces the autonomy of their unit or has little or no effect on it. Another argument for decentralizing policy to the departmental level with student involvement is to make faculty directly aware of the changing conditions of their interdependence; i.e. to make them face open discussions of the student's concern for his marketability in a glutted field and the relevance of his educational experience, to see the administrator's difficulty in obtaining funds, and/or to sense the growing concern of coordinating bodies for planning more completely the use of our public educational facilities. The faculty member's academic freedom may not be eroding, but his autonomy may be without his awareness of it.

While this paper has been addressed to the emergent conditions or contingencies which may determine criteria for evaluating the effectiveness of decision-making processes in the years ahead and has tried to relate some decision categories to appropriate decision-making and information technology structures, it has not directly considered some of our current crucial questions.

1 To what extent can crisis decisions be covered by policy or handled by an all-university senate or other structure?
2 Can any internal decision-making body make program cutbacks in some seemingly obsolete areas to permit institutional progress in a time of financial stringency and reduced growth?
3 If bargaining is the only way for faculty to get their fair share in the political distribution of public monies, is there any way that they can still retain a strong policy role? Or that students can be influential?

These questions and the capacity of the decision-making system to deal with them may constitute even longer-run criteria for evaluating this or any other decision-making model.

NOTE

1 The formal structure, I assume, refers to those legally constituted and officially recognized bodies, positions, sanctions, and rules and regulations; i.e. the *authority* system, which serves as the basis for influencing decisions. The informal structure refers to the influence on decisions possessed by individuals and groups which is based on information or expertise, on personality, on appeals to common values and attitudes, and on control of social rewards or sanctions which are not officially recognized.

REFERENCES

ANTHONY, R. (1965) *Planning and Control Systems*, Harvard Graduate School of Business Administration.
BERDAHL, R. (1970) *Statewide Coordination of Higher Education*, American Council on Education.
DILL, D. (1971) *Case Studies in University Governance*, National Association of State Universities and Land-Grant Colleges.
DYKES, A. R. (1968) *Faculty Participation in Academic Decision Making*, American Council on Education.
JOHNSON, C. and KATZENMEYER, W. (1969) *Management Information Systems in Higher Education*, Duke University Press.
KATZ, D. and KAHN, R. (1966) *The Social Psychology of Organizations*, Wiley.
MOYNIHAN, D. (1970) "Policy versus program in the '70s", *Public Interest* (Summer), No. 20, 90–100.

O'NEILL, R. (1971) "The eclipse of faculty autonomy", Paper at Campus Governance Conference, Houston, 18 Feb. 1971.

PALOLA, E. *et al.* (1970) *Higher Education by Design*, Center for Research and Development in Higher Education, University of California.

PETERSON, M. W. (1970) "The organization of departments. Research Report No. 2", *College and University Bulletin*, 1 Dec. 1970.

ROURKE, F. and BROOKS, G. (1966) *The Managerial Revolution in Higher Education*, Johns Hopkins Press.

SIMON, H. (1965) *Administrative Behavior*, Ch. 3, Free Press.

THOMPSON, J. (1963) *Comparative Studies in Administration*, University of Pittsburgh.

1.6 Models of Man and Administrative Theory

Alberto Guerreiro Ramos

To the memory of John Pfiffner who gave me the spark to develop this line of thinking.

ABSTRACT

Administrative theory can no longer legitimize the functional rationality of the organization as it largely has done. The basic problem of an earlier time was to overcome the scarcity of material goods and elementary services. In that period a great amount of toil in work settings was technically and socially necessary and even inevitable, which is not true at present. What brings about the crises in today's organizations is the fact that by design and operation they still assume that old scarcities continue to be basic, while in fact contemporary man is aware of critical scarcities belonging to another order, i.e. related to needs beyond the level of simple survival. Thus, the Social Darwinism that has traditionally validated management theory and practice has become outdated by the force of circumstances. This article is an attempt to reassess the evolution of administrative theory. It takes models of man as its point of reference (namely, the operational man, the reactive man, and the parenthetical man).

From the late 1800s to the present, a dramatic turn has taken place in the approaches to organization and work. There was a time when success in business was considered coincidental with virtue, and the teachings of Malthus, Darwin, and Spencer found ideal conditions to thrive. Thus the influential sociologist, William Graham Sumner, did not hesitate to claim that there would be no point in integrating the interest of employers and employees. Antagonism between those interests was legitimized by the "mores" and social science of that time. That the decisive criterion of human value then was success is indicated by the vogue of Elbert Hubbard's *Message to Garcia*, Orison Swett Marden's *Power of Will*, and Dale Carnegie's *How to Win Friends and Influence People*, which

---

Source: *Public Administration Review* (May-June 1972) Vol. 32, Part 3, pp. 241-6.

was published in 1936 and sold over four million copies (see Bendix, 1963).

The image of man implied in those popular books was in accord with the type of management which Taylor and the classic writers were advocating. Yet today, books which boast of wide public acceptance and are often required reading in business schools and schools of public administration are, among others, Marcuse's *Eros and Civilization*, Roszack's *The Making of a Counter Culture*, and Reich's *The Greening of America*, all of which are notorious for their indictment of established organizational and social systems.

It is a current commonplace that an atmosphere of crisis surrounds contemporary organizations and is reflected in the theorizing we do about them. Practitioners and academicians continuously experience this crisis in their everyday lives. The internal and external environment of today's organization is plagued with a high degree of ambiguity and confusion. The current literature in our field consistently shows that there is a widespread concern about how to approach the problems confronting us. In focusing on these difficulties, several scholars have implied that there is emerging a nascent model of man, the development and clarification of which is essential in order to overcome the present critical state of the art and theory of administration. For instance, James Carroll (1969) sees an "increase in awareness" which is "spilling over and inundating . . . existing social systems". He also discerns the birth of a new type of personality which no longer "fits easily into organizational and institutional value structures based upon previously fixed perceptions and concerns". And Anders Richter (1970) suggests that United States' bureaucracies are in need of what he calls "existentialist executives" whose personality structure would be similar to the psychological paradigm depicted by Carroll.

The orientation proposed by Carroll and Richter, and many others, is predicated on the idea that we need a point of reference, a central focus, in order to develop some sense of direction in dealing with administrative problems. We have to understand what types of contemporary social circumstances are now affecting each individual and in consequence the organizations. In fact, contemporary history is pregnant with a new type of man, whom elsewhere I have called the "parenthetical man".[1]

This article is an attempt to reassess the evolution of administrative theory. It takes models of man as its point of reference (namely, the operational man,[2] the reactive man, and the parenthetical man). Throughout the history of our field, theoreticians and practitioners, in their writings and actions, have uncritically made assumptions about the nature of man. Today, however, an administrative theory unconscious of its psychological implications can hardly be satisfactory.

TRADITIONAL MODELS OF MAN

In administrative theory the operational man is equivalent to *homo economicus* in classical economics; *homo sociologicus,* largely assumed by the academic model of sociology; and *homo politicus,* which David Trumen, Christian Bay, and Sheldon Wolin have described as the prevailing model of established political science.[3] Basic psychological characteristics are common to these types which lead them to conform to the criteria inherent in the industrial social system and therefore only to seek the maintenance of that system.

The validity of the operational man has been characteristically taken for granted. He has been seen as an organizational resource to be maximized in terms of measurable, physical output. Indeed, the implication of this approach for organization design can be briefly sketched. It entails (1) an authoritarian method of resource allocation in which the worker is seen as a passive being who must be programmed by experts to function within the organization; (2) a concept of training as essentially a technique for "adjusting" the individual to the imperatives of production maximization; (3) a view that man is calculative, motivated by material and economic rewards, and as a worker is detached from other individuals psychologically; (4) a view of management and administrative theory as value-free or neutral; (5) a systematic indifference to the ethical and value assumptions of the external environment; (6) the viewpoint that issues of personal freedom are extraneous to organization design; and (7) a concept of work as essentially postponement of satisfaction.

An alternative to the operational man was first suggested in the Hawthorne Studies four decades ago. This was the beginning of the Human Relations School, which viewed man as more complex than traditional theorists assumed (see Roethlisberger and Dickson, 1964). In comparison with the operationalists, the humanists (1) had a more sophisticated view of the nature of human motivation; (2) did not neglect the external social environment of the organization and therefore defined the organization as an open social system: and (3) did not overlook the role of values, sentiments, and attitudes in production.

The model of man developed by the humanists may be called "reactive man", with all that the term implies. For humanists, as well as their predecessors, the industrial system and the enterprise function as independent variables. The main objective of management is to enforce behaviors supportive of their specific rationality. Although humanists were ostensibly more concerned about workers and more knowledgeable about their motivations, the ends sought were really unchanged. They developed procedures for the co-optation of informal groups, the use of "personnel counseling", and skills in handling particular human relations to arouse positive reactions towards the purpose of the enterprise. They saw the worker as a *reactive being.* Adjustment of individuals to work settings, rather than their individual growth, was the main objective. The final outcome of mass application of "human relations" was the *total inclusion* of the worker within the organization; in other words, he was to be transformed into what W. H. Whyte, Jr. (1957) has called the *organization man*.

Has the practice of management progressed beyond this point? Viewing the evidence, the answer to this question can hardly be other than a resounding "no". The operational and reactive models are still largely shaping the organizational and social systems of this country. In intellectual milieus, these models are under strong criticism, but no widely accepted alternatives to them have yet been presented.

Yet some features of organizational settings which were largely neglected in the past are today receiving considerable attention. For instance, greater emphasis is now placed on process rather than structure, tasks rather than routines, *ad hoc* strategies rather than principles and prescriptions, and on what has been called changing organizations, nonhierarchical organizations, and participative management. The environment is more than ever a central concern, which somewhat accounts for the current influence of the systems approaches. In addition, freedom and self-actualization have become prominent themes in books and classrooms.

These are considerable improvements, but they are peripheral at best. Overall, present administrative theory and practice are not adequate for present needs. Concepts of changing organizations, for example, are framed in reactive terms, i.e. tested as to their capability to respond uncritically to fluctuations in their environment, without taking responsibility for the standards of quality and priorities of that environment. Such reactive theory seems to rely on a naive view of the nature of inputs and outputs. It considers inputs as consisting of people, materials, and energy, and loses sight of the value and ethical factors in the environment, whose rationality and legitimacy are typically ignored. The environment is accepted as given, and its episodical, vexatious framework becomes an undisputed normative pattern into which so-called changing organizations ought to fit. These are really "adaptive organizations", whereas changing organizations should be identified as those possessing capabilities of affecting and modeling the environment according to criteria not necessarily given. In other words, the management of microorganizations has to be seen as part of a general strategy geared to the management of the whole society.

Another issue involves the integration of the individual and the organization. Those who advocate such an integration overlook the basic, twofold character of rationality. There is, in fact, a rationality whose standards have nothing to do with administrative behavior. This rationality, called substantial and noetic by Karl Mannheim and Eric Voegelin[4] respectively, is an intrinsic attribute of the individual as a creature of reason, and can never be understood as pertaining to any organization.

Indeed, noetic rationality is not systematically related to coordination of means and ends from the standpoint of efficiency. It derives from the immanent imperatives of reason itself, understood as a specific faculty of man, which rules out blind obedience to requirements of efficiency. Thus, it may very well happen that historically a high degree of development in pragmatic rationality can coincide with a "high degree of irrationality in the sphere of noetic reason" (Voegelin, 1963, p. 43). Human behavior occurring under the aegis of noetic rationality only may be administrative by accident, not by necessity. The organization and its leaders can judge if a behavior is rationally instrumental to its goals but never its adequacy to noetic rationality. Indeed, it is the privilege of the noetic rationality to judge the organization. To distinguish and separate the two rationalities is therefore a condition of a sound administrative theory. Adolf Eichmann was probably a perfect bureaucrat whose crime consisted precisely in identifying noetic rationality or the Kantian categorical imperatives of "practical reason" with the "categorical imperatives of the Third Reich".[5] And, more recently, it is the chronic tension between the two rationalities that makes the decision of Daniel Ellsberg to reveal the bulk of the so-called secret Pentagon Papers so perplexing.

It is my contention that the model of the parenthetical man may provide administrative theory with conceptual sophistication to confront issues and problems involving tensions between noetic and functional rationality.

THE RISE OF THE PARENTHETICAL MAN

Actually, the parenthetical man cannot avoid being a participant of the organization. However, in striving to be autonomous, he cannot be explained by the psychology of conformity, as can those individuals who behave according to the operational and reactive models. He possesses a highly developed critical consciousness of the hidden value premises of everyday life. Indeed the adjective "parenthetical" is derived from Husserl's notion of "suspension" and "bracketing". Husserl (1967) distinguishes between natural and critical attitude. The first is that of the "adjusted" man, unconcerned with noetic rationality and locked in his immediacy. The critical attitude suspends or brackets the belief in the ordinary world, enabling the individual to reach a level of conceptual thinking and therefore freedom.

The parenthetical man is both a reflection of, and a reaction to, new social circumstances that are more perceptible now in advanced industrial societies like the United States, but which will eventually prevail throughout the entire world. As Robert Lane has pointed out, behavior patterns tend to become widespread in advanced industrial societies that only residually exist in societies in previous stages of evolution. Indeed in the past, such patterns could be detected only in exceptional individuals. Socrates, Bacon, and Machiavelli, for instance, possessed the psychological capability that Lane (1966) calls "differentiation of ego from inner world and from environment", which made them capable of seeing their respective societies as precarious arrangements. While the bulk of the population in those societies interpreted themselves and social reality according to conventionally prevailing definitions, they had the capability to suspend their circumstances, internal as well as external; by so doing, they could look at them with a critical eye. Such a capability clearly qualifies as parenthetical. Indeed, suspending is here equivalent to bracketing, to putting circumstances between parentheses. Parenthetical man is able to step from the stream of everyday life to examine and assess it as a spectator. He is able to remove himself from the familiar. He deliberately tries to become rootless, an outsider in his own social milieu, in order to maximize his understanding of it. Thus the parenthetical attitude is defined by the psychological capability of the individual to detach himself from his inner and outer circumstances. Parenthetical men thrive when the period of social innocence ends. For this reason, what Lane calls the "knowledgeable" society is the natural environment of parenthetical man.

In a survey of peasants living in the Middle East, Daniel Lerner asked villagers how they would behave in the role of governor of their country, as residents in a foreign nation, as a newspaper editor, etc. He discovered that they were so rooted in their social conditions that they could not imagine themselves in such roles. Theirs was a social world ontologically justified, the very opposite of a circumstance where chances can be exploited and possibilities can be explored.

On the other hand, Robert J. Lifton (1970) found highly rootless behaviors among Japanese youth, which he calls "protean". To illustrate, one of his respondents observed: "For me, there is not a single act I cannot imagine myself committing" (p. 319). There are many similarities between protean and parenthetical man. However, one single difference between them is basic: instead of indulging in an inconsequential relativism as the protean seems to do, the parenthetical man is ethically committed to values conducive to the primacy of reason (in the noetic sense) in social and individual life. Consequently his relationship to work and the organization is very peculiar.

The nature of this relationship can be made clear by looking at the typology Robert Presthus (1965) presents in his book, *The Organizational Society*. Were we to assume that Robert Presthus' three types of man characterize the range of persons in modern organizations, we would only be dealing with upward mobiles, ambivalents and indifferents. A fourth model, the parenthetical man, must be added to this triad. This fourth man would be one who would not over-exert himself to succeed according to conventional terms, as the upward mobile does. He would have a strong sense of self and an urge to find meaning in life. He would not uncritically accept standards of achievement, though he might be a great achiever when assigned creative tasks. He would not yield to the easy escape of apathy or indifference, because passive behavior would offend his sense of self-esteem and autonomy. He would strive to affect the environment, to draw such satisfaction from it as he could. He would be ambivalent towards the organization, but not in the manner described by Presthus. His qualified ambivalence would derive from his understanding that organizations, as bounded within the sphere of functional rationality, have to be dealt with in their own relative terms. Presthus' ambivalents are emotionally undisciplined, psychologically locked in, and easily discouraged when they fail to influence their environment. It was probably an awareness of this desolate picture of the present "organizational society" that prompted Robert Townsend (1970) to write that his book, *Up the Organization,* "does not come to grips with the problems of America's twenty million poor", but "with the eighty million psychiatric cases who do have jobs".

Administrative theory can no longer legitimize the functional rationality of the organization as it largely has done. The basic problem of an earlier time was to overcome the scarcity of material goods and elementary services. In that period a great amount of toil in work settings was technically and socially necessary and even inevitable, which is not true at present. What brings about the crisis in today's organizations is the fact that by design and operation they still assume that old scarcities continue to be basic, while in fact contemporary man is aware of critical scarcities belonging to another order, i.e. related to needs beyond the level of simple survival.[6] Thus, the Social Darwinism that has traditionally validated management theory and practice has become outdated by the force of circumstances.

An increasing number of individuals are becoming aware that the elimination of unnecessary toil is now a feasible possibility, and cognizance of this fact conditions their attitudes toward work and the organization. It is difficult to motivate this kind of person with traditional managerial practices. To manage micro-organizations without focusing on their conditioning by the macro-social system is seen as fallacious, to say the least, by an increasing number of people. A young executive, a much-honored graduate of the Yale Class of 1970, said: 'I don't want a job figuring out new ways of marketing paper plates. This society produces too much, and we ought to stop. This isn't where our priorities ought to be" (1971). Organization development and renewal only makes sense today to the extent that they represent an attempt to give people a sense of true social participation.

This is why it is not enough today to manage organizations, and why it is necessary to manage the whole society. The environment of advanced industrial societies, in which survival is no longer the main reason to work, is generating a new attitude toward the organization. The psychological syndrome described by Presthus tends to be dominant in societies in which the "fear of job loss" is pervasive (Richter, 1970, p. 419). When scarcity of jobs is perceived as a result of distorted institutionalization rather than an essential lack of social capability; when the inability to get work is no longer considered as an inherent personal defect; and when unemployment is subsidized and production of goods declines in importance; then the individual tends to see reflected in the micro-organization the same malaise of the total social fabric. As a result, he is encouraged to become less of a conforming docile worker and more of an active political being. In such a climate, politics become ubiquitous in the sense that everyone strives for the right to satisfy his own needs at all levels of interpersonal relationships. In a low level of accumulation of capital, delay of personal satisfaction may be mandatory; it no longer seems so, however, where capital accumulation is high. It is in this context that the recent expansion of the concept of management makes sense. Indeed, it is significant that the management of society is now becoming a central issue.

One of the main problems to be considered in the overall guidance of the social system is the design of new kinds of organizations or new work patterns. Galbraith (1958) has pointed out that our present affluent society is plagued by contradictions. It is a system capable of eliminating drudgery even to the point of completely abolishing labor as we have known it; nevertheless, we are not facing this concrete possibility systematically (p. 263). But the more conscious of this possibility the average individual becomes, the less he is willing to engage in unnecessary toil. The fact that the great majority of industrial workers do not find their "central life interest" in their labors is a matter of increasing social significance. There are growing indications that their off-the-job life is desolate and contaminated by their job situation. Their discontent with their job may, in turn, alienate them from the global society.

The average worker in the present advanced industrial society realizes that he is losing competence in dealing with himself and the overall environment. Instead of improving the quality of life, technology, as an uncontrolled force, is jeopardizing the possibility of man as a creature of reason. And since such an outcome is not inherent in technology but derives from the episodical political and institutional framework of advanced industrial systems, a new level of human consciousness is appearing. It encourages people (mainly the young) to jettison reactive behaviors. Such people feel that it is their responsibility to redefine the priorities and goals of both organizations and the global social system in order to develop their "own individual bents and proclivities, to consume not simply manufactured goods, but freedom itself" (Harrington, 1969). Paradoxically, technology is, in fact, the prime contributing factor to this revolution in modern society.

These are some of the reasons that are moving the affluent society toward parenthetical life-styles. While the implications of this model for organization design are beyond the scope of this article, it is well to point out that a parenthetical approach to organization design is emerging. It is visible in the behavior of many concerned individuals, scholars, and practitioners (again most of them young) who are trying to "beat" or "disestablish" existing traditional administrative systems. It is certainly implicit in the attempts at designing non-hierarchical and client-oriented

53

organizations;[7] in agencies and strategies such as those aimed at protecting citizens and consumers (e.g. the Federal Trade Commission, Citizen Group Association of California Consumers, and the various activities of such men as Ralph Nader and Saul Alinsky); in the determination of restructuring the entire social system from the standpoint of ecological imperatives,[8] new social priorities (e.g. John Gardner's *Common Cause*), and new criteria of quality of life (of which the movement of "social indicators" is indicative).[9] It is a sign of the times that *Up the Organization*, by Robert Townsend (1970), which has been a bestseller and been taken seriously in lay as well as in professional circles, was presented by the author as a "survival manual for successful corporate guerrillas" (p. ix). In its long history, the traditional organization is now reaching its moment of truth. Its lure is vanishing. Our field is now ripe for a Kantian deed, a Copernican Revolution. We need no less than a radical critique of organizational reason.

NOTES

The author has subtitled this paper "The Rise of the Parenthetical Man."
1 This article derives from a longer paper entitled "The Parenthetical Man", delivered at the National Conference of the American Society for Public Administration, Denver, Colorado, 18–21 April 1971.
2 I am indebted to John Pfiffner for this expression.
3 See Truman (1965), Bay (1965) and Wolin (1969).
4 See Mannheim (1940) and Voegelin (1963), and also Habermas (1970).
5 Phrase attributed to Hans Frank by Hannah Arendt (1968).
6 On this point see Galbraith (1958).
7 See Bennis (1966) and White (1969).
8 See Pearl and Pearl (1971). The authors advocate a "new type of ecological cost-benefit analysis, on a world-wide basis, in which planning must move us from a goods-oriented society to one oriented toward quality of life and human service" (p. 33).
9 See Gross (1969) and, on the same subject, *The Annals of the American Academy of Political and Social Science* (March 1970).

REFERENCES

ARENDT, H. (1968) *Eichmann in Jerusalem*, Viking Press, p. 136.
BAY, C. (1965) "Politics and Pseudopolitics: A Critical Evaluation of Some Behavioral Literature". *American Political Science Review*, Vol. LIX, No. 1, March 1965.
BENDIX, R. (1963) *Work and Authority in Industry*, Harper and Row, chapter 5.
BENNIS, W. G. (1966) *Changing Organizations*, McGraw-Hill.

CARROLL, J. D. (1969) "Noetic Authority", *Public Administration Review*, Sept.–Oct. 1969, p. 493.

GALBRAITH, J. K. (1958) *The Affluent Society*, New American Library.

GOODING, J. (1971) "The Accelerated Generation Moves into Management", *Fortune*, March 1971, p. 103.

GROSS, B. (1969) (ed.), *Social Intelligence for America's Future*, Allyn and Bacon.

HABERMAS, J. (1970) *Toward a Rational Society*, Beacon Press.

HARRINGTON, M. (1969) *The Accidental Century*, Penguin Books Inc., p. 272.

HUSSERL, E. (1967) "The Thesis of Natural Standpoint and Its Suspension", Kockelmans, J. J. (ed.) *Phenomenology, the Philosophy of Edmund Husserl and Its Interpretation*, Doubleday.

LANE, R. E. (1966) "The Decline of Politics and Ideology in a Knowledgeable Society", *American Sociological Review*, Oct. 1966, p. 654.

LIFTON, R. J. (1970) *History and Human Survival*, Random House, pp. 311–31.

MANNHEIM, K. (1940) *Man and Society in an Age of Reconstruction*, Harcourt, Brace and World, pp. 51–66.

PEARL, A. and PEARL, S. (1971) "Strategies for Radical Social Change: Toward an Ecological Theory of Value", *Social Policy*, Vol. 2, No. 1, May–June 1971.

PRESTHUS, R. (1965) *The Organizational Society*, Random House.

RICHTER, A. (1970) "The Existentialist Executive", *Public Administration Review*, July–Aug. 1970.

ROETHLISBERGER, F. J. and DICKSON, W. J. (1964) *Management and the Worker*, Wiley.

TOWNSEND, R. (1970) *Up the Organization*, Fawcet Publications, p. 121.

TRUMAN, D. B. (1965) "Disillusion and Regeneration: The Quest for a Discipline", *American Political Science Review*, Vol. LIX, No. 4, Dec. 1965.

VOEGELIN, E. (1963) "Industrial Society in Search of Reason", in Aron, R. (ed.) *World Technology and Human Destiny*, University of Michigan Press.

WHITE, O. F., Jr. (1969) "The Dialectical Organization: An Alternative to Bureaucracy", *Public Administration Review*, Jan.–Feb. 1969.

WHYTE, W. H., Jr. (1957) *The Organization Man*, Doubleday.

WOLIN, S. S. (1969) "Political Theory as a Vocation", *American Political Science Review*, Vol. LXIII, No. 4, Dec. 1969.

2 Aspects of Organizational Theory

INTRODUCTION

The second section opens with a long paper by Barr Greenfield which clearly rejects the convenient "duality" that has separated people and organizations. He makes the telling point that organizational structures are usually seen as constant over a period of time, and in rejecting this reified view of organization, gives a thorough analysis of the evidence available within the framework he has chosen. His conclusion, referring to the "paramount importance of the interpretation of experience", is one which is worthy of widespread attention.

"The Study of Schools as Organizations", a recent, well-known paper by Eric Hoyle, asks some extremely pertinent questions about the choice of methodology and contains a useful review of British work on the subject. It is followed by a classic paper by Weber, which is included so that students can have some first-hand knowledge of this most frequently quoted theorist in the area. The next paper, by Leonard Watson, begins by using the three types of authority posed by Weber; he does, however, bring the theorizing firmly into the school situation. Those students who, understandably, have a deep suspicion of unrelated academic theorizing will appreciate Watson's ability to place theory in a meaningful and recognizable context.

The Reader changes its focus at this point and Daniel Griffiths puts the emphasis upon change in organizations, using a systems model originally developed by Miller and Hearn which in effect is a strong plea for "open systems". Some of the main problems in achieving change are then discussed by Professor Reddin in a succinct presentation of his own perspective. The historical legacy of industry, which is much more important than we usually realize, is described by Tom Burns, who then shows how systems which can only be described as pathological continue in an age in which they are worse than irrelevant. We should be far more aware of the way in which industrial practice has shaped educational practice, and should also remember that much of the shaping has been done on the model of the first industrial revolution.

2.1 Theory about Organization: A New Perspective and its Implications for Schools

T. Barr Greenfield

In common parlance we speak of organizations as if they were real. Neither scholar nor layman finds difficulty with talk in which organizations "serve functions", "adapt to their environment", "clarify their goals" or "act to implement policy". What it is that serves, adapts, clarifies or acts seldom comes into question. Underlying widely accepted notions about organizations, therefore, stands the apparent assumption that organizations are not only real but also distinct from the actions, feelings and purposes of people. This mode of thought provides the platform for a long-standing debate about organizations and people. Is it organizations which oppress and harass people or is it fallible people who fail to carry out the well-intentioned aims of organizations? The debate continues on issues such as whether it is better to abolish organizations, to reshape them along more humane lines, or to train people to recognize the goals of organizations more clearly and to serve them more faithfully.

In contrast, this paper rejects the dualism which conveniently separates people and organizations; instead it argues that a mistaken belief in the reality of organizations has diverted our attention from human action and intention as the stuff from which organizations are made. As a result, theory and research have frequently set out on a false path in trying to understand organizations and have given us a misplaced confidence in our ability to deal with their problems. If we see organizations and individuals as inextricably intertwined, it may not be so easy to alter organizations, or to lead them, or to administer them without touching something unexpectedly human. More importantly, the view that people and organizations are inseparable requires us to reassess the commonly accepted claim that there exists a body of theory and principle which provides the touchstone for effective administrative action in organizations. The belief in the reality and independence of organizations

---

Source: An expanded version of a paper given at the Third International Intervisitation Programme on Educational Administration (1974) at Bristol, sponsored by the British Educational Administration Society and other agencies.

permits us to separate the study of organizations from the study of people and their particular values, habits and beliefs. The common view in organization studies holds that people occupy organizations in somewhat the same way as they inhabit houses. The tenants may change but, apart from wear and tear, the basic structure remains and in some way shapes the behaviour of people within. Studies have therefore focused largely on the variety of organizational structures and their effects upon people. These structures are usually seen as invariate over time and place, as universal forms into which individuals may move from time to time, bringing with them idiosyncrasies which colour their performance of the roles prescribed by the organization (Getzels, 1958, p. 156).

ORGANIZATIONAL SCIENCE AND THE PROFESSION OF ADMINISTRATION

The science of organization has found its way into studies of schools and influenced the training of those who are to administer schools. In this science, schools are a variety of the species organization which can be distinguished chiefly by the nature of their goals and their bureaucratic structure (Bidwell, 1965, pp. 973–4). The science of organization is, therefore, assumed to provide useful knowledge about schools even as it does about other kinds of organizations. Accepting this position, Griffiths (1964, p. 3) rejects "the opinion that educational administration is a unique activity, differing greatly from business, military, hospital and other varieties of administration" and endorses (p. 118) a "general theory which enables the researcher to describe, explain, and predict a wide range of human behavior within organizations".

In a profession of administration based upon organizational science, the task of the administrator is to bring people and organizations together in a fruitful and satisfying union. In so doing, the work of the administrator carries the justification of the larger social order (Getzels, 1958, p. 156), since he works to link day-to-day activity in organizations to that social order. In schools, the administrator may be director or superintendent, principal or headmaster, department head or supervisor. Whatever their titles, their tasks are always the same. They bring people and resources together so that the goals of the organization and presumably of an encompassing social order may be met (Gregg 1957, pp. 269–70). No matter what circumstances he finds himself in, the administrator mediates between the organization and the people within it. The task is difficult; he needs help with it. As the argument runs, such help is fortunately to be found in the emerging science of organizations. Since organizations do have a human component, knowledge about organizations is usually described as a social science. But social or not, this science like all others is seen as universal, timeless, and imperfect only in its incompleteness.

The claims for a science of organization and for a profession of administration based upon that science have in recent times made a marked impact upon education. For over two decades now, scholars have attempted to improve education by applying organization theory to the conduct of affairs in schools and by training educational administrators in that science (Culbertson and Shibles, 1973). Celebrating its emancipation from the press of immediate practical affairs (Griffiths, 1964), the field turned instead to discovery of the basic relationships and principles which underlie day-to-day concerns. The professor supplanted the practitioner as the source of valid knowledge about administration. If practitioners did not know or accept that they were no longer masters of the basic knowledge which underlay their craft, it did not matter. Even the scholar-practitioner, Chester Barnard, in introducing Simon's classic writings claimed that it was the scholar's knowledge of the "abstract principles of structure" rather than the practitioner's knowledge of "concrete behavior" which leads to an understanding of "organizations of great variety" (Simon, 1957, pp. xlii–xliv). Things are not what they seem, in educational administration as in other realms of reality. We need the scientist and his theory to interpret them to us. His knowledge, though it may be incomplete and is certainly subject to improvement, has the virtue of universal applicability. Acting on this conviction, scholars in educational administration have sought to understand how organizations really work and to use this knowledge towards the improvement of educational practice.

A survey of representative writing in educational administration (see Campbell and Gregg, 1957; Halpin, 1958; Griffiths, 1964; Getzels, Lipham and Campbell, 1968; Milstein and Belasco, 1973) reveals that inquiry in this field has leaned heavily on the belief that a general science of organizations has provided the needed theoretical underpinnings for understanding schools and for the training of the administrators who are to run them. While a general theory of organizations provided the rationale for understanding schools, the sister social sciences provided the research tools and the "sensitizing concepts" needed to identify and resolve their administrative problems (Downey and Enns, 1963; Tope *et al.*, 1965). Since this happy combination of theory and method yields an understanding of organizations as they really are, it then becomes possible to say how educational administrators may be trained to improve organizations and administrative practice within them (Culbertson *et al.*, 1973). Although the claim is seldom if ever made explicitly, this line of reasoning, linking a general theory of organizations to the training of administrators, implies that we have at hand both the theory and method which permit us to improve schools and the quality of whatever it is that goes on within them. That change in schools proceeds without assistance from an applied organization theory, or indeed, in contravention to it (Fullan, 1972), usually fails to shake our faith in such theory.

It will surely come as no surprise to anyone who examines the references cited to this point that most of them are American in origin, since it was in the United States that the movement to conceive educational administration as a social science arose in the late 1940s. A decade later the movement had taken hold in Canada and some time later in Australia and Britain. As the concept of educational administration as a profession and social science gains ever wider recognition and acceptance, it becomes appropriate to examine the theory and assumptions which underlie the field. In particular we need to ask whether the theory and assumptions still appear to hold in the settings where they were developed before they were recommended and applied to totally new settings. Such an examination is not only appropriate but essential in the face of an alternative view which sees organizations not as structures subject to universal laws but as cultural artefacts dependent upon the scientific meaning and intention of people within them. This alternative view, which stems from nineteenth-century German idealism (Deutscher, 1973, p. 326), bears the awkward name phenomenology (Phillipson, 1972), though it might with equal justification be called the method of understanding, as it is in the work of Max Weber (Eldridge, 1971, p. 28). What we call the view is not important. What matters is that there exists a body of theory and assumption which runs squarely at odds with that which has provided the ideological underpinnings of educational administration as it has developed over the past two decades. The ideological conflict between these views rests on two fundamentally different ways of looking at the world. One is the established view both in the study of organizations generally and in the study of educational administration. In this paper, I will outline the alternative view and recommend its application both in organization and administrative theory.

It is surely no accident that the alternative view has its roots in European philosophy and social science. And it is at least noteworthy that this view has a current flowering in Britain, where it is exerting a strong influence in both sociology (Filmer et al., 1972; Dawe, 1970; Brittan, 1973) and in education (Young, 1971; Cosin et al., 1971), I do not wish to drive the differences in the views to the point of a spurious contrast between American and European social science. The alternative view which I will outline has its supporters in the United States too (Garfinkel, 1967; Cicourel, 1964; Louch, 1966; Wilson, 1970). Two points should be made here. First, and of lesser importance, phenomenology has yet to influence the study of organizations in the United States despite the existence of a long-standing phenomenological tradition in some sociological schools of thought in that country.[1] In Britain, both theory and research on organizations reflect the phenomenological perspective (Tipton, 1973; Silverman, 1970). Second, and more important since it relates to the heart of the issue, the existence of the two competing ideologies illustrates the fundamental contention of phenomenology that there are no fixed ways for construing the social world around us. These ways are products of particular settings and circumstances rather than expressions of universal ideals and values. Our concepts of organizations must therefore rest upon the views of people in particular times and places, and any effort to understand them in terms of a single set of ideas, values and laws must be doomed to failure.

The alternative view rejects the assumption, underlying much of organization theory, that organizations belong to a single species which behaves in predictable ways according to common laws. This view finds forceful expression in the work of Mayntz (1964), a European scholar of organizations:

> Propositions which hold for such diverse phenomena as an army, a trade union, and a university ... must necessarily be either trivial or so abstract as to tell hardly anything of interest about concrete reality ... After all, the distinct character of an organization is certainly determined, among other things, by the nature, interests, and values of those who are instrumental in maintaining it [pp. 113–114].

If people are inherently part of organizations, if organizations themselves are expressions of how people believe they should relate to each other, we then have good grounds to question an organization theory which assumes the universality of organizational forms and effects. This argument suggests that organizations theorists have been so busy defining the forest that they have failed to notice differences among the trees—and worse, have ignored objects in the forest that are not trees at all. It suggests, too, that an academic industry which trains administrators by disclosing to them the social-scientific secrets of how organizations work or how policy should be made indulges at best in a premature hope and at worst in a delusion.

TWO VIEWS OF SOCIAL REALITY

The conflicting views on organizations of which I have been speaking represent vastly different ways of looking at social reality and rest on sharply contrasting processes for interpreting it. These contrasts are summarized in Table 1 in which I have compared the two views and suggested how they differ with respect to a number of critical issues. Each of these issues has implications for the theory of organizations and for research undertaken in line with such theory. Necessarily then, these contrasts also have implications for a number of practical questions in the conduct of affairs in organizations. Some of these will be explored in the concluding section of this paper. Although there are no generally accepted names for identifying the two views contrasted in Table 1, it may suffice to note that the crux of the issue is whether social reality is based upon naturally existing systems or upon human invention of social forms. Social reality is usually construed as a natural and necessary order which, as it unfolds, permits human society to exist and people within it to meet their basic needs. Alternatively, social reality may be construed as images in the mind of man having no necessary or inevitable forms

Table 1. Alternative bases for interpreting social reality

Dimensions of comparison	What is social reality?	
	A natural system	*Human invention*
Philosophical basis	Realism: the world exists and is knowable as it really is. Organizations are real entities with a life of their own.	Idealism: the world exists but different people construe it in very different ways. Organizations are invented social reality.
The role of social science	Discovering the universal laws of society and human conduct within it.	Discovering how different people interpret the world in which they live.
Basic units of social reality	The collectivity: society or organizations.	Individuals acting singly or together.
Method of understanding	Identifying conditions or relationships which permit the collectivity to exist. Conceiving what these conditions and relationships are.	Interpretations of the subjective meanings which individuals place upon their action. Discovering the subjective rules for such action.
Theory	A rational edifice built by scientists to explain human behaviour.	Sets of meanings which people use to make sense of their world and behaviour within it.
Research	Experimental or quasi-experimental validation of theory.	The search for meaningful relationships and the discovery of their consequences for action.
Methodology	Abstraction of reality, especially through mathematical models and quantitative analysis.	The representation of reality for purposes of comparison. Analysis of language and meaning.
Society	Ordered. Governed by a uniform set of values and made possible only by those values.	Conflicted. Governed by the values of people with access to power.
Organizations	Goal oriented. Independent of people. Instruments of order in society serving both society and the individual.	Dependent upon people and their goals. Instruments of power which some people control and can use to attain ends which seem good to them.

Table 1. Alternative bases for interpreting social reality—*continued*

Dimensions of comparison	A natural system	Human invention
Organizational pathologies	Organizations get out of kilter with social values and individual needs.	Given diverse human ends, there is always conflict among people acting to pursue them.
Prescription for curing organizational ills	Change the structure of the organization to meet social values and individual needs.	Find out what values are embodied in organizational action and whose they are. Change the people or change their values if you can.

except as man creates them and endows them with reality and authority. In the one perspective, organizations are natural objects—systems of being which man discovers; in the other, organizations are cultural artefacts which man shapes within limits given only by his perception and the boundaries of his life as a human animal.

The systems notion posits an organizational force or framework which encompasses and gives order to people and events within it. The system—unseen behind everyday affairs—is real; it *is* the organization. The force of "natural" in the descriptor is to evoke the view common in systems theory that organizational forms are shaped by powerful forces which in large measure act independently of man. The organizations so formed will be right and good, if the natural forces are allowed free play. Mayntz (1964, pp. 105, 115) has noted that such views in which an unseen organizational hand works for the greater social good are likely to be most congenial to scholars who share a faith in the ideals of the Western liberal democracies. In identifying organizations as social inventions, the alternative view identifies organization with man's image of himself and with the particular and distinctive ways in which people see the world around them and their place in it. This view is the perspective of phenomenology. In it organizations are the perceived social reality within which people make decisions and take actions which seem right and proper to them. (Greenfield, 1973, p. 557). The heart of this view is not a single abstraction called organization, but rather the varied perceptions by individuals of what they can, should, or must do in dealing with others within the circumstances in which they find themselves. It is noteworthy that this tradition—the decision-making tradition (Cyert and March, 1963; Simon, 1964) in organization theory—is frequently cited in scholarly writing, but seldom followed in analyses of organizations. This tradition, culminating currently in the creative insights of James March (1972) into organizational realities, reaches back into the work of Simon (1957; March and Simon, 1958) and thence into the work of Max Weber (trans.

Gerth and Mills, 1946) and the German philosophers and sociologists of the phenomenological tradition (Deutscher, 1973, p. 327; Silverman, 1972, pp. 184–5).

What are some of the particular issues involved in the contrast between the systems and phenomenological views? These are suggested in Table 1 where the two views are compared on a number of points. In the discussion which follows, the phenomenological view is emphasized, since it is assumed that the foundations of the systems view are the more familiar of the two views.

Philosophical basis

The systems view assumes that the world is knowable as it is. Although the acquisition of such knowledge requires the intervention and help of scientists, theorists and scholars, there exists an ultimate reality which may be discovered by application of the scientific method and similar forms of rational analysis. In systems theory, the prevailing image of the organization is that of an organism. Organizations exist; they are observable entities which have a life of their own. Organizations are like people, although sometimes the image is more that of the recalcitrant child rather than the mature adult. In any case, the theory endows organizations with many human properties. They have goals towards which they direct their activities; they respond and adapt to their environments. Nor can organizations escape the fate of organisms ill-adapted to their environments. Indeed, the fate of organizations depends upon their ability to adapt to an increasingly complex and turbulent environment. Following the Darwinian logic inherent in their image of the organization, systems theorists (Bennis, 1968) see small, quick-witted, democratic organizations replacing the ponderous, bureaucratic forms now expiring around us. The fact that bureaucratic organizations appear as large, robust and formidable as ever does not appear to shake belief in organizations as living entities subject to stringent laws permitting only the fittest to survive. Indeed, our belief in the living organization is likely to be so strong that we fail to notice that the systems theorists have shifted from telling us about the way organizations are to telling us how they ought to be. "If only organizations were adapted to their environments," the argument runs, "imagine how quickly these bureaucratic forms would disappear." In thinking about the dazzling prospect of a world in which organizations were creatures closely adapted to a benign, well-intentioned environment, we forget that the role of theory is to tell us the way things are rather than how they ought to be or how we should like them to be. Our image of the organization as an entity, as a living entity, rests upon an analogy. But we fail to draw the conclusion (Willer, 1967, p. 33) that the analogy is useless when discrepancies appear between the image and the phenomena observed.

The phenomenological view of reality contrasts sharply with that of systems theory. This view has its origin in the distinction Kant drew between the noumenal world (the world as it is) and the phenomenal world (the world as we see it). For Kant, a world of reality does indeed exist, but man can never perceive it directly; reality is always glossed over with human interpretations which themselves become the realities to which man responds. And man is always learning, always interpreting, always inventing the "reality" which he sees about him. In popular form, the Kantian philosophy has been expressed as follows: "Man does not create his world, but he does make it." It therefore comes as no surprise to the phenomenologist that people are killed by "empty" guns. But for the phenomenologist, beliefs are always of greater consequence than facts in shaping behaviour. The bullet may indeed be in the gun, but it is the individual's belief about an empty chamber which causes him idly to pull the trigger. Deutscher (1973) summarizes the phenomenological view as follows:

> The phenomenological orientation always sees reality as constructed by men in the process of thinking about it. It is the social version of Descartes' *Cogito, ergo sum*. For the phenomenologist it becomes *Cogitamus, ergo est*—we think, therefore it is! [1973, p. 328].

The role of social science

The implications of the phenomenological view are of critical importance in shaping our views both of the social sciences and of a study of organizations founded on them, as may be seen in the contrasting positions taken by Weber and Durkheim (Bendix and Roth, 1971, pp. 286–97). For Weber, working within his "method of understanding", "there is no such thing as a collective personality which 'acts' ", only individuals acting on their interpretations of reality. In contrast, Durkheim, convinced of an ultimate, knowable social reality, sought to eliminate the perceptions of individuals and to find "the explanation of social life in the nature of society itself" (Bendix and Roth, 1971, p. 291). Thus Durkheim spent his life building a sociology around notions of "elemental" forms which provide the invariable units out of which social life is built. Weber, on the other hand, explored the ideas, doctrines and beliefs with which men endowed their organizations and which provided the motivation for action within them. Durkheim's path leads to generality, abstraction and universality in the study of organizations; Weber's leads to the particularistic, the concrete, and the experience-based study of organizations. Durkheim's path leads to an asceptic study of organizations, Weber's to one which smells of reality.

The phenomenological view leads to the concept of organizations as "invented social reality" (Greenfield, 1973, p. 556) and to the paradox that, having invented such reality, man is perfectly capable of responding to it as though it were not of his own invention (Silverman, 1970, p. 133). More basically, however, the phenomenological perspective questions the possibility of objectivity in what Weber calls "the cultural sciences".

While it is possible for such sciences to pursue inquiry within a logically rigorous methodology and for them to take into account certain basic social facts such as where people live and what they do, it is not possible for cultural scientists to give us "a direct awareness of the structure of human actions in all their reality" (Eldridge, 1971, p. 16). Thus the notion of discovering the ultimate laws which govern social reality becomes an ever receding fantasy which retreats as we attempt to approach it. Such bogus 'laws' as the law of supply and demand were, both for Weber and Durkheim, "maxims for action", advice to people on how to protect their interests if they wished to be "fair and logical" (Eldridge, 1971, p. 18). In Weber's view, then, it is impossible for the cultural sciences to penetrate behind social perception to reach objective social reality. Paradoxically, this limitation on the cultural sciences is also their strength, since it permits them to do what is never possible in the physical sciences: the cultural scientist may enter into and take the viewpoint of the actor whose behaviour is to be explained.

> We can accomplish something which is never attainable in the natural sciences, namely the subjective understanding of the action of component individuals ... We do not 'understand' the behaviour of cells, but can only observe the relevant functional relationships and generalize on the basis of these observations [Weber, 1947, pp. 103–4].

While the cultural scientist may not discover ultimate social reality, he can interpret what people see as social reality and, indeed, he must do so according to a consistent, logical, and rigorous methodology (Eldridge, 1971, pp. 9–10). It is such a discipline for interpreting human experience which provides the science in the cultural scientist's work, not his ability to discover ultimate truths about social structure. Thus the purpose of social science is to understand social reality as different people see it and to demonstrate how their views shape the action which they take within that reality. Since the social sciences cannot penetrate to what lies behind social reality, they must work directly with man's definitions of reality and with the rules he devises for coping with it. While the social sciences do not reveal ultimate truth, they do help us to make sense of our world. What the social sciences offer is explanation, clarification and demystification of the social forms which man has created around himself. In the view of some (Dawe, 1970, p. 211), the social sciences may lead us to enlightenment and to liberation from the forces which oppress man. In the phenomenological view, these forces stem from man himself, not from abstractions which lie behind social reality and control man's behaviour within that reality.

Theory about what?
The two views give rise to opposing theories about the world and the way

it works, since each sees reality in different kinds of things. Each approaches theory building from a point of view which is normative rather than descriptive. In the natural systems view, the basic reality is the collectivity; reality is in society and its organizations. Assuming the existence of an ultimate social reality, the role of theory is to say how it hangs together or how it might be changed so that it would hang together even more effectively (Merton, 1957; Etzioni, 1960). Thus functional analysis—the theory associated with the systems view—becomes a justification of the way social reality is organized rather than an explanation of it. In this view, the theory becomes more important than the research because it tells us what we can never perceive directly with our senses: it tells us the ultimate reality behind the appearance of things and it establishes a view which is essentially beyond confirmation or disproof by mere research.

The phenomenological view begins with the individual and seeks to understand his interpretations of the world around him. The theory which emerges must be grounded (Glaser and Strauss, 1967) in data from particular organizations. That these data will be glossed with the meanings and purposes of those people and places is the whole point of this philosophical view. Thus the aim of scientific investigation is to understand how that glossing of reality goes on at one time and place and to compare it with what goes on in different times and places. Similarly organizations are to be understood in terms of people's beliefs about their behaviour within them. If we are to understand organizations, we must understand what people within them think of as right and proper to do. Within this framework we would certainly not expect people everywhere to have the same views. In fact, it is the existence of differences in belief structures which provides us with the key to interpreting them. People are not likely to think of their own views as strange. Indeed it is only in contrast to other views that we come to understand our own. Theory thus becomes the sets of meanings which yield insight and understanding of people's behaviour. These theories are likely to be as diverse as the sets of human meanings and understandings which they are to explain. In the phenomenological perspective, the hope for a universal theory of organizations collapses into multifaceted images of organizations as varied as the cultures which support them.

The view of theory as arising from our understanding is expressed by Walsh (1972):

> The point about the social world is that it has been preselected and preinterpreted by its members in terms of a series of commonsense assumptions which constitute a taken-for-granted scheme for reference ... In this manner factual reality is conferred upon the social world by the routine interpretive practices of its members. The implication of this is that every man is a practical theorist when it

comes to investigating the social world, and not just the sociologist [p. 26].

Thus, the naturalist tries to devise general theories of social behaviour and to validate them through ever more complex research methodologies which push him further from the experience and understanding of the everyday world. The phenomenologist works directly with such experience and understanding to build his theory upon them. As Kuhn (1970) points out, our theories are not just possible explanations of reality; they are sets of instructions for looking at reality. Thus choice among theories and among approaches to theory building involves normative and—especially in the social sciences—moral questions. Choice among them is in part a matter of preference, but choice may also be made on the basis of which theories direct us to the most useful problems and which provide the most helpful insights into them.

Research and methodology

In the systems view, research is directed at confirming theory. Theory, in this view, is something which scientists build, largely from the armchair, by thinking up what must be the ultimate explanation for the phenomena observed. Contrary to accepted opinion, Kuhn (1970, p. 16) has argued that such theory is never open to disproof and serves instead as a "consensual agreement among scientists about what procedures shall constitute scientific activity and hence which explanations will count as scientific explanations" (Walsh, 1972, p. 25).

From the phenomenological perspective research, theory and methodology must be closely associated. Theory must arise out of the process of inquiry itself and be intimately connected with the data under investigation. In this view, the aim of theory should be explanation and clarification. Thus research and theory which fulfils this aim must depend not only upon what is being explained but also upon to whom it is explained, and with what. Louch (1966) argues this view as follows:

> Explanation, in Wittgenstein's phrase, is a family of cases joined together only by a common aim, to make something plain or clear. This suggests that a coherent account of explanation could not be given without attending to the audience to whom an explanation is offered or the source of puzzlement that requires an explanation to be given. There are many audiences, many puzzles [p. 233].

Research in the naturalist mode is prone to use experimental methods to establish relationships among variables. The research often substitutes mathematical models for the substantive theoretical model and is satisfied if statistically significant relationships are found among the variables of the mathematical model. The aim is to relate variables x and y, usually with a host of other variables "held constant". Little effort is spent on determining whether x and y exist in any form which is meaningful to or has consequences for actors within a social situation. Nor is there much effort to ask whether holding one or more variables constant yields an interpretable result among those remaining. In physical systems, we can understand what it means to hold volume constant, for example, while we raise the temperature of a gas and observe the effect on pressure. But what does it mean when we come to a social system and speak, as some researchers do, of holding social class constant while we observe the effect of school resources upon achievement? Whereas the physicist manipulates materials and apparatus in specific, understandable ways, the social researcher frequently makes no intervention at all in the social system which he is attempting to explain. Instead, he does the manipulation of variables in his mind, or in the workings of his computer. Can we rely on the suggestion that if we manipulate variables in a social system, we will get the same results the researcher gets from his intellectual manipulation of them? The doubt is growing that we will not, as is apparent, for example, from critiques of school effects research (Spady, 1973, pp. 139–40) demonstrating that schools may account for a great deal or virtually nothing at all of pupil achievement, depending on which of several alternative but statistically acceptable procedures the researcher chooses for his analysis.

Phenomenologically based research, on the other hand, aims at dealing with the direct experience of people in specific situations. Therefore the case study and comparative and historical methods become the preferred means of analysis. These methods are perhaps found in their most developed form in the work Weber did in building ideal types for organizational analysis. These types should be seen as "characterizations or impressions of ways of thought and styles of living" which permit comparison and understanding of them (Louch, 1966, p. 172). What Weber did in building these ideal types was to worm his way into the heads of bureaucrats, clerics and commercial men in order to "discern logical connections among propositions expressing [their] beliefs about the world" (Louch, 1966, p. 173). The moral consequences of these beliefs may also be made plain and checked against "reality". The close connection among theory, research and ethics thus becomes obvious.

Thus an organizational theory based upon understanding rejects the emphasis which much of contemporary social science places upon quantification, more complex mathematical models, and bigger number crunchers in the shape of better and faster computers. As Burns (1967, p. 127) has pointed out, better manipulation of numbers cannot substitute for the emptiness of the concepts to which they apply. This fixation on numbers without concern for the concepts they are thought to represent leads to a sickness of social science which Sorokin has called "quantophrenia" and which Rothkopf (1973, p. 6) likens to the *Leerlauf* reactions described by Lorenz. In these reactions, animals go through elaborate stereotyped performances for hunting or mating when no other living creature is there to see or respond to the performances.

If we move towards improved understanding in our research we might change our image of what constitutes *the* essential research tool and supplant the computer with Weber's notion of the ideal type. An ideal type provides us with an image of a social situation at a particular time and place. We may then surround this image with others made of different organizations or of the same organization at other times. By looking at these images comparatively by seeing them almost as the frames of a motion picture, we begin to understand our world better and to comprehend its differences and the processes of change occurring within it. This direction in theory and research leads to an investigation of language and the categories it contains for understanding the world (Bernstein, 1971a; 1971b). It leads also to an investigation of the processes (Scheff, 1973; Garfinkel, 1964) by which we negotiate with each other and so come to define what we will pay attention to in our environment and our organizations.

Society and its organizations

In the systems view, the problem of society is the problem of order. Without society and its organizations, chaos and anarchy would result. The social order is seen as a basically well-working system governed by universal values. In the phenomenological view, the organization as an entity striving to achieve a single goal or set of goals is resolved into the meaningful actions of individuals. Organizations do not think, act, have goals or make decisions. People do (Georgiou, 1973; Greenfield, 1973), but they do not all think, act and decide according to preordained goals. Thus the notion of the organization as a necessary order-maintaining instrument falls and the notion of organization as the expression of particular human ideologies takes its place. In this way, the problem of order becomes the problem of control (Dawe, 1970, p. 212). Or, to put the question otherwise, the problem is not whether order shall be maintained but rather who maintains it, how, and with what consequences. The image which this view calls to mind is the organization as a battlefield rather than the organization as an instrument of order. People strive to impose their interpretations of social reality upon others and to gain command of the organizational resources which will permit them to do so. The warfare in this battlefield usually takes the form of linguistic attack and defence, although the physical forms of warfare fit just as comfortably within the perspective.

Take as an example this exchange between a principal and a new social worker after the social worker had spent considerable time and effort counselling a student who had been persistently truant and tardy.[2]

P :   It was really simpler and more effective in the old days when the truant officer just went straight to the student's home and brought him back to school.

sw: Actually, I do the work truant officers did, but I do it a different way.

p: That may be so, but we used to get results more quickly. If the students wouldn't come to school, we expelled them. They had to recognize our authority or quit school. That's what I mean by simple. Now everything is complicated. Why can't we deal with these cases without a lot of red tape?

sw: I prefer to see my work as treatment. The aim is not to wind up a case quickly but to keep the student in school and learning. And in any case, Mr. Principal, legally I am the truant officer and you need my backing to expel a student for truancy.

It is surely not hard to see in this exchange a battle going on over what the job of the social worker should be and behind that a struggle over how the school should define its responsibilities to students. The issue is how the job of the social worker shall be defined and who shall control the school's power of expulsion. Each of the protagonists is inviting (and threatening) the other to accept a particular definition of the situation and the way it is proper to act within it.

The conflict view of organizations thus links up neatly with the decision-making tradition in organizational analysis. In a recent significant contribution Perrow (1972, pp. 145–76) demonstrates how this tradition, developed brilliantly by March and Simon (1958), complements the insights of Weber. A major concern of Weber was for the way in which the power of bureaucracies would be used outside the organization. March and Simon demonstrate how power may be marshalled within the organization. As Perrow points out (p. 196), the supposed plight of professionals within bureaucracies is a minor complaint compared to what others have suffered from professionals who have been able to act out their ideological beliefs through their control of organizations.

We should also be grateful to Perrow (p. 90ff) for pointing out the contrasts between Barnard's theory and his practice. For Barnard, (1938, pp. 46–61) organizations were by their very nature cooperative enterprises. In this respect, Barnard was a good systems theorist whose theory dealt with abstractions about organizations and not with the ideologies of those who ran them. In an astonishing case study, Barnard (1948) spoke to a group of the unemployed who had recently seen "police clubs flying, women trampled, men knocked down" (p. 64) in the following terms:

I'll be God damned if I will do anything for you on the basis that you ought to have it just because you want it, or because you organize mass meetings, or what you will. I'll do my best to do what ought to be done, but I won't give you a nickel on any other basis [pp. 73–4].

In his commentary on this situation, Barnard makes it very clear that he realized he was in a position of conflict over ideology. But his theoretical concern lies not with the ideologies, but with his proposition that men under "states of tension" will do what is "utterly contrary to that which is normally observed in them" (p. 62). While he explains in detail how he won the ideological battle which gave him power to decide what the men "ought to have", he makes no mention of his final decision. The content of decisions is not important in systems theory. However, Barnard does take pains to denigrate the ideology of the unemployed workers and their claims for better treatment. He also considers in a footnote (pp. 73–4) whether a person of "superior position" should swear in front of those of "inferior status", and confides that "the oath was deliberate and accompanied by hard pounding on the table".

In this example, Barnard as theorist merely adds the notion of "states of tension" to his earlier developed principles of cooperative action in organizations. Do these ideas tell us the significant aspects about organizational life with Chester Barnard? The phenomenologist holds that Barnard's ideology is the significant variable shaping the experience of many people in the organizations which he controlled. Without understanding the ideological issues involved in an organization, and in particular without knowing what ideology is in control, the general principles of organization mean relatively little in terms of what people experience in an organization.

Organizational pathologies and cures

The systems theorist looks for pathologies in the body of the organization itself. These stem from ill adaptations of the organization to its environment, to the ultimate goals it should serve, or to the needs of individuals. The solution to these pathologies is obvious: change the structure of the organization to improve the adaptation and thus the performance of the organization. The phenomenologist, on the other hand, sees structure as simply the reflection of human beliefs. If there are problems in organizations—and problems are certainly to be expected—they must therefore rest in conflicting beliefs held by individuals. Solutions to such problems cannot be found simply by changing structures. The root of the problem lies in people's beliefs and the ability to act upon these beliefs.

> Thus the argument that we must make organizations more liveable, more congruent with human values and motives, ignores the fact that it is one set of human motives and values which is in conflict with another set of motives and values. There is no abstract entity called organization which can be held accountable—only other people [Schein, 1973, pp. 780–1].

Our penchant for thinking about organizations as entities, as things with a life of their own, blinds us to their complexity and to the human actions which constitute the façade which we call organization. It leads us to believe that we must change some abstract thing called "organization" rather than the beliefs of people about what they should do and how they should behave with each other. The more closely we look at organizations, the more likely we are to find expressions of diverse human meanings. The focus of our efforts to improve organizations should not be, "What can be done to change the structure of this organization?" but, "Whose intentions define what is right to do among people here involved with one another?" and "How might these intentions be changed?" The task of changing organizations depends, first, upon the varieties of reality which individuals see in existing organizations, and second, upon their acceptance of new ideas of what can or should be achieved through social action. We know little about either, but it is clear we should understand the first before we attempt to direct the second.

IMPLICATIONS

Where do the ideas based on phenomenology leave the notion of "organization"? And what of the science that studies organizations? And where does a profession of educational administration which bases its practice on this science now find itself? In conclusion, let me briefly develop some answers to these questions and suggest some directions for future study.

1. Organizations are definitions of social reality. Some people may make these definitions by virtue of their access to power while others must pay attention to them. Organizations are mechanisms for transforming our desires into social realities. But the transforming mechanism lies within individuals. It is found in individuals striving to change their demands or beliefs into definitions of reality that others must regard as valid and accept as limitations on their actions. This notion of organizations as dependent upon the meanings and purposes which individuals bring to them does not require that all individuals share the same meaning and purposes. On the contrary, the views I am outlining here should make us seek to discover the varying meanings and objectives that individuals bring to the organizations of which they are a part. We should look more carefully too for differences in objectives between different kinds of people in organizations and begin to relate these to differences in power or access to resources. Although the concept of organization permits us to speak of the dominating demands and beliefs of some individuals, and allows us to explore how those with dominating views use the advantage of their position, we need not think of these dominating views as "necessary", "efficient", "satisfying" or even "functional", but merely as an invented social reality, which holds for a time and is then vulnerable to redefinition through changing demands and beliefs among people. Where then may we go from here? Let me suggest some lines of development.

2. We should begin to regard with healthy scepticism the claim that a general science of organization and administration is at hand. Such

theories carry with them not only culturally dependent notions of what is important in an organization but also prescriptive ideas of how study and inquiry into organizational problems should go forward. The movement toward international associations for the study of educational administration should be welcomed, but these associations should open windows on our understanding of organizations rather than propagate received notions of organization theory. If the movement can provide a comparative and critical perspective on schools and on our notions of how they should be run, the association will serve a valuable role. Since the dominant theories of organization and administration have their source in the United States, it is these ideas which should receive searching analysis before they are blindly applied in other cultural settings. In Britain, this critical examination of theory and its policy implications has already begun (Baron and Taylor, 1969; Halsey, 1972), though one is hard pressed to find similar critical examinations in other national or cultural settings.

3. Willy nilly, the world does seem to be shrinking towards the global village. Yet there are still strong forces which maintain vivid cultural distinctions within it. Despite these forces, the interests of the mass media, which the academic community seems all too ready to ape (Perrow, 1972, p. 198), direct attention more frequently to the symptoms of social problems rather than to their sources. While the mass media are usually ready with prefabricated solutions to these problems, students of organizations should doubt the utility of solutions which ignore their sources in the truly critical and powerful organizations of our societies. If we are unwilling to understand our own organizations, or if we regard acquiring such understanding as a trivial task, we should be aware that there are often others willing and waiting to apply their own preconceptions and answers to the tasks of defining the organization, identifying its problems, and prescribing solutions to them. Our own experience of our own organizations is a valuable resource. It is with this experience that the organization theorist must begin to understand the nature of organizations. Since an understanding of organizations is closely linked to control of them and to the possibility of change within them, the phenomenological perspective points to issues of crucial importance both to the theorist and the man of practical affairs.

4. The possibility of training administrators through the study of organization theory has been seriously overestimated. Such theory does not appear to offer ready-made keys to the problems of how to run an organization. Through credentials, such training does appear to offer sound prospects for advancement within administrative systems. While such training may increase social mobility, each society must decide whether it wishes to pursue this goal, and, if it does, whether this method is the most appropriate for doing so. If training of administrators is to serve its avowed purposes, then it seems clear that the nature of the training must move in virtually the opposite direction from that advocated in

recent years. That is to say, training should move away from attempts to teach a broad social science of organizations-in-general towards a familiarity with specific organizations and their problems. That the training should continue to have critical and reflective dimensions should not conflict with this redirection of training programmes. It appears essential also for training programmes to develop a much stronger clinical base than is now common in most of them. In such training, both the theoretician and the practitioner must be intimately involved.

5. Research into organizational problems should consider and begin to use the phenomenological perspective. This redirection of research should awaken interest in the decision-making tradition of organization theory and in the institutional school of organizational analysis (Perrow, 1972, pp. 177–204) with its emphasis on the exposé and ideological analysis of specific organizations (Bendix, 1956). In methodology, research should turn to those methods which attempt to represent perceived reality more faithfully and fully than do the present highly quantified and abstruse techniques. And researchers should avoid prescribing solutions to pressing social problems on the basis of prescriptive theory and research. For example, those who concluded on the basis of the Coleman study that the achievement of black students in American schools might be raised by integrating black and white students were dazzled by the naturalist assumption that a statistical relationship represents social reality. They therefore were led to the error of believing that social relationships may be manipulated in the same way in which variables from the research design can be manipulated. In doing so, they failed to reckon with the reaction of black students to greater integration as a "solution" to their problems (Carlson, 1972). Indeed researchers and social scientists might consider the cultural imperialism which is frequently inherent in their recommendations for solving social problems and strive first to understand (Bernstein, 1971b, Sarason, 1971; Holbrook, 1964) the social and organizational world for which they hope to prescribe solutions.

What is needed for better research on schools is better images of what schools are and what goes on in them. "Better" in this case means creating images of schools which reflect their character and quality and which will tell us something of what the experience of schooling is like. Since schools are made up of different people in different times and places, it is to be expected that images which reflect the experience of schooling must be many and varied. These images would be sets of "one-sided viewpoints", as Weber called them, each throwing "shafts of light" (Eldridge, 1971, p. 12) upon social reality in schools.

As the natural systems have provided the dominating model for studies of organizations (Mayntz, 1964, p. 116), the image of the school as a unit of production has dominated investigations of schools (Levine, 1973; Spady, 1973). The production model of the school is a systems variant which sees the school as a set of roles and resources arranged to yield a product which conforms to predetermined goals. We are often so accustomed to this model that we fail to notice the enormous discrepancies between it and what typically goes on in schools. To begin with, most sets of official educational goals would justify schools doing virtually any good thing for the individual or the society in which he lives. Secondly, the products of school are nearly impossible to identify, if by product we mean something which is unmistakably due to the efforts of the school itself. The clearest measure of school product—the results students obtain on standardized and other kinds of tests—correspond poorly to the goals of education and are usually accounted for most readily by influences outside the school. Thus whether schools do anything to achieve a set of vague goals can never be determined within the model of the school as a unit of production.

If we shear from our image of schools the notion of overriding goals and visible products, what are we left with? The image is now that of pure process in which people strive to shape a social environment which is congenial to them and which they believe serves *their* purposes or the purposes which other people ought to have. The image of the school is now not the factory or the system but the public utility (Pincus, 1974) which produces a service which people use for their own ends. It is not surprising in this conception of the school that people involved with it—teachers, administrators, pupils, parents, etc.—have strong feelings about what services should be provided and how they should be provided. Moreover, it should be apparent that experience with the school's services leads to strong, though not necessarily universally accepted, beliefs about what kinds of service and conditions of service are good and bad and to convictions about which of them are effective and ineffective. However, lacking objective criteria to judge the relevance and validity of their claims, and lacking even a common basis of experience with the school's services, people holding these beliefs and convictions are likely to clash with others having different but equally firmly held convictions. We learn to believe in our own experience of school process and to doubt the validity of others' beliefs. In this way, the proposal model accounts both for the apparent stability of schools—their resistance to change—and for the continuing conflict about what schools are for and how they should be organized and run. It suggests as well that the path to understanding more about schools must lie through interpretations and analysis of the experience of people in schools, not through attempts to decide which structural elements of schools yield outcomes that best approximate their ultimate purposes.

6. The research advocated above and the rationale for it developed earlier in this paper do not imply only the description and analysis of subjective states. Weber is said to have advised researchers first to get the facts about the basic elements of social situations and then to move to a subjective interpretation of them (Eldridge, 1971, p. 19; Bendix and Roth, 1971, pp. 286–91). The "facts" Weber had in mind were such

matters as wages, costs of materials, the people involved, and descriptions of them in demographic terms. These are the typical resource variables which are of frequent concern in analyses of the school from the perspective of the production model. The questions usually investigated are whether the school is making effective and efficient use of its resources in pursuit of predetermined educational goals. Answers to such questions are complex, contradictory and unconvincing, as Spady (1973) has demonstrated. The reasons for such unsatisfactory outcomes are obvious when pointed out, as Gagné (1970) has done. Children do not learn from "environments" from "resources" or from the "characteristics of teachers". They learn from their specific involvement with people, things and events around them. Thus knowledge of the basic facts about a social situation is only the beginning of an understanding of it. What is needed beyond these basic facts is a knowledge of how people in a social situation construe it, what they see as its significant features, and how they act within it. Such knowledge can only come from the interpretation of particular experiences in specific situations.

In this respect, it might be useful to think of two kinds of variables in a social situation—outside and inside variables. The outside variables are those which lend themselves readily to quantification and which involve a minimum of interpretation. As has been suggested, these variables provide information about the characteristics of the people and resources found in a social situation. The inside variables are those which may only be expressed through interpretation of experience. Both kinds of variables are important, though in most organizational studies of schools, emphasis has usually fallen exclusively on the former category.

It would be helpful to replace our usual notion of the school as a system with the idea of the school as a set. Where the system idea implies preordained order and functions in the school, the notion of set leaves completely open both the definition of the elements of the school and the description of relationships among them. Defining the school as a set leaves as a problem for investigation what the elements of the situations are and what the meanings of relationships among the elements are. With such a view of the school, we might recognize both external and internal variables; as follows:

External variables. Pupil characteristics: their age, sex, home background, individual abilities and previous learning. School characteristics: building design, facilities and equipment. Classrooms: number of pupils, subject of study, methodology. Teacher characteristics: training and length of service, personality, intelligence, abilities and interests.

Internal variables. What is the quality of relationships among teachers, pupils and others in the school? What experiences do they have in terms of (a) their expectations for the environment, (b) the opportunities and problems they perceive, (c) the efforts they make to learn, help or teach, (d) their feelings of accomplishment or failure? What decisions do different people in the school make and why do they make them? How are people and situations defined and evaluated?

The variables listed above are intended to be suggestive rather than exhaustive. The final point to be made about them is that both of these major dimensions are essential for describing and understanding schools fully. In fact, some of the most revealing analyses will arise from contrasts between the school seen in terms of external variables and the school seen in terms of internal variables. That organizational theory has too frequently directed attention to the external variables and that it has presumed rather than explored their relationships to internal variables are points which have already been made at length.

7. A continued study of organizations from the perspectives of the social sciences is certainly warranted. Schools as one of the most significant of our social institutions deserve particular attention. It seems appropriate, however, for students of schools as organizations to consider the meaning of their studies and to redirect them towards investigations which increase our understanding of organizations as they are before attempts are made to change them. Paradoxically, the efforts which promise to yield the most penetrating insights into organizations and the most practical strategies for improving them are those efforts (March, 1972) which deal with the way people construe organizational reality and with the moral and ethical issues involved in these construings.

If, as the phenomenologist holds, our ideas for understanding the world determine our action within it, then our ideas about the world—what really exists in it, how we should behave in it—are of the utmost importance. And if our ideas about the world are shaped by our experience, then the interpretation of our experience is also of paramount importance. It is this process, the placing of meaning upon experience, which shapes what we call our organizations and it is this process which should be the focus of the organization theorist's work. And unless we wish to yield to universal forces for determining our experience, we must look to theories of organizations based upon diverse meanings and interpretations of our expereince.

NOTES

1 Deutscher (1973, pp. 324ff) describes these schools of thought and their connections with idealistic philosophy. He also points out (p. 325n) that those he calls the "Harvard functionalists" make no mention of phenomenology or its proponents in their encyclopaedic history of theories of society. See Parsons *et al.* (1961).
2 Personal communication to the author.

T. Barr Greenfield

REFERENCES

BARNARD, C. I. (1938) *The Functions of the Executive*, Harvard University Press.

BARNARD, C. I. (1948) *Organization and Management*, Harvard University Press.

BARON, G. and TAYLOR, W. (eds.) (1969) *Educational Administration and the Social Sciences*, Athlone.

BENDIX, R. (1956) *Work and Authority in Industry: Ideologies in the Course of Industrialization*, Wiley.

BENDIX, R. and ROTH, G. (1971) *Scholarship and Partisanship: Essays on Max Weber*, University of California Press.

BENNIS, W. G. (1968) "Beyond Bureaucracy", in Bennis, W. G. and Slater, P., (eds.) *The Temporary Society*, Harper and Row, pp. 53–76.

BERNSTEIN, B. (1971a) *Class, Codes and Control: Theoretical Studies towards a Sociology of Language*, Routledge and Kegan Paul.

BERNSTEIN, B. (1971b) "Education Cannot Compensate for Society" in Cosin *et al.* (eds.) (1971, pp. 61–6).

BIDWELL, C. E. (1965) "The School as a Formal Organization", in March, J. G. (ed.) *Handbook of Organizations*, Rand McNally, pp. 972–1022.

BRITTAN, A. (1973) *Meanings and Situations*, Routledge and Kegan Paul.

BURNS, T. (1967) "The Comparative Study of Organizations", in Vroom, V. (ed.) *Methods of Organizational Research*, University of Pittsburgh Press, pp. 118–70.

CAMPBELL, R. F. and GREGG, R. T. (eds.) (1957) *Administrative Behavior in Education*, Harper.

CARLSON, K. (1972) "Equalizing Educational Opportunity", *Review of Educational Research*, (42) 4, 453–75.

CICOUREL, A. (1964) *Method and Measurement in Sociology*, Free Press.

COSIN, B. R., DALE, I. R., ESLAND, G. M. and SWIFT, D. F. (eds.) (1971) *School and Society: A Sociological Reader*, Routledge and Kegan Paul.

CULBERTSON, J., FARQUHAR, R., FOGARTY, G. and SHIBLES, M. (eds.) (1973) *Social Science Content for Preparing Educational Leaders*, Charles E. Merrill.

CULBERTSON, J. and SHIBLES, M. (1973) "The Social Sciences and the Issue of Relevance", in Culbertson, J., Farquhar, R., Fogarty, G. and Shibles, M. (eds.) *Social Science Content for Preparing Educational Leaders*, Charles E. Merrill.

CYERT, R. M. and March, J. G. (1963) *A Behavioral Theory of the Firm*, Prentice-Hall.

DAWE, A. (1970) "The Two Sociologies", *British Journal of Sociology*, 21 (2), pp. 207–18.

DEUTSCHER, I. (ed.) (1973) *What We Say/What We Do: Sentiments and Acts*, Scott Foresman.

DOWNEY, L. W. and ENNS, F. (eds.) (1963) *The Social Sciences and Educational Administration*, University of Alberta.

ELDRIDGE, J. E. T. (ed.) (1971) *Max Weber: The Interpretation of Social Reality*, Michael Joseph.

ETZIONI, A. (1960) "Two Approaches to Organizational Analysis: A Critique and a Suggestion", *Administrative Science Quarterly*, **5** (2), pp. 257–78.

FILMER, P., PHILLIPSON, M., SILVERMAN, D. and WALSH, D. (1972) *New Directions in Sociological Theory*, Collier-Macmillan.

FULLAN, M. (1972) "Overview of the Innovative Process and the User", *Interchange*, **3**, (2–3), pp. 1–46.

GAGN‵, R. M. (1970) "Policy Implications and Future Research: A Response", in Mood, A. (ed.) (1970) *Do Teachers Make A Difference?* US Office of Education.

GARFINKEL, H. (1964) "The Relevance of Common Understandings to the Fact That Models of Man in Society Portray Him as a Judgemental Dope", in Deutscher (ed.) (1973, pp. 330–8).

GARFINKEL, H. (1967) *Studies in Ethnomethodology*, Prentice-Hall.

GEORGIOU, P. (1973) "The Goal Paradigm and Notes towards a Counter Paradigm", *Administrative Science Quarterly*, **18**, (3), pp. 291–310.

GETZELS, J. W. (1958) "Administration as a Social Process", in Halpin (ed.) (1958, pp. 150–65).

GETZELS, J. W., LIPHAM, J. M. and CAMPBELL, R. F. (1968) *Educational Administration as a Social Process: Theory, Research, Practice*, Harper and Row.

GLASER, B. G. and STRAUSS, A. L. (1967) *The Discovery of Grounded Theory*, Aldine.

GREENFIELD, T. B. (1973) "Organizations as Social Inventions: Rethinking Assumptions About Change", *Journal of Applied Behavioral Science*, **9**, (5), pp. 551–74.

GREGG, R. T. (1957) "The Administrative Process", in Campbell and Gregg (eds.) (1958, pp. 269–317).

GRIFFITHS, D. E. (ed.) (1964) *Behavioral Science and Educational Administration*, The Sixty-third Yearbook of the National Society for the Study of Education, University of Chicago Press.

HALPIN, A. W. (ed.) (1958) *Administrative Theory in Education*, Macmillan.

HALSEY, A. H. (ed.) (1972) *Educational Priority: E.P.A. Problems and Policies*, Vol. 1, HMSO.

HOLBROOK, D. (1964) *English for the Rejected*, Cambridge University Press.

KUHN, T. (1970) *The Structure of Scientific Revolution*, University of Chicago Press.

LEVINE, D. M. (1973) "Educational Policy After Inequality", *Teachers College Record*, **75**, (2), pp. 149–79.

LOUCH, A. R. (1966) *Explanation and Human Action*, University of California Press.

MARCH, J. G. (1972) "Model Bias in Social Action", *Review of Educational Research*, **42**, (4), pp. 413–29.

MARCH, J. G. and SIMON, H. A. (1958) *Organizations*, Wiley.

MAYNTZ, Renate (1964) "The Study of Organizations", *Current Sociology*, **13**, (3), pp. 95–155.

MERTON, R. K. (1957) *Social Theory and Social Structure*, Free Press.

MILSTEIN, M. M. and BELASCO, J. A. (eds.) (1973) *Educational Administration and the Social Sciences: A Systems Perspective*, Allyn and Bacon.

PARSONS, T. *et al.* (1961) *Theories of Society: Foundations of Modern Sociological Theory*, Free Press.

PERROW, C. (1972) *Complex Organizations: A Critical Essay*, Scott Foresman.

PHILLIPSON, M. (1972) "Phenomenological Philosophy and Sociology", in Filmer *et al.* (1972, pp. 119–63).

PINCUS, J. (1974) "Incentives for Innovation in the Public Schools", *Review of Educational Research*, **44**, (1), pp. 113–43.

ROTHKOPF, E. Z. (1973) "What Are We Trying to Understand and Improve ? Educational Research as *Leerlaufreaktion*", invited address to the meeting of the American Educational Research Association, New Orleans.

SARASON, S. B. (1971) *The Culture of the School and the Problem of Change*, Allyn and Bacon.

SCHEFF, T. J. (1973) "Negotiating Reality: Notes on Power in the Assessment of Responsibility", in Deutscher (ed.) (1973, pp. 338–58).

SCHEIN, E. H. (1973) "Can One Change Organizations, or Only People in Organizations ?" *Journal of Applied Behavioral Science*, **9**, 6, pp. 780–85.

SILVERMAN, D. (1972) "Methodology and Meaning", in Filmer *et al.* (1972, pp. 183–200)

SILVERMAN, D. (1970) *The Theory of Organisations*, Heinemann.

SIMON, H. A. (1957) *Administrative Behavior: A Study of Decision-Making Process in Administrative Organization*, 2nd ed., Free Press.

SIMON, H. A. (1964) "On the Concept of Organizational Goal", *Administrative Science Quarterly*, **9**, pp. 1–22.

SPADY, W. G. (1973) "The Impact of School Resources on Students", in Kerlinger, F. N. (ed.) *Review of Research in Education*, No. 1, Peacock, pp. 135-77.

TIPTON, BERYL F. A. (1973) *Conflict and Change in a Technical College*, Hutchinson Educational.

TOPE, D. E. *et al.* (1965) *The Social Sciences View School Administration*, Prentice-Hall.

WALSH, D. (1972) "Sociology and the Social World", in Filmer *et al.* (1972, pp. 15–35).

WEBER, M., trans. GERTH, H. H. and MILLS, C. W. (1946) *From Max Weber: Essays in Sociology*, Oxford University Press.

WEBER, M. (1947) *The Theory of Social and Economic Organizations*, (Parsons, T., ed.), William Hodge.

WILLER, D. (1967) *Scientific Sociology: Theory and Method*, Prentice-Hall.

WILSON, T. P. (1970) "Conceptions of Interaction and Forms of Sociological Explanation", *American Sociological Review*, 35, (4), pp. 697–710.

YOUNG, M. F. D. (ed.) (1971) *Knowledge and Control: New Directions for the Society of Education*, Collier-Macmillan.

2.2 The Study of Schools as Organisations

Eric Hoyle

There has long been an implicit recognition amongst educationists and laymen that schools can be regarded as entities having a distinctive organisational character. This organisational character is, of course, partly a function of school type—public, grammar, secondary modern, comprehensive—but there are variations among schools of the same type. In recent years, the attempt to understand schools as entities has been one of the growth points in educational studies. Schools have been variously conceptualised as *complex organisations, social systems,* or, occasionally, as *social institutions.* These terms are often used interchangeably, but they can have different theoretical implications. *Complex* or *formal* organisations may serve to overemphasise the formal structure of the school as against the informal structure. *Social system* usefully connotes an interrelationship of parts, but may overemphasise the degree of integration, consensus, and goal-seeking activities to be found in schools. *Social institution* has been given a rather specialised meaning which emphasises the values of an organisation (e.g. Selznick, 1957), but more generally in the sociology of education the term is best reserved for an institutional pattern (e.g. comprehensive education, private education) than for a specific organisation. In spite of the differences in terms, the central concern of these studies is to understand the functioning of schools and particularly the interplay of their various dimensions: formal structure, administrative processes, informal relationships, culture, goals, and so forth. There have been many theoretical and methodological approaches to the study of schools as organisations in recent years; there has also been a degree of optimism about a possible convergence which would provide a distinctive theoretical perspective and body of research to illustrate the functioning of schools and to resolve practical problems arising from their day-to-day operations. These expectations have been fulfilled to a lesser degree than was anticipated in the early 1960s. Some convergence has taken place, but there remain considerable differences in

---

Source: Butcher, H. J. and Pont, H. B. (1973) *Educational Research in Britain*, 3, University of London Press, pp. 32–56

approach, and it may well be that a full understanding of schools will be best derived from different sorts of study.

The study of schools as organisations emerged in the United States during the late 1950s. It was during this period that organisational analysis was in the process of becoming one of the major substantive areas of sociological study. The development of the sociology of organisations need not be documented here (see Mouzelis, 1967), but very briefly it was characterised by an attempt to develop middle-range theories of the functioning of organisations which would allow comparison between different types (e.g. factories, prisons, hospitals, schools and colleges). Thus the perspective was distinctively sociological; schools were studied more because they were organisations than because they were schools. As Corwin (1967) put it: "sociologists are beginning to appreciate the relevance of educational organisations for extending and testing theory". This orientation has had significant implications for the study of schools. One the one hand the comparative perspective of sociology has helped to identify some of the salient aspects of school organisation. On the other, the approach from sociology has not always been sensitive to the unique characteristics of schools. A concurrent development in the United States occurred in the field of educational administration. During the 1950s there emerged a dissatisfaction with the theory and research which was underpinning the administration of schools. As a result, what has come to be called the "new movement" developed. This movement was characterised by a more sophisticated theoretical and research approach to educational administration (Griffiths, 1964a, Halpin, 1967). Clearly the sociological approach to organisations was relevant to the new movement, but in fact the two traditions remained relatively distinct and the relationship between them remains problematical (Hoyle, 1969). In particular, the new movement owed more to the managerialist tradition than to the sociological approach which, in fact, partly arose from a rejection of the "classical" and "human relations" approaches to the study of industrial organisations. Although the new movement aimed to be interdisciplinary, the major figures in the field tended to be educational psychologists whose focus was leadership, morale and communication rather than formal structure, goals and culture, although certain contributors (e.g. Carlson, 1962 and Bidwell, 1965) did take a more distinctively sociological perspective. The influence of the American approach to educational administration on British thinking can be seen in Baron and Taylor (1969) and Hughes (1970).

In spite of the attention paid in the British literature of the 1960s to these American trends, the actual research carried out in this country has been largely indigenous. As we shall see, sociological studies of schools in Britain have tended to be concerned with the relationship between the differentiation of pupils, pupil subcultures, and the opportunity structure. In addition, there have been a number of studies of the implications for school organisation of new trends in education, e.g. comprehensivisation, de-streaming, and curriculum development, which have not drawn at all upon the social science approaches to organisation. Research into school administration has been carried out mainly by studies of the role of the headteacher. Thus in this country, a number of different approaches to the study of schools have emerged, and this is not surprising given the options which any student has before him when he considers potential theories and methodologies.

PROBLEMS IN THE ORGANISATIONAL ANALYSIS OF SCHOOLS

Like all organisations, schools have many dimensions which are to some degree interrelated. The researcher cannot hope to study all these relationships and must therefore make certain choices. As a means of throwing light on the problems of organisational analysis, we can consider a series of hypothetical choices—dichotomised here for the sake of simplicity—with which the researcher is confronted. (See Davies, 1970 for a valuable alternative approach.)

Theory verification or theory generation?

The investigator must decide what stance he is to take with regard to theory. He can choose to undertake a piece of research aimed at verifying a theory or he can allow the theory to emerge from the data. In the former case he would select a particular organisation theory and derive from this a series of hypotheses to test in the school situation. In the latter case he would begin his investigation without having in mind any particular theory (although as a social scientist he would not, of course, be innocent of concepts which serve to organise data) but would allow the theory to emerge. The case for generating grounded theory has been made by Glaser and Strauss (1968) who write: "We believe that the discovery of theory from data—which we call grounded theory—is the major task confronting sociology today, for as we shall try to show, such a theory fits empirical situations, and is understandable to sociologist and layman alike. Most important, it works—provides us with relevant predictions, explanations, interpretations, and applications."

General theory or specific theory?

If the investigator is concerned with verification, he must decide through his choice of theory what level of abstraction is appropriate. A range of options is open to him, namely:

1 An abstract theory of the formal properties of organisations. The most common form is *general systems theory* which has been utilised in a number of organisation studies and has been held to be relevant to the study of schools (e.g. Griffiths, 1964b).
2 A general theory of social systems. For example, Parsons (1966) examines the relevance of his theory of social systems to the understanding of school administration.

3   A comparative typology of organisations through which schools are classified according to a particular organisational type, e.g. Etzioni's (1961) comparative typology based upon the dimensions of power and compliance classifies schools as having normative power and moral compliance.

4   A comparative typology of educational organisations whereby schools are categorised as particular types, e.g. Carlson's (1964) typology categorises schools according to the two dimensions of control by the school over the admission of clients and the control by the client over his participation and derives hypotheses relating to the functioning of the different types.

5   A theory based upon one or more of the central dimensions of schools, e.g. decision-making (Griffiths, 1959), leadership role (Gross and Herriott, 1965), autonomy (Katz, 1964), bureaucracy (Anderson, 1969).

6   A theory based upon a substantive problem of educational organisations, e.g. the conservation of values (Selznick, 1951).

These different levels of abstraction serve different functions in research. The more abstract the theory, the easier it is to compare the functioning of schools with the functioning of other types of organisation; the more specific the theory, the greater the possibility of understanding schools *as such.*

Case study or comparative study?

The investigator must decide whether he is to study one organisation or several. Each approach has its advantages and its disadvantages. The considerable advantage of the case study is that it enables the investigator to become well-acquainted with the day-to-day functioning of the school. He can gain the confidence of the participants, use a variety of data-collecting techniques, and, importantly, become familiar with the under-tow which is an important determinant of organisational character. The disadvantage of the case study is that the investigator is not entitled to generalise from his findings. The advantage of a comparative study is that generalisation is theoretically possible, and the disadvantage that only limited aspects of the school can be studied and these largely by standardised modes of data collection. The choice between case study and comparative study will depend upon many factors: the purpose of the study, its theoretical perspective, and, often decisively, on the resources available to the researcher.

Synchronic or diachronic study?

A synchronic study provides a snapshot of the organisation(s) being studied at one point in time. This approach is appropriate if the main object of the investigation is to compare some formal aspect of the school, e.g. degree of bureaucratisation. A diachronic study is essential where the investigator is concerned with organisational processes, e.g. socialisation, differentiation. In order to study these processes in the school situation, it is clearly necessary to study a cohort of pupils as it passes through the year grades.

Structure or behaviour as independent variable?

The choice between these alternatives will usually turn upon the theoretical perspective of the investigator. The sociological approach tends to take structural aspects as the independent variable and explains the behaviour within the organisation in terms of the patterning imposed by the structure. On the other hand sociologists of the inter-actionist school, and most social psychologists, would take as their independent variable the interactions of members of the organisation and seek to demonstrate how these modify the formal structure. This choice is avoided at the theoretical level in the model of Getzels and Guba (1957) and Getzels, Lipham and Campbell (1968), which sees organisational behaviour as the outcome of the interaction among three dimensions: the *nomothetic* (institution-role-expectations) and the *idiographic* (individual-personality-needs) mediated by an intervening dimension: group-climate-intention, but the integration of these three dimensions at the operational level is difficult to achieve.

Research problem derived from theory or practice?

All investigators are concerned with a "problem". This may be a theoretical problem, i.e. one generated by a gap in existing theory, or a substantive problem, i.e. a practical difficulty which a school needs to resolve. This has something in common with the difference between theory verification and theory generation, but differs in that grounded theory can be developed in the absence of a specific operational problem of the school. The difference between theory-problem and practice-problem raises the difficult question of which approach ultimately has the greatest implications for practice, but we are concerned here with the initial orientation of the research. The implications can perhaps be illustrated by reference to the distinction between "sociology of education" and "educational sociology" (Hansen, 1967). The sociologist of education is not directly concerned with the resolution of practical problems but trusts that the educationist will derive his own solutions from the research findings. The educational sociologist on the other hand is centrally concerned with a school problem and draws upon sociological theory and research as and when necessary for the solution of the problem (Jensen, 1965). There is little doubt that the majority of organisational studies in education have been approached from the perspective of sociology of education. This is also true of studies in educational administration since the "new movement" was particularly concerned to avoid the "cookery book" approach which was not underpinned by a social science theory. These studies have consequently not been particularly compelling to the practising educationist. On the other hand, there have been many studies of practical school problems which have not been as useful as they might have been through not drawing on social science theory. Research on ability grouping is a good example. The rather ambivalent findings of research in this area could well have been due to the fact that ability grouping has been considered in isolation from other aspects of the school social system. The significance of factors other than grouping has been demonstrated in the NFER study of streaming in the primary school (Barker Lunn, 1970). This study took dichotomised teacher attitudes as well as streaming as a variable. Although there was no difference in the attainments of children in streamed and unstreamed schools, there were differences in attitude. In streamed schools it was the streaming structure which appeared to be important; in unstreamed schools it was the teacher. This approach might be extended to take account of the relationship between streaming and other aspects of the school social system, e.g. leadership, climate.

One means of data collection or many?
Organisational analysis can be carried out via the usual modes of data collection: questionnaires, attitude and opinion scales, structured and unstructured interviews, diaries, participant and non-participant observation, content analysis of documents, etc. The investigator must decide whether he is to rely largely on one technique or a limited number of techniques or whether he will use a variety of methods. His decision will to some degree depend upon whether he is undertaking a case study or a comparative study and upon what resources he has available. A combination of methods gives the investigator the opportunity to see the organisation in the round and to use one technique to check the validity of another. On the other hand, this does not yield an elegant research design. The use of a single means of data collection, especially if a questionnaire is used, makes comparative studies possible and is amenable to a more sophisticated statistical analysis, but, of course, it limits the investigator to a limited number of organisational dimensions. The problem has been interestingly discussed by Halpin (1967) whose own contribution to organisational studies in education has been largely through the construction of the Organizational Climate Description Questionnaire (OCDQ). This is a sixty-four item questionnaire designed to determine teachers' perceptions of the administrative climate of their schools. By means of factor analysis, Halpin identified eight dimensions of administrative relationships and, from the school profiles of these dimensions, six organisational climates. This measure has been widely used in several countries with some success. But Halpin is sensitive to the shortcomings of a single instrument and notes that it needs to be supplemented by studies within the schools themselves to establish whether the OCDQ climates were corroborated by studies carried out on the ground. As he

notes: "In a genuine sense we did not discover these Organisational Climates; we *invented* them."

Detached research or action research?

The choice to be made by the investigator is whether he simply wishes to add to the understanding of the functioning of schools and leave the practical implications to practising educationists, or whether he wishes both to understand and to participate in change on the basis of his findings. It is likely that if the research problem has been theoretically derived, the stance of the investigator will be detached. If the problem has been derived from practice, the investigator may remain detached, but may also become actively involved in the problem-solving activity. Many sociologists and social psychologists perform consultancy roles as well as researcher roles, mainly in industrial organisations. At the present time there has been relatively little involvement of social scientists in the planned organisational change of schools (Hoyle, 1970). Where the investigator does become actively involved in the organisation through action research, his entire research strategy will be different from the approach of the detached researcher. In particular he will be required to relinquish traditional modes of verification in order to manipulate the situation which he is studying and in which he himself is involved. The reader is referred to Chin (1960) for a brief summary of the differences between the various types of detached and applied research. (Related points are discussed in the chapters by Richmond and by Stenhouse.)

Are measures of output to be used or not?

The input-output model has an immediate appeal to investigators who are particularly concerned with organisational effectiveness. The paradigmatic research design in these circumstances would be to seek to predict variations in output between various categories of input on the basis of the internal characteristics of organisations. But there are some obvious difficulties—theoretical and methodological—inherent in input-output studies, e.g.

1 The identification of school goals or objectives.
2 The conceptualisation of output. In the school situation pupil achievement is an obvious "output". But what about absenteeism, teacher turnover, or—the object of an interesting British study by Power *et al.* (1967)—delinquency rates?
3 The operationalisation of output. The cognitive outcomes of schooling are *relatively* easy to assess, but the social, moral, emotional and aesthetic development of children is much more problematic. Organisational studies of schools have not so far been integrated with the movement towards the articulation and evaluation of curriculum objectives.
4 The identification of organisational patterns sufficiently different to

account for variations in output. One recent review of American research (Robbins and Miller, 1969) estimated that: "organisational arrangements of individual schools account for less than three per cent of the variance" (i.e. of pupil attainment). This review was admittedly of research which had taken school structure as the independent variable, and it could well be that other dimensions have more impact. Nevertheless, it is probably true to say that schools tend on the whole not to be very different in the internal arrangements and a low variance is to be expected in a random sample. A more appropriate method might be to study the outputs of schools which were very different in structure and process.

Students of schools as organisations have in the past been inhibited from studying outputs because of the lack of appropriate statistical models, but in recent years various models (e.g. stochastic, two stage input-output, path analysis) have been employed in assessing the effects of higher education and in some cases of schools (see Feldman, 1971 for a review of these techniques).

Is the study to be introspective or are environmental factors to be included?
A school is not a closed system. Its internal activities are affected by contextual factors. The investigator must decide whether he is to consider only the internal aspects of the school, or whether he is to take account of the influence of external factors (see Eggleston, 1967 for a review of these influences). If he decides to take account of external factors, the investigator is faced with the problem of limitation, for the school environment has its social, cultural, political, administrative, and economic components which range in extent from the immediately local to the national.

The above ten examples of the choices facing the analyst of educational organisations are by no means exhaustive. It is true that there will be a tendency for some of the solutions to these problems to be interdependent, but they nevertheless serve to illustrate perhaps why studies of schools as organisations do vary considerably in their theoretical and methodological perspectives. Each of the studies reviewed in the next section can be classified according to the particular solution adopted, but this is left to the reader rather than spelt out explicitly.

ORGANISATIONAL STUDIES OF BRITISH SCHOOLS
Although there was considerable discussion of the potentialities of organisational analysis in education during the 1960s (e.g. Hoyle, 1965), very few empirical studies have been carried out in this country. There are a number of possible ways of grouping these studies for purposes of discussion, but perhaps the most profitable distinction is between case studies and comparative studies.

Case studies

It is probably true to say that the best organisational studies of British schools so far have been case studies of single schools. Hargreaves (1967) and Lacey (1970) have both reported studies arising out of a research project initiated by the Department of Sociology at Manchester University. The orientation of the project was the analysis of social relationships amongst small groups within a school. Thus the study began with a closer affinity to small group sociology than to organisational sociology with its emphasis on structure. Hargreaves functioned as an observer-participant over a period of one year in a secondary modern school in a northern city. The central concern of his study was the pattern of pupil relationships and their cultural norms, especially amongst the fourth year boys. He outlines his research orientation as follows:

> The study is thus socio-psychological and micro-sociological in orientation. Many limitations restrict the scope of the study. Differences in individual psychology, such as personality, have been excluded, and many sociological variables receive scant attention. The study does not intend to test specific hypotheses derived from current theories. Rather, the research is exploratory in nature and focuses broadly on the structure of informal groups of pupils and the influence of such groups on the educative process.

He uses a variety of methods of data collection: observation, questionnaires with various types of item, e.g. sentence completion, orientation tests, sociometric tests, and analysis of school records, e.g. registers, house points, school fund contributions. The data on pupil subcultures revealed that these were to some degree generated by one aspect of the formal structure of the school—namely streaming. Hargreaves was able to demonstrate that in the fourth year the pupils in the A and B streams shared a distinctive "academic" subculture whilst those in the C and D streams shared a "delinquescent" subculture. He was also able to show that these subcultures had emerged over time, especially in the third and fourth years. Thus, apart from giving a valuable descriptive account of pupil subcultures, Hargreaves has made an important contribution to organisational studies by demonstrating a process of differentiation deriving from the interaction between a component of the formal structure—streaming, and a component of the informal structure—pupil interactions and friendship patterns.

As Lacey's investigation formed part of the same project as that of Hargreaves they not unnaturally have certain features in common: participant observation, the use of a variety of data gathering techniques, and a primary orientation towards studying relationships amongst pupils. Lacey begins with a detailed account of the historical development of the school and the current provision of secondary education in the city in which the grammar school in which he studied was situated. This puts the study in a macrosociological context and establishes links between the internal operations of the school and the opportunity structure of Great Britain. The middle section of the study is concerned with the issue which was central to Hargreaves' work, i.e. the relationship between ability grouping and pupil subcultures. Lacey establishes a process model with two components: *differentiation,* i.e. "the separation and ranking of students according to a multiple set of criteria which makes up the normative, academically orientated value system of the grammar school", and *polarisation* which "takes place within the student body, partly as a result of differentiation, but influenced by external factors and with an autonomy of its own". He tests some of the assumptions of this model, using sociometric techniques and various indicators of pupil subculture, at three levels: in the school as a whole, in a cohort study of one express stream, and through a number of individual case studies. Lacey is able to demonstrate that the intake of the grammar school becomes differentiated by streams in the first year, when classes are unstreamed, and further differentiated during the second year, when streaming occurs. The pupil culture is polarised into a pro-school subculture strong in the higher streams and an anti-school subculture which is strong in the lower streams. The final section of Lacey's work is concerned with the relationship between parents, teachers and pupils and is illustrated by means of case study material. As with Hargreaves' study, Lacey's work has considerable implications for the link between "labelling", opportunity, achievement, and social stratification.

Julienne Ford (1969) carried out a case study of a comprehensive school, also drawing comparative material from a secondary modern school and a grammar school situated in the same area of London as the research school. In some ways the study resembles the work of Hargreaves and Lacey both in its methodology and in its substantive concerns—especially the relationship between friendship patterns, peer values and streaming. But there are at least two important differences. Firstly, there are differences in the role which theory plays in the researches. Ford's study is basically concerned with verification, not of an organisation theory as such, but of the implicit theories of proponents of the comprehensive school. Her starting point is a set of seven propositions culled from the writings of these protagonists. Two of these propositions are used to generate five hypotheses:

1   Comprehensive schools will produce a greater development of talent than tripartite schools.
2   Comprehensive schools will provide greater equality of opportunity for those with equal talent.
3   The occupational horizons of children in comprehensive schools will be widened relative to those of children in tripartite schools.
4   Comprehensive school children will show less tendency to mix only with children of their own social type than will tripartite school children.

5 Comprehensive school children will tend to have views of the class system as a flexible hierarchy, while tripartite school children will tend to see this as a rigid dichotomy.

Data were gathered to test these hypotheses by a variety of techniques: questionnaire sociometric testing, analysis of school records, and so on. The second difference between the studies is that whereas those of Hargreaves and Lacey begin with microsociological problems and allow the macrosociological implications of their findings to emerge, Ford begins with macrosociological issues such as occupational choice, class consciousness, and ideology, and uses a single school as a test situation— a point which has evoked criticism from sociologists and also from supporters of the comprehensive idea. In fact, Ford's study is a study of an institution—comprehensive education—through a single example rather than an organisational study as such. But there is no doubt that it has made an important contribution to organisational analysis of educational organisations in Britain.

Ford does not find support for any of the hypotheses which she tests. In other words, the hopes of the protagonists of comprehensive education are not being fulfilled in this one example. It emerges from the study that again the major barrier is the process of differentiation and the "labelling" which is its consequence. In her final chapter, Ford discusses the fundamental problem of whether schools should differentiate and, if so, how this can be done in a manner which avoids the depressant effects on children who are labelled as low achievers. She offers her own solution, which is to have "schools" for children up to the age of fourteen in which there would be no differentiation within the formal structure and from which children would then pass to "colleges" offering differentiated courses.

King's (1969) case study of a grammar school was primarily concerned with the relationship between school values and pupil involvement. His three basic propositions were that education is a process of cultural transmission, that degrees of continuity exist between the culture of pupils' families and the culture transmitted by the schools, and that pupils are differentially involved in schools as social systems. From these propositions are derived a number of hypotheses which are tested by a variety of methods of data collection including interviews with pupils, questionnaires completed by staff, pupils and parents, analysis of documents including school records, and participant observation—King was a teacher in the school during the period of the investigation. For the most part the basic model is substantiated. The value system of the school was distinctively middle-class. Children from middle class homes tended to hold the school-approved middle class values. But the holding of these values was associated with involvement in school only at a low level of significance. He sums up this finding as follows:

For pupils with low stream status the degree of involvement was related to the acceptance or rejection of the school's values, but it was not for those with higher stream status. In general, school involvement does not appear to be an important mechanism for value transmission.

A research of rather a different kind is Wakeford's (1969) study of a boarding school. In one sense this is an institutional study of the public school, drawing upon documentary evidence from a variety of sources: prospectuses, lists of school rules, apologias, personal communications and interviews. But central to the study is the analysis of the single school. The main form of data collection was through observer participation—Wakeford taught in the school and had also been a pupil there— an approach which he justifies in some detail in a methodological appendix. The analysis is structured around a number of key concepts: relative deprivation, social control, adaptation. These, of course, are general sociological concepts and not specific to a middle-range theory of organisations. No distinctive theoretical perspective is adopted nor are any hypotheses tested. Wakeford's approach is to draw upon a wide range of sociological theory to give meaning to his material. For example, the section on adaptation is structured around Merton's well-known paradigm. But the main conceptual links are made with work on other forms of relatively closed organisations: prisons, military units and hospitals. The methodological orientation of Wakeford makes it difficult to summarise his main findings, since the objective of the investigation was to convey the feel of the life of such a school rather than to provide verified objective data. It is a difficult task to provide a descriptive account of the life of an organisation in all its manifestations and at the same time to make this sociologically meaningful in the sense that it articulates to familiar sociological concepts and theories. Wakeford chooses to use prior theoretical formulations to order his data in a sociologically meaningful way. The other possible approach, and the one of which Erving Goffman is the best exponent, derives new concepts from the observation of behaviour, to generate categories which cast new light on the familiar or which draw attention to the unfamiliar.

The above review of the best-known case studies of British schools indicates that although these studies have made a substantial contribution to the understanding of educational organisations, they have not done so through testing established middle-range theories of organisation. With some exceptions (e.g. a study by Turner, 1969, which applies a paradigm by Blau, 1964, for relating the macrostructure and the substructures of an organisation to a secondary modern school), British studies have been less concerned with the formal properties of schools than with seeking to understand the significance of school as an agency of cultural transmission for different categories of pupil. They have been more concerned with the pupil's world than with the staff world—the studies tell us very little about teachers in any direct sense—and it is probably the case that extant theories of organisation are more applicable to the study of the élite of an organisation than its lower participants. This must be counted as a major shortcoming of current organisation theory.

Comparative studies

Although there are very few comparative organisational studies of British schools at the present time, there are a number of comparative surveys of various dimensions of different types of school. The essential difference between a comparative organisational study and a comparative survey is that a survey is not concerned with the patterns of interaction which constitute a social system. It is concerned with comparing dimensions which are taken out of their organisational context rather than with comparing schools as entities. Surveys are valuable for many purposes, but they are not strictly organisational studies. One example is Kalton's (1966) study of sixty-six public schools conducted by means of questionnaire. Data were collected on pupils (e.g. intelligence, social class, exam results), masters (e.g. age, degree class), school structures (e.g. staffing, sixth form size) and school finances. The study is subtitled "A factual survey", and this is what it is in that it was not the purpose of the research to try to determine the organisational characters of the various schools, but to compare their dimensions. Interestingly, Kalton's book has a foreword by Royston Lambert which puts the study in a sociological context and in so doing offers a very neat account of the nature of organisational analysis:

> Any information collected by postal questionnaires from one source in a complex institution such as a school will have inevitable limitations. It can tell us much of value but not all that we need to know about a community or a system of communities. Some essential features of a school cannot be reduced to facts by this method: the wider social system or macrocosm which the school serves, the aims and values which inform it, the ethos and attitudes which permeate it, the organisation and dynamics by which it works towards its ends, the culture and underlife which it generates in the process, the effects and modes of adaptation which it induces. To examine these and other aspects of the community of the school more diverse methods are obviously needed.

Lambert has himself undertaken a comparative organisational analysis of public schools. Although the final report has not yet been published the project has so far yielded two publications: an account of pupils' perceptions of their schools as revealed in written work (Lambert, 1968) and a manual on how to conduct a comparative analysis (Lambert *et al.*, 1970).

A comparative study of direct grant schools was carried out on behalf of the Donnison Commission and constitutes Appendix 6 of Part 2 of the Report (HMSO, 1970). This provided valuable background data for the Commission but it did not provide an analysis of the organisational character of different types of Direct Grant School generated by the combination of different elements: degree of selectivity, religious affiliation, proportion of fee payers, etc. The Commission was aware of the potential value of such profiles but was disinclined to mount the necessary research which would have delayed the publication of its report.

Another large comparative study which has recently been undertaken and which will soon be published is the Sixth Form Study carried out on behalf of the Schools Council by the Department of Education, Manchester University, under the direction of Professor R. A. C. Oliver. Part of the study was considered by the Donnison Commission and has been separately published (Christie and Griffin, 1970). This showed that in a sample of highly selective schools when O-level achievements are used as a predictor of A-level achievements, there is a relative decline at A-level—although overall achievement remains high. As this is a survey rather than an organisational analysis it cannot yield the reasons for this. It might be hypothesised, however, that it could be another example of the effects of labelling whereby A-level achievements of intelligent pupils are depressed because they have not been labelled as potential Oxbridge entrants. Christie and Griffin (1971) point out that the answers could only be determined through a study of social and educational processes within the schools.

There have so far been reports of the first two stages of the Comprehensive Education Project which is being carried out by the NFER. The first report (Monks, 1968) contains a survey of several of the dimensions of a comprehensive school, e.g. structure, staffing, pupil ability. The second stage has been reported in Monks (1971) and covers a sample of 59 out of the 222 schools identified as meeting the definition of "comprehensive" in the initial survey. The report contains data on administration, attainments, friendship choices, curriculum and pupil welfare, extra-curricular activities and school-community contacts. The approach is descriptive, static, and considers one dimension at a time. The difference between a survey and an organisational analysis can be seen by comparing the chapter on administration—which includes material of pupil-teacher ratios, the distribution of responsibility allowances, and the amount of time which the head spends with visitors—with studies of school administration as a social process. One can also compare the chapter on friendship choices—which reports such data as the tendency for pupils to choose their friends from the same ability, social, behavioural and ethnic groups—with the work of Lacey and Hargreaves which considers the relationship between friendship choice, pupil subculture and streaming as a social process and examines its implications. The third stage of the project involves a study of twelve schools to determine the degree to which they are fulfilling their objectives. This stage will involve a comparative organisational study of the schools using measures developed by Banks and Finlayson.

The first major organisational study carried out on a comparative basis has been completed by King on a grant from the Schools Council. The conceptual basis of the research is given in King (1968) and a synopsis of the main findings in King (1970). The basic research problem is expressed thus: "How does the organisation of the school affect the pupils' involvement in the school?" The basic methodological problem is expressed as follows by King: "The intention of the research ... is to advance the study of schools as organisations, by attempting to evolve objective criteria of observation, simple taxonomies and actual measurements of certain organisational dimensions, all of which may enable reasonably valid and reliable comparisons to be made between schools, and also account for some of the unique features of individual schools." The basic research design involved a measure of the organisation of the school as it affects the pupils, the measurement of pupil involvement, and the relationship between organisation and involvement. The study of organisation was carried out in seventy-two secondary schools by means of questionnaire, interviews, documentary analysis and direct observation. Structural variables were characterised as being either *instrumental* or *expressive,* as being either *ritualised* or *bureaucratised,* as being age-, ability-, or sex-differentiating, and by reference to their subsystems, e.g. games, pastoral care. The results of this part of the investigation showed that the organisation of the school was most clearly related to the ability, social background and sex of pupils, its age range and its ideology; size was relatively unimportant. The study of pupil involvement was based upon 7,500 pupils drawn from a subsample of thirty schools who completed a mixed item questionnaire related to incidence in joining clubs, self-estimates of educational life, involvement, etc. The results showed that the degree of involvement varied by age, sex, ability and social class. The third element in the investigation which brought together the organisational measures and the involvement measures showed that the following organisational variables are significantly related to degrees and types of pupil involvement: the sex composition of the school, the social composition of the school, streaming, provision of out-of-school activities. This research is still very much in the British tradition, which was exemplified in the case studies, of focusing on the pupil dimension of the school, although in this case it is related to certain aspects of school organisation. As King himself notes, he has omitted from the investigation the role of teachers as agents of social control and of cultural transmission, and one might also add that the significance of the administrative process has been omitted. But this only serves to highlight the problem of attempting comparative organisational studies which will simultaneously handle all the major dimensions of the school. (The report of King's research is currently with the Schools Council from whom a synopsis can be obtained.)

There have so far been few comparative studies of the administrative dimension of schools. The issue of school administration is being largely dealt with in this country through studies of the role of the headteacher which are currently being carried out at the Universities of Bradford (see Cohen, 1970), Bristol and Leicester. Compared with the voluminous American research, there has been little in this country so far on such issues as decision-making, communication, patterns of authority, administrative climate, etc. One of the most suggestive pieces of research in this area was carried out under the direction of R. W. Revans (1965). The basic concern of the research project was to evolve a method of measuring pupils' involvement in their school work through an analysis of films of their activities during lessons in ten schools where the teachers concerned had agreed the lesson content. Significant variations in pupil involvement emerged and Revans went on to investigate the possibility that this was a function of the administrative dimension of the school. He investigated the attitudes of children towards teachers and the attitudes of teachers towards the authority structure of the school in twenty-seven schools. He summarised the findings as follows:

> ... where teachers feel either that they have a hand in the internal running of the school, or that its outside directors are aware of their internal problems, they tend to be both liked by their pupils and seen as effective teachers. If the teachers see their superiors as remote or dictatorial, they, in their turn, are seen by their pupils as unfriendly and ineffective.

A forthcoming study by Rose, Director of Research for the Central Lancashire Family and Community Project, and his colleagues will make a very valuable contribution to literature on school organisation, especially its administrative aspect. The research project was primarily concerned with the functioning of the school social workers who formed part of the project, but it became clear that the "preventative" work of the project could only be fully understood if the functioning of schools was also taken into account. Information on the schools was collected by means of interviews and observation by the project workers who were in close contact with them. Aspects covered in the report include staff ideology in relation to social work based upon a typology of teachers, the categorisation of the formal and informal aspects of the school organisation, the influence of the head, the power situation in the schools, and the flow of information. This is a case where a concern with the school as an organisation arose out of a specific problem.

POTENTIALITIES AND PROBLEMS

The preceding review indicates that in this country the study of schools as organisations has only recently begun. The purpose of this final section is threefold: to indicate possible areas for future research, to refer to relevant American work from which ideas may be derived, and to raise certain methodological issues. These aspects cannot be dealt with exhaustively and therefore three topics have been selected for discussion which give the opportunity for bringing them out.

Counselling

One of the most important recent developments in the social science of education has been the growing interest in the problem of 'labelling". The ascription of status—especially academic status—to pupils has been shown to involve a self-fulfilling prophecy at three levels: at the institutional level of allocation to different types of school, at the organisational level, and at the classroom level (e.g. Rosenthal and Jacobson, 1968). This research has contributed to a movement towards mixed ability grouping at the primary and early secondary levels. But where pupils are not "grouped by destination", as where a system of streaming operates, there arises the need for a more individualised form of guidance and counselling. This movement is only just beginning in this country, and although there are some useful studies (e.g. Moore, 1970), there is a need for further studies which will examine the relationship between guidance procedures and other elements of the school social system and particularly study the latent functions of guidance.

A number of American studies provide valuable insights in this area, and two in particular can be mentioned. Burton Clark (1960) carried out an organisational study of a Californian junior college established to provide mainly technical courses for terminal students and some academic courses for transfer students aspiring to enter a four year university course. But as an "open door" policy allowed any student to enter the junior college and choose his own courses, the majority of the students entered academic courses. The college had to reorganise its internal structure in order to provide more of these courses, but it also developed what Clark called "cooling out" procedures whereby non-academic students were persuaded to revert to technical courses. A variety of devices were used, but importantly the counsellor, armed with his files and records, became the "agent of consolation" in encouraging the less able student to drop out from academic courses on the basis of his scholastic record. Cicourel and Kitsuse (1963) studied counselling procedures in a large American high school. Using open-ended interview procedures with pupils, parents and counsellors, they demonstrated the ways in which the activities of counsellors affected the aspirations of students and parents, identified academic and other problems, and channelled students towards different courses. Their results suggested that the counselling system had become a bureaucratised form of talent hunt whereby students were differentiated on the basis of their school records, biographical and clinical data. But the bureaucratic procedures were not followed uniformly by the counsellors. They were modified on the basis of their perceptions of students as likely college material and the cases handled differently. It is clear from these two studies that the differentiation by counselling raises new problems of labelling and British investigators might begin studies of the organisation of comprehensive schools taking as the central problem of the social system the extent to which counselling replaces streaming as the basis of ascription.

Having cited these two American studies in relation to a substantive area of research, the opportunity can be taken to draw attention to the methodological contributions which they have made. Two aspects of Clark's study are of interest. Firstly, the study centres around an organisational problem which emerged during the course of investigation. In other words, the theory emerged from the data. Secondly, the study is notable for its use of documentary material as an important source of data. The study by Cicourel and Kitsuse has considerable methodological interest in that it was one of the first studies to take a sociological perspective which has since become more common. They note that most sociologists take the statistics collected by an organisation as "given" and, whilst acknowledging their questionable basis proceed to correlate these statistics with such variables as sex, class, race, etc. They reject this approach and outline their own as follows:

> In formulating our research, therefore, we proposed to address specifically the problem of investigating the processes by which persons come to be defined, classified, and recorded in the categories of the agency's statistics. If the rates of college-going students, underachievers, "academic problems", etc. are to be viewed sociologically as characteristics of the high school as a complex organisation, then the explanation for such rates must be sought in the patterned activities of that organisation and not in the behaviour of the students *per se*. The theoretical significance of student *behaviour* for variations in rates is dependent upon how the personnel of the high school interpret, type, and process the behaviour.

This orientation owes much to the work of Alfred Schutz and of Harold Garfinkel who emphasise the central importance of the perspectives of the actors whose actions produce the organisation which is under study and how organisations define persons as instances of given categories.

Authority

It has already been pointed out that there have so far been few studies of patterns of authority in British schools, and yet as these patterns are themselves undergoing change there would appear to be a need for research in this area. There are perhaps two major forces which are bringing about changes in authority patterns in British schools. Firstly, there is a change in the social climate which is leading to a demand by teachers for more participation in the running of schools. Secondly, changes in the curriculum and forms of organising for instruction (e.g. flexible grouping, team teaching, interdisciplinary enquiry) are bringing teachers into greater integration with each other at the level of their day to day work which *prima facie* might seem to be congruent with *collegial authority* whereby professional equals govern their work situation.

Research on administration has tended to conceptualise the question of authority in terms of leadership and administrative climate whereas sociologists have tended to rely upon the Weberian concept of bureaucracy. Most of the work which has operationalised bureaucracy has been carried out in North America. The standard procedure is to develop a scale of bureaucracy whereby teachers report their *perceptions* of their schools as being more or less bureaucratic. Summed scores give school profiles and it is then possible to compare schools or to correlate school scores with other variables, e.g. social class of intake, proportion of women employed, school size (Anderson, 1969), teachers' sense of power (Moeller and Charters, 1966), etc. There are, however, a number of difficulties arising from the use of the concept of bureaucracy. Firstly, it is not a unitary concept. Punch (1969) factor analysed teachers' responses to an adaptation of Hall's scale of bureaucracy and two distinctive factors emerged, a bureaucratic factor and a professional factor. Secondly, there is no single model of authority which applies to the school. Katz (1964) has suggested that the school is characterised less by authority than by autonomy, and Bidwell (1965) has suggested that the school is characterised by a mixture of authority and autonomy. This is true of the British school at the present time. The teacher has a relatively high degree of autonomy in the classroom, but relatively little involvement in decision-making on matters of school policy. The greater integration of teachers in their daily work is likely to lead to a decline in their autonomy. On the other hand, they are likely to gain a greater voice in the determination of school policy if integration is accompanied by collegiality. The paradox is that a loss in autonomy could actually increase the teacher's professionality. On the other hand, for some teachers this loss in autonomy might not be compensated for and a loss in satisfaction might result. In a highly perceptive article Lortie (1964) has pointed out that future research in team teaching should aim to assess the competing trends towards greater collegiality and towards a new form of bureaucracy.

School community relationships

A number of sociologists have argued that the central problem of organisation is that of boundary maintenance and that this, therefore, ought to be the central focus of research. The British school, as compared with its North American counterpart, has been relatively insulated from the local community and hence the problem of boundary maintenance has not been particularly acute. But at the present time there is a growing pressure to strengthen the links between school and community, particularly through the involvement of the parents in the life of the school but also through the involvement of teachers with the families of their pupils. There are obvious substantive problems here which suggest the need for research. There is little doubt that the effectiveness of the school would be improved through greater cooperation with parents, and research indicates that teachers see parental support as improving their effectiveness and satisfactions. On the other hand, there are indications that in certain circumstances teachers would see parental involvement as a threat and that a sizeable proportion of teachers do not see an involvement with the community as part of their role. Thus a boundary maintenance problem is likely to be generated by these trends. Again one can look to American experience and research in this area. The most sophisticated theoretical approach to the problem is that of Litwak and Meyer (1965, 1967) who conceptualise the problem in terms of the incompatibilities between social units of different kinds: a formal organisation (school) and a primary group (family). They develop their ideas at a theoretical level in terms of patterns of linkage which arose out of their participation in the Great Cities Project in Detroit where a variety of school-community links were established.

Apart from the work of the Central Lancashire Family and Community Project which has already been cited, the substantive problem of school community linkage is being handled in this country through the EPA Project directed by A. H. Halsey and especially through the Liverpool scheme of Eric Midwinter. The report of this project has not yet been completed and one must await its publication to see to what extent there is data which touches on this problem of the school boundary. The EPA project is a piece of action research and it may be, as Young (1965) has suggested, that school community relationships particularly lend themselves to this approach. But it is important in such a scheme to attempt to evaluate its impact upon the internal organisation of the school.

CONCLUSION

It has been the purpose of this chapter to review British research on schools as organisations. It has been shown that there are many possible approaches—both theoretical and methodological—to such studies, but that the best British studies so far published have tended to be case studies of single schools and have concentrated on pupil subculture and differentiation. A number of comparative studies have been carried out and are yet to be published, but comparative studies involve the solution of difficult problems of design. There has been little work so far in this country on the administrative dimensions of the school, perhaps partly due to the problems of access in this sensitive area but perhaps also due in part to the feeling that existing theories of organisation and administration are not particularly relevant in this context. It might well be the case that future studies will take as their starting point substantive prob-

Eric Hoyle

lems rather than theoretical problems, and three possible areas have been cited—counselling, authority in a system of integrated teaching, and school-community relationships. In either case, there would appear to be scope for, and a need for, further organisational studies of British schools.

ANDERSON, J. G. (1969) *Bureaucracy and Education*, Johns Hopkins University Press.
BARON, G. and TAYLOR, W. (1969) *Educational Administration and the Social Sciences*, Athlone Press.
BIDWELL, C. E. (1965) "The School as a Formal Organization", in March, J. G. (ed.) *Handbook of Organizations*, Rand McNally.
BLAU, P. N. (1964) *Exchange and Power in Social Life*, John Wiley.
CARLSON, RICHARD O. (1962) *Executive Succession and Organizational Change*, Midwest Administration Centre, University of Chicago.
CARLSON, RICHARD O. (1964) "Environmental Constraints and Organizational Consequences", in Griffiths, D. E. (ed.) *Behavioural Science and Educational Administration*, 63rd Yearbook of the National Society for the Study of Education, University of Chicago Press.
CHIN, R. (1960) "Problems and Prospects of Applied Research", in Bennis, W. G., Benne, K. and Chin, R. *The Dynamics of Planned Change*, Holt, Rinehart and Winston.
CHRISTIE, T. and GRIFFIN, A. (1970) "The Examination Achievements of Highly Selective Schools", *Educational Research*, **12**, *iii*, pp. 202–8.
CHRISTIE, T. and GRIFFIN, A. (1971) "A reply", *Educational Research*, **13**, *iii*, pp. 242–4.
CICOUREL, A. and KITSUSE, J. I. (1963) *The Educational Decision Makers*, Bobbs Merrill.
CLARK, B. R. (1960) *The Open Door College*, McGraw-Hill.
COHEN, L. (1970) "School Size and Headteachers' Bureaucratic Role Conceptions", *Educational Review*, **23**, *i*, pp. 50–8.
CORWIN, R. G. (1967) "Education and Sociology of Complex Organizations", in Hansen, D. A. and Gerstl, J. E. (eds.) *On Education: Sociological Perspectives*, Wiley.
DAVIES, W. B. (1970) "On the Contribution of Organizational Analysis to the Study of Educational Institutions", paper presented to the Annual Conference of the British Sociological Association.
EGGLESTON, S. J. (1967) *The Social Context of the School*, Routledge and Kegan Paul.
ETZIONI, A. (1961) *A Comparative Analysis of Complex Organizations*, Free Press.
FELDMAN, K. A. (1971) "Some Methods for Assessing College Impacts", *Sociology of Education*, **44**, *ii*, pp. 133–50.

105

FORD, J. (1969) *Social Class and the Comprehensive School*, Routledge and Kegan Paul.

GETZELS, J. W. and GUBA, E. G. (1957) "Social Behaviour and the Administrative Process", *School Review*, **65**, *iv*, pp. 423–41.

GETZELS, J. W., LIPHAM, J. M. and CAMPBELL, R. F. (1968) *Educational Administration as a Social Process*, Harper Row.

GLASER, B. and STRAUSS, A. (1968) *The Discovery of Grounded Theory*, Weidenfeld and Nicolson.

GRIFFITHS, DANIEL E. (1959) *Administrative Theory*, Appleton-Century-Crofts.

GRIFFITHS, DANIEL E. (1964a) "On the Nature and Meaning of Theory", in Griffiths, D. E. (ed.) *Behavioural Science and Educational Administration*, 63rd Yearbook of the National Society for the Study of Education Part II, University of Chicago Press.

GRIFFITHS, DANIEL E. (1964b) "Administrative Theory and Change in Organizations", in Miles, M. B. (ed.) *Innovation in Education*, Teachers College Press.

GROSS, N. and HERRIOTT, R. E. (1965) *Staff Leadership in the Public Schools*, Wiley.

HALPIN, A. W. (1967) *Administrative Theory in Education*, Macmillan.

HANSEN, D. A. (1967) "The Uncomfortable Relation of Sociology and Education", in Hansen, D. A. and Gerstl, J. E. (eds.) *On Education: Sociological Perspectives*, John Wiley.

HARGREAVES, D. H. (1967) *Social Relations in a Secondary School*, Routledge and Kegan Paul.

HMSO (1970) *Public Schools Commission Second Report*.

HOYLE, E. (1965) "Organizational Analysis in the Field of Education", *Educational Research*, **7**, *ii*, pp. 97-114.

HOYLE, E. (1969) "Organization Theory and Educational Administration", in Baron, G. and Taylor, W. *Educational Administration and the Social Sciences*, Athlone Press.

HOYLE, E. (1970) "Planned Organizational Change in Education", *Research in Education*, **3**, pp. 1–22.

HUGHES, M. (1970) *Secondary School Administration: a Management Approach*, Pergamon.

JENSEN, G. (1965) *Educational Sociology: an Approach to its Development as a Practical Field of Study*, Centre for Applied Research in Education.

KATZ, FRED E. (1964) "The School as a Complex Social Organization", *Harvard Educational Review*, **34**, *iii*, pp. 428–55.

KALTON, G. (1966) *The Public Schools: a Factual Survey*, Longman.

KING, R. (1968) "The Formal Organization of the School and Pupil Involvement", paper read to the Education Section of the British Sociological Association.

KING, R. (1969) *Values and Involvement in a Grammar School*, Routledge and Kegan Paul.

KING, R. (1970) "The Social Organization of the School", University of Exeter Institute of Education.

LACEY, C. (1970) *Hightown Grammar: the School as a Social System*, Manchester University Press.

LAMBERT, R. (1968) *The Hothouse Society*, Weidenfeld and Nicolson.

LAMBERT, R., MILLHAM, S. and BULLOCK, R. (1970) *Manual to the Sociology of the School*, Weidenfeld and Nicolson.

LITWAK, E. and MEYER, H. J. (1965) "Administrative Styles and Community Linkages", in Reiss, A. J. (ed.) *Schools in a Changing Society*, Free Press.

LITWAK, E. and MEYER, H. J. (1967) "The School and the Family: Linking Organizations and External Primary Groups", in Lazarsfeld, P. *et al. The Uses of Sociology*, Basic Books.

LORTIE, DAN C. (1964) "Proposals for Long-term Research on Team Teaching", in Shaplin, J. S. and Olds, H. *Team Teaching*, Harper Row.

LUNN, J. BARKER (1970) *Streaming in the Primary School*, National Foundation for Educational Research.

MOELLER, GERALD H. and CHARTERS, W. W. (1966) "Relation of Bureaucratisation to Sense of Power amongst Teachers", *Administrative Science Quarterly*, **10**, pp. 444–65.

MOORE, B. M. (1970) *Guidance in Comprehensive Schools: a Study of Five Systems*, National Foundation for Educational Research.

MONKS, G. (1968) *Comprehensive Education in England and Wales*, National Foundation for Educational Research.

MONKS, G. (ed.) (1971) *Comprehensive Education in Action*, National Foundation for Educational Research.

MOUZELIS, N. (1967) *Organization and Bureaucracy*, Routledge and Kegan Paul.

PARSONS, T. (1966) "Some Ingredients of a General Theory of Organizations", in Halpin, A. W. (ed.) *Administrative Theory in Education*, University of Chicago Press.

POWER, M. J. *et al.* (1967) "Delinquent schools ?", *New Society*, **10**, p. 264.

PUNCH, K. F. (1969) "Bureaucratic Structure in Schools: towards Redefinition and Measurement", *Educational Administration Quarterly*, **5**, *ii*.

REVANS, R. W. (1965) "Involvement in School", *New Society*, **6**, p. 152.

ROBBINS, M. P. and MILLER, J. R. (1969) "The Concept School Structure: an Enquiry into its Validity", *Educational Administration Quarterly*, **5**, *i*.

ROSE, GORDON *et al.* (forthcoming) *Counselling and School Social Work*.

ROSENTHAL, R. and JACOBSON, L. (1968) *Pygmalion in the Classroom*, Holt, Rinehart and Winston.

SELZNICK, P. (1941) "Institutional Vulnerability in Mass Society", *American Journal of Sociology*, **56**.

SELZNICK, P. (1957) *Leadership in Administration*, Harper Row.
TURNER, C. M. (1969) "An Organizational Analysis of a Secondary Modern School", *Sociological Review*, **17**, *i*, pp. 67–86.
WAKEFORD, JOHN (1969) *The Cloistered Elite*, Macmillan.
YOUNG, MICHAEL (1965) *Innovation and Research in Education*, Routledge and Kegan Paul.

2.3 The Three Types of Legitimate Rule[1]

Max Weber
Translated by Hans Gerth

Authority means the probability that a specific command will be obeyed. Such obedience may feed on diverse motives. It may be determined by sheer interest situation, hence by the compliant actor's calculation of expediency; by mere custom, that is, the actor's inarticulate habituation to routine behavior; or by mere affect, that is, purely personal devotion of the governed. A structure of power, however, if it were to rest on such foundations alone, would be relatively unstable. As a rule both rulers and rules uphold the internalizing power structure as "legitimate" by right, and usually the shattering of this belief in legitimacy has far-reaching ramifications.

There are but three clear-cut grounds on which to base the belief in legitimate authority. Given pure types each is connected with a fundamentally different sociological structure of executive staff and means of administration.

I

Legal authority rests on enactment; its pure type is best represented by bureaucracy. The basic idea is that laws can be enacted and changed at pleasure by formally correct procedure. The governing body is either elected or appointed and constitutes as a whole and in all its sections rational organizations. A heteronomous and heterocephalous sub-unit we shall call "public authorities" (*Behörde*). The administrative staff consists of officials appointed by the ruler; the law-abiding people are members of the body politic ("fellow citizens").

Obedience is not owed to anybody personally but to enacted rules and regulations which specify to whom and to what rule people owe obedience. The person in authority, too, obeys a rule when giving an order, namely, "the law", or "rules and regulations" which represent abstract norms. The person in command typically is the "superior" within a functionally defined "competency" or "jurisdiction", and his right to

---

Source: Etzioni, A. (ed.) (1961) *Complex Organizations: A Sociological Reader*, Holt, Rinehart and Winston, pp. 4–14.

govern is legitimized by enactment. Specialization sets limits with regard to functional purpose and required skill of the office incumbent.

The typical official is a trained specialist whose terms of employment are contractual and provide a fixed salary scaled by rank of office, not by amount of work, and the right to a pension according to fixed rules of advancement. His administration represents vocational work by virtue of impersonal duties of office; ideally the administrator proceeds *sineira et studio*, not allowing personal motive or temper to influence conduct, free of arbitrariness and unpredictability; especially he proceeds "without regard to person", following rational rules with strict formality. And where rules fail he adheres to "functional" considerations of expediency. Dutiful obedience is channeled through a hierarchy of offices which subordinates lower to higher offices and provides a regular procedure for lodging complaints. Technically, operation rests on organizational discipline.

A. Naturally this type of "legal" rule comprises not only the modern structure of state and city government but likewise the power relations in private capitalist enterprise, in public corporations and voluntary associations of all sorts, provided that an extensive and hierarchically organized staff of functionaries exists. Modern political bodies merely represent the type pre-eminently. Authority of private capitalist organization is partially heteronomous, its order is partly prescribed by the state, and it is completely heterocephalous as regards the machinery of coercion. Normally the courts and police take care of these functions. Private enterprise, however, is autonomous in its increasingly bureaucratic organization of management. The fact that, formally speaking, people enter into the power relationship (*Herrschaftsverband*) voluntarily and are likewise "free" to give notice does not affect the nature of private enterprise as a power structure since conditions of the labor market normally subject the employees to the code of the organization. Its sociological affinity to modern state authority will be classified further in the discussion of the economic bases of power and authority. The "contract" as constitutive for the relations of authority in capitalist enterprise makes this a pre-eminent type of "legal authority".

B. Technically, bureaucracy represents the purest type of legal authority. No structure of authority, however, is exclusively bureaucratic, to wit, is managed by contractually hired and appointed officials alone. That is quite impossible. The top positions of the body politic may be held by "monarchs" (hereditary charismatic rulers), or by popularly elected "presidents" (hence plebiscitarian charismatic rulers), or by parliamentary elected presidents. In the latter case the actual rulers are members of parliament or rather the leaders of the prevailing parliamentary parties. These leaders in turn may stand close to the type of charismatic leadership or to that of notabilities. More of this below.

Likewise the administrative staff is almost never exclusively bureaucratic but usually notables and agents of interest groups participate in administration in manifold ways. This holds most of all for the so-called self-government. It is decisive that regular administrative work is predominantly and increasingly performed by bureaucratic forces. The historical development of the modern state is identical indeed with that of modern officialdom and bureaucratic organization (cf. below), just as the development of modern capitalism is identical with the increasing bureaucratization of economic enterprise. The part played by bureaucracy becomes bigger in all structures of power.

C. Bureaucracy does not represent the only type of legal authority. Other types comprise rotating office holders or office holders chosen by lot or popularly elected officers. Parliamentary and committee administration and all sorts of collegiate and administrative bodies are included under the type if and when their competency rests on enacted rules and if the use they make of their prerogative follows the type of legal administration. During the rise of the modern state collegiate bodies have made essential contributions to the development of legal authority, especially the concept of "public authorities" (*Behörde*) originated with them. On the other hand, elected officialdom has played an important role in the pre-history of the modern civil service and still does so today in the democracies.

II

Traditional authority rests on the belief in the sacredness of the social order and its prerogatives as existing of yore. Patriarchal authority represents its pure type. The body politic is based on communal relationships, the man in command is the "lord" ruling over obedient "subjects". People obey the lord personally since his dignity is hallowed by tradition; obedience rests on piety. Commands are substantively bound by tradition, and the lord's inconsiderate violation of tradition would endanger the legitimacy of his personal rule, which rests merely upon the sacredness of tradition. The creation of new law opposite traditional norms is deemed impossible in principle. Actually this is done by way of "recognizing" a sentence as "valid of yore" (the *Weistum* of ancient Germanic law). Outside the norms of tradition, however, the lord's sway in a given case is restricted only by sentiments of equity, hence by quite elastic bonds. Consequently the rule of the lord divides into a strictly tradition-bound sphere and one of free favor and arbitrariness where he rules at pleasure as sympathy or antipathy move him, following purely personal considerations subject especially to the influence of "good turns".

So far as principles are followed in administration and settlement of disputes, they rest on substantive considerations of ethical equity, justice, or utilitarian expediency, not on formal considerations characteristic of the rule of law. The lord's administrative staff proceeds in the same way. It consists of personally dependent men (members of the household or domestic officials), of relatives, of personal friends (favorites), or associates bound by personal allegiance (vassals, tributary princes). The bureaucratic

111

concept of "competency" as a functionally delimited jurisdictional sphere is absent. The scope of the "legitimate" prerogatives of the individual servant is defined from case to case at the pleasure of the lord on whom the individual servant is completely dependent as regards his employment in more important or high ranking roles. Actually this depends largely on what the servant may dare to do opposite the more or less docile subjects. Personal loyalty of the faithful servant, not functional duty of office and office discipline, control the interrelationship of the administrative staff.

One may, however, observe two characteristically different forms of positional relationships, the patriarchal structure and that of estates.

A. In the purely patriarchal structure of administration the servants are completely and personally dependent on the lord; they are either purely patrimonially recruited as slaves, bondsmen-serfs, eunuchs, or extra patrimonially as favorites and plebeians from among strata lacking all rights. Their administration is entirely heteronomous and heterocephalous, the administrators have no personal right to their office, there is neither merit selection nor status honor; the material means of administration are managed under, and on account of, the lord. Given the complete dependency of the administrative staff on the lord, there is no guarantee against the lord's arbitrariness, which in this set-up can therefore have its greatest possible sway. Sultanistic rule represents the pure type. All genuine "despotism" was of this nature. Prerogatives are considered [. . .] ordinary property rights of the lord.

B. In the estate system the servants are not personal servants of the lord but independent men whose social position makes them presumably socially prominent. The lord, actually or according to the legitimacy fiction, bestows office on them by privilege or concession; or they have contractually, by purchase, tenancy or lease, acquired a title to their office which cannot be arbitrarily taken away from them; hence within limits, their administration is autocephalous and autonomous. Not the lord but they dispose over the material means of administration. This represents estate rule.

The competition of the officeholders for larger bailiwicks (and income) then determines the mutual delimitation of their actual bailiwicks and takes the place of "competency". Privilege often breaks through the heirarchic structure (*de non evocando, non apellando*). The category of "discipline" is absent. Tradition, privilege, feudal or patrimonial bonds of allegiance, status honor and "good will" regulate the web of interrelations. The power prerogatives of the lord hence are divided between the lord and the privileged and administrative staff, and this division of powers among the estates brings about a high degree of stereotypy in the nature of administration.

Patriarchal rule (of the family father, sib chief, father of his people [*Landesvater*]) represents but the purest type of traditionalist rule. Any "authorities" who claim legitimacy successfully by virtue of mere habituation represent the most typical contrast, on the one hand, to the position of a contractually employed worker in business enterprise; on the other, to the way a faithful member of a religious community emotionally relates to a prophet. Actually the domestic group [*Hausverband*] is the nucleus of traditionalist power structures. The typical "officials" of the patrimonial and feudal state are domestic officers with originally purely domestic tasks (dapifer, chamberlain, marshall, cupbearer, seneschal, major domo).

The co-existence of the strictly tradition-bound and the free sphere of conduct is a common feature of all traditionalistic forms of authority. Within the free sphere, action of the lord or of his administrative staff must be bought or earned by personal relations. (This is one of the origins of the institution of fees.) It is decisive that formal law is absent and that substantive principles of administration and arbitration take its place. This likewise is a common feature of all traditionalist power structures and has far-reaching ramifications, especially for economic life.

The patriarch, like the patrimonial ruler, governs and decides according to the principles of "cadi justice": on the one hand, decisions are strictly bound by tradition; however, where those fetters give leeway, decisions follow juristically informal and irrational considerations of equity and justice from case to case, also taking individual differences into account. All codifications and laws of patrimonial rulers embody the spirit of the so-called "welfare state". A combination of social ethical with social utilitarian principles prevails, breaking through all rigor of formal law.

The sociological distinction between patriarchal power structure and that of the estates in traditionalist rule is fundamental for all states of the pre-bureaucratic epoch. (The contrast will become fully clear only in connection with its economic aspect, that is, with the separation of the administrative staff from the material means of administration or with their appropriation by the staff.) This has been historically decisive for the question whether and what status groups existed as champions of ideas and culture values.

Patrimonial dependents (slaves, bondsmen) as administrators are to be found throughout the Mideastern orient and in Egypt down to the time of the Mamelukes; they represent the most extreme and what would seem to be the most consistent type of the purely patriarchal rule devoid of estates. Plebeian freemen as administrators stand relatively close to rational officialdom. The administration by literati can vary greatly in accordance with their nature: typical is the contrast between Brahmins and Mandarins, and both in turn stand opposite Buddhist and Christian clerics—yet their administration always approximates the estate type of power structure.

The rule of estates is most clearly represented by aristocracy, in purest form by feudalism, which puts in the place of the functional and rational duty of office the personal allegiance and the appeal to status honor of the enfeoffed.

In comparison to patriarchalism, all estate rule, based upon more or less stable appropriation of administrative power, stands closer to legal authority as the guarantees surrounding the prerogatives of the privileged assume the form of special "rights" (a result of the "division of power" among the estates). This rationale is absent in patriarchal structures, with their administration completely dependent on the lord's arbitrary sway. On the other hand, the strict discipline and the lack of rights of the administrative staff within patriarchalism is more closely related to the discipline of legal authority than is the administration of estates, which is fragmented and stereotyped through the appropriation of the means of administration by the staff. Plebeians (used as jurists) in Europe's princely service have been pacemarkers of the modern state.

III

Charismatic authority rests on the affectual and personal devotion of the follower to the lord and his gifts of grace (charisma). They comprise especially magical abilities, revelations of heroism, power of the mind and of speech. The eternally new, the non-routine, the unheard of and the emotional rapture from it are sources of personal devotion. The purest types are the rule of the prophet, the warrior hero, the great demagogue. The body politic consists in the communal relationship of a religious group or following. The person in command is typically the "leader"; he is obeyed by the "disciple". Obedience is given exclusively to the leader as a person, for the sake of his non-routine qualities, not because of enacted position or traditional dignity. Therefore obedience is forthcoming only so long as people ascribe these qualities to him, that is, so long as his charisma is proven by evidence. His rule falls if he is "forsaken" by his god[2] or deprived of his heroic strength, or if the masses lose faith in his leadership capacity. The administrative staff is selected according to the charisma and personal devotion, hence selection does not consider special qualification (as in the case of the civil servant) nor rank and station (as in the case of administration by estates) nor domestic or other forms of personal dependency (as, in contrast to the above, holds for the patriarchal administrative staff). The rational concept of "competency" is lacking as is the status idea of "privilege". Decisive for the legitimation of the commissioned follower or disciple is alone the mission of the lord and his followers' personal charismatic qualification. The administration—so far as this word is adequate—lacks all orientation to rules and regulations whether enacted or traditional. Spontaneous revelation or creation, deed and example, decision from case to case, that is—at least measured against enacted orders—irrational decisions, are characteristic of charismatic authority. It is not bound to tradition: "It is written but I say unto you" holds for the prophet. For the warrior hero the legitimate orders vanish opposite new creations by power of the sword, for the demagogue by virtue of his annunciation or suggestion of revolutionary "natural law". In the genuine form of charismatic justice and arbitration the lord or "sage" speaks the law and the (military or religious) following gives it recognition, which is obligatory, unless somebody raises a counter claim to charismatic validity. This case presents a struggle of leaders which in the last analysis can solely be decided by the confidence of the community; only one side can be right; the other side must be wrong and be obliged to make amends.

A. The type of charismatic authority has first been developed brilliantly by R. Sohn in his *Kirchenrecht* for the early Christian community without his recognizing that it represents a type of authority. The term has since been used repeatedly without recognition of its bearing.

Early history shows alongside a few beginnings of "enacted" authority, which are by no means entirely absent, the division of all power relationships under tradition and charisma. Besides the "economic chief" (sachem) of the Indians, an essentially traditional figure, stands the charismatic warrior prince (corresponding to the Germanic "duke") with his following. Hunting and war campaigns, both demanding a leader of extraordinary personal endowments, are the secular; magic is the "sacred" place of charismatic leadership. Throughout the ages charismatic authority exercised by prophets and warrior princes has held sway over men. The charismatic politician—the "demagogue"—is the product of the occidental city state. In the city state of Jerusalem he emerged only in religious costume as a prophet. The constitution of Athens, however, was completely cut out for his existence after the innovations of Pericles and Ephialtes, since without the demagogue the state machine would not function at all.

B. Charismatic authority rests on the "faith" in the prophet, on the "recognition" which the charismatic warrior hero, the hero of the street or the demagogue, finds personally, and this authority falls with him. Yet, charismatic authority does not derive from this recognition by the subjects. Rather the reverse obtains: the charismatically legitimized leader considers faith in the acknowledgement of his charisma obligatory and punishes its violation. Charismatic authority is even one of the great revolutionary forces in history, but in pure form it is thoroughly authoritarian and lordly in nature.

C. It should be understood that the term "charisma" is used here in a completely value-neutral sense. For the sociologist the manic seizure and rage of the Nordic berserk, the miracles and revelations of any pettifogging prophecy, the demagogic talents of Cleon are just as much "charisma" as the qualities of a Napoleon, Jesus, Pericles. Decisive for us is only whether they were considered charismatics and whether they were effective, that is, gained recognition. Here, "proof" is the basic prerequisite. The charismatic lord has to prove his being sent "by the grace of god" by performing miracles and being successful in securing the good life for his following or subjects. Only as long as he can do so will he be recognized. If success fails him, his authority falters. Wherever this charismatic concept of rule by the grace of god has existed, it has had decisive ramifications. The Chinese monarch's position was threatened as soon as drought, floods, military failure or other misfortune made it appear questionable whether he stood in the grace of Heaven. Public self-impeachment and penance, in cases of stubborn misfortune, removal and possible sacrifice threatened him. Certification by miracles was demanded of every prophet (the Zwickau people demanded it still from Luther).

So far as the belief in legitimacy matters for the stability of basically legal structures of authority, this stability rests mostly on mixed foundations. Traditional habituation of "prestige" (charisma) fuses with the belief in formal legality which in the last analysis is also a matter of habit. The belief in the legitimacy of authority is shattered alike through extraordinary misfortunes whether this exacts unusual demands from the subjects in the light of tradition, or destroys the prestige or violates the usual formal legal correctness. But with all structures of authority the obedience of the governed as a stable condition depends above all on the availability of an administrative staff and especially its continuous operation to maintain order and (directly or indirectly) enforce submission to the rule. The term "organization" means to guarantee the pattern of conduct which realizes the structure of authority. The solidarity of its (ideal and material) interests with those of the lord is decisive for the all important loyalty of the staff to the lord. For the relation of the lord to the executive staff it generally holds that the lord is the stronger opposite the resisting individual because of the isolation of the individual staff member and his solidarity with the lord. The lord is weak opposite the staff members as a whole when they band themselves together, as has happened occasionally in the past and present. Deliberate agreement of the staff is requisite in order to frustrate the lord's action and rule through obstruction or deliberate counter action. Likewise the opposition requires an administrative staff of its own.

D. Charismatic rule represents a specifically extraordinary and purely personal relationship. In the case of continued existence, however, at least when the personal representative of charisma is eliminated, the authority structure has the tendency to routinize. This is the case when the charisma is not extinguished at once but continues to exist in some form and the authority of the lord, hence, is transferred to successors. This routinization of charisma proceeds through:

1   Traditionalization of the orders. The authority of precedents takes the place of the charismatic leader's or his staff's charismatic creativity in law and administration. These precedents either protect the successors or are attributed to them.
2   The charismatic staff of disciples or followers changes into a legal or estate-like staff by taking over internal prerogatives or those appropriated by privilege (fiefs, prebends).

3 The meaning of charisma itself may undergo a change. Decisive in this is the way in which the problem of successorship is solved, which is a burning question for ideological and indeed often material reasons. This question can be solved in various ways: the merely passive tarrying for a new charismatically certified or qualified master usually gives way to an active search for a successor, especially if none readily appears and if any strong interests are vested in the continuity of the authority structure.

NOTES

1 Weber's "Three Types of Legitimate Rule" appeared posthumously in the *Preussische Jahrbuecher* in 1922 (187: 1–12). This exposition was not included in the first editions of *Wirtschaft und Gesellschaft* (*The Theory of Social and Economic Organization*). In the 1956 edition of *Wirtschaft und Gesellschaft* (Tuebingen: J. C. B. Mohr, 1956), which was substantially revised by J. Winckelmann, "The Three Types of Legitimate Rule" appears as Section 2 of the "Sociology of Authority" (2: pp. 551–558).

2 Translator's note: This allusion to Jesus' death and its interpretation as a downfall of his charismatic authority comes out more strongly in Webers' "Sociology of Charismatic Authority" ("Charismatismus", *Wirtschaft und Gesellschaft*, in Weber, trans. Gerth and Mills, 1946. In his later work, *Ancient Judaism* (Weber, trans. Gerth and Martindale, 1952), Weber reversed his position.

REFERENCES

WEBER, M., trans. GERTH, H. H. and MILLS, C. W. (1946) *From Max Weber: Essays in Sociology*, Oxford University Press, p. 248.

WEBER, M., trans. GERTH, H. H. and MARTINDALE, D. (1952) *Ancient Judaism*, Free Press, p. 376.

2.4 Office and Expertise in the Secondary School[1]

Leonard E. Watson

A number of changes in secondary schools are leading to consequences which can usefully be understood by reference to certain notions current in organization theory. Specifically, we shall in this article trace some of the consequences of increasing school complexity and specialization.

The trend at present is towards the larger school, with a continuing reduction in the number of smaller secondary schools. This is being influenced by the increase in school population, especially in the numbers of children remaining at school beyond the minimum leaving age, and through secondary reorganization and schemes of consolidation. Barker and Gump (1964) is one of the very small number of studies concerned with the consequences of size in schools, although many sociologists are interested in the increasing size of organizations. As schools grow larger, there is less and less likelihood that any one person will know everyone, even by sight. The "span of control" of senior staff and the need for intermediate positions of responsibility also increase. Where one teacher comprised a department in a small grammar school, the large comprehensive may have a dozen or more teachers within a department. These are not simply small schools physically enlarged. They are likely to include children varying widely in academic attainments and are expected to provide a wide variety of curricular and extra-curricular activities.

CONFLICTING PRESSURES IN THE SECONDARY SCHOOL

As formal organizations, schools are set up to achieve certain objectives —broadly covered by the term "the education of children". Those who have the effective power to set up schools and, broadly, to order their form, are generally agreed upon at least verbal specifications of what ought to happen within these schools, and they have sanctions available to make such expectations more or less effective.

Scott (1964, p. 488) defines organizations as "collectivities that have been established for the pursuit of relatively specific objectives on a more or less continuous basis". For Gouldner (1959, p. 404) "the organization

---

Source: *Educational Research* (Feb. 1969) Vol. II, No. 2, pp. 104–12.

is conceived as an 'instrument'—that is, as a rationally conceived means of realizing group goals". The components of the *rationality of action* were defined by Mannheim (1950, p. 53) as "a series of actions ... organized in such a way that it leads to a previously defined goal", and clearly may take different forms. Thus, one can see wide differences between the administration of the Sultanates of the Ottoman Empire, the hereditary nature of the office of tax-collector in eighteenth-century France, and the hierarchy of offices characteristic of a large modern government department. Maintaining effective structures is a problem for schools also: local education authorities, boards of governors, parents, teachers and others have expectations (commonly stated as goals) for schools, which they desire to see realized.

Max Weber, in his studies of the legitimacy of authority (1946, 1947, 1961 [see 2.3, p. 109] elaborated three bases of legitimacy associated with three "pure types" of authority: the charismatic, the traditional, and the legal-rational or bureaucratic. For him, bureaucracy was the most efficient means of exercising authority and realizing goals in organizations. The official operates impartially within a framework of law. His authority is that of his office; he is subordinate to his superiors, and has authority over his subordinates by virtue of his office.

It is clear that there are many bureaucratic elements in the secondary school, and many bureaucratic pressures. Offices, such as those of headmaster, head of department and assistant master, are ranked in order, with the superordinate to a large degree responsible for the actions of the subordinate. Salaries are paid according to fixed scales and tenure is according to stated contractual obligations. There is at least some attempt to ensure that the most competent are promoted to higher positions.

Similarly, there are considerable pressures towards standardization of the system. Bigger schools have accentuated problems of co-ordination; rapid changes in the technical and technological aspects of teaching have led to a need for more and more planned change, and supervision of those involved in the change; while there is an increased demand for audit and other checks. All these result in more centralization of control, and a greater emphasis on bureaucracy.

But the school is not organized completely as an "ideal" bureaucracy. It is not characterized by a single hierarchy of authority, complete subordination of individual judgement to rules and regulations, and so on. No organization, however apparently bureaucratized, can continue to function unless non-bureaucratic elements are present. If organizations have goals to fulfil, so have the individual people who work within them. The informal interaction characteristic of workplaces arises, partly from the psychological and social needs of the workers, partly because the regulations governing their behaviour are never complete in themselves; and partly because of the need for communication, discussion, consultation and other activities involving people. However important these informal factors may be—and there is no doubt that they are of crucial importance in understanding the operation of organizations—we will concentrate upon only one aspect of schools which runs counter to the bureaucratic element: professionalism.

We are familiar with the growth of "professional" orientations among occupational groups which have not always been classified as "professional". This term has been variously defined, and there is indeed some doubt as to its utility as a sociological concept (Vollmer, 1966; Habenstein, 1963). The trend at present is to see occupations, not as divided into "professions" and "non-professions", but rather as variously involved in the general process of professionalization (Vollmer and Mills, 1966). When seen in this way, the appropriate question is not, "Is this occupation a profession?" but "What are the dimensions of professionalization, and where does this occupational group lie upon each of these, in relation to other occupations?" Thus Greenwood (1957) suggests that professionalism tends to emphasize expertise, the autonomy of the occupational group, and an organizational structure emphasizing a minimal hierarchy of authority. These are not the only characteristics, but are the most important for our purpose.

When applied to teachers, we can see that the "professional orientation", with its emphasis upon the autonomy of the individual teacher, tends to be reinforced by certain structural aspects of the job. Classroom teaching is almost always conducted in isolation from colleagues—an isolation much appreciated by many teachers, who value the freedom they find within the four walls of the classroom. Lack of widely agreed criteria as to what constitutes good teaching, and the difficulty of providing behavioural definitions of educational objectives, makes standardization of teaching hazardous. Improved qualifications and training of teachers reinforces their self-confidence. But increased specialization is perhaps the most significant factor to encourage their claims for independence.

'REFERENCE GROUPS' OF TEACHERS

Under what circumstances do subordinates recognize the authority of others? Not all orders or instructions are obeyed; and some are obeyed only because of fear of the consequences of not doing so. It is also clear, however, that many people feel that their subordinate position is appropriate and that he who commands has a right to command, that he who holds the higher office does so legitimately.

The notion of *reference group* has been used extensively to refer to "those groups to which the individual relates himself as a part or to which he aspires to relate himself psychologically". These reference groups may also be seen as sources of authority, of sets of norms which serve to validate or justify the behaviour or authority claims of those who recognize these norms. Gouldner (1957) has developed a taxonomy of "latent social roles" in organizations suggesting that people, and especially professionals, may tend to identify with, and accept the authority of, the organization to which they belong (the "locals") or the wider professional group of which they are members, or to the membership of which they aspire (the "cosmopolitans"). A scientist working in an industrial company may feel that his primary loyalty is to his organization, or to the fraternity of chemists. Teachers' attitudes could be classified into three categories. Loyalty to the school, its traditions, structure, rules and leadership, may identify the "locals". Another group may feel primary identity with those who share the same academic subject and training—these we might label the "academics". Such a teacher of physics would tend to identify with his fellow physicists, wherever they were working. Others again would identify with the profession of teaching, emphasizing a set of values and an ideology which refers to the "how", the "technology" of teaching, to the child and other values, irrespective of the subject being taught. These we may refer to as the "craftsmen". These three groups of attitudes represent different modes of recognizing and ascribing authority, all three of which may overlap in any one teacher.

At present we have little evidence to clarify the area of authority and teacher response. Predominantly "academic" teachers, however, will probably be subject-centred and will resist supervision (which they may define as "interference") in this area. The "craftsmen" will probably emphasize the importance of pedagogical matters, and the "locals" will stress organizational and administrative commitments. Bidwell (1955, 1956) has suggested that teachers are most likely to accept the supervision of administrators who seem to conform to their prescriptions about what administrators should do. Thus the advice or instructions of a headmaster or head of department is much more likely to be regarded as legitimate if he is thought to have the same reference group as the teacher. Some teachers, of course, rather than being primarily "locals", "academics" or "craftsmen" may well be "indifferents". It has been suggested by some observers that the domination by occupationally "indifferent" women teachers of some teacher organizations may help to explain their relative ineffectiveness.

So far we have distinguished between authority of office (bureaucratic orientation), and of expertise (professional orientation), and have classified modes of identification with the organization, the profession of teaching and the academic tradition. We will now look at the pyramids of authority within the school with their implications for the encouragement and supervision of teachers and for the role of the headmaster.

THE PYRAMIDS OF AUTHORITY

In looking at any organization, it is important to examine any division of labour and the ways in which the varying offices are hierarchically arranged. In the secondary school, teacher specialization varies considerably according to task. Since most secondary school teachers teach only one or two subjects, the teacher is to this extent a specialist. Where size of school or lack of suitably qualified staff make it impossible

E

to teach only one or two subjects the lack of specialization is usually considered undesirable. One consequence of the division of labour of teachers by subject taught is the characteristic class-subject basis of time-tabling and the exposure of all classes to a number of different teachers during the school week.

There is a larger degree of non-specialization in general pedagogical matters. Classroom teachers are expected (and expect themselves) to decide individually questions of classroom organization and teaching method. However, this pattern appears to be changing, with increased emphasis on the role of department head responsible for the teaching in his department and for the professional guidance of his teachers, or in the development of team teaching groups. Again, on general questions of child handling and child welfare, the typical teacher in England tends to assume that he has a general "pastoral" responsibility for all his pupils, and especially for those for whom he is "form-master". However, the existence of housemasters, year-tutors and especially of school counsellors implies a division of labour which concentrates the responsibility for certain aspects of the school programme into their hands.

There has always been some division of labour in administrative and organizational matters because of the need for consultation and co-ordination. The headmaster is the final formal authority in many matters. As schools grow larger, however, many administrative concerns are delegated to specific officials, such as bursars, secretaries, clerks, school lunch supervisors, caretaking personnel and even pupils, who handle the routine work. In some cases they may make significant decisions affecting the teaching staff. Thus the school secretary will have authority to require teachers to complete pupil attendance returns, and will function bureaucratically (i.e. by virtue of office, and delegated authority from the headmaster) in making these demands.

To speak of a single hierarchy of formal authority in the secondary school staff is to oversimplify the picture. Rather we must have in mind a structure of triangles each having at its apex the headmaster, who is usually the formal superordinate of each authority system. One can distinguish several authority systems—subject teacher, head of department, head-master—classroom teacher, form-master, housemaster, headmaster (with the school counsellor, if the school has one, playing a specialized and often ambivalent role)—classroom teacher, school secretary, head teacher —classroom teacher, cleaner, caretaker, headmaster—and so on. A single person might well occupy different positions in several of the authority sub-systems. Thus a particular mistress may be a teacher of physics (and therefore responsible for certain purposes to the head of the physics de-partment); a teacher of mathematics responsible to the head of mathe-matics; a form mistress; a house-mistress; and, as a classroom teacher, responsible to the school office for certain of her functions. To complicate matters further, as a housemistress, she might have authority over heads of department (even the heads of physics or mathematics) in house activities or some aspects of pupil guidance.

The secondary school, then, is organized with a considerable but not always clear division of labour. It is a complex arrangement of specialized officials holding offices and exercising authority by virtue of this appointment but presumably having been appointed to the office by virtue of their expertise. The roles which they fulfil, however, are not necessarily clear, and the nature of their authority is frequently in doubt, especially when challenged by the "academics". The creation of superordinate offices (a tendency reinforced by the system of allowances within the Burnham scale) of itself does not necessarily create the conditions which encourage subordinates to accept the instructions or guidance of the superior official.

THE ENCOURAGEMENT AND SUPERVISION OF TEACHERS

As schools become more complex, as the pupils and teachers they recruit become more diverse and the goals of the organization more varied, maintenance of standards, of planning change and of co-ordinating activity become more pressing. The response is often increased centralization and bureaucratization, with greater supervision of teachers. This seldom causes concern to the "indifferent" teachers, for they are not firmly committed to any particular professional principle, and are likely to respond to increased pressure without enthusiasm, but without rebellion. The "local" orientation of teachers is most conducive to the smooth bureaucratic operation of schools. Schools frequently encourage this attitude, emphasizing loyalty to the school, and tending to promote staff who remain with the school. It is the "cosmopolitan" teacher who is most likely to be in conflict with bureaucratic elements within the school setting.

Blau and Scott (1963, p. 63) make clear the two sources of professional control:

> First, as a result of the long period of training undergone by the practitioner, he is expected to have acquired a body of expert knowledge and to have internalized a code of ethics which governs his professional conduct. Second, this self control is supported by the external surveillance of his conduct by peers, who are in a position to see his work, who have the skills to judge his performance, and who, since they have a personal stake in the reputation of their profession, are motivated to exercise the necessary sanctions. Professionals in a given field constitute a colleague group of equals. Every member of the group, but nobody else, is assumed to be qualified to make professional judgements.

This situation implies an essentially flat control system. The problems that arise when professionals and those professionally oriented (the "cosmopolitans") work within organizations which are to some extent bureaucratically controlled, have been studied in a number of contexts.[2] Concerning the problem of supervision of "experts" within organizations, Gouldner (1959, p. 415) writes:

> Often, not only is the expert's immediate superior unqualified to judge him, but there are only one or a few qualified judges in the entire organization. Even if there are a few, they may be close friends or fierce competitors, whose judgement about one another will, in either event, be unreliable. This means that administrative superiors must depend upon persons outside the organization to select experts or to judge the performance of those already employed. This in turn means that the technical expert himself is often dependent on persons outside his organization to validate his position within it. Consequently his work must manifest a high degree of concern for the maintenance of technical standards. This not only disposes the expert to resist imperative pressures for "results" coming from his superiors, but it also makes him less vulnerable to control from those within and in command of his organization.

Gouldner implies that the highly-qualified expert is potentially mobile and therefore independent of a particular organization. The situation in schools is less extreme, but the teacher who is well qualified in his subject often demands that his subject-knowledge competence be judged by his equals—a typically "professional" approach. Similarly, when matters of teaching method are discussed, these cannot validly be divorced from a knowledge of the subject-matter to be taught. If the headmaster is not qualified in the same field, or if the "cosmopolitan" thinks his head of department is incompetent, he is unlikely to accept their judgement. In such cases, however much he may conform for the sake of expediency, he is unlikely to be committed to the course of action he feels forced to take. He tends either to become apathetic—showing conformity without commitment—to subvert the policies of his superiors, to come into open revolt, or to leave. Occasionally he might change to a less "cosmopolitan" orientation.

What, then, are the situations most likely to irk the "academic" teacher? He tends to be resistant to rules. In a bureaucratic organization, the individual worker has no basis for making rational judgements on the choice of objectives or methods. They are selected and assigned to him. He is expected to follow rules and procedures. The tendency to follow this *rationale* of action is even present in schools. Decisions which will influence the work of the individual teacher are frequently made by a small group of senior teachers, or the headmaster himself. There are teachers, therefore, who must live with the occupational hazard of believing that they, by virtue of office, know what is best for the school and are

thereby entitled to make decisions for their subordinates. Such an attitude is not always appreciated by the "unco-operative" teachers who may
be "academics". Such teachers tend to be intolerant of rules or conventions which interfere with their freedom of action.

Conflict can arise over the criteria used in evaluating the teacher's
performance. In schools the problems can be acute because objectives are
so hard to measure and the relationship between ends and means is so
indeterminate. The young teacher, when criticized for teaching in some
particular way or using some particular method, can deny that the
method has the undesirable consequences attributed to it. This situation
can easily give rise to a clash which raises the question of the legitimacy
of the superordinate's authority.

These tensions are especially likely to occur when non-teaching staff
make demands of the teacher which he thinks interfere with his "proper"
work. In most such cases the authority of the non-teacher is that of his
office, delegated by the headmaster. If such a dispute comes to the attention of the headmaster, it can pose a difficult situation: as, for instance,
when a cleaner (who might be difficult to replace) is in conflict with one
of the teaching staff.

Heads of department, who usually encourage and supervise classroom
teachers, are among the better qualified of teachers in the school and
continue their roles as classroom teachers. But once recruited, they tend
to become more concerned with organizational and administrative matters.
Many duties bring them into conflict with teachers: not only supervisory
functions, but those concerned with co-ordinating syllabuses and allocating
resources within the department. Assistants are less likely than the department head to have an overall view of the needs of the department and of
its place within the total school programme. Thus he tends to become
more concerned with organizational values which emphasize order, coordination and other aspects of the needs of the organization. He becomes
more bureaucratic, while many of his teachers remain academically and
professionally oriented. A common consequence is the development of
considerable role strain (Goode, 1960). On the one hand, the departmental
head probably understands and sympathizes with the orientation of his
subordinates, from whose ranks he was himself recruited. On the other
hand, he is faced with organizational demands which press him towards
bureaucratic procedures, especially in the larger department. Although
responsible to the headmaster for the conduct of his department, he cannot
accomplish his work without the co-operation of his subordinates—he is
the "man in the middle" (Whyte and Gardner, 1945). Consequently,
with the conflicts and tensions characteristic of the classroom teacher (Kob,
1961; Wilson, 1962) the head of department combines those of the middle-
level administrator.

THE AUTHORITY AND ROLE OF THE HEADMASTER
In many ways these problems are complicated for the non-teaching head-

master and in some ways they are simplified. Generally the head of the larger secondary school does little if any teaching. Certainly he finds an increasing amount of his time taken up with administrative matters, as well as working with parents, teachers and difficult children. His definition of the significance of his office tends to be a hierarchical one—this is "his" school; he is its "head"; and even when these attitudes are accompanied by reference to the attitudes of teachers and the importance of delegation, there is rarely any doubt in his mind but that his is the final responsibility. As headmasters are fully aware, they are held accountable for the school to its governors.

Something is known of the dynamics of organizational tension-reduction in some settings (Orzack, 1961; Blau and Scott, 1963), but we have very little knowledge of how schools adapt to the conflicts inherent in their structure. There is a need for well-conducted case studies of educational organizations, focussing upon this question. We may, however, suggest how tensions are sometimes reduced. In highly rational and technically specialized organizations, authority tends to be legitimated on strictly legal grounds, and this is certainly so for the headship of the school. The head usually feels entitled to command. Even if his staff feel that he ought not to occupy his position he has strong controls over them through his central position in the promotion system and through his ability to make life difficult for the deviant (Becker, 1953). Thus, along with an appeal to the authority of office, there may well be an appeal to the expedience of compliance, although few headmasters would carry these requirements to dangerous lengths. It is a characteristic of the school, along with other organizations, that it cannot be maintained for long with any real effectiveness without the co-operation and involvement of those who participate in its operation.

Headmasters faced with the problem of exercising authority over specialists may give adequately qualified subordinates control of the procedures (especially the content and method of teaching) adopted in the classroom. This is part of the significance of the role and position of the department head, and increasingly of other specialists carrying special responsibility for the work of teachers. However, while this removes strain from the headmaster, it can create a new organizational tension. Now, the relationship which the headmaster establishes with his deputy, heads of department and other officials becomes crucial. Unless he can carry them with him on matters of policy, it is unlikely that he will be very effective. By creating these offices, he insulates the ordinary classroom teacher from direct communication and pressure from himself. If he wishes to influence a teacher directly he has to work through delegated authority, or risk the departmental head's resentment at being by-passed.

Heads may emphasize the extent to which they share the teacher's attitudes and orientations, their ideologies and values. They may point to years spent in the classroom and to active participation in professional bodies. While this strategy can be effective where the head and staff *do* have these elements in common, it tends to break down when the positions taken by the head and staff are fundamentally incompatible.

A further strategy often centres upon the role of the deputy head-master, who is increasingly being seen as central to the communication and authority structure of the school, and who may play a vital supplementary role (Burnham, 1965). Especially in sensitive areas where the autonomy of the teacher is concerned, many headteachers are likely to suggest or advise rather than make rules. A "collegial" relationship makes it much easier for teachers to accept innovations or guidance when they are resistant to what they define as "interference". This pattern is often found where a significant number of professionally-oriented personnel work, as in hospitals. Even where there is a formally defined medical hierarchy, "orders" are often given in the form of "consultative advice" (Goss, 1963).

Increasingly, headmasters think, like management in business, that their occupation needs experience and training, specialized skills and a systematic body of principles. This belief has been strong for some decades now in the USA where many universities confer advanced degrees in educational administration. The English headmaster is increasingly professional, seeing himself as an "expert", not in a particular subject area nor even in subject teaching, but in school management and administration. Alongside his traditional role of leader, then, we are seeing a simultaneous tendency towards both the bureaucratization of the professional, and the professionalization of the bureaucrat.

Headmasters also attempt to strengthen their authority by increasing the professional stature and competence of their staff. The school is a powerful socializing agency for teachers as well as pupils (Brim and Wheeler, 1966). Informal pressures for conformity upon the newer staff; appeals to professional values and behaviour; the use of myths, symbols and rituals; all may work towards increased commitment of the teacher, and all are used by headmasters. In so far as appropriate values are internalized and appropriate skills developed, teachers become less and less in need of close supervision and the efforts of senior teachers can be concentrated upon the more acceptable aspects of leadership. However, many factors—the lack of consistency and clarity in the normative structure of the teaching profession, the large percentage of those with a low professional commitment (Colombotos, 1963; Mason, Dressel and Bain, 1959), the high turnover of staff, and the brevity and nature of much professional training—tend to reduce the effectiveness of the college and school as a learning environment for teachers. Simultaneously, many aspects of school life lead to the reinforcement of retrogressive attitudes and practices.

CONCLUSION

Although the study of industrial and other organizations has been proceeding for many decades, and despite the early outstanding work of Waller (1932), the study of the school as a complex organization has been relatively neglected both by educationists and by theorists of organizations. This neglect has operated to the disadvantage of both those who are interested in the nature and dynamics of complex organizations, and those whose concern is for the understanding of educational processes. Nevertheless, in the last few years more research and writing has focused on the characteristics of the school as an organization. I have suggested that the tensions shown to exist in other organizations between hierarchical structure and professional teacher attitude should also be studied in the secondary school.

I make no claims that my statements are anything more than informed guesses, based upon reasoning by anaology from research conducted in organizations other than schools. As such they emphasize the need for carefully conducted studies into the structure and functioning of schools as organizations. Some questions for investigation are:

To what extent can one usefully interpret specific schools in terms of the suggestions made above?

Do the majority of teachers tend to fall into one of the categories suggested? If so, do they behave in the ways predicted?

What factors are associated with the strategies adopted by headmasters and heads of departments in the face of challenges to their authority, and with what functional consequences for the school?

Are there consistent patterns in the reference-group characteristics of those promoted to senior positions within schools?

What behavioural differences occur as a result of the promotion of people with differing orientations?

How do the careers of cosmopolitans and locals within teaching vary and with what consequences for the schools?

These questions, along with many others, would appear to bear promise of a fruitful yield.

NOTES

1 The author wishes to acknowledge with thanks the assistance of Dr. D. F. Swift, who read an earlier draft of this paper.
2 See, for example, for trade unions, Wilensky (1956, 1961); hospitals, Corwin (1961), Goss (1961, 1963), Hughes, Hughes and Deutscher (1958), Perrow (1965), Smith (1958), Stanton and Schwartz (1954); universities, Clark (1963), Davis (1961), Gross (1965); military units, Bidwell (1961), Janowitz (1961); and social welfare agencies, Blau and Scott (1963), Peabody (1964).

REFERENCES

ABRAHAMSON, M. (1967) *The Professional in the Organization,* Rand McNally.

ANDERSON, J. G. (1967) "The Teacher: Bureaucrat or Professional?", *Educational Administration Quarterly, iii,* **3**, pp. 291–300.

BARKER, R. C. and GUMP, P. V. (1964) *Big School, Small School: High School Size and Student Behavior,* Stanford University Press.

BECKER, H. S. (1953) "The Teacher in the Authority System of the Public School", *Journal of Educational Sociology,* **27**, pp. 128–44. Reprinted in ETZIONI, A. (ed.) (1965) *Complex Organizations: A Sociological Reader,* Holt.

BIDWELL, C. E. (1955) "The Administrative Role and Satisfaction in Teaching", *Journal of Educational Sociology,* **29**, pp. 41–7.

BIDWELL, C. E. (1956) "Administrative and Teacher Satisfaction", *Phi Delta Kappan,* **37**, pp. 285–8.

BIDWELL, C. E. (1961) "The Young Professional in the Army: a Study of Occupational Identity", *American Sociological Review,* **26**, 3, pp. 360–72.

BIDWELL, C. E. (1965) "The School as a Formal Organization" in March, J. G. (ed.) *Handbook of Organizations,* Rand McNally, pp. 972–1022.

BLAU, P. M. and SCOTT, W. R. (1963) *Formal Organizations,* Routledge and Kegan Paul.

BRIM, O. G. and WHEELER, S. (1966) *Socialization after Childhood: Two Essays,* Wiley.

BURNHAM, P. S. (1965) "The Role of the Deputy Head in Secondary Schools", M.Ed. thesis, Leicester University.

CLARK, B. R. (1963) "Faculty Organization and Authority", in Lunsford, T. F. (ed.) *The Study of Academic Administration,* Western Interstate Commission for Higher Education, pp. 37–51. Reprinted in Vollmer, H. M. and Mills, D. L. (eds.) *Professionalization,* Prentice-Hall, pp. 283–91.

COLOMBOTOS, J. (1963) "Sex Role and Professionalism: A Study of High School Teachers (1)", *School Review,* LXXI, 1, pp. 27–40.

CORWIN, R. G. (1961) "The Professional Employee: A Study of Conflict in the Nursing Roles", *American Journal of Sociology,* LXVI, pp. 604–15.

DALTON, M. (1961) "Conflict between Staff and Line Managerial Officers", in Etzioni, A. (ed.) *Complex Organizations: A Sociological Reader,* Holt, pp. 212–21.

DAVIS, J. A. (1961) "Locals and Cosmopolitans in American Graduate Schools", *International Journal of Comparative Sociology,* 2, **2**, pp. 212–23.

GOODE, W. J. (1960) "A Theory of Role Strain", *American Sociological Review,* **25**, pp. 483–96.

Goss, M. E. W. (1961) "Influence and Authority among Physicians in an Outpatient Clinic", *American Sociological Review*, **26**, 1, pp. 39–50.

Goss, M. E. W. (1963). "Patterns of Bureaucracy among Hospital Staff Physicians", in Freidson, E. (ed.) *The Hospital in Modern Society*, Free Press, pp. 170–94.

Gouldner, A. W. (1957) "Cosmopolitans and Locals: Toward an Analysis of Latent Social Roles", *Administrative Science Quarterly*, **2**, pp. 281–306, 444–80.

Gouldner, A. W. (1959) "Organizational Analysis", in Merton, R. K. et al. (eds.) *Sociology Today: Problems and Prospects*, Basic Books pp. 400–28.

Greenwood, E. (1957) "Attributes of a Profession", *Social Work*, **2**, 3, pp. 44–55.

Gross, Ll. (1965) "Hierarchical Authority in Educational Institutions", in Hartley, H. J. and Holloway, G. E. (eds.) *Focus on Change and the School Administrator*, School of Education, Program in Educational Administration, State University of New York at Buffalo, pp. 23–36.

Habenstein, R. W. (1963) "Critique of 'Profession' as a Sociological Category", *Sociological Quarterly*, iv, **4**, pp. 291–300.

Hall, R. H. (1968) "Professionalization and Bureaucratization", *American Sociological Review*, **33**, 1, pp. 92–103.

Hargreaves, D. (1966) *Social Relations in a Secondary School*, Routledge and Kegan Paul.

Hughes, E. C., Hughes, H. McG. and Deutscher, I. (1958) *Twenty Thousand Nurses Tell Their Story*, Lippincott.

Janowitz, M. (1961) "Hierarchy and Authority in the Military Establishment", in Etzioni, A. (ed.) *Complex Organizations: A Sociological Reader*, Holt, pp. 198–212.

Kob, J. (1961) "Definition of the Teacher's Role", in Halsey, A. H., Floud, J. and Anderson, C. A. (eds.) *Education, Economy and Society*, Free Press.

Mannheim, K. (1950) *Man and Society in an Age of Reconstruction*, Harcourt, Brace.

Mason, W., Dressel, R. J. and Bain, R. K. (1959) "Sex Role and the Career Orientations of Beginning Teachers", *Harvard Educational Review*, **29**, pp. 370–83.

Orzack, L. H. (1961) "Issues Underlying Role Dilemmas of Professionals", in Abramavitz, A. B. (ed.) *Emotional Factors in Public Health Nursing: A Casebook*, Wisconsin University Press, pp. 140–59.

Peabody, R. L. (1964) *Organizational Authority*, Atherton Press.

Perrow, C. (1965) "Hospitals: Technology, Structure and Goals", in March, J. G. (ed.) *Handbook of Organizations*, Rand McNally, pp. 910–71.

Scott, W. R. (1964) "Theory of Organizations", in Faris, R. E. L. (ed.) *Handbook of Modern Sociology*, Rand McNally, pp. 485–529.

SMITH, H. L. (1958) "Two lines of Authority: the Hospital's Dilemma", in Jaco, E. G. (ed.) *Patients, Physicians and Illness*, Free Press.

SOLOMON, B. (1967) "A Comment on 'The Authority Structure of the School' ", *Educational Administration Quarterly*, **3**, 3, pp. 281–90.

STANTON, A. H. and SCHWARTZ, M. S. (1954) *The Mental Hospital*, Basic Books.

VOLLMER, H. M. (1966) "Entrepreneurship and Professional Productivity among Research Scientists", in Vollmer, H. M. and Mills, D. L. (eds.) *Professionalization*, Prentice-Hall, pp. 276–82.

VOLLMER, H. M. and MILLS, D. (1962) "Nuclear Technology and the Professionalization of Labour", *American Journal of Sociology*, LXVII, **6**, pp. 690–6.

VOLLMER, H. M. and MILLS, D. (ed.) (1966), *Professionalization*, Prentice-Hall.

WALLER, W. (1932) *The Sociology of Teaching*, Wiley. Wiley paperbacks, 1965.

WEBER, M. (1946) *From Max Weber: Essays in Sociology*, edited and translated by Gerth, H. H., and Mills, C. W., Oxford University Press.

WEBER, M. (1947) *The Theory of Social and Economic Organization*, translated by Henderson, A. M. and Parsons, T., Free Press.

WEBER, M. (1961) "The Three Types of Legitimate Rule", in Etzioni, A. (ed.) *Complex Organizations: A Sociological Reader*, Holt, pp. 4–14.

WHYTE, W. F. and GARDNER, B. B. (1945) "Facing the Foreman's Problems", *Applied Anthropology*, **4**, pp. 1–28.

WILENSKY, H. L. (1956) *Intellectuals in the Labour Unions*, Free Press.

WILENSKY, H. L. (1961) "The Trade Union as a Bureaucracy", in Etzioni, A. (ed.) *Complex Organizations: A Sociological Reader*, Holt, pp. 221–34.

WILSON, B. R. (1962) "The Teacher's Role—a Sociological Analysis", *British Journal of Sociology*, **13**, pp. 15–32.

2.5 Administrative Theory and Change in Organizations

Daniel E. Griffiths

The observer of social organizations is forced to the conclusion that organizations are not characterized by change. Indeed, when organizations are viewed over a long period of time, their outstanding characteristic appears to be stability, rather than change. A social organization is the structural mechanism employed by a society to achieve one or more of its commonly accepted goals. Since the goals do not change noticeably and each organization's activities are rather clearly demarcated, any particular organization comes into existence with a great deal of built-in stability. The stability is so great as to constitute a powerful resistance to change.[1] On the other hand, it is clear that organizations *do* change. In many the increments of change are small, but in others change is so radical as to cause the disappearance of the original organization and the appearance of a new one.

The Roman Catholic Church is an example of a highly stable organization, existing in the same form over a long period of time. Its organizational goals have varied but little since its inception, yet it has changed. The changes have generally been small and well spaced and have tended to vary internal procedures or policies necessary to defend the Church against an unfriendly environment. Radical changes, on the other hand, are illustrated by governmental revolutions. The overthrow of the Tsarist regime in Russia and the eventual rule of the Bolshevists point up the fact that an organization (the governing body) can change to such a degree that it is completely replaced.

It should be noted in both these cases that the stimulus for change came from *outside* the organization. It would not be a far-fetched presumption to state that the hierarchies of the Catholic Church and of the Tsarist government alike would have much preferred to go on as they had been going.

There are few empirical measures of the initiation of change in organ-

Source: Miles, M. B. (ed.) (1964) *Innovation in Education*, Teachers College Press, Chapter 18, pp. 425–36; reprinted in Milstein, M. M. and Belasco, J. A. (eds.) (1973) *Educational Administration and the Behavioral Sciences: A Systems Perspective*, Allyn and Bacon.

izations. However, the one most familiar to the writer substantiates the basic assumption of this paper. A measure called Organizational Change was developed as part of the scoring procedure in a study of the administrative performance of elementary school principals in a simulated school.[2] The average score (highest possible, 70) was 5.88; standard deviation, 2.92; and odd-even reliability, .61. The observer of change must reconcile himself to study of the infrequent, not the frequent, in organizational life.

This paper attempts to state a theory of administrative change which will, at least in part, account for some of the commonly made observations concerning change in organizations. Space limitations prevent a full description of detailed observations of change in organizations. The questions to which the theory is addressed are: (1) Under what conditions does change occur? (2) Under what conditions is change least apt to occur?

DEFINITIONS: ORGANIZATION, ADMINISTRATION, CHANGE

It is necessary to say what is meant by the terms *organization, administration,* and *change.*

First of all, only *formal* organization is being considered; this term is construed to mean an ensemble of individuals who perform distinct but interrelated and coordinated functions, in order that one or more tasks may be completed. Thus we have the public school, the army, the governmental bureau, the business company. In each type of organization, the task is more or less clearly understood and approved by the public. It is obvious that organizations are, at least to some extent, a consequence of division of labor in society. It follows that any one organization functions as part of a larger social system (Griffiths, 1959).

What Kaufman (1961) has to say about organizations is also acceptable as contributing to a definition of the concept:

> The term *organization* will refer to all sets of human beings who exhibit the following five properties:
> 1. Some criterion or set of criteria by which *members* may be distinguished from non-members (i.e. demarcation of boundaries, though not necessarily territorial boundaries);
> 2. Some method of *replenishment* of materials used up by the members (also, for long-lived organizations, some method of *replacing personnel* lost by the organization through death, departure, disablement or other factors);
> 3. *Elicitation of effort* of some kind by individual members of the organization;
> 4. *Coordination* of individual activities—that is to say, some blending of the methods of eliciting effort and the methods of inhibiting activity such that the timing and character of each

member's activities facilitate, or at least do not impede, the activities of other members.

5. Some pattern of *distribution* of materials and messages among the members, and perhaps of movement of people as well.

In summary, a formal *organization* comprises a number of people who perform a task sanctioned by the society in which it functions. The members of the organization are visible as such to the public, work together, and have methods of replenishing the organization with both materials and members.

The term *administration* is used to designate the process (cycle of events) engaged in by all the members of the formal organization to direct and control the activities of the members of the organization. Though all members participate in "administration", there is of course differential distribution of influence within the organization. Those members who are officially charged with the functions of administration are called *administrators* (Griffiths, 1959).

It is assumed that educational organizations do not differ in essential characteristics from any other type of formal organization. When one uses definitions such as those employed above, it is difficult to imagine what the differences could be.

The word *change* is used to mean an alteration in the structure of the organization, in any of its processes, or in its goals or purposes. The revision of a rule, the introduction of a new procedure, or the revision of the purposes or direction of the organization are all subsumed under the concept of change. There are different degrees of change; a variation in a teacher's lunchroom assignment might be considered a minor change, and the reconstituting of a public school system to include a junior college might be considered a major change.

THE MODEL: SYSTEM THEORY

The model employed in building this theory of administrative change is system theory as discussed by Hearn (1958). Although Hearn's ideas are based upon those of Miller (1955) and other system theorists, his careful work is a definite improvement over that of his predecessors.

Systems

A system may be simply defined as a complex of elements in mutual interaction. This construct has been used in almost every area of science for a long period of time. Allport (1955) offered a more comprehensive definition:

... any recognizably delimited aggregate of dynamic elements that are in some way interconnected and interdependent and that continue to operate together according to certain laws and in such a way as to produce some characteristic total effect. A system, in other words, is something that is concerned with some kind of activity and preserves a kind of integration and unity; and a particular system can be recognized as distinct from other systems to which, however, it may be dynamically related. Systems may be complex, they may be made up of interdependent sub-systems, each of which, though less autonomous than the entire aggregate, is nevertheless fairly distinguishable in operation.

A more succinct definition is that of Hall and Fagen (1956): "A system is a set of objects together with relationships between the objects and between their attributes."

All systems except the smallest have *sub-systems,* and all but the largest have *supra-systems* which are their environments.

Systems may be *open* or *closed.* An open system is related to and makes exchanges with its environment, while a closed system is not related to and does not make exchanges with its environment. Further, a closed system is characterized by an increase in entropy, while open systems tend toward a steady state.

Open systems

Open systems, of course, have the properties of systems in general, but also have certain characteristics which distinguish them from closed systems (Hearn, 1958).

1. Open systems exchange matter, energy, and information with their environment; that is, they have *inputs* and *outputs.*

2. Open systems tend to maintain themselves in *steady states.* A steady state occurs when a constant ratio is maintained among the components of the system, given a continuous input to the system. A burning candle is often used as an example of a steady state. Upon being lighted the flame is small, but it rapidly grows to its normal size and maintains the size as long as the candle and its environment exist.

3. Open systems are *self-regulating.* In the illustration above, a sudden draft will cause the flame to flicker, but with the cessation of the draft the flame regains its normal characteristics.

4. Open systems display *equifinality;* that is, identical results can be obtained from different initial conditions. Hearn points out that equifinality in the human being (an open system) is illustrated by the case of two babies, one born prematurely, the other at full term. The babies may look very different at birth, and may be in different stages of development, but within a few months the differences will have disappeared. Even though the initial states may differ, human beings generally achieve the same stages of development.

5. Open systems maintain their steady states, in part, through the *dynamic interplay of sub-systems operating as functional processes.* This

means that the various parts of the system function without persistent conflicts that can be neither resolved nor regulated.

6. Open systems maintain their steady states through *feedback* processes. The concept of feedback as used in system theory is more elaborate than its normal usage implies. The reader is referred to Hearn (1958) for a full discussion. In general, feedback refers to that portion of the output of a system which is fed back to the input and affects succeeding outputs, and to the property of being able to adjust future conduct by reference to past performance.

7. Open systems display *progressive segregation* (von Bertalanffy, 1950). This process occurs when the system divides into a hierarchical order of subordinate systems, which gain a certain independence of each other.

Hearn (1958) summarizes the properties of *open* or *organismic systems* in this manner:

> There is a dynamic interplay among the essential functional sub-processes or sub-systems in the organismic system which enables it to maintain itself in a homeostatic steady state. Assuming a sufficient input of material from its environment, the organism develops toward a characteristic state despite initial conditions (equifinality). All of this is accomplished through an automatic self-regulatory process.

A THEORY OF ADMINISTRATIVE CHANGE

It is proposed that system theory serve as a model for a theory of administrative change. As indicated above, any open system has supra-systems and sub-systems. Let an organization be considered as an open system, comprised of human interactions, that maintains a definite boundary. Further, consider administration as an open sub-system, and the environment as a supra-system. The administration sub-system is located at the point of tangency of the three systems, as in Figure 1 opposite.

Infrequency of change

The above model for a theory of administrative change would lead one to hypothesize that change would be relatively infrequent. Open systems maintain themselves in steady states (a constant ratio is maintained among the components of the system), whereas change calls for the establishment of new ratios among the components of the system. One could also argue on purely logical grounds that society establishes organizations, or sanctions their establishment, to accomplish rather specific purposes. It is, in part, this original sanction that gives organizations their characteristic steady state.

Conditions aiding change

Although it is infrequent, change does occur in organizations; at times

Figure 1

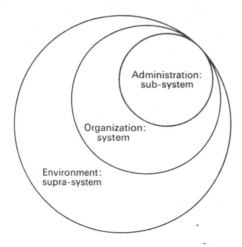

the change is radical. Under what conditions might change be expected to occur?

Several characteristics of open systems were discussed in the presentation of the model. Some of these have relevance here: input–output, steady state, self-regulation, interplay of sub-systems, feedback, and progressive segregation. An examination of these characteristics leads to several ideas about organizational change.

Since the tendency of organizations is to maintain a steady state, the major impetus for change comes from outside rather than inside an organization. Since organizations are open systems, they have a self-regulating characteristic which causes them to revert to the original state following a minor change made to meet demands of the supra-system.

Many organizations bring in outsiders as administrators, believing that change for the better will result. This apparently works in many cases, and the proposed theory can accommodate this observation. All organizations exhibit some form of progressive segregation or hierarchical order. The order makes it possible for change to occur from the top down but practically impossible for it to occur from the bottom up.

These ideas and others are now formulated as a series of propositions.

PROPOSITION 1 The major impetus for change in organizations is from the outside.
Discussion It is speculated that when change in an organization does occur, the initiative for the change is from outside the system—that is, from the supra-system. In the study of elementary school principals mentioned above, it was found that those who scored relatively higher on

Organizational Change were not aggressive leaders as such, but administrators with a tendency to make changes in the organization to please outsiders and superiors, or to comply with suggestions of subordinates (Hemphill, Griffiths and Frederiksen, 1962). The correlation between the Organizational Change score and response to outsiders was somewhat higher than the correlation between the Organizational Change score and response to subordinates. The nature of changes made in response to outsiders and insiders was not determined in this study, but it could be hypothesized that changes made in response to insiders will be concerned with clarification of rules and internal procedures, while those made in response to outsiders will be concerned with *new* rules and procedures, and possibly with changes in purpose and direction of the organization. It appears that administrators who initiate change are influenced more by those outside the system than by those inside.

Practical administrators are well aware of this proposition. The use of consultants, evaluation teams, citizens' committees and professional organizations to bring change to an organization suggests a clear recognition on the part of administrators that an organization is more apt to change in response to an external force than to an internal force.

PROPOSITION 2   The degree and duration of change is directly proportional to the intensity of the stimulus from the supra-system.
Discussion   As an illustration of the proposition (but not, of course, as proof of it), it has been noted that the rate of instructional innovation in New York State public schools more than doubled within fifteen months of the launching of the Soviet Sputnik I; this increase was maintained through 1961 (Brickell, 1961).

In order that this proposition be tested, it will be necessary to establish ways of measuring degree of change and intensity of stimulus. Duration is simply a matter of time. If the suggested measurements could be made, the proposition could be tested in all of its ramifications.

PROPOSITION 3   Change in an organization is more probable if the successor to the chief administrator is from outside the organization, than if he is from inside the organization.
Discussion   The model specifies feedback as a characteristic of open systems. Feedback tends to maintain the system in a steady state. The administrator who comes from outside does not receive feedback from his actions, since well-established channels for feedback to him do not exist. When an insider is appointed to the top post in an organization, the feedback channels which have been established over the years function to keep him operating in the steady state.

An outsider may bring change into an organization out of sheer ignorance. Not knowing the system, he will function in terms of a system which he *does* know. Being without ties in the system, he will not receive the feedback that would keep an insider from initiating procedures and policies differing from those in use.

The insider will also keep the sub-systems functioning without conflicts, since he knows how these sub-systems function to maintain the steady state. The outsider may upset the functioning of the sub-systems, through either ignorance or design. Not knowing how sub-systems function, he can inadvertently throw them into conflict through orders or expectations not customarily held for these systems. On the other hand, he may introduce conflict among the sub-systems, by purposefully changing their functions. This will, of course, upset the steady state and may in time create a state more to the liking of the chief administrator. The notion of controlled conflict as a method of change in an organization may have a sound theoretical base.

In a study of school superintendents, Carlson (1961) found that those appointed from inside the system tend to act in such a way as to maintain the system, while those appointed from outside tend to be innovators.

PROPOSITION 4 "Living systems respond to continuously increasing stress first by a lag in response, then by an over-compensatory response, and finally by catastrophic collapse of the system."

Discussion What happens to a system subjected to constantly increasing stress? Miller (1955), p. 525, has formulated the above proposition, which appears to have much relevance to education. As public education is attacked (for example, on the teaching of reading), it responds by proclaiming a strong defense. The schools claim that they have been teaching reading well. In those districts where the defense was not strong enough and the attack grew even stronger, the schools responded by changing their methods of teaching reading. The proposition has not been tested fully, because at this point the stress has always been lifted.

Revolutionary changes occur when the prediction of this proposition is carried through to completion. The collapse of the old system is followed by the establishment of a new system.

Conditions inhibiting change

Many of the characteristics of organizations are such that they make the initiation of change difficult. When organizations are viewed in terms of the system-theory model these characteristics appear very clearly.

PROPOSITION 5 The number of innovations is inversely proportional to the tenure of the chief administrator.

Discussion The longer an administrator stays in a position, the less likely he is to introduce change. The model indicates some reasons for this. All of the processes which bring about the steady state have been given time to operate. Feedback channels have become fully established. Progressive segregation has set in; the sub-systems have become structured and have gained relative independence. Change is thus more difficult, because the frequency of interaction between sub-systems is decreased, and the chances for effective communication are diminished.

PROPOSITION 6   The more hierarchical the structure of an organization, the less the possibility of change.
Discussion   The system-theory model points out that a characteristic of open systems is progressive segregation, and this occurs as the system divides into a hierarchical order of subordinate systems which gain a degree of independence of each other. The more hierarchical the sub-systems become, the more independent the sub-systems and the more difficult it is to introduce change.

PROPOSITION 7   When change in an organization does occur, it will tend to occur from the top down, not from the bottom up.
Discussion   Using the same reasoning as in Proposition 6, a hierarchical order would enable change to occur from the top down, but the relative independence of the sub-systems would tend to slow down the rate of change. The structure makes change from the bottom up very difficult; one would expect little if any change to be introduced in this way.

PROPOSITION 8   The more functional the dynamic interplay of sub-systems, the less the change in an organization.
Discussion   As a system operates, the sub-systems develop methods of interacting in which conflict is at a minimum. Each of the sub-systems has a function to perform, and each does so in such a manner as to allow it to maintain a high degree of harmony with the others. Each says to the others, in effect, "If you don't rock the boat, I won't." Change is practically synonymous with conflict, since it means that the arrangements the sub-systems have worked out no longer hold. Sub-systems resist conflict, and in the same manner resist change.

SUMMARY
Using system theory as a model, this paper develops a set of propositions concerning change in organizations. The propositions are restated briefly in the following paragraphs.

Change in organizations will be expedited by the appointment of outsiders rather than insiders as chief administrators. Such administrators will introduce change either because they do not know the system, or because they have a different concept of how the system should function. Most changes result as responses to the demands of the supra-system. The magnitude and duration of change is directly proportional to the intensity of the stimulus from outside. Revolutionary change occurs when a system is placed under continuous, unrelenting stress which is maintained in spite of over-compensating responses, and which results in the collapse of the system and its replacement by a new system.

Change is impeded by the hierarchical nature of organizations. The

Daniel E. Griffiths

hierarchical structure makes innovation from the bottom virtually impossible, and the independence of the sub-systems isolates them from innovative activity. The functional nature of the activities of each sub-system generates conflict-reducing behavior which, again, is counter to change-inducing behavior. Further, the longer the tenure of the chief administrator, the fewer the changes.

NOTES

1 See Presthus (1962), especially Chapters 1 and 2, for an analysis of the way in which system forces prevent change in organizations.
2 Hemphill, Griffiths, and Frederiksen (1962), especially Chapter 8.

REFERENCES

ALLPORT, F. H. (1955) *Theories of Perception and the Concept of Structure*, Wiley, p. 469.
BRICKELL, H. M. (1961) *Commissioner's 1961 Catalog of Educational Change*, New York State Education Department, p. 27.
CARLSON, R. O. (1961) "Succession and Performance among School Superintendents", *Administrative Science Quarterly*, June 1961, pp. 210–27.
GRIFFITHS, D. E. (1959) *Administrative Theory*, Appleton-Century-Crofts, p. 77.
HALL, A. D. and FAGEN, R. E. (1956) "General Systems", in VON BERTALANFFY, L. and RAPOPORT, A. (eds.)*Yearbook of the Society for the Advancement of General Systems Theory*, Braun-Brumfield, p. 18.
HEARN, G. (1958) *Theory Building in Social Work*, University of Toronto Press.
HEMPHILL, J., GRIFFITHS, D. E. and FREDERIKSEN, N. (1962) *Administrative Performance and Personality*, Bureau of Publications, Teachers College, Columbia University.
KAUFMAN, H. (1961) "Why Organizations Behave as They Do: An Outline of a Theory", in *Papers Presented at an Interdisciplinary Seminar on Administrative Theory*, University of Texas, p. 39.
MILLER, J. F. (1955) "Toward a General Theory for the Behavioral Sciences", *American Psychologist*, Oct. 1955, pp. 513–31.
PRESTHUS, R. (1962) *The Organizational Society*, Knopf.
VON BERTALANFFY, L. (1950) "An Outline of General Systems Theory", *British Journal of Philosophical Science*, Jan. 1950, p. 148.

2.6 Managing Organisational Change

W. J. Reddin

ABSTRACT

In this article Professor Reddin summarises the reasons why organisations start a change programme and the major strategies used to introduce change. He is an organisational change agent and the originator of the 3-D Theory of Effective Management which is used by many companies to implement major organisational change. It is now realised that to gain the maximum benefit from an organisation, it is necessary to plan its development and use its human resources to best advantage.

WHAT IS ORGANISATIONAL CHANGE?

The exciting new management function of managing planned change is beginning to emerge. Organisational Change is now attracting widespread interest and such terms as change programme and even change agent are becoming commonplace. The position of manager of organisational development is now appearing on more and more organisation charts as management recognises that the successful introduction of planned change is a key managerial function.

It is increasingly apparent to all that organisational change is a requisite for organisational improvement and that managed change is likely to be more effective than unmanaged change.

Planned organisation change started to appear in the late forties in Britain and the USA. The main forces were management's interest in the advances of the social sciences, the exciting and productive results of the work of the Tavistock Institute of Britain, the impact of the National Training Laboratories and the T-Group, and the acceptance of such style models as McGregor's Theory X and Y. It seems likely that the current interest will grow, particularly as more senior managers become better acquainted with the variety of organisational change methods available.

WHY START A CHANGE PROGRAMME?

The reasons that organisations get involved in change programmes are a

---

Source: *Industrial Training International* (March, 1970), Vol. 5, No. 3, pp. 132–4.

major force in shaping the objectives and methods of the programme. The most common reasons for senior executives to start a change programme are:

Pain. The organisation is finding its existing state painful. It may be because of a falling market share, executive turnover, decreasing profits, or too much conflict.

Image of Potential. Top management has a clear idea of what the organisation might become. This might be expressed in terms of profits, industry position, diversity, size, national role, or in other ways.

Outside Influence. Some external force, such as a government, has legislated a new function or method of operation. Technological advances often have the same effect.

Achievement Desire. Top management wants the organisation to become better. The attitude is, "if this can do us good we must use it if we want to maximise our opportunities".

Let's do Something. Line or staff want to appear to be doing something constructive. This reason is likely to lead, in the long run, to more, rather than less pain.

TWO TRADITIONAL METHODS

Two widely used traditional methods of changing an organisation might be called:

Management turnover.

Legislated change.

The method of management turnover is simply to change key people in top management. This method is more likely to be effective if the new top management has a great deal of power, some measure of human relationships skills, and sufficient resources, particularly money, for expansion. It helps still more if the new top management has a clear idea of where it wants the organisation to go, an *image of potential* and if this image is easily transmitted to the managerial force. It is not hard to understand that if all these conditions are present, a significant organisational change could be introduced with a high probability of success.

A less effective method of changing an organisation is by what might be called legislated change. This is usually in the form of an unpopular edict from the top or from outside the organisation. Such change is made more difficult if the organisation is currently operating in a reasonably efficient manner; if there were few changes in the past; if the reason for the change is difficult to explain; if the change threatens to seriously disrupt existing social relationships; or if the work force see themselves as semi-professional or professional.

PLANNED CHANGE

While both of these methods will, no doubt, continue to be used, a third method, which might be called planned change, is beginning to appear.

This planned approach goes under many names which can be used inter-
changeably:
Planned change.
Change programme.
Organisational development.
Organisational effectiveness programme.

These terms generally indicate a long-range programme of change
designed to move an organisation from one level of effectiveness to a
higher level of effectiveness and then to stabilise it at the new level. The
programme may or may not utilise an external consultant called a change
agent, and may or may not use a management style model such as those
developed by Jennings, McGregor, Blake, or Reddin. The usual function
of the style model is to make it easier to talk and think about managerial,
team, and corporate problems which retard effectiveness. It is sometimes
used to provide a utopian model. The programme often starts with some
form of management development, then to team development, inter-
team development and then to strengthening the boss-subordinate
relationship, often through management-by-objectives. The key idea is to
get managers in the organisation to take a look at themselves, their team,
their division and the organisation itself, and to make changes in a
planned direction.

TWO SCHOOLS
The two world centres for organisational change are the National Training Laboratories in the USA and the Tavistock Institute in Britain.
Virtually all change programmes and change agents are associated in
some way with one or other of these two schools.

The National Training Laboratories use what is essentially a psychological approach with the T-Group or its derivatives as the main technique. The T-Group goes under many names, including training group,
sensitivity training, development group, group dynamics, instrumented
laboratory. This approach, while concerned with organisational development, in fact appears to concentrate primarily on individual development. The basic assumption is if managers as individuals can be made to
change, then the organisation will change also. Teams are sometimes
trained using this individual approach. The team sessions then focus
more on interpersonal and emotional problems in the team rather than
job structure, responsibility, and the organisation of the team. With this
psychological approach there is more emphasis on relationships and less
on the job and on effectiveness criteria. Most USA change agents are
psychologists.

The Tavistock Institute on the other hand uses what is essentially a
sociological approach with the *change agent-client* relationship as a main
technique. The change agent is sometimes that rare consultant with training in several behavioural fields including psychology, psychoanalysis,
social psychology and sociology; or a sociologist with an interest in appli-

cation, or even a psychiatrist or psychoanalyst. The change agent usually works closely with the organisation for a few months and helps it to make the change it wants. The Tavistock School appears to deal directly with key issues and strongest variables in organisational change. Most UK change agents are sociologists.

ORGANISATIONAL EFFECTIVENESS PROGRAMMES

Broadly based programmes of organisational change have many distinct elements. These serve to differentiate them sharply from narrower programmes which are essentially equivalent to management development.

The key elements are:

—All, or practically all, managers become involved in some form of training activity such as the managerial effectiveness seminar which serves to acquaint a manager with his current behaviour and with an ideal pattern of managerial behaviour.

—A management style model, such as the 3–D theory, of effective management is used to provide a useful conceptual framework. The 3–D Model, for instance, uses effectiveness as its third dimension and by having four more-effective styles, suggests that style flexibility is the route to effectiveness.

—One or more, but preferably all, of these guide the programme:
A manager of organisational development.
A senior managerial task force.
An external change agent.

—Management teams of boss and subordinate are trained together as a unit with a view to increasing their effectiveness.

—If not already in operation, management by objectives is introduced.

—The top executive team attend a corporate strategy laboratory at which they give intensive consideration to organisational design, objectives, and philosophy.

—Organisation sub-parts meet to work through their problems: i.e. staff-line, HQ–field, research–production, sales–production.

—Multi-level meetings are held at which several layers of management discuss corporate objectives.

—The working level, unionised or not, is involved in some form of activity. This is done in order to enlist their ideas and their support for the objectives of the change programme.

—While results appear early, the programme usually runs for more than a year before all changes are successfully implemented.

OBJECTIVES

While most programmes have more than one objective, the specific objectives of some recent business and government programmes with which the author has been associated have been:

—To move decision levels downward (and sometimes upward).

—To integrate divisional objectives.

—To remove a layer of management.
—To centralise operational planning.
—To commit the work force to corporate objectives.
—To ensure smooth integration in a merger.
—To introduce management–by–objectives.
—To increase organisation flexibility.
—To make a company marketing oriented.

Some change programmes have sound, but far less precise, behavioural objectives, each open to many interpretations. Typical of these objectives are:
—To introduce participative management.
—To produce a theory–Y organisation.

THE FROZEN ORGANISATION

One of the important uses of a change programme is to change a frozen organisation into a flexible organisation.

Frozen organisations are easy to identify. Change is so difficult to introduce that many managers have stopped trying. Managers tend to stay, and prefer to stay, in one job and one division for years. Promotion is on seniority. The rule book is enormous. Past practice is the safe guideline to follow. Innovation and creativity are regarded as mavericks and are suppressed.

The fully flexible organisation, however, is the one most likely to grow profitable. New brands are introduced as soon as they are needed, the organisation structure is changed as required, resistance to change is limited or only moderate.

Criteria for individual and organisational health are the same; for both, health is a capacity to make effective adjustments to a changing environment and, where possible, to make appropriate changes in the environment.

A PROBLEM

One of the biggest problems in organisation change today is faddishness; the desire to have the latest style. Many managers, to use a management training analogy, have watched North America go through J-courses, case method, incident process, T-groups, role playing, the wheel, and the power spectrum. At any one time, one of these is the rage and the value of others often ignored. This occurs in organisational change as well. The competent manager of organisation development must understand all approaches and recognise that all have value at some time, at some place, for some purpose.

Another problem is that some think that all organisations should be treated the same way so that no diagnosis of either problems or true needs are made. The assumption is that all organisations are at the identical stage of development and all, therefore, need identical treatment. If the treatment is wrong, this can turn out to be little more than exhortation and manipulation.

SELECTING A PROGRAMME

The success of an organisational effectiveness programme depends on the appropriateness of the technique used and the commitment of senior organisational members to it. An organisation is wise to investigate several methods, conduct a pilot study with, perhaps, two of them and then make a commitment to a single approach. It should select the one programme on the basis of criteria previously established and those that may evolve as the investigation and the programme proceed. Some of the best criteria are:

—Profit potential.
—Cost and time scale.
—Proven results elsewhere.
—Availability of skilled resource people.
—Applicability of programme to the particular company.
—Flexibility in application.

2.7 Industry in a New Age[1]

Tom Burns

Industry has a long past. We are now near the end of the second century of industrialism in its recognizably modern form. To be conscious of the history of an institution like the industrial concern is to become alive to two essential considerations. First, that like any other institution— government, the church, the family, military forces, for example—industry has undergone substantial changes in its organizational form as well as in the activity or task or objectives it performs. Secondly, and in consequence, unless we realize that industrial organization is still in the process of development, we are liable to be trapped into trying to use out-of-date organizational systems for coping with entirely new situations.

A sense of the past—and the very recent past—is essential to anyone who is trying to perceive the here-and-now of industrial organization. What is happening now is part of a continuing development. A study of this process will at least help firms avoid the traps they often fall into when they try to confront a situation of the newest kind with an organizational system appropriate to an earlier phase of industrial development. Adaptation to new challenge is not an automatic process: there are many factors against it.

What we recognize as industrialism is the product of two technologies, material and social. It has developed in spasmodic fashion from the rudimentary forms of the eighteenth century by alternate advances in first one technology and then the other.

The elementary form of industrialism is Adam Smith's conjunction of the division of labour traditional in advanced society with the extension of its advantages by "those machines by which labour is so much facilitated and enlarged".

The modern industrial system was founded at a time when the perception by early mechanical scientists that natural events "obeyed" certain laws became widely diffused—in the eighteenth century. Samuel Smiles' legend that Arkwright was first struck by the feasibility of mechanical spinning "by accidentally observing a hot piece of iron become elongated by

Source: *New Society* (Jan. 1963), No. 18, pp. 17–20.

passing between iron rollers" may be fiction, but it reflects truly the commonplace terms in which the new habits of scientific thought could be used by craftsmen-inventors, who saw not just an interesting analogy but one process obeying a law which might also apply to a different and entirely new process.

At the same time that Adam Smith was observing the archetypal form of the two technologies, a third step was being taken: the creation of the first successful factory by Strutt and Arkwright. By 1835 Ure could already discount the basic principles of division of labour as outdated and misleading. The industrial system was simply the factory system as developed by Arkwright: the term, factory, meaning "the combined operation of many work people, adult and young, in tending with assiduous skill a system of productive machines continuously impelled by a central power. It is the constant aim and tendency of every improvement in machinery to supersede human labour altogether."

Factory organization stayed for three generations at the point at which Arkwright had left it. Marx's account contains the same essentials: a collection of machines, in a building all driven by one prime mover, and, preferably, of the same type and engaged on the same process. Attending the machines were men and women who themselves were attended by "feeders", most of them children, who fetched and carried away materials. There was also a "superior, but numerically unimportant" class of maintenance and repair workers. All of these worked under a master, with perhaps a chief workman or foreman. The primitive social technology of the factory system still confined it, even by the 1850s, largely to the mass production of textiles.

Technical developments in transport and communications, the impact of the international exhibitions in London and Paris, free trade, the armaments revolutions supported by the development of machine tools and of steel, and chemical technology (in Germany first) all combined during the 1850s and 1860s to form the springboard, in material technology, of the next advance in the social techniques of industrial organization.

As yet, there is no account of how that advance took place. All that can be said is that with the extension of the factory system into engineering and chemicals, iron and steel processing, food manufacture and clothing, an organizational development took place which provided for the conduct and control of many complex series of production processes within the same plant. One overt sign of this development is the increase in the number of salaried officials employed in industry. The proportion of "administrative employees" to "production employees" in British manufacturing industry had risen to 8.6 per cent by 1907 and to 20 per cent by 1948. Similar increases took place in western Europe and the United States.

The growth in the numbers of industrial administrative officials, or managers, reflects the growth of organizational structures. Production department managers, sales managers, accountants, cashiers, inspectors, training officers, publicity managers, and the rest emerged as specialized parts of the general management function as industrial concerns increased in size. Their jobs were created, in fact, out of the eighteenth century master's, either directly or at one or two removes. This gives them and the whole social structure which contains their newly created roles its hierarchical character. It is indeed a patrimonial structure. All rights and powers at every level derive from the boss; fealty, or "responsibility", is owed to him; all benefits are "as if" dispensed by him. The bond is more easily and more often broken than in pre-feudal polities, but loyalty to the concern, to employers, is still regarded not only as proper, but as essential to the preservation of the system.

Chester Barnard (1938) makes this point with unusual emphasis: "The most important single contribution required of the executive, certainly the most universal qualification, is loyalty, domination by the organization personality." More recently, A. W. Gouldner (1957/8) has pointed out "Much of W. H. Whyte's recent study of Organization Man is a discussion of the efforts by industry to attach managerial loyalty to the corporation."

The development of the bureaucratic system made possible the increase in scale of undertakings characteristic of the first part of this century. It had other aspects. The divorce of ownership and management, although by no means absolute, went far enough to render survival of the enterprise (and the survival of the existing management) at least as important a consideration as making the best profit. Profit itself wears a different aspect in the large scale corporation.

More important, the growth of bureaucracy—the social technology which made possible the second stage of industrialism—was only feasible because the development of material technology was held relatively steady. An industry based on major technological advances shows a high death-rate among enterprises in its early years; growth occurs when the rate of technical advance slows down. What happens is that consumer demand tends to be standardized through publicity and price reductions, and the technical progress is consequently restrained. This enables companies to maintain relatively stable conditions, in which large scale production is built up by converting manufacturing processes into routine cycles of activity for machines or semi-skilled assembly hands.

Under such conditions, not only could a given industrial company grow in size, not only could the actual manufacturing processes be routinized, mechanized and quickened, but the various management functions also could be broken down into specialisms and routines. Thus developed specialized management tasks: those of ensuring employee cooperation, of coordinating different departments, of planning and monitoring.

It is this second phase of industrialism which now dominates the institutional life of western societies. But while the greater part of the industrial system is in this second, bureaucratic phase of the historical development (and some older and smaller establishments remain in the first), it is now becoming clear that we have entered a third phase during the past two or three decades. J. K. Galbraith, in his *Affluent Society*, has described the new, more insecure relationship with the consumer which appears as production catches up and overtakes spontaneous domestic demand. The "propensity to consume" has had to be stimulated by advertising, by styling, and by marketing promotions guided by research into the habits, motives, and potential "needs" of consumers. At the same time, partly in an effort to maintain expansion, partly because of the stimulus of government spending on new military equipment, industry has admitted a sizeable influx of new technical developments.

There are signs that industry organized according to principles of bureaucracy—by now traditional—is no longer able to accommodate the new elements of industrial life in the affluent second half of the twentieth century. These new demands are made by large-scale research and development and by industry's new relationship with its markets. Both demand a much greater flexibility in internal organization, much higher levels of commitment to the commercial aims of the company from all its members, and an even higher proportion of administrators, controllers and monitors to operatives.

Recently, with G. M. Stalker, I made an attempt to elucidate the situation of concerns in the electronics industry which were confronted with rapidly changing commercial circumstances and a much faster rate of technical progress [see Burns and Stalker (1961)]. I found it necessary to posit two "ideal types" of working organization, the one mechanistic, adapted to relatively stable conditions, the other, "organismic", adapted to conditions of change.

In mechanistic systems the problems and tasks which face the concern as a whole are, typically, broken down into specialisms. Each individual carries out his assigned task as something apart from the overall purpose of the company as a whole. "Somebody at the top" is responsible for seeing that his work is relevant to that of others. The technical methods, duties, and powers attached to each post are precisely defined, and a high value is placed on precision and demarcation. Interaction within the working organization follows vertical lines—i.e. between superiors and subordinates. How a man operates and what he does is prescribed by his functional role and governed by instructions and decisions issued by superiors. This hierarchy of command is maintained by the assumption that the only man who knows—or should know—all about the company is the man at the top. He is the only one, therefore, who knows exactly how the human resources should be properly disposed. The management system, usually visualized as the complex hierarchy familiar in organization charts, operates as a simple control system, with information flowing upwards through a succession of filters, and decisions and instructions flowing downwards through a succession of amplifiers.

Mechanistic systems are, in fact, the "rational bureaucracy" of an earlier generation of students of organization. For the individual, it provides an ordered world of work. His own decisions and actions occur within a stable constellation of jobs, skills, specialized knowledge, and sectional responsibilities. In a textile mill, or any factory which sees itself turning out any standardized product for a familiar and steady market, one finds decision-making at all levels prescribed by the familiar.

As one descends through the levels of management, one finds more limited information and less understanding of the human capacities of other members of the firm. One also finds each person's task more and more clearly defined by his superior. Beyond a certain limit he has insufficient authority, insufficient information, and usually insufficient technical ability to be able to make decisions. He is informed quite clearly when this limit occurs; beyond it, he has one course open—to report to his superior.

Organismic systems are adapted to unstable conditions, when new and unfamiliar problems and requirements continually arise which cannot be broken down and distributed among specialist roles within a hierarchy. Jobs lose much of their formal definition. The definitive and enduring demarcation of functions becomes impossible. Responsibilities and functions, and even methods and powers, have to be constantly redefined through interaction with others participating in common tasks or in the solution of common problems. Each individual has to do his job with knowledge of overall purposes and situation of the company as a whole. Interaction runs laterally as much as vertically and communication between people of different rank tends to resemble "lateral" consultation rather than "vertical" command. Omniscience can no longer be imputed to the boss at the top.

The head of one successful electronics concern, at the very beginning of the first interview of the whole study, attacked the idea of the organization chart as inapplicable in his concern and as a dangerous method of thinking. The first requirement of a management, according to him, was that it should make the fullest use of the capacities of its members; any individual's job should be as little defined as possible, so that it would "shape itself" to his special abilities and initiative.

[The following list gives a summary of the characteristics of mechanistic and organismic systems of management.]

MECHANISTIC AND ORGANISMIC SYSTEMS OF MANAGEMENT
A mechanistic management system is appropriate to stable conditions. It is characterized by:

1   the *specialized differentiation* of functional tasks into which the problems and tasks facing the concern as a whole are

broken down.

2 the *abstract nature* of each individual task, which is pursued with techniques and purposes more or less distinct from those of the concern as a whole.

3 the reconciliation, for each level in the hierarchy, of these distinct performances by the *immediate superiors*.

4 the *precise definition* of rights and obligations and technical methods attached to each functional role;

5 the *translation of rights* and obligations and methods into the responsibilities of a functional position;

6 *hierarchic structure* of control, authority and communication;

7 a reinforcement of the hierarchic structure by the location of *knowledge* of actualities exclusively *at the top* of the hierarchy.

8 a tendency for *vertical interaction* between members of the concern i.e., between superior and subordinate;

9 a tendency for operations and working behaviour to be *governed by superiors*;

10 *insistence on loyalty* to the concern and obedience to superiors as a condition of membership;

11 a greater importance and prestige attaching to *internal* (local) than to general (cosmopolitan) knowledge, experience and skill.

The organismic form is appropriate to changing conditions, which give rise constantly to fresh problems and unforeseen requirements for action which cannot be broken down or distributed automatically arising from the functional roles defined within a hierarchic structure. It is characterized by:

1 the *contributive nature* of special knowledge and experience to the common task of the concern;

2 the *realistic* nature of the individual task, which is seen as set by the total situation of the concern;

3 the adjustment and *continual redefinition* of individual tasks through interaction with others;

4 the *shedding of responsibility* as a limited field of rights, obligations and methods. (Problems may not be posted upwards, downwards or sideways.)

5 the *spread of commitment* to the concern beyond any technical definition;

6 a *network structure* of control, authority, and communication.

7 omniscience no longer imputed to the head of the concern; *knowledge* may be located anywhere in the network, this location becoming the centre of authority.

8 a *lateral* rather than a vertical direction of communication through the organization.

F

9   a content of communication which consists of *information and advice* rather than instructions and decisions;
10 *commitment* to the concern's tasks and to the "technological ethos" of material progress and expansion is more highly valued than loyalty.
11 importance and prestige attach to *affiliations and expertise* valid in the industrial and technical and commercial milieux external to the firm.

Source: Burns and Stalker, pp. 119–22.

In this company, insistence on the least possible specification for managerial positions was much more in evidence than any devices for ensuring adequate interaction within the system. This did occur, but it was often due to physical conditions rather than to order by top management. A single-storeyed building housed the entire company, 2,000 strong, from laboratories to canteen. Access to anyone was, therefore, physically simple and direct; it was easier to walk across to the laboratory door, the office door, or the factory door and look about for the person one wanted, than even to telephone. Written communication inside the factory was actively discouraged. More im.portant than the physical set-up however was the need of each individual manager for interaction with others, in order to get his own functions defined, since these were not specified from above.

For the individual, the important part of the difference between the mechanistic and the organismic is in the degree of his commitment to the working organization. Mechanistic systems tell him what he has to attend to, and how, and also tell him what he does *not* have to bother with, what is *not* his affair, what is *not* expected of him—what he can post elsewhere as the responsibility of others. In organismic systems, such boundaries disappear. The individual is expected to regard himself as fully implicated in the discharge of any task appearing over his horizon. He has not merely to exercise a special competence, but to commit himself to the success of the concern's undertakings as a whole.

In studying the electronics industry in Britain, we were occupied for the most part with companies which had been started a generation or more ago, well within the time period of the second phase of industrialization. They were equipped at the outset with working organizations designed by mechanistic principles. The ideology of formal bureaucracy seemed so deeply ingrained in industrial management that the common reaction to unfamiliar and novel conditions was to redefine, in more precise and rigorous terms, the roles and working relationships obtaining within management, along orthodox lines of organization charts and organization manuals. The formal structure was reinforced, not adapted. In these concerns the effort to make the orthodox bureaucratic system work produced what can best be described as pathological forms of the mechanistic system.

Three of these pathological systems are described below. All three were responses to the need for finding answers to new and unfamiliar problems and for making decisions in new circumstances of uncertainty.

(1) First, there is the *ambiguous figure* system. In a mechanistic organization, the normal procedure for dealing with any matter lying outside the boundaries of one individual's functional responsibility is to refer it to the point in the system where such responsibility is known to reside, or, failing that, to lay it before one's superior. If conditions are changing rapidly such episodes occur frequently; in many instances, the immediate superior has to put such matters higher up still. A sizeable volume of matters for solution and decision can thus find their way to the head of the concern. There can, and frequently does, develop a system by which a large number of executives find—or claim—that they can only get matters settled by going to the top man.

So, in some places we studied, an ambiguous system developed of an official hierarchy, and a clandestine or open system of pair relationships between the head of the concern and some dozens of persons at different positions below him in the management. The head of the concern was overloaded with work, and senior managers whose standing depended on the mechanistic formal system felt aggrieved at being bypassed. The managing director told himself—or brought in consultants to tell him—to delegate responsibility and decision making. The organization chart would be redrawn. But inevitably, this strategy promoted its own counter measures from the beneficiaries of the old, latent system as the stream of novel and unfamiliar problems built up anew.

The conflict between managers who saw their standing and prospects depending on the ascendancy of the old system or the new deflected attention and effort into internal politics. All of this bore heavily on the time and effective effort the head of the company was free to apply to his proper function, the more so because political moves focused on controlling access to him.

(2) Secondly, the *mechanistic jungle*. Some companies simply grew more branches of the bureaucratic hierarchy. Most of the problems which appeared in all these firms with pathological mechanisms manifested themselves as difficulties in communications. These were met, typically, by creating special intermediaries and interpreters: methods engineers, standardization groups, contract managers, post design engineers. Underlying this familiar strategy were two equally familiar clichés of managerial thinking. The first is to look for the solution of a problem, especially a problem of communication in "bringing somebody in" to deal with it. A

new job, or possibly a whole new department, may then be created, which depends for its survival on the perpetuation of the difficulty. The second attitude probably comes from the tradition of productive management: a development engineer is not doing the job he is paid for unless he is at his drawing board, drawing, and so on. Higher management has the same instinctive reaction when it finds people moving about the works, when individuals it wants are not "in their place". Managers cannot trust subordinates when they are not demonstrably and physically "on the job". Their response, therefore, when there was an admitted need for "better communication" was to tether functionaries to their posts and to appoint persons who would specialise in "liaison".

(3)   The third kind of pathological response is the *super-personal* or committee system. It was encountered only rarely in the electronics firms we studied; it appeared sporadically in many of them, but it was feared as the characteristic disease of government administration. The committee is a traditional device whereby *temporary* commitments over and above those encapsulated in a single functional role may be contained within the system and discharged without enlarging the demands of individual functionaries, or upsetting the balance of power.

Committees are often set up where new kinds of work and/or unfamiliar problems seem to involve decisions, responsibilities and powers beyond the capabilities or deserts of any one man or department. Bureaucratic hierarchies are most prone to this defect. Here most considerations, most of the time, are subordinated to the career structure afforded by the concern (a situation by no means confined to the civil service or even to universities). The difficulty of filling a job calling for unfamiliar responsibility is overcome by creating a super-person—a committee.

Why do companies not adapt to new situations by changing their working organization from mechanistic to organismic? The answer seems to lie in the fact that the individual member of the concern is not only committed to the working organization as a whole. In addition, he is a member of a group or a department with sectional interests in conflict with those of other groups, and all of these individuals are deeply concerned with the position they occupy, relative to others, and their future security or betterment are matters of deep concern.

In regard to sectional commitments, he may be, and usually is, concerned to extend the control he has over his own situation, to increase the value of his personal contribution, and to have his resources possibly more thoroughly exploited and certainly more highly rewarded. He often tries to increase his personal power by attaching himself to parties of people who represent the same kind of ability and wish to enhance its exchange value, or to cabals who seek to control or influence the exercise of patronage in the firm. The interest groups so formed are quite often identical with a department, or the dominant groups in it, and their political leaders are heads of departments, or accepted activist leaders, or elected representatives (e.g. shop stewards). They become involved in issues of internal politics arising from the conflicting demands such as those on allocation of capital, on direction of others, and on patronage.

Apart from this sectional loyalty, an individual usually considers his own career at least as important as the well being of the firm, and while there may be little incompatibility in his serving the ends of both, occasions do arise when personal interests outweigh the firm's interests, or even a clear conflict arises.

If we accept the notion that a large number, if not all, of the members of a firm have commitments of this kind to themselves, then it is apparent that the resulting relationships and conduct are adjusted to other self-motivated relationships and conduct throughout the concern. We can therefore speak of the new career structure of the concern, as well as of its working organization and political system. Any concern will contain these three systems. All three will interact: particularly, the political system and career structure will influence the constitution and the operation of the working organization.

(There are two qualifications to be made here. The tripartite system of commitments is not exhaustive, and is not necessarily self balancing. Beside commitments to the concern, to "political" groups, and to his own career prospects, each member of a concern is involved in a multiplicity of relationships. Some arise out of social origin and culture. Others are generated by the encounters which are governed, or seem to be governed, by a desire for the comfort of friendship, or the satisfactions which come from popularity and personal esteem, or those other rewards of inspiring respect, apprehension or alarm. All relationships of this sociable kind, since they represent social values, involve the parties in commitments.)

Neither political nor career preoccupations operate overtly, or even, in some cases, consciously. They give rise to intricate manoeuvres and counter moves, all of them expressed through decisions, or in discussions about decisions, concerning the organization and the policies of the firm. Since sectional interests and preoccupations with advancement only display themselves in terms of the working organization, that organization becomes more or less adjusted to serving the ends of the political and career system rather than those of the concern. Interlocking systems of commitments—to sectional interests and to individual status—generate strong forces. These divert organizations from purposive adaptation. Out of date mechanistic organizations are perpetuated and pathological systems develop, usually because of one or the other of two things: internal politics and the career structure.

NOTE

1 In the main, the article follows the author's papers contributed to Welford *et al.* (1962) and to *Sociologie du Travail* (Burns, 1962).

REFERENCES

BURNS, T. (1962) in *Sociologie du Travail*.

BURNS, T. and STALKER, G. M. (1961) *The Management of Innovation*, Tavistock Publications.

BARNARD, C. I. (1938) *The Functions of the Executive*, Harvard University Press.

GALBRAITH, J. K. (1958) *The Affluent Society*, Houghton Mifflin.

GOULDNER, A. W. (1957/8) "Cosmopolitans and Locals: Towards an Analysis of Latent Social Roles", I and II, *Administrative Science Quarterly*, Vol. 2.

WELFORD, A. T., GLASS, D. V., ARGYLE, M. and MORRIS, J. N. (eds.) (1962) *Society: Problems and Methods of Study*, Routledge and Kegan Paul.

3 Individuals and Organizations

INTRODUCTION
Yukl's article, "Toward a Behavioral Theory of Leadership", contains a review of the best-known work in the field and bravely attempts a synthesis of the differing positions. A rather different perspective is put forward by Sadler, leaning fairly heavily upon the work of McGregor—who is absent from Yukl's list of references.

The section then moves on to a paper by Burnham discussing the relevance of role theory to educational administration. The final plea that those in positions of responsibility should place "much less reliance on experience *per se*, and much more on acquiring the understanding and insight that comes from a conceptual grasp of the nature of their own role, and those of their staff" is one that some students at least may find contentious. On the subject of participation and satisfaction, we have a paper by Belasco and Alutto. Perhaps the most heartfelt of the recommendations made by these two authors is the one which stresses the importance of giving greatly increased job satisfaction and participation to the younger male teachers.

It would be a rather odd Reader which, purporting to give a perspective on the behavioural approaches to educational administration, did not include a paper by Chris Argyris. Over the last few years he has been the main champion of humanistic values in the field of management studies. Although his article does not refer directly to the school or college situation, nevertheless the points raised do have a relevance which is both obvious and direct. Whilst Argyris explains conflict in general terms Gray, in his paper "Exchange and Conflict in the School", meets the problem head-on and suggests that schools do not accept (i.e. in their administrative mechanisms) the need to renegotiate constantly with their members. In this clear and concise "manifesto", Gray points out the origins of organizational resistance to change in a manner similar to that of Donald Schon in his Reith lectures. Those students working in schools in decaying city centres will certainly not consider that he overstresses the question of conflict. The concluding article, by Walton and Dutton, may seem on the surface less apocalyptic than Gray's because it is written in the convention of the Harvard Business School; however, closer inspection will reveal a similar acceptance of conflict as the norm and also a full realization of the complexity of conflict situations.

3.1 Toward a Behavioral Theory of Leadership[1]

Gary Yukl

ABSTRACT

A great deal of the apparent inconsistency in the leadership literature may be due to semantic confusion about leader behavior and to the absence of a conceptual framework which includes intermediate and situational variables. A system of three distinct leader behavior dimensions is proposed to reduce this confusion. Two of the dimensions are similar to the familiar variables, Consideration and Initiating Structure. The third dimension, Decision-Centralization, refers to the extent to which a leader allows his subordinates to participate in decision-making. A discrepancy model is developed to explain the relation between leader behavior and subordinate satisfaction with the leader. A multiple linkage model is developed to explain how the leader behavior variables interact with situational variables to determine group productivity. A review of the leadership literature revealed that the results of previous research are generally consistent with the proposed models. The compatibility of the linkage model with Fiedler's Contingency Model is discussed, and suggestions for future research are offered.

Despite over two decades of extensive leadership research, the relation of leader behavior to subordinate productivity and satisfaction with the leader is still not very clear. The apparent absence of consistent relationships in the research literature (Sales, 1966; Korman, 1966; Lowin, 1968) may be due in part to several related problems. First, there is a great deal of semantic confusion regarding the conceptual and operational definition of leadership behavior. Over the years there has been a proliferation of leader behavior terms, and the same term is often defined differently from one study to the next. Secondly, a great deal of empirical data has been collected, but a theoretical framework which adequately explains causal relationships and identifies limiting conditions has not yet emerged. Finally, the research has often failed to include intermediate

---

Source: *Organizational Behavior and Human Performance*, 6 (1971), pp. 414–40.

and situational variables which are necessary in order to understand how a leader's actions can affect his subordinates' productivity.

The purpose of this article is to begin the development of a theory which explains how leader behavior, situational variables, and intermediate variables interact to determine subordinate productivity and satisfaction with the leader. In the first section of the article, a system of three distinct and generally applicable leader behavior dimensions will be proposed. In the next two sections, these leadership dimensions will be used to develop a discrepancy model of subordinate satisfaction and a multiple linkage model of leader effectiveness. Finally, the extent to which the research literature supports these behavioral models will be evaluated.

CLASSIFICATION OF LEADER BEHAVIOR

Consideration and initiating structure
Some early investigators began with a list of very specific leadership activities (e.g. "inspection", "write reports", "hear complaints") and attempted to determine how performance of these activities or the amount of time allocated to them related to leader success. Since the number of specific leader activities that are possible is nearly endless, several Ohio State University psychologists attempted to find a few general behavior dimensions which would apply to all types of leaders. Factor analyses of leadership behavior questionnaires were carried out, and two orthogonal factors were found (Hemphill and Coons, 1957; Halpin and Winer, 1957). These factors were called Consideration and Initiating Structure. Consideration refers to the degree to which a leader acts in a warm and supportive manner and shows concern and respect for his subordinates. Initiating Structure refers to the degree to which a leader defines and structures his own role and those of his subordinates toward goal attainment.

The principal method for measuring these variables had been the use of either the Leader Behavior Description Questionnaire (Hemphill and Coons, 1957) or the Supervisory Behavior Description Questionnaire (Fleishman, 1957a). These questionnaires are administered to a leader's subordinates. A related questionnaire, called the Leadership Opinion Questionnaire (Fleishman, 1957b), is administered to the leader himself. This questionnaire is considered to be a measure of leader attitudes rather than leader behavior. Occasionally other observers, such as peers or superiors, are the source of leader behavior descriptions, and in some studies Consideration and Initiating Structure are experimentally manipulated by having leaders play predetermined roles.

Decision-centralization
A somewhat different approach to the classification of leaders was

162

initiated by Lewin's (1944) theoretical typology of democratic, autocratic, and laissez-faire leaders. Studies following in this tradition have usually focused on the relative degree of leader and subordinate influence over the group's decisions. The various decision-making procedures used by a leader, such as delegation, joint decision-making, consultation, and autocratic decision-making, can be ordered along a continuum ranging from high subordinate influence to complete leader influence. Although a leader will usually allow more subordinate participation and influence for some decisions than for others, the average degree of participation can be computed for any specified set of typical decisions. Heller and Yukl (1969) have used the term "Decision-Centralization" to refer to this average. A high Decision-Centralization score means a low amount of subordinate participation. Naturally, a leader is capable of voluntarily sharing decision-making with his subordinates only to the extent that he has authority to make decisions.

Most methods that have been used to measure participation can also be regarded as a measure of Decision-Centralization. Participation and Decision-Centralization have been measured by subordinate ratings of their perceived autonomy or influence in decision-making, by subordinate responses to a questionnaire concerning the leader's decision behavior, and by leader responses to a decision behavior questionnaire. In some studies the leader's actual decision-making behavior has been experimentally manipulated. The term Decision-Centralization was introduced for two reasons. First, this term emphasizes the behavior of the leader rather than the behavior of the subordinates. Second, the definition of Decision-Centralization explicitly encompasses a greater variety of leader decision procedures than does the typical definition of participation (Heller & Yukl, 1969).[2]

Reconciling the two approaches to leader behavior classification
Is Decision-Centralization equivalent to Consideration and Initiating Structure, or is it a distinct leadership dimension? The degree to which the three dimensions are independent depends upon the precise definitions given them. Since the definitions vary from study to study, it is not surprising that there is some disagreement regarding the relation between these dimensions. For example, Lowin (1968) has suggested that Initiating Structure is conceptually similar to autocratic supervision, Sales (1966) has suggested that "employee orientation" (which includes high Consideration) is usually associated with democratic leadership, and Newport (1962) has suggested that Consideration and Initiating Structure are similar, respectively, to democratic and autocratic leadership. On the other hand, Gomberg (1966), McMurry (1958), Schoenfeld (1959), and Stanton (1962) have claimed that high Consideration and autocratic leadership are not incompatible, or in other words, that Consideration and Decision-Centralization are separate dimensions.

There are several sound theoretical arguments for treating Decision-

Centralization as a separate dimension of leader behavior. Let us look first at the relation between Consideration and Decision-Centralization. The Consideration scale in the Ohio State questionnaires includes several items pertaining to the decision-making participation of subordinates, and Consideration is sometimes defined as including the sharing of decision-making with subordinates. However, one can argue that this sharing is only considerate of subordinates when they clearly desire participation, and the desire for participation can vary substantially from person to person and from situation to situation. Inclusion of participation items in a Consideration scale results in scores which are not comparable across persons unless first adjusted for differences in participation preferences. It is more practical to define Consideration as simply the degree to which a leader's behavior expresses a positive attitude rather than an indifferent or negative attitude toward subordinates. When defined in this manner, Consideration can be regarded as conceptually distinct from Decision-Centralization. In general, a high Consideration leader is friendly, supportive, and considerate; a low Consideration leader is hostile, punitive, and inconsiderate. A leader who acts indifferent and aloof is between these extremes but is closer to the low end of the continuum. The specific behaviors used in scaling Consideration should be generally applicable to all types of leadership situations.

What about the relation between Decision-Centralization and Initiating Structure? Although Initiating Structure is defined broadly as task-oriented behavior, it appears to include at least three types of task behavior: (1) Behavior indicating the leader's concern about productivity (e.g. goal-oriented comments to subordinates, and use of various rewards and punishments to encourage productivity), (2) behavior insuring that necessary task decisions are made, and (3) behavior insuring that these decisions and directives from higher levels in the organization are carried out (e.g. training and supervision). Note that this definition does not specify who will actually make the decisions. The task orientation of the leader does not appear to be very closely related to the amount of influence he will allow subordinates in the making of task or maintenance decisions. Even very autocratic leaders can differ considerably with respect to their task orientation and concern about group performance. Therefore, it seems reasonable to treat Initiating Structure and Decision-Centralization as separate dimensions of leader behavior.

The empirical evidence on the relation of Decision-Centralization to Consideration and Initiating Structure is scanty, and the research which will be cited should be regarded as suggestive rather than conclusive. Most of these studies use the Consideration scale of the Leader Behavior Description Questionnaire, which includes some participation items. Naturally these items increase the likelihood of finding a significant correlation between Consideration and Decision-Centralization.

In a study of 67 second-line supervisors in three companies, this author found a low but significant correlation ($r = -.24$; $p < .05$)

between Consideration and Decision-Centralization. Decision-Centraliz-ation was measured by means of leader responses on the decision pro-cedure questionnaire (Form C) described in Heller and Yukl (1968). There was no significant correlation between Decision-Centralization and Initiating Structure.

Other evidence is provided by analyses of a more recent version of the Leader Behavior Description Questionnaire, which has ten new subscales in addition to the original scales for Consideration and Initiating Struc-ture. One of the new scales, called "Tolerance of Member Freedom", can be regarded as a measure of participation or Decision-Centralization. Stogdill, Goode, and Day (1962, 1963, 1964) administered this question-naire to "subordinates" of corporation presidents, labor union presidents, community leaders, and ministers. The correlations between Consider-ation and Tolerance of Member Freedom for the four samples, respect-ively, were .41, .42, .40, and .49. For a sample of office supervisors rated by female subordinates on this questionnaire, the correlation was .50 (Beer, 1966).[3] Decision-Centralization and Initiating Structure were not significantly correlated in any of the five samples just described.

Argyle, Gardner, and Cioffi (1957) analyzed the relation among leader-ship dimensions as measured by questionnaires administered to managers in England. Democratic (vs authoritarian) leadership correlated .41 with nonpunitive (vs punitive) leadership. Democratic leadership was not significantly correlated with pressure for production, a component of Initiating Structure.

If we remember to reverse the sign of the correlation when necessary in order to correct for the fact that high participation equals low Decision-Centralization, then it is obvious that the results of these studies are remarkedly consistent. Decision-Centralization and Initiating Structure appear to be independent dimensions. Decision-Centralization and Con-sideration should probably be regarded as oblique rather than orthogonal dimensions. That is, there will tend to be a low to moderate negative correlation between them, but some leaders will have high scores on both dimensions ("benevolent autocrat") and some leaders will have low scores on both dimensions ("malevolent democrat").

A DISCREPANCY MODEL OF SUBORDINATE SATISFACTION WITH THE LEADER
In this section, a discrepancy model of satisfaction will be used to explain the relation of the three leadership dimensions to subordinate satisfaction with the leader. Discrepancy or subtraction models of job satisfaction have been proposed by a number of psychologists (Morse, 1953; Schaffer, 1953; Rosen and Rosen, 1955; Ross and Zander, 1957; Porter, 1962; Katzell, 1964; Locke, 1969). In a discrepancy model, satisfaction is a function of the difference between a person's preferences and his actual experience. The less the discrepancy between preferences and experi-ence, the greater the satisfaction. This hypothesis has received some support in the studies cited above, but the evidence is by no means

conclusive. In some versions of the discrepancy model there is a second hypothesis which states that the amount of dissatisfaction with a given discrepancy also depends upon the importance of the needs affecting the preference level. If importance varies from person to person, the discrepancy scores cannot be compared unless first adjusted for importance. Whether such a correction is necessary, and if so, how it should be made appears to be a matter of growing controversy.

Although the discrepancy model appears to be applicable to the analysis of subordinates' satisfaction with their leader, only a few studies have used it for this purpose. In two of these studies (Foa, 1957; Greer, 1961), leadership variables other than Consideration, Initiating Structure, and Decision-Centralization were used. No studies were found which included subordinate preferences for Consideration and Initiating Structure as a moderating variable. The results from studies which have included subordinate preferences for participation in decision-making tend to be consistent with the discrepancy model.

Figure 1

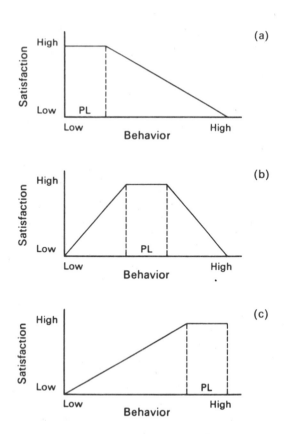

Figure 2

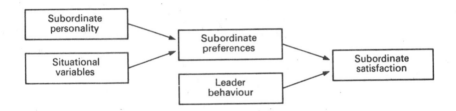

According to the proposed discrepancy model, the shape of the curve relating leader behavior to subordinate satisfaction will vary somewhat depending upon a subordinate's preference level. A preference level will be defined tentatively as a range of leader behavior acceptable to subordinates rather than as a single point on a behavior continuum. Figure 1 shows the theoretical curves for a low, medium, and high preference level. The curves represent the relation for a single subordinate. When the preference levels of group members are relatively homogeneous, the relation between leader behavior and average group satisfaction with their leader will yield a curve similar to that for an individual. However, the more variable the preferences are in a group, the less likely it is that any significant relation will be found between leader behavior and average group satisfaction.

Subordinate preference levels are determined both by subordinate personality and by situational variables (see Figure 2). Preferences can be expected to vary more for Initiating Structure and Decision-Centralization than for Consideration. Except for a few masochists, it is probably safe to assume that subordinates will desire a high degree of considerate behavior by their leaders. As a result, the function relating Consideration and subordinate satisfaction should resemble curve C in Figure 1.

Preference levels for Decision-Centralization, i.e. the subordinate's desire for participation in decision-making, may be partially determined by two personality traits: Authoritarianism (Vroom, 1959) and "need for independence" (Trow, 1957; Ross and Zander, 1957; Vroom, 1959; Beer, 1966, p. 51; French, Kay, and Meyer, 1966). Although none of these investigators assessed the relation between a personality measure and expressed behavior preferences, they did find that personality had the expected moderating effect upon the relation between Decision-Centralization and subordinate satisfaction. However, it should be noted that Tosi (1970) was not able to replicate the results of the study by Vroom (1959). The measurement of subordinate preferences in future replications may aid in clearing up the contradiction between these two studies.

The major situational determinant of the preference level for participation in making a decision is probably the importance of that decision for the subordinate (Maier, 1965, p. 165). When a decision is very important to subordinates, they are likely to prefer as much influence as possible (e.g. joint decision-making or delegation). When decisions do not involve matters of importance, consultation or even autocratic decision-making is more likely to be preferred. Of course, the more that subordinates trust their leader to make a decision favorable to them, the less need they will feel to participate in order to protect their interests. Also, when the subordinates are committed to group goal attainment or survival and the task or environment favors centralized decision-making (e.g. a crisis), then they are likely to expect the leader to make most of the decision (Mulder and Stemerding, 1963).

Preference levels for Initiating Structure are partially determined by the subordinates' commitment to group goals and their perception of the amount of structuring that is necessary to help the group attain these goals. Subordinates who are indifferent about or hostile toward the goal of maximum productivity are likely to prefer a leader who is not very task oriented in his behavior.

Summary of the discrepancy model
The major features of the proposed discrepancy model can be summarized in terms of the following hypotheses:

Hyp 1: Subordinate satisfaction with the leader is a function of the discrepancy between actual leader behavior and the behavior preferences of subordinates.
Hyp 2: Subordinate preferences are determined by the combined effect of subordinate personality and situational variables.
Hyp 3: Subordinates usually prefer a high degree of leader Consideration, and this preference level results in a positive relation between Consideration and subordinate satisfaction.

The discrepancy model in its present form is only a static model representing one-way causality at one point in time. No attempt has been made to include additional complexities such as the effects of leader behavior on subordinate preferences. For example, a leader who gradually allows greater subordinate participation may find that the subordinates' preference for decision-making increases over time. Nor does the model explicitly deal with such other determinants of subordinate satisfaction with the leader as his intelligence or the feedback effects from successful or unsuccessful group performance. Finally, the influence of various components of the model on leader behavior has also been ignored. For example, subordinate preferences represent one of several sources of role expectations for the leader, and these role expectations interact with other situational variables and leader personality to determine his behavior.

A MULTIPLE LINKAGE MODEL OF LEADER EFFECTIVENESS

When a leader is dependent upon his subordinates to do the work, subordinate performance is unlikely to improve unless the leader can increase one or more of the following three intermediate variables: (1) Subordinate task motivation (i.e. effort devoted to their tasks), (2) subordinate task skills, and (3) Task-Role Organization (i.e. the technical quality of task decisions).[4] Consideration, Initiating Structure, Decision-Centralization, and various situational variables interact in their effects on these intermediate variables. The intermediate variables interact in turn to determine group performance (see Figure 3).

Consideration, initiative structure, and subordinate motivation
Consideration and Initiating Structure interact in their effect upon subordinate task motivation. Subordinate task motivation will be highest when the leader is high on both Consideration and Initiating Structure.

Figure 3   A multiple linkage model of leader effectiveness

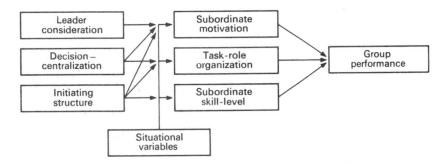

The ordering of the other combinations is less certain, because the interaction appears to be highly complex and irregular. If leaders were subgrouped according to their Initiating Structure scores, for high structuring leaders there would probably be a positive relation between Consideration and subordinate task motivation. For low structuring leaders, there is some reason to suspect that the relation between Consideration and subordinate motivation is described by an inverted U-shaped curve. In other words, subordinate task motivation can be adversely affected when the low structuring leader is either very supportive and friendly or very hostile and punitive.

There are at least two hypotheses for explaining the interaction between Consideration and Initiating Structure, and it is not yet clear if either or both are correct. From instrumentality theory (Vroom, 1964, p. 220; Galbraith and Cummings, 1967), comes the hypothesis that a leader can improve subordinate performance by being highly considerate to subordinates who make an effort to perform well, while withholding Consideration from subordinates who show little task motivation. In effect, considerate behavior is a reward which is contingent upon the display of certain task-motivated behavior by subordinates.

The "identification" hypothesis proposes that subordinate motivation is a response to previous leader Consideration rather than an attempt to obtain future Consideration. As Consideration increases, subordinate attitudes toward the leader become more favourable and his influence over the subordinates increases correspondingly. In effect, the considerate leader has greater "referent power" (French and Raven, 1959). However, in order for subordinate loyalty to be translated into task motivation, it is necessary for the leader to communicate a concern for productivity. If the leader is highly considerate but does not stress productivity, the subordinates are likely to feel that they can safely neglect their tasks.

If a leader actually becomes hostile and punitive, it is likely that subordinate task motivation will be adversely affected, regardless of the level of Initiating Structure. Punitive leadership can lead to counter-aggression by subordinates in the form of slowdowns and subtle sabotage (Day and Hamblin, 1964).

Decision-centralization and subordinate motivation

Although there is some direct evidence that subordinate participation can result in increased task motivation (Baumgartel, 1956), the nature and relative importance of the psychological processes accounting for the relation and the prerequisite conditions for their occurrence are not yet clear. A number of explanations for the effect of participation on subordinate motivation have been proposed during the last two decades.

Probably the most important of the proposed processes is the possibility that subordinates become "ego-involved" with a decision which they have helped to make. When subordinates identify with a decision, they become motivated to help make the decision successful, if only to maintain a favorable self-concept. However, there may be several limiting conditions for this causal sequence (Strauss, 1964; Vroom, 1964; Lowin, 1968). It is possible that there is some minimal amount of individual influence, actual or perceived, which is necessary before identification will occur. As a group gets larger, the influence of each member over a decision will necessarily decline; thus the size of the group may be one limiting factor. Also, it is not clear whether a person who supports a proposal that is rejected will become committed to the proposal finally selected by the group. Another prerequisite may be the subordinate's perception that the decision process is a test of his decision ability and those skills of his which are used in implementing the decision. In the case where subordinates participate in making decisions unrelated to their tasks, there is no reason to assume that any increased commitment to these decisions will generalize to task decisions. Finally, if responsibility for making decisions is thrust upon subordinates who do not want it or who see it as the legitimate role of the leader, then these subordinates may fail to identify with the decisions (French, Israel, and As, 1960).

Another explanation of the relation between Decision-Centralization and task motivation is that participation facilitates reduction of subordinate resistance to change (Coch and French, 1948). One way this could occur is through direct persuasion. Since the leader is usually not aware of all the subordinates' fears and doubts regarding a proposed change, consultation provides him with an opportunity to uncover these fears and to persuade subordinates that the change will be beneficial rather than harmful. When a leader's proposal involves features which clearly are detrimental to subordinates, mere persuasion is not likely to win their support. However, consultation or joint decision-making provides the opportunity for bargaining and agreement on a compromise proposal which the subordinates can support (Strauss, 1964).

When the leader allows his subordinates to make a group decision, the interaction dynamics of the group are yet another possible source of increased task motivation. If the work group is cohesive, its members are subject to direct social pressure to conform to group norms (Schachter, Willerman, Festinger, and Hyman, 1961; Berkowitz, 1954; Seashore, 1954). In addition, the work group may function as a "reference group" for its members (Newcomb, 1965, p. 109). Subordinates who have positive attitudes toward their work group will tend to support group norms, including group decisions made in a legitimate manner. This tendency for member attitudes and behavior to be consistent with reference group norms will occur even in the absence of direct social pressure.

Of course, increased commitment to carry out decisions is not conceptually equivalent to increased task motivation. Subordinates can make task decisions which in effect restrict output or resist change. Subordinate attitudes toward the leader and the organization constitute an important situational variable which moderates the effect of participation upon task motivation. If relations between the leader and the subordinates are very poor, or the subordinates are in opposition to the goal of maximum group performance, then participation in decisions involving production goals, standards, quotas, etc., is not likely to result in increased subordinate task motivation (Strauss, 1964). Since Consideration is an important determinant of subordinate attitudes toward the leader, participation is more likely to be effective if combined with high Consideration than if combined with low Consideration.

Leader behavior and subordinate task skill
The second way in which leaders can increase group performance is to increase the ability of subordinates to perform their individual tasks. A number of studies (reviewed in Vroom, 1964, p. 197) support Maier's (1965) hypothesis that performance is a function of a person's Motivation

X Ability. According to this hypothesis, even highly motivated subordinates will not perform well if they lack the necessary knowledge or skills to carry out their assignments. Therefore, one way for a leader to improve group performance is to correct deficiencies in subordinate task skills and knowledge by means of on-the-job instruction and improved downward communication of task-relevant information. Instruction and communication of this nature are, by definition, elements of Initiating Structure. A more complex analysis of the relation between Initiating Structure and subordinate task skill was beyond the scope of this article.

The nature of task-role organization

Task-Role Organization refers to how efficiently the skill resources of subordinates are utilized to perform the group's formal tasks. Adequacy of Task-Role Organization depends upon how well job assignment decisions and work method decisions are made. The making of job assignment decisions is usually referred to in industrial psychology as "placement" or "classification". When the jobs of each subordinate are identical and subordinates work independently of each other, it doesn't matter what subordinates are assigned to what jobs. However, when jobs are highly specialized, each job has different skill requirements, and skill differences among subordinates are substantial, then job assignments are an important type of task decision. If work assignments are not made carefully, the skills of some workers will not be fully utilized, while other workers will be placed in jobs which they cannot perform adequately. Furthermore, if the jobs are interdependent, bottlenecks will occur at various points in the flow of work.

Work method decisions are important whenever a task can be performed in many different ways, and some ways are better than others. Work methods and procedures can be designed with the available skills of a particular work group in mind, but it is common practice in industrial engineering to ignore individual differences and develop methods which maximize the efficiency of the typical worker. Decisions about work procedures are not always the responsibility of the leader. In some organizations, work methods are designed by staff specialists or are rigidly prescribed by company or union regulations.

Task-Role Organization was included in the multiple linkage model to account for any variability in group productivity which is not attributable to subordinate motivation, subordinate ability, or to extraneous events such as an improvement in the flow of material inputs, a breakdown in equipment, etc. The identification of Task-Role Organization as a separate variable is analogous to Maier's (1965) distinction between the quality of a decision and group acceptance of the decision. Although Task-Role Organization is an important conceptual component of the multiple linkage model, measurement of this variable is likely to prove troublesome. Any measure of Task-Role Organization will be highly specific to a given set of tasks and subordinates. Within a specific situation, one could attempt to scale the adequacy of job assignment decisions by evaluating the match between job requirements and subordinate skills for all possible combinations of job assignments. Adequacy of work method decisions could be evaluated in several ways. In some situations, the accumulated knowledge of industrial engineering specialists may permit the subjective ranking of various possible work procedures according to their relative efficiency. When objective measures of group performance (e.g. quantity or quality of output, labor time, errors) are available to use as a criterion of efficiency, then alternative work methods may be experimentally compared. However, it may be difficult to hold task motivation constant, even within a single work group, because job design can affect the intrinsic motivation of workers as well as their efficiency.

Initiating structure, decision-centralization, and task-role organization
Both Initiating Structure and Decision-Centralization appear to be related to Task-Role Organization. By definition, a leader who is high in Initiating Structure will attempt to improve the efficiency of his group. However, simply engaging in structuring behavior does not guarantee that Task-Role Organization will improve. The leader's success depends upon his organizing skills, technical knowledge, and the extent to which he taps the knowledge of his subordinates by allowing them some degree of participation in making task decisions. The relation between Decision-Centralization and Task-Role Organization is moderated by the relative amount of leader and subordinate organizing skills and task knowledge. When the leader is very capable in this respect but the subordinates lack the appropriate talents, then there will be a negative relation between participation and Task-Role Organization. When the subordinates have more relevant knowledge and organizing talent than the leader, we would expect a positive relation between participation and Task-Role Organization. We have already seen that Decision-Centralization can affect the task motivation of subordinates as well as the quality of task decisions. This means that in the situation where there is a negative relation between participation and Task-Role Organization, there may also be a positive relation between participation and subordinate motivation. When such a trade-off dilemma occurs, some intermediate degree of Decision-Centralization will probably be optimal with respect to group performance.

In some situations, the quality of task decisions involves a time dimension. That is, the effectiveness of decisions depends in part upon how quickly they are made (Strauss, 1964; Lowin, 1968). Autocratic decision-making is faster than other decision procedures because little communication with subordinates is necessary. Therefore, participation is likely to be negatively related to group performance when rapid decision-making is required. The magnitude of this negative relation will be greatest when the leader already has the necessary knowledge and ability to make good decisions, the subordinates are motivated by the urgency of the situation, and the task group is very large.

Summary of the multiple linkage model
The major features of the multiple linkage model of leadership effectiveness can be summarized by means of the following hypotheses:

Hyp 1: Group productivity is a function of the interaction among subordinate task motivation, subordinate task skills, and Task-Role Organization for the group.

Hyp 2: Initiating Structure and Consideration interact in the determination of subordinate task motivation. Task motivation is highest when the leader is high on both behavior variables.

Hyp 3: Decision-Centralization is negatively correlated with subordinate task motivation (i.e. high participation causes high motivation) when subordinate relations with the leader are favorable, the decisions are relevant to subordinate tasks, and subordinates perceive their participation to be a test of valued abilities.

Hyp 4: Initiating Structure interacts with Decision-Centralization in the determination of Task-Role Organization. The relationship is moderated by the level and distribution of task knowledge and planning ability in the group.

Hyp 5: Initiating Structure is positively related to the level of subordinate task skill.

REVIEW OF RELATED RESEARCH
Most studies of the relation between leader behavior and subordinate satisfaction with the leader have not measured subordinate preferences or the personality and situational variables which determine these preferences. Most studies of the relation between leader behavior and group productivity have not included measures of the intermediate and situational variables in the proposed linkage model. The approach typical of most leadership research has been to look for a linear relation between leader behavior and one of the criterion variables. Nevertheless, previous research does provide some direct and some indirect evidence for evaluating the proposed models.

In the following sections of this article, relevant leadership research will be reviewed. The review will include studies dealing with variables which are reasonably similar to those in the proposed discrepancy and linkage models. However, it should be emphasized that in many of these studies, the operational measurement of a variable only approximates the conceptual definition presented in this article. Studies using scales which can be regarded as a measure of leader attitudes (e.g. LPC scale, F scale, Leadership Opinion Questionnaire) rather than leader behavior were not included. Also excluded were studies of general vs close supervision. This leadership dimension, as usually defined, confounds Decision-

Centralization with Initiating Structure. Finally, the review does not include studies of emergent leaders in informal groups, studies using children, studies involving an entire organization rather than individual work groups or departments, and studies in which leader behavior is obviously confounded with organizational variables such as the incentive system.

Consideration and satisfaction

In seven studies of the relation between Consideration and subordinate satisfaction with their leader, Consideration was measured by means of subordinate responses on leader behavior description questionnaires. In five of these studies (Halpin, 1957; Halpin and Winer, 1957; Nealey and Blood, 1968; Yukl, 1969a; Anderson, 1966) there was a strong positive relation between Consideration and subordinate satisfaction. In the remaining two studies (Fleishman and Harris, 1962; Skinner, 1969) there was a significant curvilinear relation between Consideration and two objective measures which reflect subordinate satisfaction, namely turnover and grievances. The curve describing the relation corresponded roughly to curve C in Figure 1. If subordinate preferences were homogeneous, this curve would represent supporting evidence for the concept of a zone of indifference within which leader behavior does not affect subordinate satisfaction. Below this indifference zone, the relation between Consideration and satisfaction was positive.

In research reported in Likert (1961, p. 17), aspects of Consideration such as "supervisor takes an interest in me and understands my problems" and "supervisor thinks of employees as human beings rather than as persons to get the work done", were related to favorable attitudes on job-related matters. In two laboratory experiments (Day and Hamblin, 1964; Misumi and Shirakashi, 1966) punitive leader behavior (i.e. low Consideration) was associated with low subordinate satisfaction. In another laboratory experiment, Lowin (1969) found a significant positive relation between subordinates' satisfaction and their ratings of leader Consideration, but the difference in satisfaction between high and low Consideration conditions, although in the right direction, was not significant.

Only two studies were found in which a positive relation between Consideration and subordinate satisfaction with the leader did not occur. In a study by Argyle, Gardner, and Cioffi (1958), leader self-reports of punitive behavior did not correlate significantly with subordinate turnover and absences. Pelz (1952) found an interaction between the degree to which a leader acts as a representative of his subordinates when dealing with higher management (one form of Consideration) and the leader's upward influence in the organization. For leaders with little upward influence, subordinates were less satisfied when the leader "went to bat" for them than when he did not go to bat. Presumably the leader representation raised expectations which he could not fulfill, thereby frustrating subordinates. In terms of the discrepancy model, the subordinates' preferences for leader representation are probably lower when it repeatedly causes frustration. Whether the negative effects of unsuccessful representation can completely cancel out the positive effects of other considerate behavior by the leader is not clear. It does not seem likely.

In summary, the research literature indicates that in most situations, considerate leaders will have more satisfied subordinates. Although none of the investigators included subordinate preferences in their analysis, the results are consistent with the discrepancy model if we can make the relatively safe assumption that most subordinates prefer considerate leaders.

Initiating structure and satisfaction

A consistent linear relation between Initiating Structure and subordinate satisfaction was not found, even within sets of studies using comparable measures. Unfortunately, none of the studies reviewed included subordinate preferences. Baumgartel (1956), Halpin and Winer (1957), Argyle *et al.* (1958), Misumi and Shirakashi (1966), Lowin (1969), Anderson (1966), and Likert (1961, pp. 16–18) failed to find a significant relation. Halpin (1957) and Yukl (1969a) found positive correlations. Vroom and Mann (1960) found a significant negative correlation between pressure for production and job satisfaction for delivery truck drivers but not for loaders. Nealey and Blood (1968) found a negative correlation between Initiating Structure and subordinate satisfaction for second-level supervisors and a positive correlation for first-level supervisors.

Only three studies were found which examined the possibility of a curvilinear relation between Initiating Structure and subordinate satisfaction. Likert (1955) found that the relation between pressure for productivity and subordinate satisfaction took the form of an inverted U-shaped curve which is similar to curve B in Figure 1. Fleishman and Harris (1962) and Skinner (1969) found a curvilinear relation between Initiating Structure and both turnover and grievances. Although subordinate preferences were not measured, the relationships in these studies were roughly comparable to curve A in Figure 1.

Fleishman and Harris also tested for an interaction between Initiating Structure and Consideration. The results of their analysis suggest that Consideration has a greater effect upon subordinate satisfaction than does Initiating Structure. High Consideration leaders could increase Initiating Structure with little accompanying increase in turnover or grievances. Fleishman and Harris provide two possible explanations for this interaction. One explanation is that considerate leaders are more likely to deal with any dissatisfaction caused by high structuring behavior before the dissatisfaction results in official grievances or withdrawal (i.e. turnover). Another explanation is that Consideration affects the way subordinates perceive structuring behavior. In terms of the discrepancy model, subordinates of highly considerate leaders are more likely to have a higher preference level for Initiating Structure because they do not perceive leader structuring as threatening and restrictive.

Decision-centralization and satisfaction

Six studies were found which examined the correlation between subordinate satisfaction and participation as perceived either by the leaders or by the subordinates (Baumgartel, 1956; Argyle *et al.*, 1958; Vroom, 1959; Bachman, Smith, and Slesinger, 1966; Yukl, 1969a; Tosi, 1970). In each of these studies, evidence was found to support a positive relation between participation and subordinate satisfaction, although within some of the studies, a significant relation was not obtained for every subsample or for every alternative measure of the variables. A significant positive relation was also found in each of five studies in which participation was experimentally manipulated (Coch and French, 1948; Shaw, 1955; Morse and Reimer, 1956; Solem, 1958; Maier and Hoffman, 1962). The results of these studies are generally consistent with the discrepancy model if one can assume that the subordinates preferred a substantial degree of participation.

In those cases where a significant relation between participation and subordinate satisfaction was not found, there was usually some reason to expect that the subordinates preferred a moderate or low amount of participation. In the study by Vroom (1959), a positive correlation occurred for subordinates with a high need for independence but not for subordinates with a low need for independence. Bass (1965, pp. 169–170) and French *et al.* (1960) found that subordinate participation did not result in more favorable attitudes toward a leader unless the subordinates perceived the decision-making as a legitimate part of their role. Further evidence for the moderating effect of subordinate preferences can be found in a study by Baumgartel (1956) and in two unpublished studies (Jacobson, 1951; Tannenbaum, 1954) which were reported in Likert (1961, pp. 92–93). In the Tannenbaum study, some subordinates reacted adversely to a sudden substantial increase in participation. Finally, Morse (1953, p. 64) found that, regardless of whether workers made some decisions or none, they reported more intrinsic job satisfaction when the amount of decision-making equalled the amount desired than when they were not allowed to make as many decisions as they desired. Although intrinsic job satisfaction is conceptually distinct from satisfaction with the leader, these two variables are probably highly correlated when the leader determines how much responsibility a subordinate has for making task decisions.

Consideration, initiating structure, and productivity

Considering the complexity of the interaction between Consideration and Initiating Structure, it is not surprising that research on the relation between Consideration and productivity does not yield consistent results. In the large majority of studies there was either a significant positive

177

relation (Katz, Maccoby, Gurin, and Floor, 1951; Argyle *et al.*, 1958; Besco and Lawshe, 1959; Schachter *et al.*, 1961; Kay, Meyer, and French, 1965) or there was no significant linear relation (Bass, 1957; Halpin, 1957; Rambo, 1958; Day and Hamblin, 1964; Anderson, 1966; Nealey and Blood, 1968; Rowland and Scott, 1968). Lowin (1969) found a positive relation for objectively manipulated Consideration in an experiment but not for subordinate ratings of Consideration. A significant negative relation was found by Halpin and Winer (1957) for aircraft commanders and by Fleishman, Harris, and Burtt (1955, p. 80) for foremen of production departments but not for nonproduction departments. In both of these studies, productivity was measured by superior ratings, and the highest ratings went to leaders low on Consideration but high on Initiating Structure. It is possible that the ratings were influenced more by the raters' task-oriented stereotype of the ideal leader than by actual group performance.

Turning to research on the relation between Initiating Structure and productivity, we again find mixed results. In a number of studies a significant positive relation was reported (Fleishman *et al.*, 1955; Likert, 1955; Halpin and Winer, 1957; Maier and Maier, 1957; Besco and Lawshe, 1959; Anderson, 1966; Nealey and Blood, 1968). For some subsamples in three of these studies, and for leaders studied by Argyle *et al.* (1958), Bass (1957), Halpin (1957), Rambo (1958), and Lowin (1969), a significant relation was not found. In no case was a significant negative relation reported.

It is unfortunate that so few investigators measured intermediate variables or tested for an interaction between Consideration and Initiating Structure. However, the few studies which are directly relevant to the proposed linkage model do provide supporting evidence. In a laboratory experiment in Japan, Misumi and Shirakashi (1966) found that leaders who were both task oriented and considerate in their behavior had the most productive groups. Halpin (1957) found that aircraft commanders were rated highest in effectiveness when they were about the mean on both Consideration and Initiating Structure. Hemphill (1957) obtained the same results for the relation between the behavior of department chairmen in a Liberal Arts College and faculty ratings of how well the department was administered. Fleishman and Simmons (1970) translated the Supervisory Behavior Description into Hebrew and administered this questionnaire to the superiors of Israeli foremen. Proficiency ratings for the foremen were also obtained from their superiors. Once again, the foremen with the best ratings tended to be high on both Consideration and Initiating Structure. Patchen (1962) found that personal production norms (i.e. task motivation) of workers were highest when the leader encouraged proficiency as well as "going to bat" for them. These production norms were related in turn to actual group production. Finally, although he didn't measure Consideration, Baumgartel (1956) found a significant positive relation between subordinate motivation and the concern of research laboratory directors for goal attainment (i.e. Initiating Structure).

Decision-centralization and productivity

Seventeen studies were found which examined the relation between Decision-Centralization and group productivity. A significant positive relation between participation and productivity was found by Bachman *et al.* (1966), Coch and French (1948), Fleishman (1965), French (1950), French, Kay, and Meyer (1966), Lawrence and Smith (1955), Likert (1961, p. 20), Mann and Dent (1954), McCurdy and Eber (1953), Meltzer (1956), and Vroom (1959). Argyle *et al.* (1958) found a positive relation only for departments without piece rates, suggesting that the organizational incentive system, a situational variable, interacts with Decision-Centralization in determining the subordinates' task motivation. Tosi (1970), French *et al.* (1960), and McCurdy and Lambert (1952) failed to find a significant relation between participation and productivity. In two other studies (Shaw, 1955; Morse and Reimer, 1956) a significant negative relation was found. Several of these studies demonstrate that various situational variables can moderate the effects of leader decision behavior on group performance. Nevertheless, the high percentage of studies reporting a positive relation is an indication that some degree of participation leads to an increase in group performance in most situations. However, this generalization is *not* equivalent to concluding "the more participation there is, the greater will be group productivity". For a particular group, there is probably some optimal pattern of decision-making which will consist of various amounts of delegation, joint decision-making, consultation, and autocratic decision-making (Heller and Yukl, 1969). The optimal pattern is likely to involve some intermediate amount of subordinate influence, rather than the greatest possible amount.

DISCUSSION

The Multiple Linkage Model and Fiedler's Contingency Model

A considerable number of leadership studies have been conducted by Fred Fiedler and his associates at the University of Illinois (Fiedler, 1967). Fiedler has developed a theory of leadership effectiveness to explain the results of this research. According to Fiedler's theory, group performance is a function of the interaction between the leader's "esteem for his least preferred co-worker" (LPC) and three situational variables: task structure, leader-member relations, and the position power of the leader. Leaders with low LPC scores have the most productive groups when the leadership situation, in terms of the three situational variables, is either very favorable or very unfavorable. Leaders with high LPC scores are more effective when the situation is intermediate in favorableness. Although Fiedler provides a behavioral explanation for these hypothesized relations, most of his studies did not measure leader behavior.

The few studies which have attempted to identify the behavioral correlates of LPC scores have not yielded consistent results (Sample and Wilson, 1965; Fiedler, 1967, p. 53; Nealey and Blood, 1968; Yukl, 1970; Gruenfeld, Rance, and Weissenberg, 1969; Reilly, 1969). Thus, it is not possible at this time to determine whether Fiedler's model is compatible with the proposed linkage model. Both theories are generally supported by their own separate bodies of empirical research. Reconciliation of the two approaches will probably require additional research which includes variables from both theories.

DIRECTION FOR FUTURE RESEARCH

The theoretical framework and the literature review presented earlier point out some empirical gaps which badly need filling. The central feature of the linkage model is the set of intermediate variables. A leader can do little to improve group productivity unless he can alter one or more of these variables. Yet the mediating role of these variables, their relation to each other, and their interaction in the determination of productivity have seldom been investigated in leadership studies. Future research should be more comprehensive in scope. Leader behavior variables, intermediate variables, situational variables, subordinate preferences, criterion variables (i.e. satisfaction and productivity), and relevant leader traits should all be included. Situational variables other than those discussed in this article also need to be investigated. Likely candidates are the organizational limiting conditions for participation suggested by Lowin (1968) and Strauss (1964), the structural variables found to be associated with leader decision behavior by Heller and Yukl (1969), the situational variables in Fiedler's model, the situational variables cluster-analyzed by Yukl (1969b), and Woodward's (1965) system for classifying production technology. Finally, the way in which the three behavior dimensions interact in determining the intermediate variables should be investigated. If possible, the leader behavior variables should be experimentally manipulated in order to avoid the measurement problems associated with leader behavior descriptions by subordinates.

The analysis of leader effectiveness has utilized leader behavior variables which maintain a basic continuity with traditional conceptualization and research. However, in speculating about future research, it is appropriate to evaluate the continued usefulness of these broadly defined behavior dimensions. It is obvious that Consideration and Initiating Structure are composed of relatively diverse elements, while Decision-Centralization is an average based on many different types of decisions. In order to improve the predictive power of the model, it may be necessary to identify which components of the behavior variables are the most important determinants of each intermediate variable.

The discrepancy model and the multiple linkage model provide only the skeleton of a static leadership theory which purposely ignores the additional complexities of feedback loops and circular causality. Much additional research and revision will be necessary to transform the skeleton into a full-fledged dynamic model which permits accurate predictions about leader effectiveness in formal task groups.

NOTES

1 The author is grateful to Ken Wexley and Alexis Anikeeff for their helpful comments.
2 Despite my preference for the term Decision-Centralization, the more familiar term participation will usually be used when discussing the direction of correlations in order to avoid confusion.
3 Significance levels for the correlations were not given, but judging from the sample sizes, they should all be significant at the .05 level or better.
4 The leader can also improve productivity by obtaining necessary information, resources, and cooperation from other organization members and outside agencies, but this involves leader behavior outside the context of the work group.

REFERENCES

ANDERSON, L. R. (1966) "Leader behavior, member attitudes, and task performance of intercultural discussion Groups", *Journal of Social Psychology*, **69**, pp. 305–19.

ARGYLE, M., GARDNER, G. and CIOFFI, F. (1957) "The measurement of supervisory methods", *Human Relations*, **10**, pp. 295–313.

ARGYLE, M., GARDNER, G. and CIOFFI, F. (1958) "Supervisory methods related to productivity, absenteeism, and labor turnover", *Human Relations*, **11**, pp. 23–40.

BACHMAN, J. G., SMITH, C. G. and SLESINGER, J. A. (1966) "Control, performance, and satisfaction: An analysis of structural and individual effects", *Journal of Personality and Social Psychology*, **4**, pp. 127–36.

BASS, B. M. (1957) "Leadership opinions and related characteristics of salesmen and sales managers", in Stogdill, R. M. and Coons, A. E. (eds.) *Leader Behavior: Its Description and Measurement*, Bureau of Business Research, Ohio State University.

BASS, B. M. (1965) *Organizational Psychology*, Allyn and Bacon.

BAUMGARTEL, H. (1956) "Leadership, motivations, and attitudes in research laboratories", *Journal of Social Issues*, **12** (2), pp. 24–31.

BEER, M. (1966) *Leadership, employee needs, and motivation*, Bureau of Business Research, Ohio State University, Monograph No. 129.

BERKOWITZ, L. (1954) "Group Standards, cohesiveness, and productivity", *Human Relations*, **7**, pp. 509–19.

BESCO, R. O. and LAWSHE, C. H. (1959) "Foreman leadership as perceived by supervisor and subordinate", *Personnel Psychology*, **12**, pp. 573–82.

COCH, L. and FRENCH, J. R. P. (1948) "Overcoming resistance to change", *Human Relations*, 1, pp. 512–32.

DAY, R. C. and HAMBLIN, R. L. (1964) "Some effects of close and punitive styles of supervision", *American Journal of Sociology*, 16, pp. 499–510.

FIEDLER, F. E. (1967) *A theory of leadership effectiveness*, McGraw-Hill.

FLEISHMAN, E. A. (1957a) "A leader behavior description for industry", in Stogdill, R. M. and Coons, A. E. (eds.) *Leader Behavior: Its Description and Measurement*, Bureau of Business Research, Ohio State University.

FLEISHMAN, E. A. (1957b) "The Leadership Opinion Questionnaire", in Stogdill, R. M. and Coons, A. E. (eds.) *Leader Behavior: Its Description and Measurement*, Bureau of Business Research, Ohio State University.

FLEISHMAN, E. A. (1965) "Attitude versus skill factors in work group productivity", *Personnel Psychology*, 18, pp. 253–66.

FLEISHMAN, E. A. and SIMMONS, J. (1970) "Relationship between leadership patterns and effectiveness ratings among Israeli foremen", *Personnel Psychology*, 23, pp. 169–72.

FLEISHMAN, E. A. and HARRIS, E. F. (1962) "Patterns of leadership behavior related to employee grievances and turnover", *Personnel Psychology*, 15, pp. 43–56.

FLEISHMAN, E. A., HARRIS, E. F. and BURTT, H. E. (1955) *Leadership and supervision in industry*, Bureau of Educational Research, Ohio State University, Research monograph No. 33.

FOA, U. G. (1957) "Relation of worker's expectations to satisfaction with his supervisor", *Personnel Psychology*, 10, pp. 161–8.

FRENCH, J. R. P. (1950) "Field experiments: Changing group productivity", in J. G. Miller (ed.) *Experiments in Social Process: A Symposium on Social Psychology*, McGraw-Hill.

FRENCH, J. R. P., ISRAEL, J. and AS, D. (1960) "An experiment on participation in a Norwegian factory", *Human Relations*, 13, pp. 3–19.

FRENCH, J. R. P., KAY, E. and MEYER, H. (1966) "Participation and the appraisal system", *Human Relations*, 19, pp. 3–20.

FRENCH, J. R. P. and RAVEN, B. (1959) "The bases of social power", in Cartwright, D. (ed.) *Studies in Social Power*, Institute for Social Research, University of Michigan.

GALBRAITH, J. and CUMMINGS, L. L. (1967) "An empirical investigation of the motivational determinants of task performance: Interactive effects between instrumentality-valence and motivation-ability", *Organizational Behavior and Human Performance*, 2, pp. 237–57.

GOMBERG, W. (1966) "The trouble with democratic management", *Transaction*, 3 (5), pp. 30–5.

GREER, F. L. (1961) "Leader indulgence and group performance", *Psychological Monographs*, 75 (12, Whole No. 516).

GRUENFELD, L. W., RANCE, D. E. and WEISSENBERG, P. (1969) "The behavior of task-oriented (low LPC) and socially-oriented (high LPC) leaders under several conditions of social support", *Journal of Social Psychology*, **79**, pp. 99–107.

HALPIN, A. W. (1957) "The leader behavior and effectiveness of aircraft commanders", in Stogdill, R. M. and Coons, A. E. (eds.) *Leader Behavior: Its Description and Measurement*, Bureau of Business Research, Ohio State University.

HALPIN, A. W. and WINER, B. J. (1957) "A factorial study of the leader behavior descriptions", in Stogdill, R. M. and Coons, A. E. (eds.) *Leader Behavior: Its Description and Measurement*, Bureau of Business Research, Ohio State University.

HELLER, F. and YUKL, G. (1969) "Participation, managerial decision-making and situational variables", *Organizational Behavior and Human Performance*, **4**, pp. 227–41.

HEMPHILL, J. K. (1957) "Leader behavior associated with the administrative reputations of college departments", in Stogdill, R. M. and COONS, A. E. (eds.) *Leader Behavior: Its Description and Measurement*, Bureau of Business Research, Ohio State University.

HEMPHILL, J. K. and COONS, A. E. (1957) "Development of the leader behavior description questionnaire", in Stogdill, R. M. and Coons, A. E. (eds.) *Leader Behavior: Its Description and Measurement*, Bureau of Business Research, Ohio State University.

JACOBSON, J. M. (1953) "Analysis of interpersonal relations in a formal organization", unpublished doctoral dissertation, University of Michigan.

KATZ, D., MACCOBY, N., GURIN, G. and FLOOR, L. (1951) *Productivity, Supervision, and Morale among Railroad Workers*, Survey Research Center, University of Michigan.

KATZELL, R. A. (1964) "Personal values, job satisfaction, and job behavior", in Borrow, H. (ed.) *Man in a World of Work*, Houghton Mifflin.

KAY, E., MEYER, H. H. and FRENCH, J. R. P. (1965) "Effects of threat in a performance appraisal interview", *Journal of Applied Psychology*, **49**, pp. 311–7.

KORMAN, A. K. (1966) "Consideration, initiating structure, and organizational criteria—A review", *Personnel Psychology*, **19**, pp. 349–62.

LAWRENCE, L. C. and SMITH, P. C. (1955) "Group decision and employee participation", *Journal of Applied Psychology*, **39**, pp. 334–7.

LEWIN, K. (1944) "The dynamics of group action", *Educational Leadership*, **1**, pp. 195–200.

LIKERT, R. (1955) "Developing patterns in management", in *Strengthening Management for the New Technology*, American Management Association.

LIKERT, R. (1961) *New Patterns of Management*, McGraw-Hill.

LOCKE, E. A. (1969) "What is job satisfaction?" *Organizational Behavior and Human Performance*, 4, pp. 309–36.

LOWIN, A. (1968) "Participative decision-making: A model, literature critique, and prescriptions for research", *Organizational Behavior and Human Performance*, 3, pp. 68–106.

LOWIN, A., HRAPCHAK, W. J. and KAVANAGH, M. J. (1969) "Consideration and Initiating Structure: An experimental investigation of leadership traits", *Administrative Science Quarterly*, 14, pp. 238–53.

MAIER, N. R. F. (1965) *Psychology in Industry*, Third ed., Houghton-Mifflin.

MAIER, N. R. F. and HOFFMAN, L. R. (1962) "Group decision in England and the United States", *Personnel Psychology*, 15, pp. 75–87.

MAIER, N. R. F. and MAIER, R. A. (1957) "An experimental test of the effects of 'developmental' vs. 'free' discussions on the quality of group decisions", *Journal of Applied Psychology*, 41, pp. 320–3.

MANN, F. C. and DENT, J. (1954) "The supervisor: Member of two organizational families", *Harvard Business Review*, 32 (6), pp. 103–12.

McCURDY, H. G. and EBER, H. W. (1953) "Democratic vs. authoritarian: A further investigation of group problem-solving", *Journal of Personality*, 22, pp. 258–69.

McCURDY, H. G. and LAMBERT, W. E. (1952) "The efficiency of small groups in the solution of problems requiring genuine cooperation", *Journal of Personality*, 20, pp. 478–94.

McMURRAY, R. N. (1958) "The case for benevolent autocracy", *Harvard Business Review*, 36 (1), pp. 82–90.

MELTZER, L. (1956) "Scientific productivity in organizational settings", *Journal of Social Issues*, 12 (2), pp. 32–40.

MISUMI, J. and SHIRAKASHI, S. (1966) "An experimental study of the effects of supervisory behavior on productivity and morale in a hierarchical organization", *Human Relations*, 19, pp. 297–307.

MORSE, N. (1953) "*Satisfaction in the white-collar job*", Institute for Social Research, University of Michigan.

MORSE, N. C. and REIMER, E. (1956) "The experimental change of a major organizational variable", *Journal of Abnormal and Social Psychology*, 52, pp. 120–9.

MULDER, M. and STEMERDING, A. (1963) "Threat, attraction to group and strong leadership: A laboratory experiment in a natural setting", *Human Relations*, 16, pp. 317–34.

NEALEY, S. M. and BLOOD, M. R. (1968) "Leadership performance of nursing supervisors at two organizational levels", *Journal of Applied Psychology*, 52, pp. 414–22.

NEWCOMB, T. H., TURNER, R. H. and CONVERSE, P. E. (1965) "*Social psychology*", Holt, Rinehart and Winston.

NEWPORT, G. (1962) "A study of attitudes and leadership behavior", *Personnel Administration*, 25 (5), pp. 42–6.

PATCHEN, M. (1962) "Supervisory methods and group performance norms", *Administrative Science Quarterly*, **7**, pp. 275–94.

PELZ, D. C. (1952) "Influence: A key to effective leadership in the first-line supervisor", *Personnel*, **29**, 209–17.

PORTER, L. W. (1962) "Job attitudes in management: I. Perceived deficiencies in need fulfillment as a function of job level", *Journal of Applied Psychology*, **46**, pp. 375–84.

RAMBO, W. W. (1958) "The construction and analysis of a leadership behavior rating form", *Journal of Applied Psychology*, **42**, pp. 409–15.

REILLY, A. J. (1969) "The effects of different leadership styles on group performance: A field experiment", Paper presented at the American Psychological Association Convention, Washington, D.C., 1 Sept. 1969.

ROSEN, R. A. H. and ROSEN, R. A. A. (1955) "Suggested modification in job satisfaction surveys", *Personnel Psychology*, **8**, pp. 303–14.

ROSS, I. C. and ZANDER, A. (1957) "Need satisfactions and employee turnover", *Personnel Psychology,* **10**, pp. 327–38.

ROWLAND, K. M. and SCOTT, W. E. (1968) "Psychological attributes of effective leadership in a formal organization", *Personnel Psychology*, **21**, pp. 365–78.

SALES, S. M. (1966) "Supervisory style and productivity: Review and theory", *Personnel Psychology*, **19**, pp. 275–86.

SAMPLE, J. A. and WILSON, T. R. (1965) "Leader behavior, group productivity, and rating of least preferred coworker", *Journal of Personality and Social Psychology*, **1**, pp. 266–70.

SCHACHTER, S., WILLERMAN, B., FESTINGER, L. and HYMAN, R. (1961) "Emotional disruption and industrial productivity", *Journal of Applied Psychology*, **45**, pp. 201–13.

SCHAFFER, R. H. (1953) "Job satisfaction as related to need satisfaction in work", *Psychological Monograph*, **67**, (14, Whole No. 364).

SCHOENFELD, E. (1959) "Authoritarian management: A reviving concept", *Personnel*, **36**, pp. 21–4.

SEASHORE, S. (1954) *"Group cohesiveness in the industrial work group"*, Institute for Social Research, University of Michigan.

SHAW, M. E. (1955) "A comparison of two types of leadership in various communication nets", *Journal of Abnormal and Social Psychology*, **50**, pp. 127–34.

SKINNER, E. W. (1969) "Relationships between leadership behavior patterns and organizational-situational variables", *Personnel Psychology*, **22**, pp. 489–94.

SOLEM, A. R. (1958) "An evaluation of two attitudinal approaches to delegation", *Journal of Applied Psychology*, **42**, pp. 36–9.

STANTON, E. S. (1962) "Which approach to management—democratic, authoritarian, or . . . ?" *Personnel Administration*, **25** (2), pp. 44–7.

STOGDILL, R. M., GOODE, O. S. and DAY, D. R. (1962) "New leader behavior description sub-scales", *Journal of Psychology*, **54**, pp. 259–69.

G

STOGDILL, R. M., GOODE, O. S. and DAY, D. R. (1963) "The leader behavior of corporation presidents", *Personnel Psychology*, **16**, pp. 127–32.

STOGDILL, R. M., GOODE, O. S. and DAY, D. R. (1964) "The leader behavior of presidents of labor unions", *Personnel Psychology*, **17**, pp. 49–57.

STRAUSS, G. (1964) "Some notes on power equalization", in Leavitt, H. J. (ed.) *The social science of organizations: Four perspectives*, Prentice-Hall.

TOSI, H. (1970) "A re-examination of personality as a determinant of the effects of participation", *Personnel Psychology*, **23**, pp. 91–9.

TANNENBAUM, A. S. (1954) "The relationship between personality and group structure", unpublished doctoral dissertation, Syracuse University.

TROW, D. B. (1957) "Autonomy and job satisfaction in task-oriented groups", *Journal of Abnormal and Social Psychology*, **54**, pp. 204–9.

VROOM, V. H. (1959) "Some personality determinants of the effects of participation", *Journal of Abnormal and Social Psychology*, **59**, pp. 322–7.

VROOM, V. H. (1964) "Work and Motivation", Wiley.

VROOM, V. H. and MANN, F. C. (1960) "Leader authoritarianism and employee attitudes", *Personnel Psychology*, **13**, pp. 125–40.

WOODWARD, J. (1965) *Industrial Organization: Theory and Practice*, Oxford University Press.

YUKL, G. A. (1969a) "Conceptions and consequences of leader behavior", paper presented at the annual convention of the California State Psychological Association, Newport Beach, January, 1969.

YUKL, G. A. (1969b) "A situation description questionnaire for leaders", *Educational and Psychological Measurement*, **29**, pp. 515–8.

YUKL, G. A. (1970) "Leader LPC scores: Attitude dimensions and behavioral correlates", *Journal of Social Psychology*, **80**, pp. 207–12.

3.2 Leadership Style, Confidence in Management, and Job Satisfaction

Philip J. Sadler

ABSTRACT

A sample of persons drawn from all functions and from all levels of two companies in the United Kingdom were invited to express a preference for one of four leadership styles—the *tells,* the *sells,* the *consults,* and the *joins.* Each respondent was then asked to state which style most closely described his own immediate manager. (Alternatively, he could reply that his own manager did not correspond at all closely to any of the styles.) These answers were then related to replies to other questions concerned with describing managerial behaviour and with measuring job satisfaction, satisfaction with the employing organisation, and confidence in management.

The results indicate that the four descriptions of leadership styles are meaningful to people. The consultative style was the one most consistently preferred. Most people were able to see their own managers as fitting one of the four descriptions. Those who felt that their own managers did not correspond at all closely to any one of the four styles showed least confidence in management and relatively low job satisfaction. Their descriptions of managerial behaviour show that they regard their bosses as weak, indecisive, inconsistent, incompetent, and lacking in human relations skills.

INTRODUCTION

The qualities of leaders and the processes of leadership have long been considered an important field for study, and from the beginnings of social psychology researchers have repeatedly explored this area. Early speculation about the personality traits or qualities of the successful leader has largely given way to the study of actual leadership behaviour and analysis of situational factors, such as the type of the group and the nature of the group's task.

Several of those who have studied leadership behaviour have sought to classify and categorise different approaches to leadership and different

---

Source: *The Journal of Applied Behavioral Science* (1970), Vol. 6, No. 1, pp. 3–19.

ways of exercising the leadership role. In studies of this kind the two leadership styles which have most often been identified and compared are usually described as "authoritarian" or "autocratic" on the one hand and "democratic", "consultative", "participative", or "permissive" on the other.

In 1939 and 1940 some classic experiments comparing these two leadership styles were carried out by Lewin, Lippitt, and White (White and Lippitt, 1959). Their first experiment compared "autocratic" and "democratic" styles; in the second experiment a third leadership style, described as "laissez faire", was included in the research design. In this latter study four groups of 11-year-old boys, matched as closely as possible in terms of personality and interests, were formed. Four adults acted as leaders of these groups, employing the autocratic, democratic, and laissez faire styles in rotation, so that every adult eventually employed each style in each group. In groups where the leader acted in an autocratic way all activities and methods were decided upon by him and he kept aloof from group members except when issuing orders or making decisions. In groups which were democratically led all decisions were made by group discussion, with the leader taking an active role as discussion leader. In the laissez faire groups the boys were left to make their own decisions, and the leader took no active part in the process.

The productivity of each group was measured by observing and estimating the percentage of time spent in "high activity involvement". When overall productivity ratings for the three groups were compared, the autocratic groups were found to be highest on quantity, while the democratically led groups were judged to have produced work of the highest quality.

One of the most striking findings of the study related to the behaviour of groups while the leader was absent. In the autocratically led groups productivity dropped sharply when the leader was out of the room. In the democratic groups there was virtually no change in the level of activity, while in the laissez faire groups productivity actually rose during the leader's absence.

This piece of research, although, undoubtedly a classic in its field, has been criticised on the grounds that the studies were carried out with schoolchildren and that the findings are of doubtful validity for adult leadership in the industrial field.

Among those who have been concerned with studying approaches to leadership in the industrial setting are McGregor and Blake. McGregor (1960) distinguishes between two kinds of leadership but bases his analysis not so much on the behaviour of leaders as on their beliefs and attitudes. He describes two opposing sets of beliefs. The first, Theory X, includes these assumptions:

The average human being has an inherent dislike of work and will avoid it if he can.

Because of this human characteristic of dislike of work most people must be coerced, controlled, directed, threatened with punishment, to get them to put forth adequate effort toward the achievement of organizational objectives.

The average human being prefers to be directed, wishes to avoid responsibility, has relatively little ambition, wants security above all.

The second, Theory Y, is characterised by these beliefs:

The expenditure of physical and mental effort in work is as natural as play or rest.

External control and the threat of punishment are not the only means for bringing about effort toward organizational objectives.

Commitment to objectives is a function of the rewards associated with their achievement.

The average human being learns under appropriate conditions not only to accept but to seek responsibility.

As McGregor points out, these two sets of assumptions involve very different implications for managerial leadership. Theory X, in fact, can be regarded as the rationale for the autocratic leadership style, while Theory Y forms the basis for democratic leadership.

Blake (Blake and Mouton, 1964) also initially hypothesises two approaches to executive leadership—"concern for production" and "concern for people". However, he puts forward the idea of measuring the *degrees of concern* under each heading on a nine-point scale and describes actual leader behaviour in terms of the degrees of each kind of concern that it exhibits. For example, 9.1 leadership shows maximum concern for production but minimum concern for people, while 1.9 leadership is the reverse. In theory this analysis enables 81 styles of leadership to be identified, but in practice Blake confines his categories to 9.1 and 1.9 as already described: 1.1, where concern is minimal both for production and people; 5.5, which represents compromise between the interests of production and the needs of people; and 9.9, which is characterised by maximum concern for production combined with maximum concern for people. It is of course this latter style which Blake holds out as the ideal. In a sense his analysis is an answer to those who charge the proponents of democratic leadership with being unrealistic idealists who ignore the fact that in practice decisions have to be made and work has to be done.

The classification of styles of leadership which has been adopted as the starting point for this research is based on one proposed by Tannenbaum and Schmidt (1958). They suggest that leadership behaviour varies along a continuum from "boss-centered leadership" at one extreme to "subordinate-centered leadership" at the other. As one moves along this continuum away from the boss-centered style of leadership the amount of authority and control exercised by the leader diminishes, while the amount of freedom granted to subordinates increases. For example, the authors describe decision-making behaviour as it occurs at various points in the range. Where leadership is extremely boss-centered the leader makes his own decisions and announces them to the group. As one moves along the continuum the degree of participation by subordinates in the decision-making process gradually increases until, under extremely subordinate-centered leadership, group members very largely make their own decisions within broad limits defined by the leader. They point out that extremely subordinate-centered leadership of this kind is only very rarely encountered in formal organisations.

The *Styles of leadership* film (1962) based on this analysis distinguishes four specific styles of leadership relating to points on the Tannenbaum-Schmidt continuum. These are:

1   The *tells* style. The manager who employs this style habitually makes his own decisions and announces them to his subordinates, expecting them to carry them out without question.
2   The *sells* style. The manager using this approach also makes his own decisions, but rather than simply announcing them to his subordinates he tries to persuade the latter to accept them. Recognising the possibility of resistance on the part of those who will be faced with the decisions, he seeks to reduce this by "selling" them.
3   The *consults* style. Where the manager uses this style he does not make his decision until he has presented the problem to members of the group and listened to their advice and suggestions. The decision is still his but he does not make it until he has consulted his staff.
4   The *joins* style. This approach to leadership involves delegating to the group (which includes the manager himself as a member) the right to make decisions. The manager's function is to define the problem and to indicate limits within which the decision must be made. Normally the decision will reflect majority opinion in the group once the problem has been freely discussed.

This film was shown to the members of a number of management courses at Ashridge Management College, Berkhamsted, Hertfordshire, England, during 1965 and 1966. It invariably generated lively discussions which centered around such questions as whether these four styles of leadership were recognisable in practice and, if so, whether they had different effects on efficiency and morale. Out of these discussions arose the idea of a piece of research designed to test the validity of these concepts in an industrial setting and to explore relationships between leadership style and employee satisfaction. In more precise terms, tentative answers were sought to the following questions:

1 Do people feel able to state a clear preference for one of the four styles?
2 Where preferences are expressed, what kind of leadership is most often preferred?
3 Do people see their own managers as exercising one of the four styles?
4 Where they do, which style is most frequently perceived?
5 What kinds of behaviour are associated with managers who are seen as exercising each of the four styles?
6 What kinds of behaviour are associated with managers who are not perceived as corresponding to one of the four types of leaders?
7 What are the relationships between people's perceptions of the leadership styles of their managers and:
   a. their job satisfaction?
   b. their satisfaction with the company as an employer?
   c. their confidence in their managers?
   d. their view of the helpfulness of the appraisal interviews conducted by their managers?
8 Irrespective of the particular style of leadership preferred or perceived, how much more satisfied are those who see their managers as exercising the style they prefer than those whose perceptions differ from their preferences?

METHOD

The data which form the basis of this paper were collected in a series of opinion surveys carried out on behalf of two related companies—one engaged in the marketing of data-processing equipment, office equipment, and computer services, and the other engaged in research and development in the computer field. In all, four separate surveys were carried out:

1 A survey of the opinions of the entire staff of the research and development company (n = 581);
2 A survey of salesmen concerned with data-processing equipment in the marketing company (n = 215);
3 A survey of systems analysts in the marketing company (n = 282);
4 A survey of all employees in computer service bureaux in the marketing company (n = 511).

This report is concerned with the analysis of replies to seven questions which formed part of a larger questionnaire containing 45 items. It is not possible to reproduce the questions in full in this article, but a brief indication of their content is given below.[1] They are listed in the same order in which they were presented to respondents.

Job satisfaction. This question called for an indication of attitude to the job on a five-point scale ranging from "I like it very much indeed" to "I dislike it".

191

Satisfaction with employing company. Respondents were invited to rate the organisation as a place to work on a five-point scale from "One of the best" to "One of the worst".

Confidence in immediate management. This called for people tò express a degree of confidence in their immediate managers on a four-point scale ranging from "A lot of confidence" to "No confidence".

Management characteristics. Respondents were shown a list of 20 items describing aspects of managerial behaviour ("Keeps you informed about company policies and operations", "Is fair to everybody", "Gives you enough responsibility", "Deals with work problems and crises effectively", and so on). They were invited to mark any which particularly applied to their own managers.

Preferred leadership style. The four styles suggested by Tannenbaum and Schmidt (1958) were described. They were not given any titles, but simply called Boss A, Boss B, Boss C, and Boss D. Respondents were asked to say under which boss they thought they would most enjoy working.

Perceived leadership style. Respondents were then asked to indicate to which of the four styles their own manager most closely corresponded. A fifth response category was, "He does not correspond at all closely to any of them".

Helpfulness of counseling and appraisal interview. Those who had been counseled by their managers within the previous 12 months were asked to say how helpful the interview had been. The scale ranged from "Very helpful" to "Did more harm than good".

The questionnaires were anonymous and completed voluntarily. Although people were asked some very pointed questions about their own managers, it was not possible to identify either the respondents or the particular managers referred to.

RESULTS

Preferred leadership style
Asked to express a preference for one of the four styles of leadership described in the questionnaire, respondents replied as follows:

	Men (n = 1,270) %	Women (n = 319) %
Tells	8	15
Sells	23	25
Consults	61	35
Joins	5	17
No reply	2	8

Among men, there is clearly a marked preference for the *consults* style, while both *tells* and *joins* find little favour. The fact that only 2% did not express a preference for a particular style implies that respondents saw the question as meaningful and regarded the descriptions of different types of leaders as reflecting real differences in leader behaviour.

The replies of women were more widely spread across the various styles. *Consults* is again the most favoured but in this case by a much smaller margin. On the other hand, higher proportions of women than men express preferences for the *tells* and *joins* styles.

Differences in perceptions by job

The sample was broken down into the following job groupings:

Managers (n = 126)
Engineers (n = 132)
Programmers (n = 219)
Systems analysts (n = 309)
Other computer personnel
  (n = 230)

Skilled engineering workers
  (n = 113)
Administrative personnel
  (n = 124)
First-line supervisors (n = 61)
Salesmen (n = 196)

1 First-line supervisors most frequently (18%) and engineers least frequently (5%) expressed preferences for the *tells* style.
2 *Sells* was most often preferred by first-line supervisors (31%) and by salesmen (30%) and least often by managers (16%) and skilled engineering workers (19%).
3 *Consults* was the most frequently preferred style in all groups. However, the proportion expressing this preference ranged from over two-thirds among managers, engineers, and programmers to less than half among administrative personnel, computer personnel, and skilled engineering workers.
4 The *joins* style was the least frequently preferred style in all groups with the exception of skilled engineering workers and computer personnel. In both groups 17 per cent expressed a preference for this style.

Perceived leadership styles

Respondents were next asked to state to which of the four styles their own immediate manager most closely corresponded. A fifth response category, "He does not correspond at all closely to any of them", was provided in this question.

The replies were distributed as shown below:

	Men (n = 1,270) %	*Women* (n = 319) %
Tells	18	29
Sells	24	14
Consults	26	14
Joins	5	6
None of these	24	24
No reply	3	13

193

Among the men very similar proportions (about 25%) perceive their managers as *selling, consulting,* and as not representative of any of the four styles. Only one in 20 perceives his manager as *joining.* The clear preference for the *consults* style is not therefore reflected in employees' perceptions of actual managerial behaviour.

Among women *tells* is the most frequently perceived style. As with the men, approximately one in four feels that her manager does not correspond closely to any one of the four styles.

Differences in perceived styles by job
The *tells* style is most frequently perceived by first-line supervisors (34%) and least often by systems analysts (11%).

The *consults* style is most frequently perceived by managers (36%), systems analysts (28%), and salesmen (27%) and least frequently by computer personnel (14%), first-line supervisors (15%), and skilled engineering workers (16%).

The *sells* style is most frequently perceived by managers (30%) and least often by skilled engineering workers (16%).

In no group was the *joins* style perceived by more than 8 per cent.

Particularly high proportions replying that their managers do not correspond to any one of the four styles were found among the professional-level engineers and engineering craftsmen and technicians.

It is interesting to speculate on the meaning of the reply, "He does not correspond at all closely to any of them". It may imply that the manager concerned does have a distinctive leadership style but one which does not fall under any of the descriptions given, or it may mean that the manager concerned has no style at all in the sense that his subordinates do not know what to expect of him. A third possibility is that the manager varies his style from one situation to another according to his view of what is appropriate. The next analysis throws some light on these possibilities.

Perceived leadership styles and characteristic managerial behaviour
Respondents were presented with a list of 20 statements which described possible managerial behaviour and were invited to mark any which they felt applied to their own manager. All 20 statements were favourable with the exception of one, "Has too much on his plate to manage you properly", which could be regarded as mildly critical.

The replies were analysed in relation to employees' perceptions of their own manager's leadership style. The results of this analysis involve considerable detail but can be summarised as follows:

1 Managers who *tell* receive the highest ratings for efficiency, discipline, and decisiveness, but achieve low scores on human relations items.
2 Managers who *sell* receive average scores on most items.
3 Managers who *consult* receive the highest ratings for helpfulness,

letting people know where they stand, helping people get ahead, inspiring subordinates with enthusiasm, building team spirit, being familiar with subordinates' work, and for forward planning, delegation, problem solving, and trust. They also achieve high scores on items reflecting efficiency.

4 Managers who *join* receive the highest ratings for consideration, fairness, ability to judge quality of subordinates' work, and for giving support and right amounts of praise and criticism. They receive generally low scores on efficiency items.

5 Managers not regarded as corresponding to any one of the four styles *receive the lowest ratings on all 19 favourable characteristics and the highest score on the one critical statement.* Scores were particularly below the norm on the following characteristics:

Letting people know where they stand;
Standing up for people;
Helping people get ahead;
Dealing with problems and crises effectively;
Running things efficiently;
Making decisions and standing by them;
Inspiring people with enthusiasm;
Giving the right amount of praise and criticism;
Building team spirit.

The results of this analysis fit in remarkably well with some of Blake's categories of leader (Blake and Mouton, 1964). The *tells* style, for example, which gets the highest score on efficiency and a low score on human relations, is very similar to his 9.1 style, showing maximum concern for production and minimum concern for people. The *sells* approach, with average scores all around, is not unlike Blake's 5.5 style, representing a compromise between the demands of production and the needs of people. The *joins* style, with high scores on human relations items and low scores on those reflecting efficiency, resembles his 1.9 approach—maximum concern for people and minimum concern for production. The 9.9 style—maximum concern for production and maximum concern for people—is exemplified by the *consults* type of leader who scores highly on both efficiency and human relations items. Finally, the manager who does not correspond closely to any of the four styles and who scores lowest on both efficiency and human relations statements appears to match Blake's description of the 1.1 leader, who exhibits minimum concern for both production and people.

Two conclusions can be drawn from this analysis. First, the way in which people allocate their own managers to one of the four leadership styles is meaningful and relates in the way one would expect to the more specific behavioural characteristics of their managers. Second, it is, on the whole, the manager who is regarded as weak, indecisive, inconsistent, and incompetent, as well as lacking in human relations skills, who cannot easily be classified in terms of the four leadership styles.

Perceived leadership style and job satisfaction
People were asked to indicate their level of job satisfaction. Their replies were analysed in relation to their perceptions of leadership style.

An index of job satisfaction was constructed from these replies in the following day. The most favourable response was given the weight 4 and the least favourable response the weight 0. Weighted mean scores for each group were then expressed as percentages of the maximum possible score. The indices of job satisfaction for each group perceiving a different leadership style were as follows:

Style of leadership preferred	Job satisfaction index
Tells (n = 320)	75
Sells (n = 352)	79
Consults (n = 367)	82
Joins (n = 79)	80
None of these (n = 381)	72
No reply (n = 81)	75

There is a statistically significant association between the style of leadership perceived and the level of job satisfaction. The *consults* style is associated with a high level of satisfaction, while the lowest level of satisfaction is found among those who consider that their manager does not correspond to any of the four styles.

Perceived leadership style and satisfaction with company as employer
A similar satisfaction index was constructed for a question which provides a measure of satisfaction with the employing company. The indices of satisfaction for each group perceiving a different leadership style are shown.

Style of leadership perceived	Company satisfaction index
Tells (n = 319)	82
Sells (n = 352)	85
Consults (n = 366)	87
Joins (n = 78)	85
None of these (n = 382)	80
No reply (n = 79)	75

The association between perceived leadership style and satisfaction with the employing company is significant. Once again, the highest level of satisfaction is associated with the *consults* style of leadership.

Perceived leadership style and confidence in management
A third index, of confidence in immediate management, was constructed, and the indices for each group perceiving a different style follow:

Style of leadership perceived	Confidence in management
Tells (n = 320)	64
Sells (n = 352)	72
Consults (n = 365)	75
Joins (n = 77)	61
None of these (n = 386)	49
No reply (n = 71)	68

The association between perceived leadership style and confidence in management is obvious. Managers who *consult* or *sell* inspire the highest levels of confidence, while a very low level of confidence is associated with those who cannot be classified under any one of the four styles. It is interesting to note that while those who see their managers as exercising the *joins* style have relatively high levels of job and company satisfaction their confidence in management is relatively low.

Perceived leadership style and helpfulness of the appraisal interview
Both companies in which the research was carried out operate a very similar staff counseling and appraisal system which involves each manager in carrying out an annual interview with his subordinates. The tabulation below shows the relationship between the perceived leadership style of a manager and the attitude of his subordinates to the helpfulness of this interview.

Style of leadership perceived	Percentage describing interview as "Not very helpful" or "Did more harm than good" %
Tells (n = 201)	29
Sells (n = 210)	29
Consults (n = 232)	27
Joins (n = 48)	27
None of these (n = 238)	45

The extent to which the interview is seen as unhelpful does not vary at all in relation to the particular leadership style of the appraiser. However, where the appraiser is not regarded as corresponding to any one of the four styles, the proportion regarding the interview as unhelpful is significantly higher.

Preferred style, perceived style, and job satisfaction
Thus far, in relating perceptions of leadership style to the criteria of

satisfaction, no account has been taken of the extent to which the styles that people perceive are the ones for which they have expressed a preference. For example, the generally higher levels of satisfaction among those who perceive the *consults* style may well be due in part to the fact that it is this group who are most likely to be receiving the style of leadership they prefer. The figures below show—for each group perceiving a particular leadership style—the percentage who had previously expressed a preference for that same style.

Style of leadership perceived	*Proportion preferring same style*
	%
Tells (n = 318)	21
Sells (n = 348)	40
Consults (n = 365)	77
Joins (n = 78)	32
None of these (n = 375)	—

Clearly, those who perceive the *consults* style are much more likely to be getting the kind of leadership they prefer than those who perceive the *tells* style. A further analysis has therefore been carried out for the job satisfaction criterion in which the relationship between preferences and perceptions is taken into account. The results are shown below:

	Job satisfaction index
Preferring and perceiving the *tells* style (n = 66)	80
Preferring and perceiving the *sells* style (n = 138)	83
Preferring and perceiving the *consults* style (n = 279)	83
Preferring and perceiving the *joins* style (n = 25)	81
Perceiving *tells* but preferring other styles (n = 251)	73
Perceiving *sells* but preferring other styles (n = 206)	78
Perceiving *consults* but preferring other styles (n = 96)	78
Perceiving *joins* but preferring other styles (n = 53)	77
Perceiving no particular style (n = 362)	72

No one particular style of leadership is more likely to be associated with high job satisfaction than any other, provided it be the preferred style of the persons perceiving it. Where the style a person perceives is not the same as the one he prefers, a lower level of satisfaction is associated with perceiving the *tells* style and with perceiving no particular style at all.

These results indicate, therefore, that style of leadership affects job satisfaction only in a negative sense. The *tells* style, for example, is only likely to produce a significantly lower level of job satisfaction when it is perceived by those who have expressed preferences for other styles.

SUMMARY AND CONCLUSIONS

The main conclusions indicated to date by this study follow.

1 The four descriptions of leadership styles are meaningful to people in that the vast majority are able to express a preference for one of them.

2 The consultative style of leadership is most often preferred.

3 Different patterns of preferences are held by different categories of employees.

4 Most people are able to describe their own managers in terms of one of the four styles. Approximately one in four, however, feels that his manager does not correspond closely to any one of them. Although three-fifths prefer consultative leadership, only one in four perceives his manager as exercising this style.

5 People's allocations of their managers among the four styles fit in very well with their descriptions of the behaviour of the same managers.

6 In general, managers who exhibit a distinctive style of leadership are more effective in promoting confidence and satisfaction among employees than managers who are not seen as having a distinctive style.

7 High job satisfaction is associated with being led in the way one prefers to be led. In interpreting this finding, the possibility that high job satisfaction in turn promotes satisfaction with leadership cannot be discounted.

8 Among those who feel that they are not receiving the type of leadership they prefer, the lowest level of job satisfaction is among those who perceive their manager as using the *tells* approach and those who feel that their manager displays no particular style.

Of these conclusions, perhaps the most significant is that leaders who are seen as having distinct and identifiable styles of leadership are more effective in promoting confidence and satisfaction, *whatever style they adopt,* than those who do not have a distinctive style. This suggests that one important characteristic of the successful leader is consistency of behaviour, which enables subordinates to know where they stand with him and to predict his actions and reactions. In relation to the implications which this has for management training, it would be useful in future research to focus attention more sharply on the group of managers lacking a distinctive style. It would be of value to know, for example, what their personal and background characteristics are and what attitudes and beliefs they hold about the managerial process. A controlled study to assess the effect of management training on the way managers are classified by their subordinates would also be likely to provide some interesting results.

The present research provides support for the widely held view of the superiority of the consultative style of leadership, since it is the only style to receive above average ratings on both efficiency and human relations criteria.

It must be stressed that the above conclusions are held to be valid only for the type of social climate typified by the two companies in which the research was carried out. These firms operate in a young and progressive industry and they employ a relatively high proportion of graduate and qualified manpower. The author's aim, therefore, is to repeat the investigation in other industries in order to extend the generality of the findings.

NOTE

1 Mimeographed tables showing the actual wording of the questions together with detailed results and tests of statistical significance are available on request from the author at Ashridge Management College, Berkhamsted, Hertfordshire, England.

REFERENCES

BLAKE, R. and MOUTON, JANE S. (1964) *The Managerial Grid*, Gulf.
McGREGOR, D. (1960) *The human side of enterprise*, McGraw-Hill.
Styles of Leadership (1962) 16mm. film, 3 reels, 26 min, B/w and color, Roundtable Productions (Room 333, 275 South Beverly Drive, Beverly Hills, California).
TANNENBAUM, R. and SCHMIDT, W. H. (1958) "How to choose a leadership pattern", *Harvard Business Review*, March-April 1958, **36** (2).
WHITE, R. and LIPPITT, R. (1959) "Leader behavior and member reaction in three social climates", in Cartwright, D. and Zander, A. (eds.) *Group Dynamics: Research and Theory*, Tavistock Publications.

3.3 Role Theory and Educational Administration

Peter S. Burnham

1

In the developing field of administrative theory, resulting in the main from the contributions of American social scientists working in a variety of organisational settings, the importance of role theory as a "tool of analysis" has been increasingly recognised. While not yet fully fledged and clearly defined (Biddle and Thomas, 1966), it has shown itself capable of throwing a good deal of light on the behaviour of people in the educational field, from teachers and deputy heads to principals and local authority administrators.

The concept of role has been widely used in the larger field of organisational theory (Hoyle, 1965). Institutions, such as colleges and schools, are organised agencies designed to carry out specialised tasks for the social system. Any organisational group facing a common task or problem will experience the need for certain identifiable functions to be performed. Rather than leave the performance of these behaviours to chance—as in the informal group—they are combined into separate "offices" and arranged in some form of organisational structure of positions. Institutional behaviour, then, may be thought of as being organised around offices or positions which are compounded of the various functions and behaviours vital to the well-being and purposes of the organisation.

These positions are collections of rights and duties, distinguished from one another, and designated by a title such as principal, deputy head or teacher. Other symbols of identification include dress or badge of rank, and the physical setting within which the incumbent operates: the teacher in his classroom, the caretaker in his boiler-room or the head in his study with a name-plate on the door. Positions are also defined by the social and educational attributes required to occupy the position (middle class values, a degree, wide experience, a teaching certificate); by psychological characteristics such as temperament or intelligence; and by the relationship to other people or positions (Oeser and Harary, 1962).

Source: George Baron and William Taylor (eds.) (1969) *Educational Administration and the Social Sciences*, Athlone Press, pp. 72–94.

Within the organisation, positions are ordered hierarchically in terms of status, and may be thought of as locations on an organisational chart.

Associated with every position in an organisation is a set of expectations concerning what is appropriate behaviour for a person occupying that position, and these "appropriate behaviours" comprise the role associated with the office. In order to differentiate these two terms—position and role—one might say that a person *occupies* a position but *plays* or *performs* a role (Levinson, 1959). A role is the dynamic aspect of a position (Linton, 1952).

Each role incumbent is expected to perform certain kinds of functions, and to act in certain specific and differentiated ways in his relations with the persons with whom he interacts. For a head, these include pupils, parents, teachers and other heads.[1] The concepts of role and role expectation thus provide one way of thinking about administrative behaviour. In this sense, administration can be seen as the process of defining, allocating and integrating roles and personnel to maximise the probability of achieving the goals of the organisation (Hills, 1960). Clearly, the role expectations must be oriented towards such ends. It is these normative behavioural expectations which represent the institutional (or what has been called the nomothetic) dimension of behaviour within an organisation (Getzels, 1963).

The role is linked with position and not with the person who is only "temporarily" occupying that position. However, as each person occupying a position brings his own individual personality to bear on the role, actual role performance may be thought of as a fusion of role expectations and "self".[2] In this way, as Getzels (1958) points out, each individual stamps the particular role he plays with the unique style of his own personality. Hence, while *what* one is expected to do is prescribed, *how* one actually plays the role will be distinguished by personal nuances. So, just as the institution can be defined by positions, roles and role expectations, individuals can be defined by their personalities and need-dispositions. This personal aspect of an organisation is referred to as the idiographic dimension.[3]

It is obvious that administrators need to take both role and personality into account when allocating persons to positions within the organisation, if they are to deal with the factors which contribute to conflict, efficiency and job satisfaction. It is far more than a once-and-for-all fitting of round pegs into round holes, for the playing of a role is both dynamic and creative.

If they are to maximise the staffing potential within the institution and create an organisation that is both efficient and effective, administrators need to encourage the creative fusion of personality and role among their staff, to reinforce those personality attributes which enhance the roles particular individuals are playing, and to make wise "marriages" between personalities and positions. Effectiveness can be held to relate to the co-operative achievement of organisational goals and is thus institutional and non-personal in character; efficiency can be held to relate to the satis-faction of individual needs and is personal in character (Barnard, 1938). It is the function of the administrator to secure the right balance between these two dimensions; it is not sufficient that he concerns himself with nomothetic considerations alone. As Westwood (1966) has pointed out, neither the nomothetic leader (the tough bureacratic boss) stressing insti-tutional requirements, procedures and rules, nor the idiographic leader (the easy going head whose paramount concern is the contentment of his staff) emphasising the interests, needs and personalities of the staff, is necessarily appropriate. What seems to be required is the "transactional" leader, who achieves and maintains the necessary equilibrium in the organisation (Getzels, Lipham and Campbell, 1968). In a large school, for example, this may be the function of the total *leadership situation* towards which a number of positions will be contributing (the deputy head, senior mistress, housemasters, heads of departments, and so on, as well as the head).

A major part of the administrator's job is to stake out the differentiated roles of the staff in such a way as to make the best match between institutional demands and staff personality needs (Campbell, 1964b). Who is to take 4c and who 1A? Who is to be careers master and who the year master of the first form? In a college of education who should be nominated as Chairman of the Academic Review Board, who upgraded as senior woman tutor to deal with the students' personal problems, and who selected as co-ordinator of the professional studies? As schools and colleges become bigger and more complex, differentiation of function increases, calling for further role specification. What used to be done by one person is now a job for two or three. Administrators need periodi-cally to re-define the roles in a changing instituition, to expand certain roles to cover behavioural gaps in the task structure, to be aware of role confusion or role ambiguity, and to arbitrate in cases of dispute over role demarcation.

In these days of social change, educational innovation and school re-organisation, there is a recurring need for the educational administrator to be both vigilant and sensitive regarding the role fabric of his school or college organisation. For instance, the introduction of ancillary staff into schools has led to the increased interaction of professional and artisan roles (science master and lab technician; games master and groundsman; duty teacher and dinner lady), heightening the possibility of role conflict in the institution. The introduction of auxiliary staff into schools on a greater scale than at present (teachers' aides and part-time helpers) and the possible differentiation of the teaching force itself into generalists and specialists or in the team teaching situations associated with inter-disciplinary enquiry, may create many new and delicate role definition problems for the head. Often there is little or no tradition to help in these matters.

Campbell notes that specialist positions within the large school have highly differentiated roles and the incumbents tend to perceive the organisation in the light of their own discriminative needs, interests and knowledge. The sixth form physics master may have little interest in, or patience with, the needs and problems of the teacher of the slow learners; or the French expert in his language laboratory with the concerns of the nongraduate careers master grappling with the vocational aspirations of the lower streams. Instead of dealing with fairly diffuse and generalised roles among which teachers are easily interchangeable—as in the primary school or the old elementary school—the secondary school head is challenged with finding ways of understanding and utilising dozens of specialists, with defining their roles, and with mediating the bird's-nest tangle of differing and often conflicting expectations. Increased school size supports a more complex division of labour, bringing into the school a more heterogeneous array of highly trained specialists who desire and are competent to exercise independent judgment within their realms of expertise (Charters, 1964). Yet these very same forces increase the necessity of delimiting the autonomy of such persons in the interests of co-ordination. The resolution of this dilemma is one of the important challenges confronting the educational administrator. Role specification, or the outlining in detail of the rights, privileges and responsibilities of each position, and role co-ordination, are major organisational tasks.

A changing school environment demands a changing school (Herriott and St. John, 1966). The change from grammar school to comprehensive school—from a clientele largely aspiring towards middle class values to one including a sizeable proportion with working class values—necessitates more than a change of methods and procedures. The teachers need to take on new role elements; to adjust their attitudes and expectations; and to re-formulate their objectives and approaches. The head must diagnose the changing needs of the pupils and effect the necessary adjustments to the role structure of the school, leading the teachers to understand and accept a new interpretation of their role. And because schools are embedded in a culture with both local and national orientations, it is essential that the roles created shall be consonant with a wide spectrum of social and individual needs.

The genius of administration, according to Nolte (1966), lies in this endless process of diagnosing, defining, classifying and interpreting roles, in the context of an intimate knowledge of the personalities of a large and varied staff. It is a competency which requires to be based on a clear understanding of the social and educational goals of the institution, a thorough analysis of the jobs to be done, and a perceptive awareness of the interests, skills and idiosyncrasies of the staff.

2

A role, then, is concerned with what a person does, whereas role expectations consist of shared attitudes held by persons defining the role— attitudes about what a role occupant should or should not do

(Lieberman, 1956). However, it is not the formal system alone which sets up role expectations; individuals and groups within the informal system also play a considerable part. As the teachers interact with one another in the gossip groupings of the staffroom, as they meet in their friendship groups at social evenings and in their homes outside school, as they knock up against one another in the daily routine of school life, so the pointed comments and asides build up a climate of expectations about colleagues. It is a commonplace of the organisational scene to talk about "the old man". Turner (1962) has said that the formalised roles are to the full roles as detonators to explosives, merely devices to set them off. This is particularly true of those roles which involve close and/or friendly contact with the staff, parents or children, such as the head, the deputy head, the school secretary and the school counsellor. The administrator is thus not the only person who defines roles in the institution, though he may be the first and the most decisive.

Three important factors can be said to have relevance for the structure of role expectations. First, apprehension of the expectations of others, awareness of just how one is supposed to behave, will depend on the role incumbent's perceptual acuity and accuracy (Argyle, 1952; Brookover, 1955). The finer points of a role definition may be acquired only by a perceptually sophisticated person able to "read" the fleeting or esoteric cues and gestures: the smile, the pause, the significance of the raised eyebrow, the meaningful absence of a member of staff, and such subtle responses to one's first tentative steps in the role. Each tiny cue and response acts as a gentle shaper of the role incumbent's behaviour. At first, only the iceberg-tip of a role prescription will be spelled out; at the interview for the job, during the initial briefing sessions, and in the duty rostas and standing orders on the staff notice-board. A few salient "boundary-stones" will be set out, the rest being left for the individual to find out in more informal ways; this "filling-in" stage being high on the list of priorities for the newcomer to any organisation. In some cases, helping the new member of staff to fit in may be a responsibility attached to the role of the deputy head as social-emotional leader of the informal system; in others, it may be carried out even more informally by an experienced and friendly colleague.

It is at this stage that the administrator must be aware of the significance of his own behaviour to a newcomer eager to do the right thing, in that his every gesture and response will be analysed for clues as to his degree of approval or disapproval. For a head to forget to greet a young teacher with his first name, or to fail to notice him when passing in the corridor, may be enough to trigger off in the young teacher a long and searching review of his recent role behaviour. The head, himself, should also be concerned to "read" the responses of his staff to ascertain whether he is meeting their expectations for administration or leadership.

Second, the intensity or narrowness with which an expectation is defined will range from "strongly required" or "must" at one end of the continuum, to "prohibited" or "must not" at the other, with an indeterminate area of tolerated or openly permissive behaviour in between (Levinson, 1959). For instance, the head may be strongly required by the teachers to keep parents away from the classrooms; the teachers may be strongly required by the head to leave the staffroom when the bell rings; parents may be prohibited from entering school premises; and the teachers' code may require that they must not criticise a colleague in the presence of other staff or children. About these more extreme role prescriptions, there will usually be little doubt. However, the teacher might experience considerable difficulty in determining whether he may or may not (as *he* pleases) wear a bright red shirt to school, join the local Labour club, teach with his coat off, or smoke as he goes about the school; the head as to whether he may or may not (as *he* pleases) go into the staffroom for a chat on other than formal occasions, be an irregular church-goer, or decline to participate in local community affairs. In all such cases, the newcomer will need to explore his role in a very chary "now I am warm, now I am cold" way.

The third important factor having relevance for the structure of role expectations, is the role incumbent's perceptions of the legitimacy or illegitimacy of the expectations of others to which he is exposed. Gross, Mason and McEachern (1958) define a legitimate expectation as one which the incumbent of a position feels others have a right to hold. At one time, if the principal and staff of a teacher training college held strong expectations for the personal and social behaviour of the students, an example of which might be the requirement that they be in their beds with lights out by a fixed time in the evening, these were perceived as legitimate by the students of the day. Now, in a different social climate, such expectations would be rejected as illegitimate by most students and seen as a violation of their personal freedom. In the same way, head-teachers sometimes require certain responses from their staff that may not be construed as legitimate by the staff. In one school, the head strongly required the men teachers to wear a suit with the middle button done up, much to the dismay and annoyance of a number of young teachers who did not concede that this was a legitimate expectation. In a changing society, there is obviously considerable scope here for conflict and dissatisfaction among staff. Even changes in teaching methods may give rise to difficulties of this kind; for instance, certain teachers who have grown up with the belief that "pedagogic isolation" is a right may feel that it is illegitimate to be expected to teach with other teachers present, as in team-teaching.

To the extent that the role incumbent conforms to the expectations for his position, so he permits the other people with whom he interacts to anticipate his behaviour. In this way, he enables them to respond adequately. Roles are complementary and interdependent, in that each and every role derives its meaning from other related roles in the organisation. What is seen as a "right" for one role may be prescribed as an "obligation" for a related role; and conversely, the "obligation" of one role may be the "right" of a colleague. Rights may be thought of as the behaviours "due" to the role incumbent; obligations the behaviours he "owes" to the occupants of related positions. To the extent that he meets with the expectations directed at him, so the rights associated with his role will be accorded; to the extent that he fails to meet with the expectations, so his rights will be withdrawn (Lieberman, 1956). In this sense, the role behaviours of related positions act as role sanctions for the individual. As we have already noted, should the head of a school fail to meet with the legitimate expectations of the teachers, examples of which might be the requirement that he consults them over important matters or sets an acceptable tone for the school, then the teachers may decide to disavow some of their obligations towards the head and withdraw their support for his policies. They may decide to "work to rule" and carry out only the mandatory behaviours. It can be seen from this that a head's authority really lies in the teachers' evaluations of his behaviour; the head must clearly earn his authority. Bates (1957) states that it is the anticipatory nature of role reciprocity which enables the interacting individuals in an organisation to articulate their roles, and to function collectively as an integrated unit.

3

Any individual will have a whole series of role relationships based on the many roles he plays in society. In addition to his professional role, the headmaster may also play the roles of husband, father, uncle, lay preacher, examiner, secretary to the local tennis club, freemason, and so on. This collection of roles Merton (1957a) called the "status-set", and it is clear that these multiple roles can present many problems of compromise and co-ordination. The head may find it difficult to reconcile the competing role expectations for his behaviour associated with the widely different positions he occupies. As a professional person, he will give precedence to the occupational role, but this may still leave him with role problems. If he lives in the school community, he may find that he is expected to take on various "outside" roles conditional upon his being head of the school, such as those of church elder or chairman of the fete committee. It is for this reason that some headteachers withdraw completely from the local community in order to compartmentalise the role of the head, and limit the strain resulting from too extensive a repertoire for the role.

However, with regard solely to his professional position, the administrator will be involved in a whole series of role relationships (Southall, 1959). His position might be visualised as at the centre of a web of relationships, a pattern referred to by Merton (1957b) as the "role-set". For the head of a school, the role-set would include the director of education, the inspectorate, the staff of the school (though here one might easily find the staff divided into several "audience groups"), the caretaker, the deputy head, the school secretary, the children, the parents, the governors and the community as a whole through its various committees and pressure groups.

Obviously, some expectations are more directly and importantly involved than others; some will come from superiors and some from subordinates; some from people with whom the head is in constant touch and some from those in peripheral positions. The basic problem is one of integrating the role expectations of all the members of the role-set. It is clear that there exists in the role-set a considerable potential for differing, conflicting and, sometimes, quite incompatible role expectations. Gross, Mason and McEachern (1958) found that superintendents of schools were faced with conflicting expectations from parents, teachers and school boards. In a study of the role of the deputy head, Burnham (1964) discovered that heads and teachers were perceived as holding quite contrary expectations for the deputy head's role. The heads were perceived by the deputy head as wanting him to engage in behaviour concerned with school organisation, such as timetable making or assigning teachers to school duties, while the teachers were perceived as wanting him to carry out behaviours manifesting concern for them, such as listening to their problems or relaying their suggestions to the head.

This last study shows that the concept of role is further complicated by the fact that the expectations are not necessarily simple and direct in form. What counts is not only what teachers, governors, parents and others in the role-set *really* expect of the head, or what they *say* they expect, but what the head *perceives* them to be expecting—a fact which is often at the bottom of many of the misunderstandings that occur in organisations. It is at this point, also, that the possibility exists of "perceptual seduction" in that factors such as power, high status, propinquity, affiliation and the threat of sanctions, may "persuade" the role incumbent to perceive one set of expectations as being more legitimate than another, irrespective of any objective importance or relevance. The administrator is constantly faced with the difficulty of assessing the legitimacy of expectations, and the relative weightings which are to be given to different sets of expectations, and he must be vigilant in guarding against perceptual distortion.

There is also the complication that the concept of role has to be considered from three different points of view (Levinson, 1959). First of all, in the sense that we have already been discussing it, are the *role demands* emanating from the role-set which seek to channel, guide, support, adjust and prescribe the behaviour of a position. Second, there is the individual's own inner definition of the role or *role conception,* what he personally and ideally thinks he ought to do. Third, there is the actual *role performance* or observed behaviours resulting from the interaction of the role demands, the individual's role conception and the characteristics of his personality. Many deputy heads, after adjusting their role performance to meet the perceived role demands of their headteachers, found that their greatest source of conflict lay in the disparity between this actual role behaviour and their ideal conception of the role (Burnham, 1964). It is at this point that we realise how great is the propensity for conflict in any role, but particularly for those with a wide and varied role-set, such as that faced by the administrator of a large institution.

The leadership role in schools and colleges is particularly vulnerable to role conflict. Perhaps the simplest kind of conflict situation, and certainly the one viewed most apprehensively by the administrator, is that between role expectations and personality (Getzels, 1963). Many aspiring teachers must have wondered if they were going to be able to live up to the role expectations associated with the job of head. The primary aim of most interviewing committees would seem to be that of selecting on the basis of personality relative to the needs of "leadership". In some organis- ations, quite elaborate personality tests and structured situations are used to select those most fitted temperamentally and psychologically for the top jobs. Yet the trait approach to leadership has been shown to be inadequate and unproven. Studies of leaders in different situations have failed to discover any particular syndrome of personality traits that regu- larly characterise such individuals and differentiate clearly between leaders and non-leaders (Stogdill, 1948; Gibb, 1954). This does not mean, of course, that personal qualities are not relevant to the adminis- trator role. Clearly, administrative style is likely to depend a good deal on personality.

The possibility that personality may conflict with role expectations in the school can be seen when one imaginatively considers the case of the gentle natured, easy-going head of a small village school suddenly promoted into a bigger and tougher urban school, being forced by the situational expectations to adopt a tough-minded, more authoritatian manner. If one looks at the role of the teacher, it is possible to sympathise with the rather traditional and authoritarian old-timer trying to "maintain standards" in a school de-streamed by a new and permissive headmaster.

Lipham (1960) showed that principals of schools were expected to exert themselves energetically, to strive for higher status, and to relate themselves successfully to other people—situations requiring high levels of drive, social ability, mobility and emotional control. The study sug- gested that persons having a basic personality structure characterised by such needs and dispositions would suffer less strain in fulfilling the head's role.

Psychologically distant heads of task groups were shown by Fiedler (1960) to be more effective than heads who tend towards warmer and psychologically closer relations with subordinates. He maintains that it is for this reason that in large organisations intercourse between leaders and followers is limited by an elaborate system of rules and institutionalised barriers (Fiedler, 1957). In a school or college, these might include such

209

things as a separate toilet for the head, separate arrangements for tea-breaks, a personal study distant from the staffroom, a secretary to "bar the way", a rule or understanding that the head is only available to staff at certain times, and a notice-board for the head's communications. Fiedler goes on to point out that while it is commonly thought that these barriers exist to prevent subordinates becoming too familiar with the head, they primarily serve to protect the head from emotional involvement with the staff. The leader is then less likely to have the opportunity to form close friendships which could lead to favouritism towards some and poor discipline among the rest. Should he do so, he would find it difficult to reach unpopular decisions uninfluenced by his feelings. An emotionally dependent head is easily exploited by his staff.

It would seem that an administrator must choose whether he is to fulfil his own individual personality needs or the institutional requirements of his role. To try to satisfy both is to increase the possibility of role strain. However, if he chooses simply to indulge his own needs, he is likely to be an unsatisfactory administrator and thus fail to meet the expectations of the role-set; if he chooses to fulfil the requirements of his role to the letter, he may well be frustrated personally. In his study of school executives, Seeman (1960) concludes that there is a danger that heads may come to be alienated from their staff (and often from themselves as persons), for "to the leader we seem to offer position and advancement at a minimum cost of isolation".[4]

If we examine a second major type of conflict situation, we shall find that a good deal of the conflict in the leadership role is rooted in the norms and values of society. These cultural imperatives impose mutually conflicting demands with which institutional leadership must deal (Seeman, 1953). First, there is the conflict between the success ideology and the equality ideology, whether in relation to staff or pupils. On the one hand, the head is expected to stress competition, differentiation of staff and pupils, rank orders and mark-lists, job techniques, rewards and punishments, talk about the job, and task goals; on the other hand, to emphasise shared feelings, mutual support, friendship groupings, personal interests and social functions.

Second, there is the conflict between the needs for dependence and independence. While some teachers are submissive and like to be told what to do, others demand more independence, initiative and personal responsibility. But as we have seen, too much autonomy among teachers in a large school can give rise to problems of control and co-ordination for the head.

Third, the head is often faced with the choice between *universalistic* as against *particularistic* criteria for his behaviour. As a key figure in the distribution of resources and sanctions, the head must operate from a universalistic frame of reference, in that he must treat everyone alike, be seen to be fair and just, and have no personal favourites. If the school is to avoid having "blue-eyed boys", "inner cabinets" and "creepers", the head must renounce too intimate ties with his staff. Much as the head might like to assess and relate to members of staff in particularistic terms, as "friends", he is forced to judge them according to such universalistic criteria as professional qualifications and job competence. Getzels (1952) suggests that in large bureaucratic organisations, the allocation of roles is made according to universalistic criteria, and not, as in very small schools, on more personal grounds. With the bureaucratisation of comprehensive schools, the trend is likely to be towards universalistic principles of organisation which may involve heart-searching conflict situations for the head, as in taking old Tom off the important examination work because he is so out of date, or in giving the headship of an expanding department to a young newcomer over the heads of two or three established old-timers.[5]

One might also point to the conflict that exists between the motivation of the staff, requiring warm and encouraging support, and their organisation for work and assessment for promotion or report, requiring a cool objectivity and differentiation based on job performance (Wilson, 1962). These two aspects are similar to the two main leader-behaviour factors teased out by Halpin and Winer (1957) from the Ohio State University Leader Behaviour studies. (See also Stogdill, Scott and Jaynes, 1956; Stogdill and Shartle, 1955.) They suggested that "initiating structure", or behaviours indicating that the leader was organising, defining roles and establishing new ways of getting things done, and "consideration", or behaviours indicative of warmth, friendship and mutal trust in the relationship between the leader and his staff, accounted for 83 per cent of the total leader behaviour variance. These two leadership roles seem to be linked to the two major goals of any organisation, namely, goal achievement and group maintenance. It is suggested that specialists in these functions emerge, one the task leader and the other the social-emotional leader (Cartwright and Zander, 1960).

In his study of the role of the deputy head in secondary schools, Burnham (1968) suggests that the leadership role in a large school might be divided into its instrumental and expressive aspects, the head concentrating on the task functions while the deputy head fulfils the social-emotional leadership role. In a large organisation, for a number of cogent reasons, such as the very different personality attributes required for each of these two specialist roles and the increasing amount of time needing to be spent on each area of behaviour, these two aspects of leadership are basically incompatible. However, the two leaders can constitute a dominant or central pair, supporting each other, and dividing between them the performance of the behaviours needed for leadership in the instrumental and expressive areas of the organisation (Bales and Slater, 1956). It would seem that the administration of schools and colleges would be much improved if there was a greater realisation and awareness of the functional aspects of such a leadership alliance.[6]

In a very large school, both the instrumental and expressive functions of the leadership role may be further differentiated, certain elements of each being delegated to other senior members of staff. The instrumental function might be divided between the head and a "procedural" deputy responsible for detailed organisation; while the expressive function might be shared by a number of people, including the deputy head, the senior mistress, the housemasters, and the school counsellor. (It would seem that the title of deputy head is rapidly becoming obsolescent when leadership is viewed in this functional way.) The extension of the leadership role into a more complicated leadership pattern involving several senior administrators does not alter the basic principle that all concerned should form a co-operating and supportive leadership coalition.

Lastly, in the field of role conflict there is the conflict which results from the clash of divergent expectations from members of the role-set. Seeman (1953) highlighted the clash between those expectations of teachers for the administrator which stressed the instrumental aspects of his role, and those which emphasised the expressive aspects. In his study of Ohio school superintendents, Seeman showed that those superintendents who were most successful in securing salary increases for the teachers—and one can assume that this is a permanent expectation— were described by these same teachers as men who did not spend enough time in personal contact with them. The superintendents were perceived as "stand-offish". With a limited amount of time at his disposal, the administrator may have to decide whether to carry out the instrumental functions of his role or engage in expressive contact with his staff.

A number of situations come to mind manifesting divergent sets of role expectations for the head. The young teachers on a staff may expect the head to delegate responsibility and encourage innovation, whereas the old guard may want him to leave them alone and maintain the traditions of the past. There will be those on the staff who stress to the head the importance of informal activities, such as school outings and concerts, much to the annoyance of those who want the school to concentrate on the formal task of preparing children for examinations and vocational requirements. Some teachers may expect the head to visit their classrooms to see what is going on, and to offer help and advice, while others would rather he left them alone, trusting them as professional people. In a college of education setting, one can see that the principal may be expected to emphasise academic education by some of the staff and by the university boards of studies, but by others on the staff and by the representatives of practising teachers in the schools to stress practical teaching and classroom know-how.

4

Finally, we might differentiate between the "leadership" and "administrative" aspects in the role of the administrator of an organisation (Lipham, 1964). While these behaviours are different in orientation, they are, nevertheless, integral parts of a broadly conceived administrator-role, and both aspects are concerned with the achievement of the goals and objectives of the institution. As Taylor points out in Chapter 6, the head of a school ". . . not only administers but also makes policy—sometimes with only a minimum of consultation with those most likely to be affected"—and needs to develop an ". . . understanding of how educational objectives are defined and the means whereby resources may be organised to achieve them".

We have seen that "leadership" is associated with those behaviours which are concerned with initiating new structure and procedures within the organisation for accomplishing or changing the goals of the institution. It is an important part of the head's job to diagnose the needs of the school and to identify new educational objectives. In this role as a "leader", the head would be carrying out the functions of an innovator. In that sense, he would be playing a role that is somewhat disruptive of the *status quo*.

When the administrator is emphasising the "administrative" aspect of his role, he will be concerned with making use of existing structure and procedures to achieve the goals of the institution. He concentrates upon maintaining and strengthening rather than changing the established arrangements within the organisation. Hence, in his role as an "administrator" the head is a stabilising force, a traditionalist, and in that sense, a "conformist".

We can now see that the "administrative-leadership" dimension gives rise to a basic paradox in the role of the head of an organisation. At one time, as Lipham puts it, he must wear an "administrative hat", and at other times, a "leadership hat"—the expectations for his behaviour on many occasions seeming to be quite self-contradictory. Having but one head, he has to be aware of which hat he *is* wearing and, in the context of the situational needs of the organisation, he must decide which hat he *should* be wearing, a decision that clearly requires very great understanding and insight. He must judge when it is more appropriate to move towards change and development, and when it is more politic to integrate changes and consolidate the organisation. To play the role of leader too long, or too often can be dysfunctional for the organisation in that it is likely to impose too great a strain. It is in the making of such decisions that one distinguishes the wise administrator.

It follows, then, that it is for the administrator to determine when he should "administrate" and when he should "lead". The extent to which he carries out these two functions will be determined by his diagnosis and assessment of the school and its task in the social setting. The situation may well vary from term to term. The introduction of comprehensive schools, the upsurge of curriculum reform, the awareness of new vocational and parental expectations, and the recruitment of new members of staff, will all necessitate change in the institution. At such times, a good deal of leadership will be expected of the head.

In defining their concept of *executive professional leadership*, Gross and Herriott (1965) consider that the head needs to keep up with current thinking and research as the intellectual leader of the school; to study the latest methods of teaching, and to work closely with the staff to effect curriculum innovation, as the pedagogic leader of the school; while as educational leader his chief function is to identify problems, co-ordinate the various aspects of new ventures in the school, and consult with individual teachers and groups of teachers regarding their problems.

Whereas leadership may be required only on occasions, administration is a constant requirement. As an administrator, the head is responsible for managing a largely professionally staffed organisation, and for operating a rationally contrived set of arrangements whereby problems can be discovered and discussed, and decisions made. Amongst other duties, he will be responsible for planning, organising, directing, co-ordinating, communicating, decision-making, budgeting, reporting, allocating resources and evaluating (Gulick and Urwick, 1966; Gregg, 1957; Griffiths, Hemphill *et al.*, 1961). In carrying out such duties, he will need to relate to such people as inspectors and organisers, school health service personnel, officials at county hall, school meals staff, the caretaker and the school secretary, local bigwigs, publishers' representatives and so on. Not surprisingly, the teachers on his staff will often feel that he has little or no time for them.

In this respect, Nolte (1966) suggests that many heads become "wrapped in the embrace of the office". They become over-concerned with attendance sheets and mark-lists, stationery and supplies, ringing the bell on time, checking dinner money accounts, writing letters to each other, looking over buildings with men from the architect's department, discussing the use of the school hall with the secretary of the local women's guild, and drawing up detailed schemes and standing orders which few have time to read. (See also Katz, 1955.) As the staffroom cynic would put it, there is real danger that the head will become a glorified clerk and tea-brewer.

In the past, it is true, many heads have overstressed the administrative function of their role. Holing-up in their studies for long periods of time, busying themselves with petty routine and simple clerical duties, they have tended to let the school organisation run itself. In discussing superintendents of schools, Halpin (1966) considers that far too many of them allow their main responsibilities to become obscured by trivia, with the result that they abdicate the leadership role and degenerate into mere functionaries. Leadership and innovation generate costs for members of staff and give rise to increased tension and conflict within the organisation. This, in turn, creates anxieties and problems for the head, as the negative affect and annoyance is directed his way. It is tempting to seek the quiet life, to avoid the dilemmas of leadership, by a retreat into "busywork" and perfunctory activity. The situation is often rationalised by heads as that of a contented staff ticking over quite happily, getting on with the age-old task of educating the pupils, when it is perfectly clear to the outsider that the school has got into a rut and needs a thoroughly good shake-up. This a process that all too often has to await the appointment of a new head, thus establishing a "shake-up cycle" for schools of a generation long. For some reason, conflict is construed as "bad" by many headteachers and principals, when it might more rationally be perceived as the healthy concomitant of innovation and change. Generally speaking, it might be thought that there is too little conflict as a result of leadership in our schools.

It is now clear the the occupants of top positions in educational institutions will need to place much less reliance on experience *per se*, and much more on acquiring the understanding and insight that comes from a conceptual grasp of the nature of their own role, and those of their staff (Campbell, 1964a). So far, principals of colleges and heads of schools have not received adequate professional preparation for their positions. It would seem sensible to include in their training, at some stage, a grasp and understanding of role theory in so far as it illuminates the work of the administrator.

The training of high school principals in techniques of administration is receiving a good deal of attention in the U.S.A. Hughes (1967) concludes his article on the subject of training in school management for headteachers in this country with the assertion that we would do well to introduce our school administrators to the study of administrative theory, with its new emphasis on the insight to be obtained from the social sciences. Lonsdale (1964) suggests that by analysing and studying their own role, and the role structure of the organisation, the administrator can reduce the amount of role conflict within the institution, and help staff to become more sensitive and responsive to others' rights through a better understanding of the nature of their roles. This more rational view of one's job, and of the structure of the educational organisation, is essential if our large schools and colleges are to be adaptive and responsive to the needs of a changing society.

NOTES

1 Throughout this chapter, illustrations will be largely concerned with the role of the headmaster. There is no intention, however, to limit the relevance of role theory to this one position; the head is used as one example from a whole range of administrators in the field of education.

2 Sarbin (1954) defines "self" as the organisation of qualities (traits, attitudes, habits, personal skills) and need-dispositions (sentiments and drives).

3 For a discussion of the nomothetic and idiographic dimensions of an organisation, see Getzels (1963).

4 Anyone who has regularly visited schools as an "informed outsider"

will have sensed and experienced the professional and psychological hunger of many lonely heads, eager for some confirmation of their ideas, for some sympathy with their disenchantment over young teachers' attitudes, and, very often, for sheer human friendship and conversation.

5 For further discussion of these "pattern variables" or dilemmas of choice see Parsons, 1951 and 1956; and Laulicht, 1955.

6 Bales (1955) and Parsons (1954) both point to the functional similarity of the leadership alliance in the organisation and the incest taboo in the nuclear family as socialising mechanisms.

REFERENCES

ARGYLE, M. (1952) "The Concepts of Role and Status", *The Sociological Review*, **44**, pp. 39–52.

BALES, R. F. (1955) "The Equilibrium Problem in Small Groups", in, Hare, A., Borgatta, E. and Bales, R. F. (eds.) *Small Groups: Studies in Social Interaction*, Alfred Knopf.

BALES, R. F. and SLATER, P. E. (1956) "Role Differentiation in Small Decision-making Groups", in Parsons, T. and Bales R. F. (eds.) *Family: Socialization and Interaction Process*, Routledge and Kegan Paul.

BARNARD, C. I. (1938) *The Functions of the Executive*, Harvard University Press.

BATES, F. L. (1957) "A Conceptual Analysis of Group Structure", *Social Forces*, **36**, p. 103.

BIDDLE, B. J. and THOMAS, E. J. (1966) *Role Theory: Concepts and Research*, Wiley.

BROOKOVER, W. B. (1955) "Research on Teacher and Administrator Roles", *Journal of Educational Sociology*, **29**, pp. 2–13.

BURNHAM, P. S. (1964) *The Role of the Deputy Head in Secondary Schools* unpublished M.Ed. thesis, University of Leicester.

BURNHAM, P. S. (1968) "The Deputy Head", in Allen, B. (ed.) *Head-teachers for the Seventies*, Blackwell.

CAMPBELL, R. F. (1964a) "The Superintendent—his Role and Professional Status", *Teachers' College Record*, as quoted in M. C. Nolte, (ed.) *An Introduction to School Administration: Selected Readings*, Macmillan, pp. 308–17.

CAMPBELL, R. F. (1964b) "Implications for the Practice of Administration", in Griffiths, D. E. (ed.) *Behavioral Science and Educational Administration*, University of Chicago Press, ch. XIII.

CARTWRIGHT, D. and ZANDER, A. (1960) "Leadership and Group Performance", in their *Group Dynamics: Research and Theory*, Tavistock Publications, 2nd. edn.

CHARTERS, W. W. (1964) "An Approach to the Formal Organization of the School", in Griffiths, D. E. (ed.) *Behavioral Science and Educational Administration*, University of Chicago Press, ch. XI.

CHASE, F. S. and GUBA, E. G. (1955) "Administrative Roles and Behaviour", *Review of Educational Research*, **25**

FIEDLER, F. E. (1957) "A Note on Leadership Theory: the Effect of Social Barriers between Leaders and Followers", *Sociometry*, **20**, p. 87.

FIEDLER, F. E. (1958) *Leader Attitudes and Group Effectiveness*, University of Illinois Press, p. 44.

FIEDLER, F. E. (1960) "The Leader's Psychological Distance and Group Effectiveness", in Cartwright, D. and Zander, A. (eds.)

GETZELS, J. W. (1952) "A Psycho-sociological Framework for the Study of Educational Institutions", *Harvard Educational Review*, **22**, pp. 234–46.

GETZELS, J. W. (1958) "Administration as a Social Process", in Halpin, A. W. (ed.) *Administrative Theory in Education*, Midwest Administrative Center, University of Chicago, pp. 153–5.

GETZELS, J. W. (1963) "Conflict and Role Behaviour in the Educational Setting", in Charters, W. W. and Gage, N. L. (eds.) *Readings in the Social Psychology of Education*, Allyn and Bacon, p. 309.

GETZELS, J. W., Lipham, J. M. and Campbell, R. F. (1968) *Educational Administration as a Social Process: Theory, Research, Practice*, Harper and Row.

GIBB, C. A. (1954) "Leadership", in Lindzey, G. (ed.) *Handbook of Social Psychology 2*, Addison Wesley.

GREGG, R. T. (1957) "The Administrative Process", in Campbell, R. F. and Gregg, R. T. (eds.) *Administrative Behaviour in Education*, Harper and Row.

GRIFFITHS, D. E., HEMPHILL, J. *et al.* (1961) *Administrative Performance and Personality*, Teachers' College, Columbia University.

GROSS, N., MASON, W. S. and McEACHERN, A. W. (1958) *Explorations in Role Analysis: Studies of the School Superintendency Role*, Wiley.

GROSS, N. and HERRIOTT, R. E. (1965) *Staff Leadership in Public Schools: a Sociological Inquiry*, Wiley.

GULICK, L. and URWICK, L. (1966) "POSDCORB", in Nolte, M. C. (ed.) (1966).

HALPIN, A. W. (1966) *Theory and Research in Education*, Collier-Macmillan.

HALPIN, A. W. and WINER, B. J. (1957) "A Factorial Study of the Leader Behaviour Descriptions", in Stogdill, R. M. and Coons, A. E. (eds.) *Leader Behaviour: Its Descriptions and Measurement*, The Ohio State University, Bureau of Business Research Monograph No. 88, Section III.

HERRIOTT, R. E. and ST. JOHN, N. H. (1966) *Social Class and the Urban School*, Wiley.

HILLS, R. J. (1960) "A New Concept of Staff Relations", in Nolte, M. C.

H

(ed.) (1966) *An Introduction to School Administration; Selected Readings*, p. 372.

HOYLE, E. (1965) "Organizational Analysis in the Field of Education", *Educational Research*, VII, 97.

HUGHES, M. G. (1967) "Simulated Situations", *Trends in Education*, 7, p. 34.

KATZ, R. L. (1955) "Skills of an Effective Administrator", *Harvard Business Review*, 33, pp. 33–42.

LAULICHT, J. (1955) "Role Conflict, the Pattern Variable Theory, and Scalogram Analysis", *Social Forces*, 33, p. 250.

LEVINSON, D. J. (1959) "Role, Personality and Social Structure in the Organizational Setting", *Journal of Abnormal and Social Psychology*, 58, p. 170.

LIEBERMAN, S. (1956) "The Effects of Changes in Roles on the Attitudes of Role Occupants", *Human Relations*, 9, p. 385.

LINTON, R. (1952) 'Concepts of Role and Status", in Swanson, G. E., Newcomb, T. M. and Hartley, E. L. (eds.) *Readings in Social Psychology*, revised edition, Holt, Rinehart.

LIPHAM, J. M. (1960) *Personal Variables Related to Administrative Effectiveness*, unpublished doctoral dissertation, University of Chicago, quoted in Charters, W. W. and Gage, N. L. (eds.) (1963) p. 313.

LIPHAM, J. M. (1964) "Leadership and Administration", in Griffiths, D. E. (ed.) *Behavioral Science and Educational Administration*, University of Chicago Press, ch. VI.

LONSDALE, R. C. (1964) "Maintaining the Organization in Dynamic Equilibrium", in Griffiths, D. E. (ed.) *Behavioral Science and Educational Administration*, University of Chicago Press, ch. VII.

MERTON, R. K. (1957a) *Social Theory and Social Structure*, revised and enlarged edition, The Free Press of Glencoe.

MERTON, R. K. (1957b) "The Role-set: Problems in Sociological Theory", *British Journal of Sociology*, 8.

NOLTE, M. C. (ed.) (1966) *An Introduction to School Administration: Selected Readings*, Macmillan, p. 259.

OESER, O. A. and HARARY, F. (1962) "A Mathematical Model for Structural Role Theory: I", *Human Relations*, 15, p. 89.

PARSONS, T. (1951) *The Social System*, Tavistock Publications.

PARSONS, T. (1954) "The Incest Taboo in Relation to Social Structure and the Socialization of the Child', *British Journal of Sociology*, 5, p. 101.

PARSONS, T. (1956) "A Sociological Approach to the Study of Organizations: I and II", *Administrative Science Quarterly*, 3.

SARBIN, T. R. (1954) "Role Theory", in Lindzey, G. (ed.) *Handbook of Social Psychology: I*, Addison-Wesley.

SEEMAN, M. (1953) "Role Conflict and Ambivalence in Leadership", *American Sociological Review*, 18, p. 373.

SEEMAN, M. (1960) *Social Status and Leadership: the Case of the School Executive*, The Ohio State University, Bureau of Educational Research, Monograph No. 35.

SOUTHALL, A. (1959) "An Operational Theory of Roles", *Human Relations*, **12**, 17.

STOGDILL, R. M. (1948) "Personal Factors associated with Leadership: a Survey of the Literature", *Journal of Psychology*, **25**.

STOGDILL, R. M. and SHARTLE, C. L. (1955) *Methods in the Study of Administrative Leadership*, The Ohio State University, Bureau of Business Research, Monograph No. 80.

STOGDILL, R. M., SCOTT, E. L. and JAYNES, W. E. (1956) *Leadership and Role Expectations*, The Ohio State University, Bureau of Business Research, Monograph No. 86.

TURNER, R. H. (1962) "Role-taking: Process vs. Conformity", in Rose, A. M. (ed.) *Human Behaviour and Social Processes*, Routledge and Kegan Paul.

WESTWOOD, L. J. (1966) "Re-assessing the Role of the Head", *Education for Teaching*, **71**, p. 65.

WILSON, B. R. (1962) "The Teacher's Role: a Sociological Analysis", *British Journal of Sociology*, **13**.

3.4 Decisional Participation and Teacher Satisfaction

James A. Belasco and Joseph A. Alutto

INTRODUCTION

The level of satisfaction experienced by organizational members has been a persistent concern of educational researchers. One of the most frequently mentioned sources of dissatisfaction has been the frustration of the expanding desires of various organizational members (particularly teachers) for participation in the organization's decision-making process. This study examined the relationship between the levels of satisfaction experienced by teachers and their state of decisional participation. Following March and Simon and Katz and Kahn, satisfaction was defined as a willingness to remain within the current school organization despite inducement to leave. Decisional participation was defined as the discrepancy between current and preferred levels of participation.

CONCEPTUAL BACKGROUND OF THE STUDY

Educational organizations exist in a symbiotic relationship with their environment, importing human and fiscal resources and utilizing them in the production of educated and socialized students (Katz and Kahn, 1965; Thompson, 1967). In addition to its dependency on such environmental input supplying units as local taxpayers and state legislators, the school organization is also dependent upon those who supply human inputs such as teachers and administrators. For example, the organization must be assured of a sufficient supply of skilled manpower to carry out its basic tasks, and a willingness on the part of organizational members both to prosecute dependably their current organizational assignments and adapt to changing future conditions. In an effort to deal with this dependency, the educational organization must be concerned with the satisfaction of the needs and expectations of individual system members. Therefore, member satisfaction is a crucial organizational concern.

Considerable prior research has concentrated on the relationship between employee satisfaction and such extrinsic factors as economic salary and benefit levels (Morse, 1953), physical environments (Katz and Kahn, 1951; Patchen, 1962), organizational climate (Argyris, 1964) and

Source: *Educational Administration Quarterly* (Winter 1972),Vol. 8, No. 1, pp. 44–58.

supervisory style (Katz *et al.*, 1950; Herzberg *et al.*, 1959). A persistent theme throughout this research is that satisfaction levels vary directly with a sense of distributive justice concerning these important issues. That is, the denial of what organizational members deem to be "fair" or "just" treatment concerning issues of importance to them, is inevitably associated with lower levels of satisfaction (Patchen, 1960). For example, the Likert studies linking supervisory style to member satisfaction point out that those employees who accept current supervisory behavior do not record low levels of satisfaction. Rather, the relationship between low satisfaction levels and certain supervisory styles is a phenomenon which arises primarily from the desire of certain less satisfied employees to modify the kind of supervision they receive (Likert, 1961).

Recently, participation in organizational decision making has emerged as a central concern of teachers. Data presented by Sharma (1955), Belasco and Alutto (1969), and Findley (1968), indicates the centrality of participation in organizational decision making for public school teachers. Stinnett, Kleinman, and Ware (1967) further argue that teacher militancy, in part, is a reflection of this increased desire for participation. Prior research has indicated that decisional participation may be measured through a discrepancy approach which compares current with preferred levels of participation (Alutto and Belasco, 1971). This approach isolates three states of decisional participation—decisional deprivation (participation in fewer decisions than preferred), decisional equilibrium (participation in as many decisions as desired), and decisional saturation (participation in more decisions than desired). Such a method also provides an indication of a teacher's sense of distributive justice concerning his or her participation in organizational decision making. Given the centrality of the distributive justice concept to varying satisfaction levels, this discrepancy definition of decisional participation is of particular relevance in a study of teacher satisfaction.

Other research has indicated that neither the desire for increased participation nor employee satisfaction levels are equally distributed throughout the teacher population. For example, data demonstrate that the desire for increased participation in organizational decision making is not equally and widely distributed throughout the population. Rather a certain substratum of teachers desire more participation than they currently enjoy (are decisionally deprived), while others desire less participation (are decisionally saturated), while still others desire no change in the current rate of participation (Alutto and Belasco, 1971). Furthermore, other research evidence indicates a wide heterogeneity in the distribution of the various attitudinal characteristics within the teaching population. For example, teachers who are younger (Ryans, 1960), married male (Mason *et al.*, 1959), employed in secondary schools (Lieberman, 1956), coming from higher social class backgrounds (Colombotos, 1962) tend to be more professional in orientation. Satisfaction, as one attitudinal characteristic of teachers, has been demonstrated to be differentially distributed throughout an organizational population by Herzberg *et al.* (1959) Gurin, Veroff and Feld (1960), Porter (1961), Blauner (1960), and Kornhauser (1965). This suggests that this study should expect a differential distribution of both the desire for participation and its relationship to satisfaction levels throughout the teacher group.

Lastly, many previous researchers have postulated that higher levels of satisfaction are associated with various desirable organizational outcomes. Patchen, for instance, in his research among professional employees in the TVA, suggests that greater job satisfaction is associated with higher work achievement (Patchen, 1970). Likert (1961) and Bennis (1967) have found that higher levels of satisfaction are associated with increased trust, more productivity, and in general a more effective organization. Corwin has similarly argued that satisfaction and role conflict are inversely related (Corwin, 1965), while Kahn has presented data which indicate that satisfaction is also inversely related to job tension (Kahn *et al.*, 1964). Thus, higher levels of satisfaction are often postulated as correlates of such desirable organizational outcomes as higher trust, lower role conflict, less job related tension, and more positive attitudes towards the organization.

This raises the three research questions which are the focus of this paper. They are:

1 Is the state of decisional participation (as indicated by decisional deprivation, saturation or equilibrium) systematically associated with varying levels of teacher satisfaction?
2 Are levels of satisfaction differentially distributed throughout the teaching population?
3 Are varying levels of satisfaction associated with varying organizational outcomes?

METHODOLOGY
Relevant data for this study were collected through use of questionnaire survey techniques. Subjects were teachers employed in two school districts located in Western New York State. Research site 1 was a small urban center (population 50,000) and site 2 a medium-sized rural district. Complete useable responses from teachers in each district resulted in return rates of 60% in system 1 and 75% in system 2. Analysis of the demographic characteristics of respondents and non-respondents in each district revealed no significant differences when considering population and survey sample distributions of attributes such as age, sex, marital status, and teaching level.

The age, sex, teaching level, and employing district of each subject were taken directly from completed questionnaires. Use of the characteristics listed below as variables for analytical purposes required the computation of specific indices as outlined in the following paragraphs.

Satisfaction

Satisfaction has been measured in many different ways. These various methods share a common focus on the affective feeling states which people experience in the course of their employment (Katz and Kahn, 1951). Such a focus has been of interest not only because of its intrinsic value (for example, many share the humanistic position that people should enjoy their work) but also because such affective states directly related to the continuance and regularity of employee participation in organizational activities (Metzner and Mauer, 1953).

In the light of the importance of continued employee participation in the organization, March and Simon suggest that a more organizationally relevant measure of employee satisfaction would be the willingness of an employee to remain within the organization (Simon and March, 1958). Beyond the humanistic position valuing satisfaction for its own sake, continuance of service is a crucial organizational concern. In other words, dissatisfaction which does not lead to either lower productivity (and research has failed to uncover a systematic relationship between productivity and satisfaction [Vroom, 1964]) or a desire to leave the organization may not be an organizationally relevant concern. Therefore, for the purposes of this paper, satisfaction was defined as the willingness of organizational members to leave the organization. Satisfaction was ascertained from a series of questions which focused on the inducements necessary for a teacher to leave the employ of the school district. By satisfaction, therefore, we mean the probability that a person would continue in his organization despite a variety of inducements to leave. Specifically, factor analysis indicated that responses to the following four items discriminated among respondents' satisfaction levels a slight increase in pay, a slight increase in status, a position allowing slightly more creativity, and a position in which individuals were slightly more friendly (Alonzo, 1970). This measure of satisfaction was employed in the study.

Decisional participation

Decisional participation was computed from teacher responses to a series of questions which posed 12 decisional situations which occur in school systems (see Table 1). Teachers indicated whether they currently participated and whether they desire to participate in each decision. An index was derived by summing over the number of decisions in which each teacher currently participated and those in which he wished to participate, and then computing the absolute difference between these two figures. These absolute differences became the index of decisional discrepancy. Teachers were then placed in groups characterized by: 1) decisional deprivation (current participation less than preferred); 2) decisional equilibrium (current participation equal to desired participation); 3) decisional saturation (current participation greater than desired).

223

Trust

Interpersonal trust was conceived as teachers' predisposition towards their social environment, particularly the degree to which the social context of their lives was perceived as either benign and friendly or hostile and unpredictable. Subjects were asked to respond to a set of six items by denoting their agreement in full, agreement in part, or disagreement. Examples of trust included "most people can be trusted" and "if you don't watch yourself people will take advantage of you". All items in the scale focused on beliefs concerning the fundamental cooperativeness and trustworthiness of human nature. These items were derived from the work of Kluckholm and Murray (1967). The higher an individual score the greater his interpersonal trust.

Table 1. Decisional situations

---
1 Hiring new faculty members
2 Selecting specific instructional texts
3 Resolving learning problems of individual students
4 Determining appropriate instructional methods and techniques
5 Establishing general instructional policies
6 Establishing classroom disciplinary policies
7 Planning school budgets
8 Determining specific faculty assignments
9 Resolving faculty member grievances
10 Planning new buildings and facilities
11 Resolving problems with community groups
12 Determining faculty salaries

Job tension

The measure of job related tension was an adaptation of that reported by Kahn *et al.* (1964), and Lichtman (1970) and involved teacher responses on a five point scale to various aspects of job related tension (e.g., I never know what's expected of me, my work interferes with my home life, I find work rules confusing). The greater the numerical tension score the greater the tension or anxiety being experienced by each teacher.

Authoritarianism

It was anticipated that given the character of the authoritarian personality as spelled out by Adorno (1950), the degree of authoritarianism exhibited by teachers would be related to varying levels of satisfaction. A shortened version (13 questions) of the F scale was employed for this purpose (Rokeach, 1965).

Role conflict

Several authors, including Corwin (1965) and Alutto (1968), cite data which indicates that there is an inverse relationship between satisfaction levels and experienced role conflict. As a means of determining degrees

224

of perceived role conflict, each teacher indicated the percentage of working time that is now, and that should be devoted to a series of ten physical teaching activities (such as classroom teaching, course preparation, supervisory non-educational activities and professional development). The sum or absolute magnitude of the differences between desired and current time allocation was the index of perceived role conflict. The higher the sum, the greater the degree of role conflict.

Perceptions of administrative influence
Teachers were asked to rank order as to how a series of role performers, including the school superintendent and principal, currently do and should preferably influence their teaching activity. Such a ranking indicated current influence ratings for these two officials and levels of preferred influence as well. Given the ranking procedure, the lower the rank the more influential the official.

Attitudes
Prior research has indicated that one correlate of increased desire to participate in decision making among teaching personnel is greater attitudinal militancy (Alutto and Belasco, 1971). In an attempt to discover whether or not satisfaction levels were differentially related to attitudinal predispositions, teacher evaluations of strikes, unions and collective bargaining were measured through semantic differential techniques. For interpretive purposes, the greater each subject's attitudinal score the more positive his evaluation of each activity.

Reliability for the entire instrument was established at .85 on a test-retest pattern involving 100 elementary school teachers and 51 secondary school teachers in the New York City area.

FINDING
Examination of the data reported in Table 2 indicates that there are significant systematic relationships between individual member satisfaction levels and the state of decisional participation. Examining first the relationship between membership satisfaction and overall decisional participation, it is apparent that those teachers who are decisionally deprived report significantly lower satisfaction levels. For instance, the mean score for the high satisfaction group indicates that it is composed of a larger number of individuals who are decisionally saturated or at equilibrium than is the low satisfaction group ($\bar{x}$ of the high satisfaction group is 1.70 vs. $\bar{x}$ of the low satisfaction group of 1.54). This bears out the centrality of the relationship between distributive justice and satisfaction levels. Those teachers with lower satisfaction levels participate in fewer decisions than desired which reflects a violation of their sense of distributive justice.

Examining the three decisional groups separately, this relationship is even clearer. For the decisionally deprived group taken alone, these

Table 2. Decisional climate and satisfaction

(N = 427)
Decisional condition: 1 = Deprived; 2 = Equilibrium; 3 = Saturated

		Satisfaction Level			
		Low	Moderate	High	F
Total 12 Decisions	$\bar{x}$	1.54	1.47	1.70	3.8795
	S.D.	.77	.71	.81	
Deprived Only	$\bar{x}$	3.58	3.36	2.66	5.2193
	S.D.	2.2	2.0	1.75	
Equilibrium Only	$\bar{x}$	3.37	3.43	3.53	.0300
	S.D.	2.91	3.02	2.34	
Saturated Only	$\bar{x}$	1.88	2.06	1.78	.2532
	S.D.	1.02	1.91	1.23	
Rank Principal is	$\bar{x}$	3.08	3.33	3.18	.6344
	S.D.	1.84	1.58	1.62	
Rank Principal Should be	$\bar{x}$	3.75	3.82	3.61	.5406
	S.D.	1.83	1.79	1.85	
Rank Superintendent is	$\bar{x}$	3.06	3.70	3.83	3.1325
	S.D.	2.63	2.54	2.43	
Rank Superintendent Should be	$\bar{x}$	4.97	5.24	4.95	.6752
	S.D.	2.43	2.39	2.30	

teachers with high satisfaction levels were less deprived ($\bar{x} = 2.66$) than those with low satisfaction ($\bar{x} = 3.58$). For teachers experiencing either equilibrium or saturation, satisfaction levels did not vary significantly with the extent of their decisional condition.

As a probable correlate of this relationship between decisional deprivation and lower satisfaction, is the observation that less satisfied teachers attribute more current influence to the superintendent ($\bar{x}$ of the ranks = 3.06) than do more satisfied teachers ($\bar{x}$ of the ranks = 3.83). Both decisional deprivation and current influence levels of the superintendent are facets of the decisional climate in an organization. Where the superintendent exercises more influence over the daily activities of the organization, there is likely to be less opportunity for decisional participation on the part of such lower level organizational members as teachers. This restriction of the opportunity to participate increases the probability that teachers will be decisionally deprived. Thus, the centralization of influence in the superintendent's office may be associated with increased teacher decisional deprivation, both of which, in turn, are associated with lower levels of teacher satisfaction. Decisional climate appears to be a major factor in teacher satisfaction, thus answering the first research question in the affirmative.

Turning to the second research question, the data presented in Table

3 indicate that satisfaction levels are not uniform throughout the school population. Rather the most satisfied teachers tend to be older ($\bar{x}$ of the age of the high satisfaction group = 38.61 vs. $\bar{x}$ of the age of the low satisfied group = 32.11), female ($\bar{x}$ of the sex of the high satisfied group = 1.79 vs. $\bar{x}$ of the sex of the low satisfied group = 1.56), teaching in the elementary school ($\bar{x}$ of the location of the high satisfied group = 1.25 vs. $\bar{x}$ of the location of the low satisfied group = 1.44). Previously reported data indicated that such individuals were also the most likely to be decisionally saturated (Alutto and Belasco, 1971). Combined with the previously stated data in Table 2, this indicates that decisional saturation may be the most satisfying decisional state, and that this is usually found in at least one stratum in the school population.

Analysis of the data reveals several interesting relationships between satisfaction and certain organizational outcomes. In the case of job tension, as predicted by Kahn, those teachers reporting higher satisfaction levels report lower job tension ($\bar{x}$ of the tension levels for the high

Table 3. Satisfaction level, personal characteristics and organizational Outcomes

(N = 427)

		Satisfaction Level			
		Low	Moderate	High	F
Trust	$\bar{x}$	13.41	13.84	13.97	1.06
	S.D.	2.75	3.06	3.18	
Authoritarianism	$\bar{x}$	35.29	33.45	34.92	1.40
	S.D.	9.67	8.96	9.15	
Role Conflict	$\bar{x}$	36.47	33.06	29.47	2.03
	S.D.	33.52	28.21	26.54	
Sex—1 = Male					
2 = Female	$\bar{x}$	1.56	1.62	1.79	9.94
	S.D.	.54	.53	.41	
Age	$\bar{x}$	32.11	32.36	38.61	10.54
	S.D.	16.20	12.97	14.17	
Tension	$\bar{x}$	40.39	36.27	29.98	34.55
	S.D.	13.12	10.88	9.10	
Evaluate Collective					
Bargaining	$\bar{x}$	53.74	51.70	49.84	1.34
	S.D.	19.07	18.85	20.12	
Evaluate Strikes	$\bar{x}$	33.12	32.10	25.59	8.47
	S.D.	18.83	18.41	16.27	
Evaluate Unions	$\bar{x}$	38.02	40.00	30.80	9.48
	S.D.	20.40	20.97	19.35	
Teaching Level					
1 = Elementary					
2 = Secondary	$\bar{x}$	1.44	1.45	1.25	
	S.D.	.50	.44	—	

satisfied group = 29.98 vs. x̄ of the tension levels of the low satisfied group = 40.39). Similarly, those same high satisfaction level teachers report less militant attitudes. Thus high satisfaction levels do seem to be associated with the desirable organizational outcomes of reduced job tension and less militant attitudes.

On the other hand, however, it was clear from the data that high trust and low role conflict, as other desirable organizational events, were not significantly associated with varying satisfaction levels. The trust score of those teachers with high satisfaction levels (x̄ = 13.97) was not significantly different from those teachers with lower satisfaction levels (x̄ = 13.84 and 13.42). Similarly, while the role conflict score for higher satisfied teachers (x̄ = 29.47) was lower than those for the less satisfied group (x̄ = 33.06 and 36.47), the differences were not large enough to reach the level of statistical significance. In short, in response to the third research question, teachers' satisfaction levels are associated with varying organizational outcomes in the case of felt job tension and attitudes toward militancy, but not in the instances of trust and role conflict.

CONCLUSIONS

This study in two school districts explored the relationship between decisional participation and teacher satisfaction. The variable decisional participation was conceptualized as the discrepancy between current and preferred levels of participation. This approach led to the identification of three decisional states: deprivation, equilibrium and saturation. Satisfaction, in turn, was defined as the willingness to remain within the organization despite a variety of inducements to leave.

It is apparent that if a given educational organization is to sustain itself over time it must be concerned with both the attraction and retention of teachers and the faithful performance of their inter-related role activities. Levels of teacher satisfaction have been inexorably linked with these crucial organizational concerns. Therefore, for both humanistic and organizational reasons, educational institutions must create the conditions which enhance the probability of high satisfaction levels among their teaching personnel.

The data reported in this study indicate that decisional climate is a major factor influencing teacher satisfaction levels. Those teachers with lower satisfaction levels (e.g. those who are most willing to consider leaving their current employment) also possess the highest level of decisional deprivation. These teachers with the highest mobility propensity also view the influence/authority structure as being more centralized in the superintendent's office. These decisionally deprived, more mobility oriented teachers tended to be found among the younger males teaching in the secondary schools. Older females teaching in the elementary schools, on the other hand, tended to experience both decisional saturation and highest levels of satisfaction. Furthermore, those teachers experiencing highest levels of satisfaction also reported less felt job tension and less militant attitudes, though different satisfaction levels were not associated with varying perceived role conflict or trust propensities. Thus, at least some of the teaching population experienced dissatisfactions which were associated with their state of decisional participation and which could have a deleterious effect on the educational system.

While the data are tentative and may be limited by the single geographic region and the relatively small sample, it does suggest the utility of the decisional discrepancy approach to the study of teacher satisfaction levels. Neither the desire for increased participation in organizational decision making nor high levels of satisfaction are equally distributed throughout the teacher group. Rather there are certain substrata of teachers who both desire more participation in organizational decision making than they currently enjoy and report low levels of satisfaction, while others concurrently desire less participation than they currently have and report high levels of satisfaction.

These findings further suggest modification of some of the assumptions concerning the organizational outcomes associated with high satisfaction. While satisfaction was associated with lower job tension and less militant attitudes, it was not related to either reduced role conflict or increased trust. The absence of any relationship between satisfaction and role conflict is particularly puzzling. Research by Kahn, among others, indicates a strong relationship between conflict and satisfaction. Perhaps, for teachers, the low visibility of actual classroom activities reduces substantially both the possibility and the negative effects of role conflict. Alternatively, teachers may have come to accept the inevitability of role conflict, and through such acceptance reduce the cognitive dissonance which is an inevitable concomitant of lower satisfaction and heightened desire to leave the situation.

The absence of a significant relationship between trust and satisfaction may be traced to the observation that trust may not be a relevant organizational variable. Much of the research from which the presumed relationship between trust and satisfaction has been drawn has been based on small group populations. Few, if any of the studies have been conducted in large scale organizational systems. Relationships which emerge in small group populations may not hold in large scale organizations. Furthermore, the question may legitimately be asked: would persons participate in decision making and have high levels of satisfaction whether or not they trusted each other personally? In other words, is trust, as it has been defined, more of a personal rather than organizational nature? Consider an organization composed of five dyads, in which the parties trust each other in each dyad, but the ten individuals are not willing to trust one or more members of a different dyad. In such a situation, although the members do not trust each other in different dyads, they may still be willing to participate in the decision-making process of the overall organization. Furthermore, since they are willing to participate in the organization's decision-making process, such participation may be associated with high levels of satisfaction. Therefore, trust may not be related to satisfaction since trust may not be related to participation in organizational decision-making.

By the same token, several of the more deleterious organizational effects of low levels of satisfaction did emerge from the data. For example, those less satisfied teachers experienced considerably more felt job tension. While a certain amount of tension may be desirable, the concurrent emergence of low satisfaction and high tension is often accompanied by such dysfunctional activities as reduced levels of organizational performance and withdrawal from the situation through either lateness, absenteeism or various kinds of "on-the-job" mental absences. Another possible response to dissatisfaction is the hostile agressive act. Not unsurprisingly, then, those teachers who report lowest levels of satisfaction also reported the most militant attitudes towards such aggressive actions as joining unions and striking. Thus, low levels of satisfaction may pose serious potential problems for educational organizations in their efforts to secure and retain the necessary flow of human resources.

Lastly, the data suggest the necessity for a management strategy which recognizes that a similar decisional participation approach will have a varying impact on satisfaction levels in different strata of the teaching population. It is thus necessary to identify those substrata within the teaching group which are particularly deprived, then design a participative management program which meets the needs of those particular teachers. For example, it is apparent that increased participation should be afforded to younger males in the secondary school in order to increase their levels of satisfaction. It is particularly crucial for the system to meet the needs of this group of teachers since, in many respects, they possess the newest, most modern pedagogical and up-to-date curriculum skills. Such teachers potentially can provide the opportunity for the educational system to renew and strengthen its educational performance. By the same token, older females teaching in elementary school should receive neither more nor less participation since they already are quite satisfied. Thus, to increase satisfaction levels there is a pressing need for differential participative management approaches to meet the differential participation desires of various substrata in the overall school population. Such a differential strategy is necessary if the educational organization is to effectively retain and insure the high quality performance of its most critical resource—the classroom teacher.

REFERENCES

ADORNO, T. (1950) *The Authoritarian Personality*, Harper.
ALONZO, R. (1970) "An Analysis of Commitment Orientations among

Professional Nurses", Ph.D. Dissertation, State University of New York at Buffalo.

ALLUTO, J. (1968) "Role Theory in Propositional Form", Ph.D. Dissertation, Cornell University.

ALLUTO, J. and BELASCO, J. (1971) "Decisional Deprivation, Equilibrium and Saturation as Variables in Educational Research", Working Paper No. 93, State University of New York at Buffalo.

ARGYRIS, C. (1964) *Integrating the Individual and the Organization*, Wiley.

BELASCO, J. and ALUTTO, J. (1969) "Organizational Impacts of Teacher Negotiations", *Industrial Relations*, Vol. 9, No. 1, pp. 67–79.

BENNIS, W. (1967) "Beyond Bureaucracy", in Hollander, E. P. and Hunt, R. G. (eds.) *Current Perspectives in Social Psychology*, 2nd edition, Oxford University Press.

BLAUNER, R. (1960) "Work Satisfaction and Industrial Trends in Modern Society", in Galenson, W. and Lipset, L. (eds) *Labour and Trade Unionism*, Wiley, pp. 341–6

COLOMBOTOS, J. L. (1962) *Sources of Professionalism: A Study of High School Teachers*, Cooperative Research Project No. 330, University of Michigan Department of Sociology.

CORWIN, R. (1965) "Professional Persons in Public Organizations", *Educational Administration Quarterly*, Vol. 1, pp. 1–26.

FINDLEY, D. (1968) "The Secondary Principal: Evaluation and Supervision", *Contemporary Education*, Vol. XXXIX, May 1968, pp. 276–7.

GURIN, G. *et al.* (1960) *Americans View Their Mental Health*, Basic Books, pp. 148–51.

HERZBERG, F. *et al.* (1959) *The Motivation to Work*, Wiley.

KAHN, R. *et al.* (1964) *Organizational Stress*, Wiley.

KATZ, D. *et al.* (1950) *Productivity, Supervision and Morale in an Office Situation*, Institute for Social Research.

KATZ, D. and KAHN, R. (1965) *The Social Psychology of Organizations*, Wiley.

KATZ, D. and KAHN, R. (1951) "Human Organization and Worker Motivation", in Tripp, L. R. (ed.), *Industrial Productivity*, Industrial Relations Research Association, pp. 146–71.

KLUCKHOLM, C. and MURRAY, H. (1967) *Personality in Nature and Society in Culture*, Knopf, A. A. pp. 146–84.

KORNHAUSER, A. W. (1965) *Mental Health of the Industrial Worker*, Wiley.

LICHTMAN, C. (1970) "Some Interpersonal Response Correlates of Organizational Rank", *Journal of Applied Psychology*, Vol. 54, No. 1. pp. 77–80.

LIEBERMAN, M. (1956) *Education as a Profession*, Prentice-Hall.

LIKERT, R. (1961) *New Patterns in Management*, McGraw-Hill.

MASON, W. S. *et al.* (1959) "Sex Role and the Career Orientations of

Beginning Teachers", *Harvard Educational Review*, Vol. 29, pp. 370–83.

METZNER, H. and MAUER, F. C. (1953) "Employee Attitudes and Absences", *Personnel Psychology*, Vol. VI, pp. 467–85.

MORSE, N. C. (1953) *Satisfaction in the White Collar Job*, Institute for Social Research.

PATCHEN, M. (1960) "Absence and Employee Feelings about Fair Treatment", *Personnel Psychology*, Vol. 13, No. 3, Autumn 1960, pp. 349–60.

PATCHEN, M. (1962) "Supervisor Methods and Group Performance Norms", *Administrative Science Quarterly*, Vol. 7, No. 3, Dec. 1962, pp. 275–94.

PATCHEN, M. (1970) *Participation, Achievement and Involvement on the Job*, Prentice-Hall.

PORTER, L. W. (1961) "A Study of the Perceived Need Satisfactions in Bottom and Middle Management Jobs", *Journal of Applied Psychology*, Vol. XLV, No. 1, Feb. 1961.

ROKEACH, M. (1965) *The Open and Closed Mind*, Basic Books.

RYANS, D. C. (1960) *Characteristics of Teachers: Their Description, Comparison and Appraisal*, American Council on Education.

SHARMA, C. L. (1955) "Who Should Make What Decisions", *Administrators Notebook*, Vol. 3, No. 8, April 1955.

SIMON, H. and MARCH, J. (1958) *Organization*, Wiley.

STINNETT, T. M., KLEINMAN, J. H. and WARE, M. L. (1967) *Professional Negotiations in Public Education*, Macmillan, p. 7.

THOMPSON, J. D. (1967) *Organizations in Action*, McGraw-Hill.

VROOM, V. (1964) *Work and Motivation*, Wiley.

3.5 The Individual and Organization: Some Problems of Mutual Adjustment[1]

Chris Argyris

It is a fact that most industrial organizations have some sort of formal structure within which individuals must work to achieve the organization's objectives.[2] Each of these basic components of organization (the formal structure and the individuals) has been and continues to be the subject of much research, discussion, and writing. An extensive search of the literature leads us to conclude, however, that most of these inquiries are conducted by persons typically interested in one or the other of the basic components. Few focus on both the individual and the organization.

Since in real life the formal structure and the individuals are continuously interacting and transacting, it seems useful to consider a study of their simultaneous impact upon each other. It is the purpose of this paper to outline the beginnings of a systematic framework by which to analyze the nature of the relationship between formal organization and individuals and from which to derive specific hypotheses regarding their mutual impact. Although a much more detailed definition of formal organization will be given later, it is important to emphasize that this analysis is limited to those organizations whose original formal structure is defined by such traditional principles of organization as "chain of command", "task specialization", "span of control", and so forth. Another limitation is that since the nature of individuals varies from culture to culture, the conclusions of this paper are also limited to those cultures wherein the proposed model of personality applies (primarily American and some Western European cultures).

The method used is a simple one designed to take advantage of the existing research on each component. The first objective is to ascertain the basic properties of each component. Exactly what is known and agreed upon by the experts about each of the components? Once this information has been collected, the second objective follows logically. When the basic properties of each of these components are known, what

Source: Milstein, M. M. and Belasco, J. A. (eds.) (1973) *Educational Administration and the Behavioral Sciences: A Systems Perspective*, Allyn and Bacon, pp. 296–317.

predictions can be made regarding their impact upon one another once they are brought together?

The research on the human personality is so great and voluminous that it is indeed difficult to find agreement regarding its basic properties.[3] It is even more difficult to summarize the agreements once they are inferred from the existing literature. Because of space limitations it is only possible to discuss in detail one of several agreements which seems to the writer to be the most relevant to the problem at hand. The others may be summarized briefly as follows. Personality is conceptualized as (1) being an organization of parts where the parts maintain the whole and the whole maintains the parts; (2) seeking internal balance (usually called adjustment) and external balance (usually called adaptation); (3) being propelled by psychological (as well as physical) energy; (4) located in the need systems: and (5) expressed through the abilities. (6) The personality organization may be called "the self" which (7) acts to color all the individual's experiences, thereby causing him to live in "private worlds", and which (8) is capable of defending (maintaining) itself against threats of all types.

The self, in this culture, tends to develop along specific trends which are operationally definable and empirically observable. The basic developmental trends may be described as follows. The human being, in our culture:

(1) tends to develop from a state of being passive as an infant to a state of increasing activity as an adult. (This is what Erikson, 1950, has called self-initiative and Bronfenbrenner, 1951, has called self-determination; see also Kotinsky, 1952).

(2) tends to develop from a state of dependence upon others as an infant to a state of relative independence as an adult. Relative indpendence is the ability to "stand on one's own two feet" and simultaneously to acknowledge healthy dependencies.[4] It is characterized by the individual's freeing himself from his childhood determiners of behavior (e.g. the family) and developing his own set of behavioral determiners. The individual does not tend to react to others (e.g. the boss) in terms of patterns learned during childhood (White, 1952 pp. 339 ff.).

(3) tends to develop from being capable of behaving in only a few ways as an infant to being capable of behaving in many different ways as an adult.[5]

(4) tends to develop from having erratic, casual, shallow, quickly dropped interests as an infant to possessing a deeping of interests as an adult. The mature state is characterized by an endless series of challenges where the reward comes from doing something for its own sake. The tendency is to analyze and study phenomena in their full-blown wholeness, complexity, and depth (White, 1952, pp. 347 ff.).

(5) tends to develop from having a short time perspective (i.e. the

present largely determines behavior) as an infant to having a much longer time perspective as an adult (i.e. the individual's behavior is more affected by the past and the future).[6]

(6) tends to develop from being in a subordinate position in the family and society as an infant to aspiring to occupy at least an equal and/or superordinate position relative to his peers.

(7) tends to develop from having a lack of awareness of the self as an infant to having an awareness of and control over the self as an adult. The adult who experiences adequate and successful control over his own behavior develops a sense of integrity (Erikson, 1950) and feelings of self-worth (Rogers, 1951).

These characteristics are postulated as being descriptive of a basic multidimensional developmental process along which the growth of individuals in our culture may be measured. Presumably every individual, at any given moment in time, could have his degree of development plotted along these dimensions. The exact location on each dimension will probably vary with each individual and even with the same individual at different times. Self-actualization may now be defined more precisely as the individual's plotted scores (or profile) along the above dimensions.[7]

A few words of explanation may be given concerning these dimensions of personality development:

(1) They are only one aspect of the total personality. All the properties of personality mentioned above must be used in trying to understand the behavior of a particular individual. For example, much depends upon the individual's self-concept, his degree of adaptation and adjustment, and the way he perceives his private world.

(2) The dimensions are continuous, where the growth to be measured is assumed to be continuously changing in degree. An individual is presumed to develop continuously in degree from infancy to adulthood.

(3) The only characteristic assumed to hold for all individuals is that, barring unhealthy personality development, they will move from the infant toward the adult end of each continuum. This description is a model outlining the basic growth trends. As such, it does not make any predictions about any specific individual. It does, however, presume to supply the researcher with basic developmental continua along which the growth of any individual in our culture may be described and measured.

(4) It is postulated that no individual will ever obtain maximum expression of all these developmental trends. Clearly all individuals cannot be maximally independent, active, and so forth all the time and still maintain an organized society. It is the function of culture (e.g. norms, mores, and so forth) to inhibit maximum expression and to help an individual adjust and adapt by finding his optimum expressions.

A second factor that prevents maximum expression and fosters optimum expression are the limits set by the individual's own personality. For example, some people fear the same amount of independence and activity that others desire, and some people do not have the necessary abilities to perform certain tasks. No given individual is known to have developed all known abilities to their full maturity.

(5) The dimensions described above are constructed in terms of latent or genotypical characteristics. If one states that an individual needs to be dependent, this need may be ascertained by clinical inference, because it is one that individuals are not usually aware of. Thus one may observe an employee acting as if he were independent, but it is possible that if one goes below the behavioral surface the individual may be quite dependent. The obvious example is the employee who always seems to behave in a manner contrary to that desired by management. Although this behavior may look as if he is independent, his contrariness may be due to his great need to be dependent upon management which he dislikes to admit to himself and to others.

One might say that an independent person is one whose behavior is not caused by the influence others have over him. Of course, no individual is completely independent. All of us have our healthy dependencies (i.e. those which help us to be creative and to develop). One operational criteria to ascertain whether an individual's desire to be, let us say, independent and active is truly a mature manifestation is to ascertain the extent to which he permits others to express the same needs. Thus an autocratic leader may say that he needs to be active and independent; he may also say that he wants subordinates who are the same. There is ample research to suggest, however, that his leadership pattern only makes him and his subordinates more dependence-ridden.

SOME BASIC PROPERTIES OF FORMAL ORGANIZATION

The next step is to focus the analytic spotlight on the formal organization. What are its properties? What are its basic "givens"? What probable impact will they have upon the human personality? How will the human personality tend to react to this impact? What sorts of chain reaction are probable when these two basic components are brought together?

Formal organizations as rational organizations

Probably the most basic property of formal organization is its logical foundation or, as it has been called by students of administration, its essential rationality. It is the planners' conception of how the intended consequences of the organization may best be achieved. The underlying assumptions made by the creators of formal organization is that within respectable tolerances man will behave rationally, that is, as the formal plan requires him to behave. Organizations are formed with particular objectives in mind, and their structures mirror these objectives. Although man may not follow the prescribed paths, and consequently the objectives may never be achieved, Herbert A. Simon (1955) suggest that by and large man does follow these prescribed paths:

Organizations are formed with the intention and design of accomplishing goals; and the people who work in organizations believe, at least part of the time, that they are striving toward these same goals. We must not lose sight of the fact that however far organizations may depart from the traditional description ... nevertheless most behavior in organizations is intendedly rational behavior. By "intended rationality" I mean the kind of adjustment of behavior to goals of which humans are capable—a very incomplete and imperfect adjustment, to be sure, but one which nevertheless does accomplish purposes and does carry out programs [p. 30].

In an illuminating book, L. Urwick (1944) eloquently describes this underlying characteristic. He insists that the creation of a formal organization requires a logical "drawing-office" approach. Although he admits that "nine times out of ten it is impossible to start with a clean sheet", the organizer should sit down and in a "cold-blooded, detached spirit ... draw an ideal structure". The section from which I quote begins with Urwick's description of how the formal structure should be planned. He then continues:

Manifestly that is a drawing-office job. It is a designing process. And it may be objected with a great deal of experience to support the contention that organization is never done that way ... human organization. Nine times out of ten it is impossible to start with a clean sheet. The organizer has to make the best possible use of the human material that is already available. And in 89 out of those 90 per cent of cases he has to adjust jobs around to fit the man; he can't change the man to fit the job. He can't sit down in a cold-blooded, detached spirit and draw an ideal structure, an optimum distribution of duties and responsibilities and relationships, and then expect the infinite variety of human nature to fit into it.

To which the reply is that he can and he should. If he has not got a clean sheet, that is no earthly reason why he should not make the slight effort of imagination required to assume that he has a clean sheet. It is not impossible to forget provisionally the personal facts —that old Brown is admirably methodical but wanting in initiative, that young Smith got into a mess with Robinson's wife and that the two men must be kept at opposite ends of the building, that Jones is one of those creatures who can think like a Wrangler about other people's duties but is given to periodic amnesia about certain aspects of his own [pp. 36–9].[8]

The task of the organizer, therefore, is to create a logically ordered world where, as Fayol suggests, there is a "proper order" and in which there is a "place for everything [everyone]".[9]

The possibility that the formal organization can be altered by personalities, as found by Arensberg and McGregor (1942) and Stogdill and Koehler (1952), is not denied by formal organizational experts. Urwick, for example, states in the passage below that the planner must take into account the human element. But it is interesting to note that he perceives these adjustments as "temporary deviations from the pattern in order to deal with idiosyncrasy of personality". If possible, these deviations should be minimized by careful preplanning.

> He [the planner] should never for a moment pretend that these (human) difficulties don't exist. They do exist; they are realities. Nor, when he has drawn up an ideal plan of organization, is it likely that he will be able to fit in all the existing human material perfectly. There will be small adjustments of the job to the man in all kinds of directions. But those adjustments are deliberate and temporary deviations from the pattern in order to deal with idiosyncrasy. There is a world of difference between such modification and drifting into an unworkable organization because Green has a fancy for combining bits of two incompatible functions, or White is "empire-building" . . . or Black has always looked after the canteen, so when he is promoted to Sales Manager, he might as well continue to sell buns internally, though the main product of the business happens to be battleships.
>
> What is suggested is that problems of organization should be handled *in the right order*. Personal adjustments must be made, insofar as they are necessary. But fewer of them will be necessary and they will present fewer deviations from what is logical and simple, if the organizer first makes a plan, a design—to which he would work if he had the ideal human material. He should expect to be driven from it here and there. But he will be driven from it far less and his machine will work much more smoothly if he *starts* with a plan. If he starts with a motley collection of human oddities and tries to organize to fit them all in, thinking first of their various shapes and sizes and colors, he may have a patchwork quilt; he will not have an organization [pp. 36–9, quoted by permission of Harper and Brothers].

The majority of experts on formal organization agree with Urwick. Most of them emphasize that no organizational structure will be ideal. None will exemplify the maximum expression of the principles of formal organization. A satisfactory aspiration is for optimum expression, which means modifying the ideal structure to take into account the individual (and any environmental) conditions. Moreover, they urge that the people must be loyal to the formal structure if it is to work effectively. Thus Taylor emphasizes that scientific management would never succeed without a "mental revolution".[10] Fayol has the same problem in mind when he emphasizes the importance of *esprit de corps*.

It is also true, however, that these experts have provided little insight into *why* they believe that people should undergo a "mental revolution", or why an *esprit de corps* is necessary if the principles are to succeed The only hints found in the literature are that resistance to scientific management occurs because human beings "are what they are" or "because it's human nature". But *why* does "human nature" resist formal organizational principles? Perhaps there is something inherent in the principles which causes human resistance. Unfortunately too little research specifically assesses the impact of formal organizational principles upon human beings.

Another argument for planning offered by the formal organizational experts is that the organization created by logical, rational design, in the long run, is more human than one created haphazardly. They argue that it is illogical, cruel, wasteful, and inefficient not to have a logical design. It is illogical because design must come first. It does not make sense to pay a large salary to an individual without clearly defining his position and its relationship to the whole. It is cruel because, in the long run, the participants suffer when no clear organizational structure exists. It is wasteful because, unless jobs are clearly predefined, it is impossible to plan logical training, promotion, resigning, and retiring policies. It is inefficient because the organization becomes dependent upon personalities. The personal touch leads to playing politics, which Mary Follett has described as a "deplorable form of coercion" (quoted in Bendix, 1956, pp. 36–9).

Unfortunately, the validity of these arguments tends to be obscured in the eyes of the behavioral scientist because they imply that the only choice left, if the formal, rational, predesigned structure is not accepted, is to have no organizational structure at all, with the organizational structure left to the whims, pushes, and pulls of human beings. Some human-relations researchers, on the other hand, have unfortunately given the impression that formal structures are "bad" and that the needs of the individual participants should be paramount in creating and administering an organization. A recent analysis of the existing research, however, points up quite clearly that the importance of the organization is being recognized by those who in the past have focused largely upon the individual (Argyris, 1954b).

In the past, and for the most part in the present, the traditional organizational experts based their "human architectural creation" upon certain basic principles or assumptions about the nature of organization. These principles have been described by such people as Urwick (1944), Mooney, Holden *et al.*, Fayol, Dennison, Brown, Gulick, White, Gaus, Stene, Hopf, and Taylor. Although these principles have been attacked by behavioral scientists, the assumption is made in this paper that to date no one has defined a more useful set of formal organization principles. Therefore the principles are accepted as givens. This frees us to inquire about their probable impact upon people, *if they are used as defined.*

Task (work) specialization

As James J. Gillespie (1948) suggests, the roots of these principles of organization may be traced back to certain principles of industrial economics, the most important of which is the basic economic assumption held by builders of the industrial revolution that "the concentration of effort on a limited field of endeavor increases quality and quantity of output". It follows from the above that the necessity for specialization should increase as the quantity of similar things to be done increases.

If concentrating effort on a limited field of endeavor increases the quality and quantity of output, it follows that organizational and administrative efficiency is increased by the specialization of tasks assigned to the participants of the organization (Simon, 1947). Inherent in this assumption are three others. The first is that the human personality will behave more efficiently as the task that it is to perform becomes specialized. Second is the assumption that there can be found a one best way to define the job so that it is performed at greater speed.[11] Third is the assumption that any individual differences in the human personality may be ignored by transferring more skill and thought to machines.[12]

A number of difficulties arise concerning these assumptions when the properties of the human personality are recalled. First, the human personality, we have seen, is always attempting to actualize its unique organization of parts resulting from a continuous, emotionally laden, ego-involving process of growth. It is difficult, if not impossible, to assume that this process can be choked off and the resultant unique differences of individuals ignored. This is tantamount to saying that self-actualization can be ignored. The second difficulty is that task specialization requires the individual to use only a few of his abilities. Moreover, as specialization increases, the less complex motor abilities are used more frequently. These, research suggests, tend to be of lesser psychological importance to the individual. Thus the principle violates two basic givens of the healthy adult human personality. It inhibits self-actualization and provides expression for few, shallow, superficial abilities that do not provide the "endless challenge" desired by the healthy personality.

Wilensky and Lebeaux (1955) correctly point out that task specialization causes what little skill is left in a job to become very important. Now small differences in ability may make enormous differences in output. Thus two machine-shovel operators or two drill-press operators of different degrees of skill can produce dramatically different outputs. Ironically, the increasing importance of this type of skill for the healthy, mature worker means that he should feel he is performing self-satisfying work while using a small number of psychologically unchallenging abilities, when in actuality he may be predisposed to feel otherwise. Task specialization, therefore, requires a healthy adult to behave in a less mature manner, but also requires that he feel good about it!

Not only is the individual affected, but the social structure as well is modified as a result of the situation described above. Wilensky and

Lebeaux, in the same analysis, point out that placing a great emphasis on ability makes "who you are" become less important than "what you can do." Thus the culture begins to reward relatively superficial, materialistic characteristics.

Chain of command

The principle of task specialization creates an aggregate of parts, each performing a highly specialized task. An aggregate of parts, each busily performing its particular objective, does not form an organization, however. A pattern of parts must be formed so that the interrelationships among the parts create the organization. Following the logic of specialization, the planners create a new function (leadership) the primary responsibility of which is to control, direct, and coordinate the interrelationships of the parts and to make certain that each part performs its objective adequately. Thus the planner makes the assumption that administrative and organizational efficiency is increased by arranging the parts in a determinate hierarchy of authority in which the part on top can direct and control the part on the bottom.

If the parts being considered are individuals, then they must be motivated to accept direction, control, and coordination of their behavior. The leader, therefore, is assigned formal power to hire, discharge, reward, and penalize the individuals in order to mold their behavior in the pattern of the organization's objectives.

The impact of such a state of affairs is to make the individuals dependent upon, passive, and subordinate to the leader. As a result, the individuals have little control over their working environment. At the same time their time perspective is shortened because they do not control the information necessary to predict their futures. These requirements of formal organization act to inhibit four of the growth trends of the personality, because to be passive, subordinate, and to have little control and a short-time perspective exemplify in adults the dimensions of immaturity, not adulthood.

The planners of formal organization suggest three basic ways to minimize this admittedly difficult position. First, ample rewards should be given to those who perform well and who do not permit their dependence, subordination, passivity, and so forth to influence them in a negative manner. The rewards should be material and psychological. Because of the specialized nature of the worker's job, however, few psychological rewards are possible. It becomes important, therefore, that adequate material rewards are made available to the productive employee. This practice can lead to new difficulties, since the solution is, by its nature, not to do anything about the on-the-job situation (which is what is causing the difficulties) but to pay the individual for the dissatisfactions he experiences. The result is that the employee is paid for his dissatisfaction while at work and his wages are given to him to gain satisfactions outside his work environment.

Thus the management helps to create a psychological set which leads the employees to feel that basic causes of dissatisfaction are built into industrial life, that the rewards they receive are wages for dissatisfaction, and that if satisfaction is to be gained the employee must seek it outside the organization.

To make matters more difficult, there are three assumptions inherent in the above solution that also violate the basic givens of human personality. First, the solution assumes that a whole human being can split his personality so that he will feel satisfied in knowing that the wages for his dissatisfaction will buy him satisfaction outside the plant. Second, it assumes that the employee is primarily interested in maximizing his economic gains. Third, it assumes that the employee is best rewarded as an individual producer. The work group in which he belongs is not viewed as a relevant factor. If he produces well, he should be rewarded. If he does not, he should be penalized even though he may be restricting production because of informal group sanctions.

The second solution suggested by the planners of formal organizations is to have technically competent, objective, rational, loyal leaders. The assumption is made that if the leaders are technically competent presumably they cannot have "the wool pulled over their eyes" and that therefore the employees will have a high respect for them. The leaders should be objective and rational and personify the rationality inherent in the formal structure. Being rational means that they must avoid becoming emotionally involved. As one executive states, "We try to keep our personality out of the job." The leader must also be impartial; he must not permit his feelings to operate when he is evaluating others. Finally, the leader must be loyal to the organization so that he can inculcate the loyalty in the employees that Taylor, Fayol, and others believe is so important.

Admirable as this solution may be, it also violates several of the basic properties of personality. If the employees are to respect an individual for what he does rather than for who he is, the sense of integrity based upon evaluation of the total self which is developed in people is lost. Moreover, to ask the leader to keep his personality out of his job is to ask him to stop actualizing himself. This is not possible as long as he is alive. Of course, the executive may want to feel that he is not involved, but it is a basic given that the human personality is an organism always actualizing itself. The same problem arises with impartiality. No one can be completely impartial. As has been shown, the self-concept always operates when we are making judgments. In fact, as Rollo May (1953) has pointed out, the best way to be impartial is to be as partial as one's needs predispose one to be but to be aware of this partiality in order to correct for it at the moment of decision. Finally, if a leader can be loyal to an organization under these conditions, there may be adequate grounds for questioning the health of his personality make-up.

The third solution suggested by many adherents to formal organizational principles is to motivate the subordinates to have more initiative and to be more creative by placing them in competition with one another for the positions of power that lie above them in the organizational ladder. This solution is traditionally called "the rabble hypothesis". Acting under the assumption that employees will be motivated to advance upward, the adherents of formal organizations further assume that competition for the increasingly (as one goes up the ladder) scarcer positions will increase the effectiveness of the participants. Williams (1956), conducting some controlled experiments, shows that the latter assumption is not necessarily valid. People placed in competitive situations are not necessarily better learners than those placed in noncompetitive situations. Deutsch (1949), as a result of extensive controlled experimental research, supports Williams' results and goes much further to suggest that competitive situations tend to lead to an increase in tension and conflict and a decrease in human effectiveness.

Unity of direction

If the tasks of everyone in a unit are specialized, then it follows that the objective or purpose of the unit must be specialized. The principle of unity of direction states that organizational efficiency increases if each unit has a single activity (or homogeneous set of activities) that are planned and directed by the leader.[13]

This means that the goal toward which the employees are working, the path toward the goal, and the strength of the barriers they must overcome to achieve the goal are defined and controlled by the leader. Assuming that the work goals do not involve the egos of the employees (i.e. they are related to peripheral, superficial needs), then ideal conditions for psychological failure have been created. The reader may recall that a basic given of a healthy personality is the aspiration for psychological success. Psychological success is achieved when each individual is able to define his own goals, in relation to his inner needs and the strength of the barriers to be overcome in order to reach these goals. Repetitive as it may sound, it is nevertheless true that the principle of unity of direction also violates a basic given of personality.

Span of control

The principle of span of control[14] states that administrative efficiency is increased by limiting the span of control of a leader to no more than five or six subordinates whose work interlocks (Urwick, 1938).

It is interesting to note that Dale (1952), in an extensive study of organizational principles and practices in one hundred large organizations, concludes that the actual limits of the executive span of control are more often violated than not, while in a recent study Healey (1956) arrives at the opposite conclusion. Worthy (1950) reports that it is formal policy in his organization to extend the span of control of the top management much further than is theoretically suggested. Finally, Suojanen

(1955), in a review of the current literature on the concept of span of control, concludes that it is no longer valid, particularly as applied to the larger government agencies and business corporations.

In a recent article, however, Urwick (1956) criticizes the critics of the span-of-control principle. For example, he noted that in the case described by Worthy, the superior has a large span of control over subordinates whose jobs do not interlock. The buyers in Worthy's organization purchase a clearly defined range of articles; therefore they find no reason to interlock with others.

Simon (1947) criticizes the span-of-control principle on the grounds that it increases the "administrative distance" between individuals. An increase in administrative distance violates, in turn, another formal organizational principle that administrative efficiency is enhanced by keeping at a minimum the number of organizational levels through which a matter must pass before it is acted on (pp. 26–8). Span of control, continues Simon, inevitably increases red tape, since each contact between agents must be carried upward until a common superior is found. Needless waste of time and energy result. Also, since the solution of the problem depends upon the superior, the subordinate is in a position of having less control over his own work situation. This places the subordinate in a work situation in which he is less mature.

Although the distance between individuals in different units increases (because they have to find a common superior), the administrative distance between superior and subordinate within a given unit decreases. As Whyte (1956) correctly points out, the principle of span of control, by keeping the number of subordinates at a minimum, places great emphasis on close supervision. Close supervision leads the subordinates to become dependent upon, passive toward, and subordinate to, the leader. Close supervision also tends to place the control in the superior. Thus we must conclude that span of control, if used correctly, will tend to increase the subordinate's feelings of dependence, submissiveness, passivity, and so on. In short, it will tend to create a work situation which requires immature, rather than mature, participants.

AN INCONGRUENCY BETWEEN THE NEEDS OF A MATURE PERSONALITY AND OF FORMAL ORGANIZATION

Bringing together the evidence regarding the impact of formal organizational principles upon the individual, we must conclude that there are some basic incongruencies between the growth trends of a healthy personality in our culture and the requirements of formal organization. If the principles of formal organization are used as ideally defined, then the employees will tend to work in an environment where (1) they are provided minimal control over their work-a-day world, (2) they are expected to be passive, dependent, subordinate, (3) they are expected to have a short time perspective, (4) they are induced to perfect and value the frequent use of a few superficial abilities, and (5) they are expected to produce under conditions leading to psychological failure.

All of these characteristics are incongruent to the ones healthy human beings are postulated to desire. They are much more congruent with the needs of infants in our culture. In effect, therefore, formal organizations are willing to pay high wages and provide adequate seniority if mature adults will, for eight hours a day, behave in a less mature manner. If this analysis is correct, this inevitable incongruency increases (1) as the employees are of increasing maturity, (2) as the formal structure (based upon the above principles) is made more clear-cut and logically tight for maximum formal organizational effectiveness, (3) as one goes down the line of command, and (4) as the jobs become more and more mechanized (i.e. take on assembly-line characteristics).

As in the case of the personality developmental trends, this picture of formal organization is also a model. Clearly, no company actually uses the formal principles of organization exactly as stated by their creators. There is ample evidence to suggest that they are being modified constantly in actual situations. Those who expound these principles, however, probably would be willing to defend their position that this is the reason that human-relations problems exist; the principles are not followed as they should be.

In the model of the personality and the formal organization, we are assuming the extreme of each in order that the analysis and its results can be highlighted. Speaking in terms of extremes helps us to make the position sharper. In doing this, we make no assumption that all situations in real life are extreme (i.e. that the individuals will always want to be more mature and that the formal organization will always tend to make people more dependent, passive, and so forth, all the time).[15] The model ought to be useful, however, to plot the degree to which each component tends toward extremes and then to predict the problems that will tend to arise.

Returning to the analysis, it is not difficult to see why some students of organization suggest that immature and even mentally retarded individuals probably would make excellent employees in certain jobs. There is very little documented experience to support such a hypothesis. One reason for this lack of information is probably the delicacy of the subject. Examples of what might be obtained if a systematic study were made may be found in a recent work by Mal Brennan (1953). He cites the Utica Knitting Mill, which made arrangements during 1917 with the Rome Institution for Mentally Defective Girls to employ twenty-four girls whose mental age ranged from six to ten years of age. The girls were such excellent workers that they were employed after the war emergency ended. In fact, the company added forty more in another of their plants. It is interesting to note that the managers praised the subnormal girls highly. According to Brennan, in several important reports they said that:

When business conditions required a reduction of the working staff, the hostel girls were never "laid off" in disproportion to the normal girls; they were more punctual, more regular in their habits, and did not indulge in as much "gossip and levity". They received the same rate of pay, and they had been employed successfully at almost every process carried out in the workshops.

In another experiment reported by Brennan, the Works Manager of the Radio Corporation, Ltd., reported that of five young morons employed, "the three girls compared very favourably with the normal class of employee in that age group. The boy employed in the store performed his work with satisfaction ... Although there was some doubt about the fifth child, it was felt that getting the most out of him was just a matter of right placement." In each of the five cases, the morons were reported to be quiet, respectful, well behaved, and very obedient. The Works Manager was especially impressed by their truthfulness. A year later the same Works Manager was still able to advise that "in every case, the girls proved to be exceptionally well-behaved, particularly obedient, and strictly honest and trustworthy. They carried out work required of them to such a degree of efficiency that *we were surprised they were classed as subnormals for their age*."[16]

SUMMARY OF FINDINGS

If one were to put these basic findings in terms of propositions one could state:

Proposition 1.   There is a lack of congruency between the needs of healthy individuals and the demands of the formal organization.

If one uses the traditional formal principles of organization (i.e. chain of command, task specialization, and so on) to create a social organization, and

if one uses as an input agents who tend toward mature psychological development (i.e. who are predisposed toward relative independence, activeness, use of important abilities, and so on),

then one creates a disturbance, because the needs of healthy individuals listed above are not congruent with the requirement of formal organization, which tends to require the agents to work in situations where they are dependent, passive, use few and unimportant abilities, and so forth.

Corollary 1. The disturbance will vary in proportion to the degree of incongruency between the needs of the individuals and the requirements of the formal organization.[17]

An administrator, therefore, is always faced with a tendency toward continual disturbance inherent in the work situation of the individuals over whom he is in charge.

Drawing on the existing knowledge of the human personality, a second proposition can be stated.

Proposition 2.   The results of this disturbance are frustration, failure, short time perspective, and conflict.[18]

If the agents are predisposed to a healthy, mature self-actualization, the following results will occur:

1   They will tend to experience frustration because their self-actualization will be blocked.
2   They will tend to experience failure because they will not be permitted to define their own goals in relation to their central needs, the paths to these goals, and so on.
3   They will tend to experience short-time perspective, because they have no control over the clarity and stability of their future.
4   They will tend to experience conflict, because, as healthy agents, they will dislike the frustration, failure, and short-time perspective which is characteristic of their present jobs. If they leave, however, they may not find new jobs easily, and even if new jobs are found, they may not be much different.[19]

Based upon the analysis of the nature of formal organization, one may state a third proposition.

Proposition 3.   The nature of the formal principles of organization cause the subordinate, at any given level, to experience competition, rivalry, intersubordinate hostility, and to develop a focus toward the parts rather than the whole.

(1) Because of the degree of dependence, subordination, and so on of the subordinates upon the leader, and because, the number of positions above any given level always tends to decrease, the suborindates aspiring to perform effectively and to advance will tend to find themselves in competition with, and receiving hostility from, each other.[20]

(2) Because, according to the formal principles, the subordinate is directed toward and rewarded for performing his own task well, the subordinate tends to develop an orientation toward his own particular part rather than toward the whole.

(3) This part-orientation increases the need for the leader to coordinate the activity among the parts in order to maintain the whole. This need for the leader, in turn, increases the subordinate's degree of dependence, subordination, and so forth. This is a circular process whose impact is to maintain and/or increase the degree of dependence, sub-

ordination, and so on, as well as to stimulate rivalry and competition for the leader's favor.

A BIRD'S EYE, CURSORY PICTURE OF SOME OTHER RELATED FINDINGS
It is impossible in the short space available to present all of the results obtained from the analysis of the literature. For example it can be shown that employees tend to adapt to the frustration, failure, short time perspective, and conflict involved in their work situations by any one or a combination of the following acts:

1   Leaving the organization.
2   Climbing the organizational ladder.
3   Manifesting defense reactions such as daydreaming, aggression, ambivalence, regression, projection, and so forth.
4   Becoming apathetic and disinterested toward the organization, its make-up, and its goals. This leads to such phenomena as: (a) employees reducing the number and potency of the needs they expect to fulfill while at work; (b) employees goldbricking, setting rates, restricting quotas, making errors, cheating, slowing down, and so on.
5   Creating informal groups to sanction the defense reactions and the apathy, disinterest, and lack of self-involvement.
6   Formalizing the informal group.
7   Evolving group norms that perpetuate the behavior outlined in (3), (4), (5), and (6) above.
8   Evolving a psychological set in which human or non-material factors become increasingly unimportant while material factors become increasingly important.
9   Acculturating youth to accept the norms outlined in (7) and (8):

Furthermore, it can also be shown that many managements tend to respond to the employees' behavior by:

1   Increasing the degree of their pressure-oriented leadership.
2   Increasing the degree of their use of management controls.
3   Increasing the number of "pseudo"-participation and communication programs.

These three reactions by management actually compound the dependence, subordination, and so on that the employees experience, which in turn cause the employees to increase their adaptive behavior, the very behavior management desired to curtail in the first place.

Is there a way out of this circular process? The basic problem is the reduction in the degree of dependency, subordination, submissiveness, and so on experienced by the employee in his work situation. It can be shown that job enlargement and employee-centered (or democratic or participative) leadership are elements which, if used correctly, can go a long way toward ameliorating the situation. These are limited, however, because their success depends upon having employees who are ego-involved and highly interested in the organization. This dilemma between individual needs and organization demands is a basic, continual problem posing an eternal challenge to the leader. How is it possible to create an organization in which the individuals may obtain optimum expression and, simultaneously, in which the organization itself may obtain optimum satisfaction of its demands? Here lies a fertile field for future research in organizational behavior.

NOTES

1 This analysis is part of a larger project whose objectives are to integrate by the use of a systematic framework much of the existing behavioral-science research related to organization. The total report has been published as a book (Argyris, 1957). The project has been supported by a grant from the Foundation for Research on Human Behavior, Ann Arbor, Michigan, for whose generous support the writer is extremely grateful.

2 Temporarily, "formal structure" is defined as that which may be found on the organization charts and in the standard operating procedures of an organization.

3 The relevant literature in clinical, abnormal, child, and social psychology, and in personality theory, sociology, and anthropology was investigated. The basic agreements inferred regarding the properties of personality are assumed to be valid for most contemporary points of view. Allport's "trait theory", Cattell's factor analytic approach, and Kretschmer's somatotype framework are not included. For lay description see Argyris (1954a).

4 This is similar to Erikson's sense of autonomy and Bronfenbrenner's state of creative interdependence.

5 Lewin (1935) and Kounin (Barker et al., 1943) believe that as the individual develops needs and abilities the boundaries between them become more rigid. This explains why an adult is better able than a child to be frustrated in one activity and behave constructively in another.

6 Lewin (1948a) reminds those who may believe that a long time perspective is not characteristic of the majority of individuals of the billions of dollars that are invested in insurance policies.

7 Another related but discrete set of developmental dimensions may be constructed to measure the protective (defense) mechanisms individuals tend to create as they develop from infancy to adulthood. Exactly how these would be related to the above model is not clear.

8 Extracts from Urwick (1944) are quoted by permission of Harper and Brothers.

I

9 Cited in Koontz and O'Donnell (1955).

10 For a provocative discussion of Taylor's philosophy, see Bendix (1956) pp. 274–319.

11 For an interesting discussion see Friedmann (1955) pp. 54ff.

12 Friedmann (1955) p. 20. Friedmann reports that 79 per cent of Ford employees had jobs for which they could be trained in one week.

13 The sacredness of these principles is questioned by a recent study. Gunnar Heckscher (1955) concludes that the principles of unity of command and unity of direction are formally violated in Sweden: "A fundamental principle of public administration in Sweden is the duty of all public agencies to cooperate directly without necessarily passing through a common superior. This principle is even embodied in the constitution itself, and in actual fact it is being employed daily. It is traditionally one of the most important characteristics of Swedish administration that especially central agencies, but also central and local agencies of different levels, cooperate freely and that this is being regarded as a perfectly normal procedure".

14 First defined by V. A. Graicunas (1947).

15 In fact, much evidence is presented in the book from which this article is drawn to support contrary tendencies.

16 Mr. Brennan's emphasis.

17 This proportion does not hold under certain conditions.

18 In the full analysis, specific conditions are derived under which the basic incongruency increases or decreases.

19 These points are taken, in order, from Barker *et al.* (1941), Dollard *et al.* (1939), Lewin *et al.* (1944), Lippitt and Bradford (1945), Lewin (1948b) and Newcomb (1950).

20 These problems may not arise for the subordinate who becomes apathetic, disinterested, and so on.

REFERENCES

ARENSBERG, C. M. and McGREGOR, D. (1942) "Determination of Morale in an Industrial Company", *Applied Anthropology*, 1, (Jan.-March 1942), pp. 12–14, Massachusetts Institute of Technology.

ARGYRIS, C. (1957) *Personality and the Organization*, Harper.

ARGYRIS, C. (1954a) *Personality Fundamentals for Administrators*, revised edition, Yale University Press, Chapter 1.

ARGYRIS, C. (1954b) *The Present State of Research in Human Relations*, Yale University Press.

BARKER, R. G., DEMBO, T. and LEWIN, K. (1941) "Frustration and Regression: an Experiment with Young Children", *Studies in Child Welfare* Vol. XVIII, No. 2, University of Iowa Press.

BARKER, R. G., KOUNIN, J. and WRIGHT, H. R. (eds.) (1943) *Child Behavior and Development*, McGraw-Hill, pp. 179–98.

BENDIX, R. (1956) *Work and Authority in Industry*, Wiley.

BRENNAN, (1953) *The Making of a Moron*, Sheed and Ward, pp. 13–18.
BRONFENBRENNER, U. (1951) "Toward an Integrated Theory of Personality", in Blake, R. R. and Ramsey, G. V. (eds.) *Perception: an Approach to Personality*, Ronald Press Co. pp. 206–57.
DALE, E. (1952) *Planning and Developing the Company Organization Structure*, American Management Association, Chapter XX.
DEUTSCH, M. (1949) "An Experimental Study of the Effects of Co-operation and Competition upon Group Process", *Human Relations*, 2, pp. 199–231.
DOLLARD, J. *et al.* (1939) *Frustration and Aggression*, Yale University Press.
ERIKSON, E. H. (1950) *Childhood and Society*, Norton.
FRIEDMANN, G. (1955) *Industrial Society*, Free Press.
GILLESPIE, J. J. (1948) *Free Expression in Industry*, Pilot Press, pp. 34–7.
GRAICUNAS, V. A. (1947) "Relationship in Organization", in Gulick, L. and Urwick, L. (eds.) *Papers on the Science of Administration*, 2nd edition, Institute of Public Administration, Columbia University, pp. 183–7.
HECKSCHER, G. (1955) *Swedish Public Administration at Work*, Stuieförbundet Naringsliv Och Samhalle, p. 12.
HEALEY, J. H. (1956) "Coordination and Control of Executive Functions", *Personnel*, 33, Sept. 1956, pp. 106–17.
KOONTZ, H. and O'DONNELL, C. (1955) *Principles of Management*, McGraw-Hill, p. 24.
KOTINSKY, R. (1952) *Personality in the Making*
LEWIN, K. (1935) *A Dynamic Theory of Personality*, McGraw-Hill.
LEWIN, K. (1948a) *Resolving Social Conflicts*, Harper, p. 105.
LEWIN, K. (1948b) "Time, Perspective and Morale", in Lewin, G. W. (ed.) *Resolving Social Conflicts*, Harper, pp. 103–24.
LEWIN, K. *et al.* (1944) "Level of Aspiration", in Hunt, J. McV. (ed.) *Personality and the Behavior Disorders*, New York, pp. 333–78.
LIPPITT, R. and BRADFORD, L. (1945) "Employee Success in Work Groups", *Personnel Administration*, 8, Dec. 1945, pp. 6–10.
MAY, R. (1953) "Historical and Philosophical Presuppositions for Understanding Therapy", in Mowrer, O. H. *Psychotherapy and Research*, New York, pp. 38–9.
NEWCOMB, T. M. (1950) *Social Psychology*, Dryden, pp. 361–73.
ROGERS, C. R. (1951) *Client-centered Therapy*, Houghton Mifflin.
SIMON, H. A. (1947) *Administrative Behavior*, MacMillan, pp. 80–81.
SIMON, H. A. (1955) *Research Frontiers in Politics and Government*, Washington, D.C.
STOGDILL, R. M. and KOEHLER, K. (1952) *Measures of Leadership Structure and Organization Change*, Columbus, Ohio.
SUOJANEN, W. W. (1955) "The Span of Control—Fact or Fable?", *Advanced Management*, 20, pp. 5–13.
URWICK, L. (1944) *The Elements of Administration*, Harper.

URWICK, L. (1956) "The Manager's Span of Control", *Harvard Business Review*, **34**, May/June 1956, pp. 39–47.

URWICK, L. (1938) *Scientific Principles and Organization*, New York, p. 8.

WHITE, R. W. (1952) *Lives in Progress*, Dryden.

WHYTE, W. (1956) "On the Evolution of Industrial Sociology," paper presented at the 1956 meeting of the American Sociological Society.

WILENSKY, H. L., and LEBEAUX, C. N. (1955) *Industrialization and Social Welfare*, New York, p. 43.

WILLIAMS, D. C. S. (1956) "Effects of Competition between Groups in a Training Situation", *Occupational Psychology*, **30**, April 1956, pp. 85–93.

WORTHY, J. C. (1950) "Organizational Structure and Employee Morale", *American Sociological Review*, **15**, April 1950, pp. 169–79.

3.6 Exchange and Conflict in the School

Harry L. Gray

The purpose of this article is to look at the school as an organization in which conflict is seen to arise as the result of the different demands that members make on the institution. This is not the only way of looking at a school, but it is a fundamental way of looking at any kind of organization. The premise is that all organizations are in a complex state of internal (and external) conflict and that when conflicts can be resolved easily and quickly the organization is in a healthy state; but when they are suppressed there is a build-up of frustration that leads to unmanageable crises. These conflicts have their origin in the wide variety of changing needs felt by members of the schools, needs which require them constantly to renegotiate their terms of membership in an unspoken psychological contract. Administrative mechanisms in schools and other organizations ignore the need to renegotiate and assume a much too simplistic view of membership. Hence there are no overt means for resolving the conflicts that arise from incompatibilities in member requirements. The negotiation process involves social and psychological exchange—that is, members commit themselves to an organization only in so far as they receive in return an acceptable reward or "exchange". Thus there is a need to develop structures for schools that can respond to the negotiation process and the need for perceived return on commitment.

ORGANIZATIONS SERVE PURPOSES
There can be no doubt that organizations serve purposes, and schools are no exception. The mere fact of organization is a proof of purposeful activity. But to go further than this presents problems, for while organizations may *serve* purposes it seems unlikely that they can have objectives, since objectives require conscious target setting and organizations, while being made up of human beings, are not themselves animate. An initial difficulty arises because most of us think of organizations as having the characteristics of a sort of collective human being, and this presents us with difficulties when we try to understand what actually happens in an organization. It is sometimes said that people have objectives but that

---

Source: Commissioned for this volume by The Open University.

organizations do not;[1] however, it is easier to think of organizations as serving the purposes of their members in the first instance and then to examine the consequences of member demands, rather than confuse objectives as being organizational and at the same time those shared by members.

Some leading members of organizations identify with them in such a way that they personify the organizations in themselves. How they do this needs to be examined in detail, but it would seem that, in some cases, they accept leadership resonsibilities at a time when the climate is good and the organization is under no threat; they then consolidate their influence and power so that when the organization meets hard times they are well ensconced. Alternatively, they are brought in when the organization is under threat and given power during the crisis which they are able to retain afterwards. It is because certain members—not always key members—identify closely with the organization that it appears to have its own aims. We can see how this happens in the case of a school. The first head personifies the objectives of the school because he goes for the things he wants and believes in. When he leaves, many of the old staff will have identified with his objectives too and they continue to speak of their personal objectives as those of the school.

In voluntary organizations a ruling clique or cabal always rises into pre-eminence and those who do not share its beliefs and values leave, perhaps to form their own organization. Something similar can happen in commercial organizations when some members withdraw their capital and set up a rival company. But in organizations where there is a public monopoly or near monopoly, quittance and setting up a competing organization is seldom possible. Indeed, as in the case of the school, many of the members may have psychological attachment to the school and believe their values and objectives to be as valid as those of their colleagues. Since, to them, a given school merely represents a location in which their ideological educational objectives may be expressed, there is no *prima facie* reason why they should leave, but rather every reason why they should stay and try to influence matters.

ORGANIZATIONAL RESISTANCE TO CHANGE

In some way personal purposes, particularly those of the leaders, become institutionalized. Political parties exemplify this in their debates about the pure political doctrine. What is interesting is not so much the debate that goes on, but the way in which organizations appear to deal with it. It is a characteristic of organizations that they should seek to perpetuate a simple unified doctrine and that they should be highly resistant to change of almost any fundamental kind. If one had to choose one major aspect of an organization as being the most critical for understanding that organization's development, one could most usefully choose the ways in which it resists change. Yet if one speaks of a natural tendency of organizations to resist change, this is clearly not a characteristic of "the organisation", but of the people in it; the empirical evidence is that organizational change can be quite fundamental, given a sufficiently significant change in the membership.

To understand the situation one must examine the nature of vested interests. A vested interest is simply an involvement in an organization which gives a valued reward to an individual. When the reward is at risk the individual will make every effort to retain it. In financial terms this interest is a salary or return on investment, but it is also a whole complex of other things of which monetary return may be the least consequential. Membership of any organization is dependent upon an individual receiving a return on his investment—whether that investment be time, money or labour. According to "exchange theory"[2] active membership is conditional upon some kind of valued return[3] and passive membership on there being no negative return. In other words, one only joins an organization if one is going to get something out of it; what that return is may be irrational or ridiculous to others, but so long as the member values it positively it is an adequate return on investment in social, psychological, emotional, financial or material terms. In order to obtain the acceptable exchange or return each member enters into a psychological negotiation with other members of the organization to ensure that the demanded return continues to be forthcoming.

THE PSYCHOLOGICAL INVESTMENT

But this psychic investment is not an inert activity, as it may be with financial investment. One does not join an organization and stay outside. To obtain a return on commitment one must have some involvement with other members, and involvement means seeking influence, status, power and/or authority. Some people will be content with quite minor roles and involvement in an organization. For some a condition of membership will be that very little is demanded of them and an increased demand will be an inducement to leave. But for everyone, a requirement of membership will be to have that control over membership which leaves the individual free to continue negotiating the conditions of membership that he himself requires. Too often it is assumed that all members of an organization seek ultimate power over others. For many this will not be so, but in order to have freedom for oneself one will need to have some power over some others. While everyone always has the option of leaving an organization, the cost of leaving may be greater than the cost of staying; hence to stay and receive the required reward may mean an increased involvement—more than initially required.

What happens is that in order to negotiate the original exchange (or to negotiate a new exchange in changed circumstances) a member has to change his relationship with the other members. Once this occurs the change in relationships represents threats to some members which can only be resolved if yet other members ease their demands or a change in the balance of power can be negotiated. The trouble with organizations is that power tends to be critically balanced and changes in demand from any section of membership upsets the balance and threatens some positions or roles. In the face of threat, most people over-react and see a strong challenge to their status which must be violently resisted. Hence conflict is a potential factor in all organizations, and in most organizations potential conflict is suppressed.

It must be understood that all models of organizations represent only a part of reality. A model is simply a way of looking at an organization so that what happens can be more clearly understood. A model does not have to be "true", but it does have to make things clearer, to give possible and reasonable explanations and, in all likelihood, enable us to predict certain behaviour in other organizations. The "exchange-conflict" model has certain important characteristics. It assumes that organizations can usefully be described in terms of the people who are members of them. The concept of membership is important and includes "users" of the organization—like parents of pupils in the school. A member may be anyone who has to do with the organization. Exchange theory describes behaviour in terms of the interest that people have in being members and it highlights the ways in which the personal interests of members become issues of potential conflict. It follows from this view that since all members have a range of interests in the organization and they are not all reconcilable, at least at any given moment, a fruitful way of describing what happens in organizations is to view them as areas of conflict. Any demand made on an organization by any individual or group of individuals is a potential threat even when initially essential to the life of the organization. Members of an organization need to be prepared for the conflicts that are bound to arise when changes of membership occur (increases or decreases), because changes bring about the need for further negotiations on returns, a situation fraught with conflict potential.

THE ROOTS OF ORGANIZATIONAL CONFLICT

The "exchange-conflict" model shows how all organizations are in a state of tension over the rewards given to members; because these rewards cannot be guaranteed, due to the changing needs of individuals, each member will either withdraw or attempt to secure his position, probably by over-compensating. Since all positions in the structure hold a degree of power, each member will attempt to secure more power, and in so doing he threatens the status of some other members of the organization. Power changes require that individuals make alliances, formally or informally, and as power blocks grow other groups will attempt to counteract the threat to themselves. We may illustrate the situation for all organizations as having four areas: potential conflict; conflict avoidance; active conflict; conflict resolution.

It is not enough merely to state the existence of conflict without explaining the consequences and how they may be dealt with. It can be argued that avoiding or ignoring conflict is a satisfactory way of dealing with it. In fact most organizations do just that and, in addition to not recognizing it, they actively suppress it. But three points must be made about conflict in addition to its recognition. First, if ignored it becomes dysfunctional in that energy is wasted in avoiding it which could be released into other activities; secondly, it is possible to work through conflict situations so that nobody loses face or their return on investment; and thirdly, conflict is basic to the creative exchange among members of the organization in that it is the only way in which the organization can be brought to serve the purposes of the members. Avoiding conflict resolution leads to inequitable returns for individuals which encourage them to weaken their contributions to the organization. (An equitable return is one which an individual recognizes to be fair to him and is also at an acceptable expense to other members.)

It will be clear that the idea of contract is not so much economic as psychological. The psychological aspect of the contract is important because satisfaction is basically a complex psychic response. Simple "recognition" by colleagues may be more significant to an individual than a high salary and the interest here is in the reward "set" or "cluster"—all those things that are considered by an individual to be rewarding.[4] Likewise the investment "set" will include everything an individual puts into his membership of an organization. We are thinking of individuals as complex social beings[5] with any number of facets to their make-up—material and spiritual—and it is this complexity of needs, talents, wants and contributions that we are examining in terms of social exchange and organizational membership.

EXCHANGE AND CONFLICT IN THE SCHOOL

If we translate the "exchange-conflict" concepts to the school then the following description emerges. Membership of the school would be anyone who makes an investment in the school on an economic, social or psychological dimension. Organizations construct boundaries around themselves at a point where control can most conveniently be exercised by those who see themselves as "in charge". Hence the boundary that the headmaster chooses to work within is different from that of the Chief Education Officer. The head chooses within his boundary teaching staff and pupils, with perhaps the ground staff, some kitchen staff and some caretaking staff. The Chief Education Officer includes all ancillary and support staff and possibly parents and advisory staff. While it may be argued that the boundaries of the school are defined for it by the Local Education Authority on the basis of historical precedent, the question arises as to where the head *in practice* draws the boundaries. It is clear from the examination of particular schools that boundaries are differently drawn and have different degrees of permeability—for example, some infant schools never allow parents beyond the door while others use parents as ancillary teaching staff. Equally, the influence of parents is different in a maintained comprehensive school from a minor fee-paying private school. Parents represent, *per se,* a threat to the exchange possibilities of staff in the school by adding another group with vested interests. There are various ways of handling this threat, of which the most creative is to legitimize parental rights to bargaining and to use the ensuing increased investment to bring about change in the organization of the school. To do so is to share control.

PROBLEMS OF PERSONAL STATUS

The unwillingness of most traditional leaders to share control *within* the system (as opposed to control over the system) is a factor which prevents resolution of conflict. The resolution of conflict involves give and take on all sides and this is often interpreted as defeat and weakness. The traditional view of leadership is that it exists to maintain the *status quo,* whereas in fact the maintenance of the *status quo* is a means of defence against perceived attack. For the individual leader, inability to change arises from varying degrees of self-identification with the organization—one of the most persistent factors going against proper negotiation and bargaining because he sees negotiation as providing a personal threat. If a teacher wishes to introduce a new idea or project into the school, the headmaster may approve of it so long as it reinforces his own position. If he supports it strongly he may be seeing it as a means of strengthening his bargaining position; if he merely supports it he may simply see it as no positive threat. Unfortunately, if he supports it strongly the initiator may find himself at a disadvantage, since what was initially for the teacher a means of strengthening his own position has now been transferred to support the head's position and hence becomes a weakness of his (the teacher's) bargaining position. In extreme cases, the initiator finds he has become the creature of the headmaster and is forced now to capitalize on the situation in unanticipated ways. What is certain is that the control of the idea passes to the headmaster and the initiator has increased his dependence on an authority figure. Often initators make suggestions simply to increase their bargaining position and not really because they are committed to the idea itself. Thus an English teacher might suggest that the school produce a summer revue because other dramatic presentations have been cornered by other teachers. The head accepts the idea and the revue is successful to such an extent that the head expects a revue each summer under circumstances which add to the head's reputation. In these situations the head is likely to see his interests and "the school's" to be identical and in argument will claim that the school is more dependent on him than colleagues perhaps for such reasons as "I shall still be here after you have moved on". The teacher has now to decide what return he will receive in playing along with the head.

Proprietorship is a critical aspect of the contract-conflict syndrome. While it may well be that in terms of his career, the school will have the head as a member longer than some of his colleagues[6], length of membership is no criterion for evaluating the contribution or contract of members. Indeed, to do so is to engage in just another avoidance of conflict. For if one member sees himself as having a greater interest than another in an organization, then that represents an area of potential conflict that requires to be worked through. Any member may believe himself to have the interests of the organization most near to his heart. This is never so in actuality—though one individual may be more *dependent* on an organization for more things than another. Hence the stereotype of the old stager who dedicates his life to the school and becomes increasingly upset as more and more of the other teachers want to do things differently.

CONTINUOUS RENEGOTIATION

If, on the basis of "exchange-conflict" theory members make contracts with organizations and enter into an essentially continuous negotiating relationship with their other colleagues, then the organizational structure that best fits the situation is one where roles and duties change and are shared on a continuously renegotiated basis. When roles are constant for quite considerable periods the condition is that the members of the organization are in a stable situation. When the situation changes either for a short time or altogether, the roles will change and involve a fresh process of negotiating. Few, if any, organizations are of this kind; almost all have persistent structural characteristics which vary in their ability to meet the needs of members. Yet the success of an organization depends on its ability to satisfy member needs. Many organizations cope by varying degrees of flexibility—which generally means simply bending while the pressure is on. What organizations require is a basic morphogenic quality or inherent quality of change. Schools have nothing like this quality and it remains open to examination to what extent they "ought" to be like this if so many other organizations are rigid too.

NEEDS OF MEMBERS

The first question about school structure or organization concerns its relationship to the members and the contractual situation the school serves. If it is agreed that the school has no existence apart from its members and no *a priori* organizational aims but the complex "set" of member objectives and needs, then we can examine the nature of the contract and the structure for working out that contract. If we take three groups of "members"—parents, teachers and students—it is clear that their needs are different, their demands are different and their manner of involvement different. In the simplest way, the needs of parents are proxy needs in that they will be fulfilled through their children, while teacher needs are "professional" in that their needs will be fulfilled as they do their jobs. The needs of the pupils are highly individual, and both immediate and future. For instance, a teacher of English is satisfying a personal and professional need to teach a subject she likes, but none of the children in the class may like English (or they may all like it, or some of them may) and even if they do like it during the lesson the usefulness of English to them will be different for each child. But additionally, the pupils will not fully make use of their "education" until they leave school, which may be five or six years later. The teacher may leave at the end of the term. Thus for most of the members of the school (parents and children) the time scale for rewards of membership is quite different from that of the teachers (though a teacher reward may be "getting a lot of children through O level"). Because of the professional or cosmopolitan orientation of many teachers, the contract tends to be with the education service rather than the school or even the children; teachers leave, children stay.

The structure of the school reinforces the time-scale by using the examination timetable as a control mechanism. The majority of secondary schools are organized on the basis of a need to obtain a high number of A level (and consequently O level) passes.[7] While this would appear, at face value, to suggest a concern for pupils' long-term interests, in fact it simply protects the positions of the teachers because it reinforces their structural and career needs to be, say, head of an English department, rather than the needs of the pupil in school in the future as against the present. Such a structure cannot be amenable to pressing current needs and hence is not open to contractual negotiation. Indeed, the initial contract that the pupil and parent makes when the child joins the school places all the advantages firmly on the side of the school and against the pupil. Since the contract is not continuously (or even initially) open to negotiation, there can be no wonder that children, especially as they grow older, become alienated.[8] On the basis of this model one part of a cure for truancy would be negotiation. (Primary schools, because there is more open negotiation between pupils and teachers, have fewer problems both in deciding who the members are and in entering into negotiation with them.)

CONSEQUENCES OF FAILURE TO NEGOTIATE

The development of an "exchange-conflict" model for the school (or for any organization) illustrates the consequences of a failure in the negotiating process since conflict can be stored up when negotiation is ignored or incomplete. Conflict arises when adequate negotiation does not take place. Negotiation is a complex continuous process, for the most part unplanned and even unconscious. In reality all human relationships involve some form of negotiation and contract-making and we are all conscious of the bargains[9] we have struck either when joining an organization or at critical periods during our membership. Unfortunately, many leaders and other members are unaware of this bargaining relationship, possibly seeing their behaviour in terms of "leadership" or "good management". Continually in schools one hears raised the question of responsibility and delegation which heads like to see as implying that they must hold ultimate responsibility for everyone and everything. There is no need to pursue the argument fully here[10] except to draw attention to the fact that in so far as any individual believes that he is "ultimately responsible" he will enter all negotiations with an area of bargaining sealed off, and hence there can be no full negotiation. The effect of this is for him to aim to retain personal power, but also to attempt personal protection against erosion of his status. In practice no single individual ever carries the whole can and no one can be held responsible for the failings of others, even subordinates, so to claim total personal responsibility is a form of special pleading with unfortunate organizational consequences. In schools the idea of ultimate responsibility is a myth to bolster up the status of the head, who is in any case subordinate to school governors and the local education authority, to reduce the areas of negotiation and hence to increase conflict in the areas of conflict avoidance and active conflict. The relevance of the exchange concept is equally true of hierarchial situations as of situations where all the members are equals. The added dimension that hierarchies produce is of greater intransigence in conflict potential situations. Hierarchies by their very nature increase the incidence of conflict by repression, except in so far as hierarchy is negotiated (as is probably the case in peace-time armies where lower ranks may require their superiors to dominate them —as part of the bargain). Far from resolving problems, hierarchies actually make them worse, because designated leaders insist on being more "responsible" than the other members require.

WHO SERVES WHOM?

One of the problems of the school is the question of who is there to serve whom. Hospitals have a similar dilemma in the customer/client/patient relationship to the professional/medical practitioner. While hospitals undoubtedly exist to serve the needs of patients they also undoubtedly exist to serve the needs of nurses and doctors. Indeed, from the way the hospital service functions, it would often seem that the needs of doctors and nurses are the more important. The case of schools is not dissimilar if we look at who determines the structure, sets the norms and determines the rewards. There can be little doubt that the condition for entering the contract, as the teachers make it, is that they should determine all the conditions for membership. Thus teachers decide who shall be members and in what manner (banding, streaming, even selection), what the behavioural norms will be (pupils respond to the initiatives of the teacher), what the rewards will be (which examination can be passed), what the punishments will be (by restricting opportunities available for qualifying in a limited range of subjects), and so on. It must be recalled that the only examinations that a school permits are controlled by teachers or teacher-dominated organizations; teachers choose the subjects to be studied in school and determine the status of subjects by allocating time and resources in the timetable; and teachers decide on the kind of behaviour to be permitted from members of the school. In mitigation it may be argued that education and initiation in all societies is determined by the elders and that teachers are merely surrogates for parents/elders at large; the implication in British culture may be debated, but it is significant that the structures provided for the pupils are also provided for the adult teacher, in which case they lead to a good deal of potential and active conflict. There can be little doubt that the very structures designed for the education of the child are equally dysfunctional for the adult teacher, who is hoist with his own petard of subjects chosen, working and membership norms, rewards and punishments. (For instance, teachers of low status subjects are accorded low organizational and social status.) In order to change the system, teachers are finding it necessary to think of staff much more as "collective" and this makes a very uncomfortable situation for traditionalist teachers.

CONTINUOUS NEGOTIATION

Exchange theory enables us to examine an organization in terms of the negotiation an individual makes as a condition of his membership. He himself makes a psychological contract, generally unexpressed, that his contributions will be conditional upon his personal evaluation of the returns to him. Given, however, that he perceives a threat to a just return he will try to improve his position at the expense of others. Indeed, sometimes the unspoken contract is that he should be able to achieve power at the expense of others—a greater temptation for designated leaders than other members. The exchange contract involves negotiation, which is a continuous psycho-sociological process. Mutually successful negotiation leads to harmony while unsuccessful negotiation (uni- or bi-lateral) leads to conflict. Conflict can only be resolved by successful renegotiation, though the terms of settlement may well change in the process. Many people prefer power, however precarious, to fair negotiation and most organizations like schools and hospitals are so ordered as to prevent fair exchange and negotiation. Hence they contain large numbers of people in active conflict who desire to negotiate only in unilaterally favourable ways.

THE PREVENTION OF NEGOTIATION

Schools inhibit negotiation in a number of quite clear and distinct ways, the effect of which is to place power in an increasingly limited number of hands. Briefly, these ways are problems of membership expressed structurally in the reward and punishment systems, environmental links and economic organization. In addition, though this is not dealt with here, is the whole complexity of individual personality, for to all organization models must be added the dimension of personal and interpersonal psychology.[11]

MEMBERSHIP

The school determines who shall join the conditions of membership. Individuals cannot choose to be members or not, hence they cannot negotiate conditions of entry. There can be no guarantee that the purposes of the controlling members of the school will coincide with the needs of the coerced members. Even where there is a choice of school, there is no choice of "no school". All selection systems by their very nature are discriminating and schools have quite subtle ways of showing that only a limited range of behaviours and achievements are acceptable. A different kind, and range, of behaviours is expected of student members from that expected of teaching members and there are undoubtedly many more restraints on entry negotiation for pupils and parents than teachers.

REWARDS AND PUNISHMENTS

Schools are very clear about the rules that condition rewards and punishments. The standards applied to pupils tend to be applied also to teachers, even when inappropriate, such as with regard to lateness, absence or being out of school when not teaching. Heads have very great freedom to determine their own behaviour and attendance, pupils have very little, while with teachers it varies according to age and status. Punishments tend to be summary, exemplary and statutory. Often they are strictly illegal in terms of national law but, like churches, schools can give their own standards legal standing. Rewards go to those who conform to general norms; punishments are given to deviants. In few cases are rewards or punishments negotiable, nor are they to be influenced by the general membership.

STRUCTURE

The major elements of structure are subject departments with high-status departmental heads. The timetable, which is generally inordinately complex and hence not amenable to change, is also a powerful instrument of control. The decision-making structure is usually a naive form of democracy interpreted either as taking majority decisions or representation by the head in the interests of the majority. Few schools have made any attempt to find alternative ways of helping the membership to share in decision-making. Such devices as school councils are firmly controlled by headmasters in a wide variety of traditionally unsubtle ways (such as calling a full council only once a term and then making it clear that its purpose is "advisory").

FILTERING OF ENVIRONMENT

Every member of an organization brings his perception of the environment, and of the organization, with him. How do schools select the relevant environments with which they will interact? (For example, public schools concern themselves with university entrance, the respected professions, and upper middle-class values—downtown comprehensives with getting the best number with O levels irrespective of job opportunities.) The staff decide what qualification pupils can legitimately aim at. The problem of inner city schools is that many teachers have no sense or experience of urban decline. Hence members (pupils and parents) find it impossible to discover the terms on which to open negotiations with the school staff.

ECONOMICS

The material provision of all schools is based upon an administrative model of the type of school. Each local education authority has a formula for setting up and furnishing a school which ignores the realities of membership. With some large authorities a minimal amount of negotiation is possible, but only by teaching staff, never by parents or other users. Since the school is handed over to the governors in a fixed state, there is little point in anyone negotiating a contract; at best one settles for an accommodation to the *fait accompli*. Once the school starts functioning, administrative considerations override everything and the administrators become very powerful people over *everyone* else in the system. Staff salaries, too, are only marginally negotiable; student grants are never so.

CONFLICT RESOLUTION

According to the exchange-conflict theory, individuals compensate for inadequate or fruitless negotiation by seeking power (generally higher up in the system). Successfully negotiated mutual contracts lead to commitment and no conflict. Unsuccessful negotiation leads to frustration and compensation-seeking, which in turn leads to power-seeking and conflict. However, the vitality of an organization lies in its ability to allow members to continue negotiation, which is in itself a form of conflict. This kind of conflict does not lead to frustration, but to enhanced commitment and more fully active membership. The problem arises as to how to apply this simple model (which is in fact very complex once its ramifications in terms of an actual organization become clear) to the school situation, which is itself complex. The answer can only be that if the school is aware of the nature of negotiation and contract and responds to what that means, then the whole structure will be more open and receive more support from members. The starting point is open negotiation among the members; some teachers, as well as pupils, would be simply delighted to be asked if there were any changes they would particularly like to see—and to realize that their suggestions would actually be given a try.

NOTES

1 There are many reasons for this; some of them are explored in, for instance, Kahn *et al.* (1964), where the problems of individuals as members of organizations are discussed.

2 Cf. Homans (1958) and Jacobs (1974).

3 The return can be anything, or a combination of things, that the individual requires. It may be economic, but, whatever it is, it is also a "psychic set". See below.

4 See Maslow (1964); economic rewards are a part of a complete set of personal "needs" that must be satisfied.

5 See Schein (1965) on Complex Man.

6 In these days a pupil who spends seven or eight years in school may well have a longer membership than most of his teachers, including the head.

7 Apart from teachers' salaries, one of the largest single committed financial investments is in the examination system. In many secondary schools the cost of examination entry fees is as great as the cost of an extra teacher.

8 Where pupils are not alienated the reason is that they buy off present discontents against future rewards (examination successes), but in so far as there is no negotiation the school avoids creative confrontation, since avoiding contractual problems in the present prevents their being recognized for future action.

9 See Smith (1973), especially Chapter VI, "The Problems of Integration".

10 See Gray (1973).

11 See, for example, Kahn et al. (1964).

REFERENCES

GRAY, H. L. (1973) "The Function of the Head of a School", *Journal of Moral Education*, Vol. 2, No. 2.

HOMANS, G. C. (1961) *Social Behavior*, Routledge and Kegan Paul.

HOMANS, G. C. (1958) "Social Behaviour as Exchange", *American Journal of Sociology*, **63**, pp. 597–606.

HOPPER, Earl L. (ed.) (1971) *Readings in the Theory of Educational Systems*, Hutchinson.

JACOBS, T. O. (1974) "Leadership and Social Exchange", in Tilley, K. W. (ed.) *Leadership and Management Appraisal*, pp. 193–210, English Universities Press.

KAHN, R. L. et al. (1964) *Organizational Stress: Studies in Role Conflict and Ambiguity*, Wiley.

MASLOW, A. (1964) *Motivation and Personality*, Harper and Row.

SCHEIN, E. (1965) *Organisational Psychology*, Prentice-Hall.

SILVERMAN, D. (1970) *The Theory of Organisation*, Heinemann.

SMITH, P. B. (1973) *Groups within Organisations*, Harper and Row.

3.7 The Management of Interdepartmental Conflict: A Model and Review

Richard E. Walton and John M. Dutton

ABSTRACT

A general model of interdepartmental conflict and its management is presented, together with a review of the relevant literature. The model intergrates the contextual determinants of organizational conflict emphasized by sociologists and the dynamics of conflictful relationships studied by social psychologists. The general feedback linkage in the model is provided by the adaptive and maladaptive reactions of higher executives to conflict and the consequences of conflict between units. Each of these several aspects of the model has implications for a strategy of modifying interdepartmental patterns.

Horizontal interactions are seldom shown on the organizational chart, but transactions along this dimension are often at least as important as vertical interactions (Simpson, 1959; Landsberger, 1961; Burns and Stalker, 1961). This paper presents a general model of interdepartmental conflict and its management, together with a review of the relevant literature.[1] The model includes five sets of related variables: antecedents to conflict, attributes of the lateral relationship, management of the interface, consequences of the relationship, and responses of higher executives. Figure 1 shows the general relationship among these sets of variables.

The general model is postulated as applicable to all lateral relations between any two organizational units (departments, divisions, sections, and so on) that engage in any type of transaction, including joint decision making, exchanging information, providing expertise or advice, and auditing or inspecting.

ANTECEDENTS TO INTERUNIT CONFLICT AND COLLABORATION

Manifest conflict results largely from factors which orginate outside the particular lateral relationship under consideration or which antedate the relationship. Hypotheses and models that use external factors to predict lateral relations have been advanced by March and Simon (1958), Thompson (1961), Caplow (1964), Lawrence and Lorsch (1967a, 1967b)

Source: *Administrative Science Quarterly*, (1969), Vol. 14, pp. 73–84.

and Pondy (1967). The present model describes nine major types of antecedents: mutual dependence, asymmetries, rewards, organizational differentiation, role dissatisfaction, ambiguities, common resources, communication obstacles, and personal skills and traits.

Mutual task dependence
Mutual task dependence is the key variable in the relevance of the interunit conflict model in general and the impact of the postulated conflict antecedents in particular. Task dependence is the extent to which two units depend upon each other for assistance, information, compliance, or other coordinative acts in the performance of their respective tasks. It is assumed here that dependence is mutual and can range from low to high. Asymmetry in the interdependence is treated later.

According to Miller (1959), the more performance of one unit depends on the performance of all other units, the more likely is the system to perform without external control. Other studies, however, Dutton and Walton (1966), for example, indicate that task interdependence not only provides an incentive for collaboration, but also presents an occasion for conflict and the means for bargaining over interdepartmental issues. A related factor, task overload, has similarly mixed potential for conflict and collaboration. Overload conditions may intensify the problem of scarce resources and lead to bargaining; may increase tension, frustration, and aggression; and may decrease the time available for the social interactions that would enable the units to contain their conflict. On the other hand,

Figure 1 General model of interunit conflict

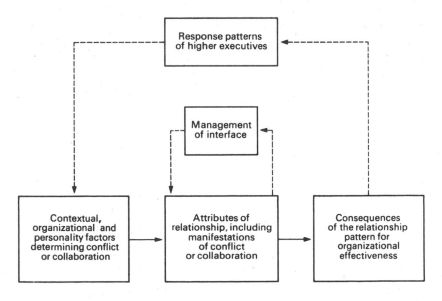

overload may place a premium on mutual assistance. The net directional effects of high task interdependence and overload are therefore uncertain.

Other implications of the extent of mutual task dependence are more predictable. High task interdependence and overload tend to heighten the intensity of either interunit antagonisms or friendliness, increase the magnitude of the consequences of unit conflict for organizational performance, and contribute to the difficulty of changing an ongoing pattern.

Task-related asymmetries

Symmetrical interdependence and symmetrical patterns of initiation between units promote collaboration; asymmetrical interdependence leads to conflict. For example, in a study by Dalton (1959), a staff group resented the asymmetries in their relationship with line groups. The staff group had to understand the problems of the line groups, had to get along with them, promote their ideas, and justify their existence; but none of these relations were reciprocal requirements imposed on the line groups. Strauss (1962) reported that asymmetrical high dependence of purchasing agents on another group led them to make more attempts to influence the terms of requisitions they received and thereby force interaction to flow both ways.

The adverse effects of asymmetrical conditions are sometimes related to the fact that one unit has little incentive to coordinate. The more dependent unit may try to increase the incentive of the more independent unit to cooperate by interfering with their task performance. The assumption is that once the independent unit is made aware of their need for the cooperation of the dependent unit (i.e. to desist from interfering acts), they will behave more cooperatively (supply the assistance necessary). This tactic may indeed achieve its purpose, and the conflict-interfering acts may cease; but frequently interference elicits a retaliatory response.

Conflict is also produced by differences in the way units are ranked along various dimensions of organizational status, namely direction of initiation of action, prestige, power, and knowledge. Seiler (1963) studied in an organization in which it was generally agreed that research had more prestige than engineering and engineering had more prestige than production. When the sequential pattern of initiation and influence followed this status ordering, it was accepted. However, where a lower-status industrial engineering group needed to direct the higher-status research group to carry out routine tests, the result was a breakdown in relationships between the departments.

Inconsistency between the distribution of knowledge among departments and the lateral influence patterns are also a source of conflict. Lawrence and Lorsch (1967a) advanced the idea that the more the influence of each unit is consistent with key competitive factors, the more effectively will interunit issues be resolved. They noted that in container firms, customer delivery and product quality were crucial for competitive success; therefore, sales and production were required to have the most influence in the resolution of interunit conflict. By contrast, in the food industry, where market expertise and food science were essential, sales and research were required to be the more influential. Landsberger (1961) also found that the locus of power among three plants in the same industry was affected by their different market positions.

Zald (1962) in a study of correctional institutions offered a power-balance proposition about the effect of relative power: assuming task interdependence and divergent values among three units (teachers, cottage parents, and social service workers), conflict is most likely to occur between units that are unable to control the situation and those perceived as being in control. He found that the patterns of conflict among these three units were generally consistent with predictions based on this power balance hypothesis.

Performance criteria and rewards

Interunit conflict results when each of the interdependent departments has responsibility for only one side of a dilemma embedded in organiz-ational tasks. Dutton and Walton (1966) noted that the preference of production units for long, economical runs conflicted with the preference of sales units for quick delivery to good customers. Dalton (1959) observed that staff units valued change, because that was one way they proved their worth; whereas line units valued stability, because change reflected unfavorably upon them or inconvenienced them. Also, staff units were strongly committed to preserving the integrity of control and rule systems, whereas line personnel believed they could be more effective by flexible reinterpretation of control and incentive schemes, and by ignoring many discipline and safety violations. A study by Strauss (1962) showed that engineers preferred to order brand items, whereas purchas-ing agents sought specifications suitable for several vendors. Similar instances abound. Landsberger (1961) postulated several basic dilemmas which probably underlie many interdepartmental differences: flexibility versus stability; criteria for short-run versus long-run performance; emphasis on measurable results versus attention to intangible results; maximizing organizational goals versus responding to other societal needs.

Although the dilemmas may be inherent in the total task, the reward system designed by management can serve either to sharpen or to blunt their divisive effective: the more the evaluations and rewards of higher management emphasize the separate performance of each department rather than their combined performance, the more conflict.

Close, one-to-one supervisory styles have generally been assumed to promote more conflict among peers than general supervision in which the superior also deals with subordinates as a group (Likert 1961). One might speculate that group supervisory patterns are taken to indicate emphasis on group rather than individual performance criteria; and that group patterns allow the supervisor to observe the process and to reward co-operative acts.

Organizational differentiation

Litwak (1961) postulated that uniform tasks require a bureaucratic type of organization, characterized by impersonality of relations, prior specification of job authority, emphasis on hierarchical authority, separation of policy and administration, and emphasis on general rules and specialization; whereas nonuniform tasks require a human-relations organization with the contrasting characteristics. In contemporary society, most large-scale organizations have to deal with both uniform and nonuniform tasks, and must combine these contradictory forms of social relations into a professional model. Litwak regards the inclusions of these contradictory forms as a source of organizational conflict.

Lawrence and Lorsch (1967a) emphasized the effects of differentiation. Where each unit (such as research, sales, or production) performs a different type of task and copes with a different segment of the environment, the units will develop significant internal differences. Such units may differ from each other (*a*) in the degree of structure, that is, tightness of rules, narrowness of span of supervisory control, frequency and specificity of performance review; and in the orientation of its members; (*b*) toward the environment, such as, new scientific knowledge versus customer problems and market opportunities versus costs of raw materials and processing; (*c*) toward time, such as planning time perspective; and (*d*) toward other people, such as, openness and permissiveness of interpersonal relationships. Lawrence and Lorsch measured these differences in six plastics organizations with the results shown in Table 1.

Table 1. Differences related to environment of departments*

Departments	Orientation toward environment	Orientation toward time	Degree of formality in departmental structure	Permissiveness versus directiveness in orientation toward others
Applied research	Techno-economic	Long	Medium	Medium
Sales	Market	Short	High	Low
Production	Techno-economic	Short	High	High

* After Lawrence and Lorsch (1967a).

Lawrence and Lorsch believe this fourfold differentiation is largely a response to the degree of uncertainty in the environments of the different departments. They use a notion of optimum degree of differentiation, which depends upon the task environments. Thus, either overdifferentiation or underdifferentiation has implications for the coordinative processes. Although greater differentiation apparently results in more *potential* for conflict, these authors do not assume that more manifest conflict will automatically result. In their study of six plastics organizations, the degree of integration did not, in fact, vary strictly with the degree of differentiation.

Role dissatisfaction

Role dissatisfaction, stemming from a variety of sources, can be a source of conflict. Blocking status aspirations in purchasing agents (Strauss, 1962) and in staff members (Dalton, 1959) led to conflict with other units. In these cases, professionals felt they lacked recognition and opportunities for advancement. Similarly, White (1961) stated that members might feel that the growth of their units and its external status did not meet their needs, and therefore might enter another unit or withdraw from contacts which were painful reminders of the lack of status. Where one unit informally reports on the activities of another unit, resentment can occur, as with staff units reporting to management on production irregularities (Dalton, 1959). Argyris (1964) and Dalton (1959) both argued that role dissatisfaction and conflict followed where one unit with the same or less status set standards for another.

Where there is role dissatisfaction, ambiguities in the definition of work responsibilities further increase the likelihood of interunit conflict. Landsberger (1961) pointed out that ambiguities tempted the dissatisfied unit to engage in offensive maneuvers so as to improve its lot, and thus induced other units to engage in defensive maneuvers.

Role dissatisfaction and ambiguity are related to more basic organizational variables, including growth rate, organizational level, and hierarchical differences. Organizational growth appears to have offsetting consequences. Slower rates of organizational growth and of opportunities for promotion increase role dissatisfaction, but are also accompanied by fewer ambiguities. Interfaces higher in the organization are more likely to be marked by conflict to redefine departmental responsibilities. At the higher levels, jurisdictional boundaries are less clear (Pondy, 1967), and the participants perceive more opportunity to achieve some restructuring. Steep and heavily emphasized hierarchical differences in status, power, and rewards were seen by Thompson (1961) as responsible for some lateral conflict, because these factors tended to activate and to legitimate individual aspiration for increased status and power and tended to lead to increased upward orientation toward the desires of one's superiors, rather than to problem orientation and increased horizontal coordination.

Ambiguities

In addition to its interaction with role dissatisfaction, ambiguity contributes to interunit conflict in several other ways. Difficulty in assigning credit or blame between two departments increases the likelihood of conflict between units. Dalton (1959) attributed part of the staff-line conflict he observed to the fact that although improvements required collaboration between line and staff units, it was later difficult to assess the contribution of each unit. Similarly, disputes resulted between production and sales units, when it could not be determined which department made a mistake (Dutton and Walton, 1966).

Low routinization and uncertainty of means to goals increase the potential for interunit conflict. This proposition is supported by Zald (1962) in his study of interunit conflict in five correctional institutions. Similarly, ambiguity in the criteria used to evaluate the performance of a unit may also create tension, frustration, and conflict (Kahn, Wolfe, *et al.*, 1964). Organization planning, which includes clarity of rule definition, correlated positively with measures of lateral coordination and problem solving in a study of ten hospitals by Georgopoulas and Mann (1962).

Dependence on common resources

Conflict potential exists when two units depend upon a common pool of scarce organizational resources, such as, physical space, equipment, manpower, operating funds, capital funds, central staff resources, and centralized services (e.g. typing and drafting). If the two units have interdependent tasks, the competition for scarce resources will tend to decrease interunit problem solving and coordination. Also, if competition for scarce resources is not mediated by some third unit and they must agree on their allocation, they will come into direct conflict.

Communication obstacles

Semantic difficulties can impede communications essential for cooperation. Strauss (1964) observed that differences in training of purchasing agents and engineers contributed to their conflicts. March and Simon (1958) stated that organizational channeling of information introduced bias.

Common experience reduces communication barriers and provides common referents. Miller (1959) proposed that the less units know about each other's job, the less collaboration and that lack of knowledge can lead to unreasonable interunit demands through ignorance. Cozer (1956) argued that accommodation is especially dependent on knowledge of the power of the other unit.

Personal skills and traits

Walton and McKersie (1965), reviewing experimental studies, found that certain personality attributes, such as high authoritarianism, high dogmatism, and low self-esteem, increased conflict behavior. Kahn *et al.* (1964,

p. 256) found that in objective role conflict persons who scored lower on neurotic anxiety scales tended to depart more from "cordial, congenial, trusting, respecting, and understanding relations", and introverts tended to lose their confidence, trust, and respect for work associates more than extroverts.

Most interunit relationships are mixed-motive situations, which require high behavioral flexibility to manage optimally. A person with a narrower range of behavioral skills is less likely to exploit the integrative potential fully in an interunit relationship. He may either engage in bargaining to the exclusion of collaborative problem solving, or withdraw or become passive (Walton and McKersie, 1966). Dalton (1959) and Thompson (1960) found that personal dissimilarities, such as, background, values, education, age, social patterns lowered the probability of interpersonal rapport between unit representatives, and in turn decreased the amount of collaboration between their respective units. Personal status incongruities between departmental representatives, that is, the degree to which they differed in rank orderings in various status dimensions (such as length of service, age, education, ethnicity, esteem in eyes of superiors, pay and so on) increase the tendency for conflict (Dutton and Walton, 1966).

Personal satisfaction with the internal climate of one's unit decreases the likelihood that a member will initiate interunit conflict. Seiler (1963) observed that in one firm, constructive handling of interdepartmental differences occurred in part because the members of each department derived social satisfaction from their work associates, had high job interest and good opportunities for promotions, and were not in conflict with each other.

INTERDEPARTMENTAL RELATIONSHIP

Tactics of conflict and indicators of collaboration
The literature on interdepartmental relations has been most vivid in its description of manifest conflict and collaboration process. Dalton (1959) observed that staff units were encouraged by top management to monitor and report on the activities of line units, and the line units retaliated by resisting the ideas of the staff units and discouraging their promotions. He also observed power struggles between line units and documented the conflict tactics of coalitions, distortion of information, and misappropriation of resources.

Strauss (1962) observed the tactics of purchasing agents who wished to increase their authority and influence over decisions shared with engineering and production. The purchasing agents made restrictive rules for the other units, evaded their rules, relied on personal contacts and persuasion to subvert the other units, and altered organization structure.

Focusing on positive relations, Georgopoulos and Mann (1962) used coordination as their broadest concept, which included the extent to which the various interdependent parts of an organization function each according to the needs and requirements of the other parts of the total system. In a study of ten hospitals, they found that over-all coordination correlated positively with (a) shared expectations, (b) absence of intra-organizational tension, (c) awareness of problems and solving of problems, and (d) ease of communication.

System characteristics of an interunit relationship

Attempting to incorporate aspects of the approaches just described, Walton (1966) developed a theory which also explains the system dynamics of conflict and collaboration in the interunit relationship. Three components of the relationship are considered: (a) exchange of information in the joint process, (b) structure of interunit interactions and decision making, and (c) attitudes toward the other unit. Two opposite types of relationships, "integrative" and "distributive", are postulated as frequently encountered systems of interunit behavior (see Table 2). This particular model now appears to be most applicable to lateral relations where the dominant transaction at the interface is joint decision making; where there is relative symmetry in interdependency; and where the transactions required are relatively frequent and important.

Table 2. Components and characteristics of contrasting types of lateral relationships*

	Type of lateral relationship	
Component	Integrative	Distributive
Form of joint decision process	Problem-solving: free exchange of information, conscientious accuracy in transmitting information	Bargaining: careful rationing, and deliberate distortion of information.
Structure of interaction and framework of decision	Flexible, informal, open	Rigid, formal, circumscribed.
Attitudes toward other unit	Positive attitudes: trust, friendliness, inclusion of other unit	Negative attitudes: suspicion, hostility, dissociation from other unit.

* After Walton (1966).

In the most general sense, the chain of assumptions underlying Walton's systems theory of lateral relationships (and explaining the distributive syndrome, in particular) is as follows: first, an antecedent, say goal competition between participants engaged in joint decision making, induces the units to engage in concealment and distortion tactics in their exchange of information, such that joint decision making takes on the character of bargaining. Second, in order to ration and distort information effectively and systematically, a unit will attempt to place limitations on the interactions and other behavior of their counterpart in order to make them more predictable and keep them within certain boundaries. Third, the way information is handled (concealment, distortion, etc.) and the way interactions are patterned (circumscribed, rigid, etc.) results in suspicion and hostility. Furthermore, these negative attitudes have a feedback effect which tend to reinforce the same interaction structure and information-handling pattern.

Regardless of the antecedents, the theory hypothesizes that the conflict relationship will become fixed as a result of: the tendency to generalize a conflictful orientation to the many areas of interunit decision making, the self-reinforcing nature of the various elements of a relationship pattern the reciprocal nature of a conflictful orientation between units, and the tendency toward socialization and institutionalization of these orientations within a unit.

The individual propositions contained in the model are generally supported by a review of the relevant literature in experimental social psychology (Walton, 1966). The hypothesized variation of attributes of a relationship are also generally supported by a comparative field study of production-sales relationships in six plants (Walton, Dutton, and Fitch, 1966). The hypothesized dominant cause-effect relationships among process, structure, and attitude are anecdotally supported in a comparison of two plants (Dutton and Walton, 1966).

The theory suggests that the total lateral relationship is influenced or determined by contextual factors operating first upon the way the parties exchange information, with the effects on interaction structure and interunit trust as subsequent reactions. However, although the process of exchanging information may be the most frequent determinant, it is not exclusively the point of entry in the lateral relationship. For instance, personality and status may first influence attitudes such as trust and friendliness in which case the pattern of information exchange and interaction structure are a secondary reaction.

MANAGEMENT OF THE INTERFACE

The relationship between units is largely a function of the conflict potential inherent in the factors already discussed; but it is also subject to control by the participants, their effectiveness depending upon how much conscious effort they invest in management of the interface and the appropriateness of the techniques they use.

Interface conflict will be managed best where the attention devoted to interface management corresponds to the degree of differentiation between departments. Lawrence and Lorsch (1967a) compared integrative devices used by three high-performing organizations selected from industries with high, medium, and low differentiation. The most differentiated firm had the most elaborate array of interface management techniques, including a separate integrative department with the primary purpose of coordinating the basic functional units, permanent teams consisting of representatives of members from functional units together with the integrative department, direct contact across hierarchies at all levels, procedures for appeal to a common superior, and a coordination system involving written communications. As expected, when all three organizations were compared, the same rank order obtained for the differentiation scores as for the degree of elaboration of integrative devices. Explicit conflict-resolution mechanisms can be overelaborate, however. For example, a formal coordinative unit was used between slightly differentiated units in a *low*-performing unit. Lawrence and Lorsch concluded that the units were not sufficiently differentiated to justify the coordinative unit, and the result was that the superfluous unit added noise to the system, actually decreasing coordination.

In their comparison of six plastics firms, Lawrence and Lorsch found that three factors promoted effective resolution of interdepartmental conflict and thus high organizational performance. First, where there is a separate coordinating person or unit, the coordinating unit will be most effective if its degree of structure and the goal, time, and interpersonal orientations of its personnel are intermediate between those of the units linked. Second, where there is a separate coordinating unit, conflict resolution will be more effective if its personnel have relatively high influence based on perceived expertise, and if they evaluated and rewarded on over-all performance measures embracing the activities of the several departments. Third, interunit cooperation will be more effectively achieved and over-all organizational performance will be higher to the extent that managers openly confront differences rather than smooth them over or force decisions. The more subtle aspects of confrontation are discussed by Schmidt and Tannenbaum (1960) and Walton (1968), who analyze the advantages and risks of confronting differences, the timing and skill required, as well as the conditions under which confrontation is most appropriate.

Seiler (1963) observed techniques for management of interunit conflict. A department may keep its own records, so as to reduce requests for information and thus avoid distasteful contact; a junior member may be assigned as the liaison person, where his presence will not arouse status conflict; and inventories may be introduced to reduce scheduling interdependence.

CONSEQUENCES OF INTERUNIT CONFLICT

The manifest characteristics of interunit conflict include: a competitive orientation, bargaining and restrictions on information, circumscribed interaction patterns, and antagonistic feelings. To determine whether the conflict has an adverse effect on organizational performance, one must assess the consequences of these characteristics. Whether a competitive orientation is in fact energizing or debilitating for members of the unit will depend in part on the personalities of the participants. For some, competition is motivating and arouses energies not otherwise available for organizational tasks; for others conflict is a major threat. Whether competitive energy will contribute to over-all performance depends upon whether a unit can improve its performance without interfering with the performance of another unit.

Another factor governing the motivational effect of conflict is the degree of symmetry in tactics between units. Crozier (1961) reported that managers who were not able to retaliate when conflict was initiated responded by withdrawing commitment from their job. Seiler (1963) postulated that internal social stability, value sharing between units, and a legitimate authority hierarchy between units were important in influencing whether interunit competition would result in destructive conflict.

According to Strauss (1964), the competitive orientation that accompanies conflict behavior may also contribute to a system of checks and balances, increase the availability of new ideas to compete with established ones, and decrease the type of collusion among middle managers, deprives higher-level top management of information.

It seems reasonable to assume that the more important the interdependence, the more a restriction on interunit information becomes damaging. When a lateral relationship involves joint decision making, each unit can bias the decisions in its own favor by controlling information relevant to these decisions. Even minor concealment or distortion can be of great importance, if the decisions are key ones.

The structural attributes of a conflictful relationship are not necessarily variable in the lateral relationship, as for example, the number of liaison contacts between departments, which may be specified by higher authorities. Whether a structural attribute has a positive or an adverse effect on over-all performance depends on factors other than structure. For example, in a conflictful pattern more problems are referred to the superiors. On the one hand, referral may overload a superior; on the other, a superior may find himself more informed about operations and subordinates. Similarly, referral of problems requiring new policy may also be organizationally useful. Also, the inability of a decision-making pair to change decision rules or apply them flexibily may result in decisions that are not innovative. However, given the larger network of task relationships in which the pair is embedded, the inflexibility may produce a degree of predictability, which is valuable for some other reason.

Channeling all interunit interactions through a few liaison persons in a conflict syndrome often reduces over-all performance; for where other persons are either affected by an interunit decision or have potentially relevant information or opinions, ignoring their contribution decreases the quality of the decisions and lowers the commitment to decisions.

Apart from their influence on the quality of decisions, the attributes of an interunit relationship may impinge upon coordinative activities. For example, a tendency to avoid contact can result in implementation that lacks coordination. The seriousness of the effect of conflict in decreasing the rate of interaction between the units therefore depends in part upon how much coordination is required to implement joint decisions.

Conflict relationships involve stereotyping and include *attitudes* of low friendliness, low trust, and low respect. Such attitudes indirectly affect performance. For example, low trust limits the flow of relevant task information and decreases coordinative interactions. Furthermore, some persons experience psychological strain when other persons dislike or distrust them. Dalton (1959, p. 95) reported that staff men were shocked by the need to engage in conflict that required them to use their interpersonal skills as much as their academic skills. The stress of this interpersonal or intergroup climate may result in higher turnover or withdrawal from interdepartmental relations.

A positive by-product of interunit rivalry is more unit cohesion, which contributes to cooperation within the unit. Each unit may become more receptive to directives from their own hierarchy; but sometimes the centralization of control within the unit causes frustration in subordinates (Seiler, 1963). Competition may serve as a useful training device. Managers' insight into how the respective goals of interdependent units contribute to over-all goals may be sharpened. Negotiating and policy-making skills of prospective top managers may be increased, and tolerance of unavoidable conflict may be developed.

Some of the postulated relationships between attributes of a conflictful syndrome and consequences for over-all performance are shown in Table 3. Each of the relationships is subject to limiting conditions, some of which were noted earlier. The point being made is that conclusions about the effect of a generally competitive or conflictful relationship can only be made on the basis of an analysis of the specific components of the pattern together with an analysis of the task. Comparative field data are needed to evaluate the validity of the concept of an optimum degree of competitiveness and rivalry. The optimum might be expected to vary, depending upon the type of interunit interdependence, the type of work of each unit, and the personalities of unit representatives.

RESPONSES OF HIGHER EXECUTIVES

Response tendencies of executives
The response of executives refers to how superiors react to information about subordinate organizational units; that is, to low performance and attributes of the interunit relationship itself. Here "low performance" means inadequate productivity, low adaptability, or inability of the units to conserve their human and other resources.

A manager's response is a combination of his habitual patterns,

Table 3. Consequences of interunit conflict

Attributes of conflictful lateral relationships	Illustrative consequences
Competition in general	Motivates or debilitates Provides checks and balances
Concealment and distortion	Lowers quality of decisions
Channeled interunit contacts	Enhances stability in the system
Rigidity, formality in decision procedures	Enhances stability in the system Lowers adaptability to change
Appeals to superiors for decisions	Provides more contact for superiors May increase or decrease quality of decisions
Decreased rate of interunit interaction	Hinders coordination and implementation of tasks
Low trust, suspicion, hostility	Psychological strain and turnover of personnel or decrease in individual performance

emotional reactions, and deliberate responses. This idiosyncratic element in the system of interunit conflict shown in Figure 1 is a major problem in developing a general explanatory or predictive model of the total system. For the same reason, however, it is an opportunity for improving the interunit relationship. Several automatic responses to low performance can be noted for illustration. If the joint performance of two units is considered inadequate, higher executives may place particular emphasis on observable, short-run measures of performance for each subunit. Thus, poor performance, whatever its source, may lead to the very rewards, controls, and styles of supervision here shown to be antecedents to conflict. If the relationships hypothesized are valid, reinforcing feedback will lead to more interunit conflict and still lower performance. White (1961) reported that higher executives who were dissatisfied with the performance of subordinate units frequently responded by reorganizing the units. The feelings of status depreciation or power deprivation and the ambiguity which frequently follow a reorganization may increase the potential for conflict.

Executive responses in relation to the model
The model has implications both for determining what needs changing and for developing a strategy for achieving the change. Executive responses can either reinforce and intensify a conflict pattern, or create pressures to change it. Much depends upon how sophisticated a diagnostic model the manager uses. Ideally he would take into account all the

valid implications of a model of the antecedents, dynamics, and consequences of conflict.

The model as a diagnostic tool. Cause-and-effect relationships can be traced back through the model as follows:

1   Are there manifestations of conflict or low collaboration in the lateral relationship? If not, this interunit conflict model is not relevant. If so, determine the particular aspects of the relationship processes that are impinging upon performance; for instance, distortion of information, infrequent interaction, and lack of mutual assistance.

2   Are these dysfunctional elements of the conflict process inherent in a competitive interunit relationship? If not, determine how the management activities at the interface are inadequate, and whether these can be modified by suggesting or requiring changes in them. If they are, determine what particular contextual variables are responsible for the competitive orientation; for example, scarce resources, competitive reward system, asymmetrical task interdependence, or personalities of key liaison personnel.

3   Which of the contextual factors that create the interunit conflict are not inherent in the technology or are not essential parts of the administrative apparatus? Determine which of these might be modified to have a significant influence on the relationship.

An exhaustive treatment of the factors which are instrumental in altering a conflictful interunit relationship and which executives can modify would review the entire model. Instead, only a few relevant executive responses that have been treated in the literature are considered.

Thompson (1960) identified three areas of executive response: first, "within limits, administrative allocations (of rewards, status symbols, resources, etc.) determine the relative deprivation experienced by organizational members, and thereby control potential conflict inherent in modern technologies" (392). Second, "to the extent that recruitment and selection procedures limit or maintain it within manageable pattern, the organization can manage the potential conflict in latent role diversity" (394). By latent role diversity, Thompson means differences in socioeconomic status, ethnic background, and so on. Third, "by varying the distinctiveness of the organization, the proportion of members exposed, and the frequency and regularity of their exposure, the organization gains a measure of control over conflict stemming from potential reactions to competing pressures" (396). Here he is referring to organizational conflict induced by ideas or pressures from the organization's environment.

Landsberger (1961) states that horizontal differences in authority can be more strongly supported by organizational logic, and need be less dependent on arbitrary fiat than vertical authority. On the other hand, differences in lateral authority are less obvious and are less likely to be stated explicitly, and therefore tend toward conflict. Consequently, one executive response is to make explicit rules allocating final authority for decisions on interunit activities, so as to depersonalize the order. A related response is for higher executives to develop rules to cover an increasing proportion of interunit transactions, and thereby confine decisions to exceptional situations, a practice noted by both Brown (1960) and Landsberger (1961).

Pondy (1967) refers to other devices which are not only available to those who manage the interface, but which can also be included in the executive response repertory: reducing dependence on common resources, transfer pricing between units, loosening schedules, or introducing buffer inventories. Litwak (1961) suggests many "mechanisms or segregation", used to reduce the conflict generated by contradictory social forms which modern organizations must incorporate, including stricter role separation between those for whom affect and those for whom strict objectivity is important; physical separation, such as moving the research facility away from the production facility; and transferral occupations, such as engineers who maintain involvement with a product from research to production stages.

Implications of the model for change of strategy. Ideally, higher executives would develop a strategy for modifying the level of interunit conflict and collaboration which not only acts on the problem diagnosed, but also takes into account the self-perpetuating characteristics of conflict relationships. The analysis of the dynamics of lateral relationship not only underscored the self-reinforcing tendencies of conflictful processes of information exchange, interaction patterns, and attitudes between units; it is also stressed the reciprocal and regenerative tendencies of conflictful approaches to the interface.

These self-reinforcing, regenerative and reciprocal tendencies lead to persistence of a conflict process; therefore, higher management needs to engage in activities designed to replace existing patterns. Blake, Shepard and Mouton (1964), and Walton (1968) have outlined theories and techniques of third-party consulting interventions. The underlying assumption is that the units must find a new culture in which to view and understand each other. Various techniques of re-education can be used to change intergroup perceptions based on stereotypes, misunderstanding the intention of others, and past history of hostile relations. Thus, whether higher executives conclude that basic contextual factors or techniques for interface management need to be modified, change effort will be effective only if it includes some interventions which help change the existing pattern.

CONCLUSIONS

Several features of the model of interunit conflict deserve emphasis: First, no *a priori* assumption is made that interunit conflict should be reduced. Second, the model recognizes a large number of potential determinants of conflict and conflict-reinforcement syndromes. Third, the model incorporates contextual and structural factors emphasized by sociologists and economists, as well as interpersonal interaction phenomena

K

studied by social psychologists. These approaches are integrated in the explanatory model and in the action implications of the model. Fourth, the model of the internal dynamics of the relationship particularly throws light on the problems of unfreezing the existing patterns. Fifth, the ability to manage interunit conflict is shown to require sophistication in executive response.

NOTE

1 This research was supported by a grant from the McKinsey Foundation for Management Research, Inc.

REFERENCES

ARGYRIS, CHRIS (1964) *Integrating the Individual and the Organization*, Wiley.

BLAKE, R. R., SHEPARD, H. A. and MOUTON, J. S. (1964) *Intergroup Conflict in Organizations*, Foundation for Research on Human Behavior.

BROWN, W. (1960) *Explorations in Management*, Tavistock Publications.

BURNS, T., and STALKER, G. M. (1961) *The Management of Innovation*, Tavistock Publications.

CAPLOW, T. (1964) *Principles of Organizations*, Harcourt, Brace and World.

COZER, L. A. (1956) *The Functions of Social Conflict*, Free Press.

CROZIER, M. (1961) "Human Relations at the Management Level in a Bureaucratic System of Organization", *Human Organization*, **20**, pp. 51–64.

DALTON, M. (1959) *Men Who Manage*, Wiley.

DUTTON, J. M., and WALTON, R. E. (1966) "Interdepartmental Conflict and Cooperation: Two Contrasting Studies", *Human Organization*, **25**, pp. 207–20.

GEORGOPOULOS, B. and MANN, F. (1962) *The Community General Hospital*, MacMillan.

KAHN, R. L., WOLFE, D. M., QUINN, R. P., SNOEK, J. D. and ROSENTHAL, R. A. (1964) *Organizational Stress: Studies in Role Conflict and Ambiguity*, Wiley.

LANDSBERGER, H. A. (1961) "The Horizontal Dimension in a Bureaucracy", *Administrative Science Quarterly*, **6**, pp. 298–333.

LAWRENCE, P. R. and LORSCH, J. W. (1967a) *Organization and Environment*, Division of Research, Graduate School of Business Administration, Harvard University.

LAWRENCE, P. R. and LORSCH, J. W. (1967b) "Differentiation and Integration in Complex Organizations", *Administrative Science Quarterly*, **12**, pp. 1–47.

LIKERT, R. (1961) *New Patterns of Management*, McGraw-Hill.

LITWAK, E. (1961) "Models of Bureaucracy which Permit Conflict", *American Journal of Sociology*, **67**, pp. 177–84.

MARCH, J. G. and SIMON, H. A. (1958) *Organizations*, Wiley.

MILLER, E. J. (1959) "Technology, Territory and Time", *Human Relations*, **12**, pp. 243–72.

PONDY, L. R. (1967) "Organizational Conflict: Concepts and Models", *Administrative Science Quarterly*, **12**, pp. 296–320.

SCHMIDT, W. and TANNENBAUM, R. (1960) "The Management of Differences", *Harvard Business Review*, **38**, Nov.-Dec. pp. 107–15.

SEILER, J. A. (1963) "Diagnosing Interdepartmental Conflict", *Harvard Business Review*, **41**, Sept.-Oct., pp. 121–32.

SIMPSON, R. L. (1959) "Vertical and Horizontal Communication in Formal Organization", *Administrative Science Quarterly*, 4, pp. 188–96.

STRAUSS, G. (1962) "Tactics of Lateral Relationship: the Purchasing Agent", *Administrative Science Quarterly*, **7**, pp. 161–86.

STRAUSS, G. (1964) "Work-flow Frictions, Interfunctional Rivalry, and Professionalism: a Case Study of Purchasing Agents", *Human Organization*, **23**, pp. 137–49.

THOMPSON, J. D. (1960) "Organizational Management of Conflict", *Administrative Science Quarterly*, **4**, pp. 389–409.

THOMPSON, V. A. (1961) *Modern Organization*, Alfred A. Knopf.

WALTON, R. E. (1966) "Theory of Conflict in Lateral Organizational Relationships", in Lawrence, J. R. (ed.) *Operational Research and the Social Sciences*, pp. 409–28, Tavistock Publications.

WALTON, R. E. (1968) "Interpersonal Confrontation and Basic Third-party Roles", *Journal of Applied Behavioral Sciences*.

WALTON, R. E., DUTTON, J. M. and FITCH, H. G. (1966) "A Study of Conflict in the Process, Structure, and Attitudes of Lateral Relationships", in Haberstroh and Rubenstein (eds.) *Some Theories of Organization*, revised edition, pp. 444–65, Irwin

WALTON, R. E., and MCKERSIE, R. B. (1965) *A Behavioral Theory of Labor Negotiations*, McGraw-Hill.

WALTON, R. E. and MCKERSIE, R. B. (1966) "Behavioral Dilemmas in Mixed-motive Decision Making", *Behavioral Science*, **11**, pp. 370–84.

WHITE, J. (1961) "Management Conflict and Social Structure", *American Journal of Sociology*, **67**, pp. 185–91.

ZALD, M. N. (1962) "Power Balance and Staff Conflict in Correctional Institutions", *Administrative Science Quarterly*, **7**, pp. 22–49.

4 Theory and Practice

INTRODUCTION
The final section of the Reader begins with a paper by George Baron outlining the Victorian legacy of the "headmaster tradition"; some students might like to compare this paper with the one referring to the industrial legacy by Burns (2.7, p. 148). This is followed by a British research study by Meredydd Hughes which, besides giving some fascinating live case material, concludes by emphasizing (as have other articles in the Reader) that one of the most crucial tasks of the "professional-as-administrator" is the "acceptability" of his approach to the professional colleagues working with him. There follows a short discussion by Eric Hoyle, highly relevant to the contemporary situation, upon the use of the word "profession" as it is used in teaching.

The section then changes its perspective to look at a conflict model with regard to decision making in the school curriculum. This paper by John Eggleston carries on from M. D. F. Young the notion that the social perspective of both teachers and children is a critical factor in the occurrence of change in the school curriculum.

The greatest merit of Sugarman's paper, "The School as a Social System", is probably its clear and complete analysis of both the problems and the sub-systems involved in them. More clearly than any other paper in this volume it stresses the need to examine outputs in the educational system. Students will have to make up their own minds as to whether Sugarman has produced a method of making "case studies of individual schools mutually comparable". Joyce Oldham's article, which follows, outlines some of the difficulties and opportunities in planning an empirical study in a school; the author stresses the need to take into account the importance of power distribution and its effect on decision-making, not just in school but also in the wider society.

The two concluding papers in the Reader reflect basic concerns of the course as a whole as well as a general point that management must be a dynamic activity. The first, by Newell, describes an important and comparatively new approach in schools using the work which has been done in Organization Development, a set of techniques derived from the behavioural sciences which represents a useful addition to the conceptual armoury of management in education. The final paper, by Ray Bolam, brings together several themes which have been apparent in many articles throughout the Reader. It attempts to synthesize a number of approaches and tentatively suggests a way forward.

4.1 Some Aspects of the "Headmaster Tradition"[1]

George Baron

"It is a tradition of English life," wrote Norwood (Norwood and Hope, 1909) "that the Headmaster is an autocrat of autocrats, and the very mention of the title conjures up in the minds of most people a figure before which they trembled in their youth, and with which they have never felt quite comfortable even in mature life. The Headmaster, in most English schools, certainly holds a position of absolute power, for which no analogy can be found in any other profession whatever, a position, further, of authority and in influence far surpassing all that is exercised by those of the same rank in other countries."

The assessment is no longer generally valid,[2] but the position of the headmaster, both in old-established public and grammar schools and even in the "new" secondary schools, still continues to be a distinctive feature of English education and attracts, as it has always done, the attention and surprise of foreign visitors. Whilst he can no longer, without arousing opposition or ridicule, exert the autocratic powers which made his Victorian predecessors legendary figures, he is still, in a very real sense, the pivot and focus of his school, whether it is controlled by an independent governing body or by a local education authority. A headmaster is expected, if not to rule, certainly to lead, both by staff and pupils alike and one who is "weak", in that he fails to protect his colleagues from outside interference, or who cannot make decisions and enforce them within his school, is little esteemed, no matter what qualities of personal charm, sympathetic understanding or academic distinction he may possess. Moreover, he is expected to have sufficient acquaintance with each of the hundreds of pupils in his school to satisfy parents who wish to discuss details of their children's education with him. Indeed, a major popular criticism made of the comprehensive schools now being opened in London is that no head could conceivably know personally two thousand children and the suggestion that this particular responsibility should be assumed by his colleagues does not give widespread satisfaction.[3]

Source: University of Leeds, Institute of Education (June, 1956) Researches and Studies, 14 with a postscript by the author (1974) commissioned for this volume by The Open University.

In spite of the importance attached to his office, little examination has been made of the evolution of this concept of the "Headmaster". At most, it is ascribed to the respect for "tradition" usually considered characteristic of the English approach to social institutions. But this is merely to note that what exists now has existed for an appreciable span of years and furnishes no explanation as to why a particular institution has survived, nor what successive and diverse influences have sustained and modified its original form and later growth. Close examination of such influences may, however, show that what is termed "tradition" is in reality not merely due to inertia and an aversion to change, but to a delicate counterpoise resulting from a series of dissimilar but compensating social factors.

In the case of the headmaster the tradition is not one distantly seated in our history. Until the beginning of the nineteenth century the "Headmaster", as distinct from the "Master", hardly existed, save in a few of the larger and better known schools. A school consisted of one man and his pupils. Even when an "Usher" was appointed it was not unusual for him to be quite independent of the Master and to be responsible to the trustees of the foundation alone. Only exceptionally, when numbers rose and when the Master wished to lighten his duties, did he engage personal assistants at his own expense.

The rapid development of the more famous Public Schools in the first half of the nineteenth century, however, resulted in the Master being obliged to engage a number of assistants, whose numbers rose or fell with the fortunes of the school. In some cases their position was little better than that of the ill-paid and half-literate teachers in some of the private schools of the time; in others they enjoyed profits earned from boarding pupils in their own houses or augmented their stipends by fees received for private tuition. In the newer schools, such as the City of London School and University College School, founded to meet rising middle-class demands, the need for a "staff" in the modern sense of the term was apparent from the earliest days and the number of assistant masters and their conditions of service were determined by energetic Governing Bodies.

At this stage in the development of secondary education the position of the headmaster was by no means as stable as it was later to become. At Eton, Westminster and Winchester he was "an officer and subordinate member of the Foundation or College, and subject to the superintendence of its head, the Provost, Warden or Dean" (Public Schools Commission, 1864); and at the newly founded Liverpool Institute School his office hardly existed at all in that its powers were shared in turn, on the Scottish pattern,[4] by a number of masters of equal status. It was, indeed, by no means certain how a large school should be organised and especially where the centre of power should lie. Had it not been for the appointment of Arnold to Rugby the issue might conceivably have been a major one.

The originality of Arnold lay in his regarding his school first and foremost as a community which shaped the characters of his boys as well as their minds. Moreover, because of his sense of pastoral mission, which expressed and was supported by the liberal evangelism of his time, he was convinced that he must be the centre of that community and exercise his influence on every individual member of it. Thus he developed his well-known prefect system through which he enlisted, though not without difficulties, the aid of older boys to discipline and guide the younger and placed his carefully chosen assistant masters in charge of the "houses" hitherto run by "dames". Throughout, to parents, old boys and his many friends and correspondents, he never tired of showing how his work at Rugby was a vocation.

It is understandable that the example of Arnold spread to other boarding schools of similar status and importance: the conditions under which boys were taught, the absence of effective organisation, the misuse of endowments and, above all, the low moral tone of school life became increasingly repugnant to the awkening conscience of early Victorian England. It was not inevitable, however, that it should exert the profound influence that it did on the wide range of endowed grammar schools, both boarding and day, which were so drastically reformed in the middle of the century, nor that it should be adopted in the many new foundations which came into being. That this was the case resulted from other factors, including the determination of the rising industrial and commercial interests to break down institutions based upon privilege and patronage and to apply, in their reconstruction, the lessons learnt in the business firm and the factory in which rewards, and, indeed, security depended upon day-to-day performance. What took place, then, was an "organisational" as well as an industrial revolution, which produced the Civil Service, the Army of the Cardwell reforms and later the organs of local government which we know today. In educational matters the Public Schools Commissions of 1864 and the subsequent Public Schools Act of 1868, though by no means root and branch in their approach, firmly remodelled the government of the major Public Schools and made their headmasters responsible to, and dismissible by, the governing bodies of their schools, whilst at the same time affirming their control over internal organisation.

Four years later, the members of the Schools Inquiry Commission (1868), in the course of their thorough and detailed examination of all other schools providing secondary education in some form, found many extraordinary instances of gross mismanagement and neglect. They recommended, therefore, that in all cases a Master should be dismissible by his governing body and that, furthermore, his emoluments should be "largely and intimately connected with his success". It was indeed urged by Sir John Coleridge with the formidable backing of Mr. John Stuart Mill and Mr. Morley that the Master should be guaranteed nothing save house and grounds rent free. Beyond this he should receive a fixed sum for each boy admitted to his school. Other Commissioners felt, however, that a small regular income should also be guaranteed in order to give new Masters time to build up their schools (Vol. I, p. 599).

This approach, the counterpart in secondary education of "payment by results" in the elementary field, reflected the current belief that the methods which had proved so successful in the industrial field would be similarly beneficial elsewhere.

W. E. Forster certainly espoused it wholeheartedly. "We had," he said in the House of Commons, when introducing the Endowed Schools Bill of 1869, "to consider carefully this question—whether it is desirable that masters should have any payment out of the endowment or should entirely depend upon school fees. I confess that I formed my opinion on this point in a great measure from my trade experience. I looked upon masters as persons employed by the trustees to do certain work and—I hope that they will not feel the comparison a disparaging one—I thought it would be right to treat them as I should treat persons whom I employed to do any commercial work. Now, I have found that the way to get the best service in such cases is to give a small fixed income, which makes a man independent of great want and calamity and then make the remainder of his income depend, fairly and generously, upon the success of the undertaking in which he is engaged. I believe that will be the system by which we can best regulate the payments to the masters of these schools whereas very frequently their income is entirely independent of the success of the school and in those cases the school does not succeed" (Hansard, 1869).

In the revision of school schemes which followed the passage of the Endowed Schools Act the recommendations of Forster and his colleagues were substantially accepted and the personal fortunes of headmasters intimately linked with those of their schools. More important still, the staffing of the schools was, in the great majority of cases, placed wholly in the hands of the headmasters. They were given full powers to appoint and dismiss their assistants and, provided that the total expenditure did not exceed a fixed sum, to pay them whatever salaries they considered advisable. The supremacy of the nineteenth-century headmaster in his school was thus based upon his possessing all the powers of the nineteenth-century employer.[5]

Many consequences followed. Since the emoluments of a headmaster depended upon his success in increasing the numbers in his school, he had not only to make a show of efficiency, but he had to bow to the increasing pressure to bring scientific subjects, modern languages and geography into the curriculum. Similarly, he had to respond to the demands of parents and employers for visible results and hence sought to enter as many pupils as possible for examinations such as the Oxford and Cambridge "Locals", the London Matriculation and those of the College of Preceptors. Another important result of the widening of the curriculum and the development of new specialisms was that the prestige of a headmaster came to be based less upon his scholarship, although this might on occasion be considerable, but upon his organisational powers; his capacity for maintaining and developing the "tone" of his school and for fostering its corporate life through athletics and out-of-school activities; his sense of occasion as expressed through morning assemblies and speech days; and the personal links which he established with parents, old boys and civic leaders.

The Schools Inquiry Commission (1868) had reported adversely on the virtual monopoly of headmasterships by clergymen. "It is said," they wrote, "and we think with justice, that the profession suffers from the frequent restriction of valuable masterships to men in Holy Orders—and we believe those of our witnesses are right, who consider that their abolition would go a long way to give the profession of teaching a position and importance of its own" (Vol. I, pp. 611–12).

Despite the subsequent removal from many schemes of clauses requiring headmasters to be in Orders, the replacement of clerics by laymen proceeded slowly. The evidence submitted to the Royal Commission on Secondary Education (1895) by the Assistant Masters' Association showed that of the 596 headmasters of the public secondary schools of which details had been obtained, as many as 283 were clerics (Vol. IV, Minutes of Evidence No. 13, 099). It was not until local education authorities, influenced by their nonconformist voters, began to be represented on governing bodies after 1902 that the possession of Holy Orders ceased to be an important qualification for a headmastership of an endowed grammar school. Moreover, the long continuance of the clerical headmaster tradition could not fail to influence the attitudes of those who were laymen. They assumed, and were expected to assume, something of the moral purpose of their predecessors and often paid particular attention to religious training. Indeed, even at the present day, the headmaster, because he conducts the "daily act of worship" and not infrequently takes upon himself the religious education of his senior boys, is linked with the older order.

From the point of view of the consolidation of the "idea of the headmaster" an important factor was the influence of reform in creating a community of understanding among those so clearly responsible for the well-being of their schools. The Headmasters' Conference brought together the leaders of the most prominent schools from 1869 onwards, whilst by the end of the century the Headmasters' Association, set up in 1890, had enrolled practically every headmaster of a secondary school of note. Through the latter body in particular, the man working in some obscure country grammar school or some newly-founded municipal secondary school was brought into touch with the great figures of the day, heard them declare with passion their determination to defend their independence against the central authority and local authorities proposed by the Royal Commission on Secondary Education and was strengthened in his own resolve to assert his authority over his school and its destiny.

The headmaster remained no longer an isolated figure, dependent only upon his school and his personal qualities for his status, but was a member of a well-organised body of vigorous and active men, who, through the Conference and the Association, constantly voiced their disapproval of any infringement of their authority and their autonomy. Thus when the Board of Education and the local education authorities eventually came into being they entered an area in which the chief vantage points had already been seized by well-organised and determined forces.

By comparison with the headmasters, their employees, the assistant masters, were slow in developing a sense of identity and common purpose. This was largely because of the very great diversity of men staffing the schools. They ranged from graduates of Oxford and Cambridge, whiling away a few years before entering upon a good "living", to youths who remained at their schools for two or three years as underpaid drudges. Between these two extremes there were ex-elementary school teachers, who had, in some cases, secured degrees of London University by part-time study; athletic young men prepared to "look upon cricket not only as their pleasure but as their duty" (*The Journal of Education*, 1886); and a motley and changing assembly of others who had failed to make good in a recognised profession. Tenure, even for well-qualified men, was insecure and not infrequently a change of headmaster meant the dismissal of the entire existing staff of the school.[6]

Salaries, too, were low, even by the standards of the day, and there could be little hope of increments for length of service. Finally, nothing in the way of superannuation existed, save in the most well-endowed schools.

Nevertheless, the expansion of the older Universities following the reforms of the mid-century and, more particularly, the increasing number of graduates produced by London, Wales and Victoria, meant that the core of well-qualified men serving as assistant masters was growing. It was not until 1891, however, that their frustration first expressed itself in an organised form through the Assistant Masters' Association. It is significant that the earliest energies of the latter were not devoted to campaigns for adequate salaries or pensions, but to securing that its members should no longer be regarded as the employees of their headmasters and should be accorded equal status with them as employees of the same governing bodies.

This first objective was attained with the passing of the Endowed Schools (Masters) Act of 1908 and the assistant masters in grammar schools ceased to be the paid servants of their headmasters.[7] From this time their position was closer to that of teachers in elementary schools and secondary schools maintained by local education authorities in which head teachers and staff alike were employed by the latter or by appropriate governing bodies.

As has been suggested, there was, during the last decade of the nineteenth century, considerable nervousness among the well-established headmasters of existing grammar schools lest the proposed Board of Education and local education authorities would bring about the loss of their independence and oblige them to conform to rigid codes and regulations of the kind associated with the elementary school world.

In the event, the Board proved to be their ally and lost no opportunity for emphasising that all secondary schools should, through the institution of individual governing bodies, enjoy a wide measure of independence and that headmasters and headmistresses alike should retain the pre-eminence which they had attained during the preceding century.[8]

Some of the new local education authorities, however, were not always of this mind. They, and particularly their Secretaries and Directors of Education, were striving to establish their position in respect of schools which had hitherto held them at a distance and in respect also of their own higher grade and day technical schools which, in some cases at least, were seeking to secure something of the independence of the secondary schools proper. Hence they were anxious to acquire or retain control of staffing and tended to treat headmasters with scant respect. Close local control was, nevertheless, strongly resisted by the Board. Its officials were men educated in schools of national status and prestige and they viewed secondary education as a vehicle for the cultural life and traditions of the nation as a whole rather than for local and sectional interests. It was therefore, to protect the headmaster against undue interference that they stressed the importance of every secondary school having its own governing body, composed not only of members of the local education committee but also of men and women with special knowledge and interests in educational matters. It is interesting to note that, from this time, governing bodies were intended to become the protectors of the independence of the headmasters of the new secondary schools rather than, as envisaged by the nineteenth-century reformers, the means for checking their excesses.

During the vital formative years between 1902 and 1914, moreover, the influence of the Board made itself insistently felt through its indefatigable teams of inspectors. They did not hesitate to recommend the removal of an inefficient headmaster, but they emphasised the importance of his office by the detailed attention which they paid to it during full inspections and by the support which they strove to give to men who could bring the spirit of the established grammar schools and of the older Universities into the new county and municipal schools. In many areas local authorities began to think on similar lines and show a preference for men with distinguished educational antecedents.

To some extent, the years following the first world war saw a shift in what might be termed the "centre of gravity" of secondary education. The rapid increase in the number of secondary schools maintained or controlled by local education authorities meant that their staffs, benefiting from the activities of the National Union of Teachers in the elementary school field, secured a standard salary scale through the Burnham settlement, a nation-wide superannuation scheme and, as a result of stubbornly fought battles with individual local authorities, a vastly increased security of tenure. In that headmasters in such schools were now dealing with men independent of them as regards their salaries and tenure, they were in a far less autocratic position than before. Similarly, in independent and direct-grant schools, whilst headmasters retained their powers to appoint and, with the approval of their governing bodies, to dismiss their assistant masters and whilst salaries and pensions depended upon the custom of each individual school, the ability of any school to attract able and well-qualified masters depended upon it offering them conditions of service at least as favourable as those available to them if they joined the service of a local education authority.

Yet despite these factors and despite also the changed social atmosphere of the post-war years, the headmaster, both in maintained and in less closely-regulated schools, still continued to enjoy a distinctive position. Paradoxically enough, a major reason for this was the freedom which the Board of Education sought to give to each school and indeed to each assistant master in his actual work in the classroom. Since the duties of the latter were not defined and still less the precise content of his teaching or the methods he should use, he had, within the school itself, no clearly formulated professional rights. He could be required by his headmaster, who alone was responsible for internal organisation, to teach subjects for which he had little liking, or to accept what he considered an undue proportion of difficult or backward forms. Furthermore, although his headmaster could not bring about his dismissal, save after a hard-fought and wearing struggle with his professional association, he could exercise an often decisive influence through the open testimonial or the confidential reference. On the other hand, the increasing uniformity of the academic and professional background of headmasters and assistant masters, combined with the revolt in the twenties and the thirties against the authoritarianism prevalent in many occupations in Victorian and Edwardian times, made the confident exercise of such powers less attractive to headmasters themselves.

It remains to be seen how far the greatly expanded conception of secondary education resulting from the Act of 1944 will bring new elements into the situation. There has been a reversion, as regards the basis of the headmaster's salary, to the principle of it being closely linked to the number of pupils in his school, but the motive has not been to encourage headmasters to attract more pupils but to ensure that salaries roughly correspond to existing responsibilities. The former inflexibility of the Burnham scales has also been modified, so that headmasters can exercise decisive influence over the allocation of allowances for advanced work to assistant masters. On the other hand, the difficulty of finding men to staff the schools, at least in science subjects, restricts any tendency towards arbitrary and capricious action in any side of school organisation. Furthermore, the interlinking of all forms of school with the agencies of the welfare state brings constant pressure on a headmaster to think in terms of immediate administrative necessity, of compromise to meet the wishes of the many bodies and individuals concerned with his school and of quick and effective response to the social situation in which he works.

So far, however, there are few signs of any significant change, on a scale commensurate with that which took place in the last century, in fundamental thinking concerning the headmaster's office. It might perhaps be expected that, just as the prevailing industrial philosophy of a hundred years ago affirmed his autonomy and his personal responsibility, so might the present-day development of managerial training lead to attempts to analyse and assess his position in a world of increasingly complex inter-relationships. But, despite the vast scope of secondary education and the incorporation within it of secondary modern schools and secondary technical schools, some of the roots of which lie deep in the old traditions of elementary education, very little has yet been said or written bearing on the subject. In particular, no thought appears to have been given to examining how assistant masters might, before entering upon headmasterships, prepare themselves through organised and intensive study for their new duties.[9] There is, of course, no intention here to suggest that the headmaster is less sensitive to changing circumstances than the businessman or the civil servant. The reverse is frequently true. What is argued is that serious thinking and consequently popular speculation about his role and about school structure is dogged by recollections of earlier stereotypes derived from the time-hardened images of the great Victorian individualists and hence difficult to assess within the close-knit patterns of shared responsibility characteristic of present-day enterprise. As a result the demands made by rapid social change and by the vast network of welfare services linked with the school tend to be regarded as extraneous, or at most peripheral, to the main task of leadership within the school itself.

It has been seen that, quite apart from considerations of social philosophy, the increase in the size of schools and their staffs was a major factor in the growth of the "Headmaster Tradition" in the nineteenth century. It seems more than likely that the stimulus to remodel it will come from the new comprehensive schools which, by reason of their complexity as well as, in some cases, their size, will make the distribution of authority essential. If this is so, it is to be hoped that its basis, though widened, will remain within the school itself and not be imperceptibly transferred, owing to the weight of administrative considerations and outside influences, to the "community" or its representatives. A stand on this issue, which will only be successful if based on careful thought by those concerned, will preserve the essence of the position taken up by those who, like Thring and many others, fought for the independence of the school from directed political and social pressures and who, in their day, could only achieve their ends by stressing their own personal privileges and authority.

POSTSCRIPT (1974)

This paper provides a bench mark from which the developments of the past twenty years can be measured. Its publication did, in fact, coincide with the beginnings of interest in the role of the head and in the management of schools. Since then there has grown up a wide range of literature seeking to throw light on the position of the head and on his part in decision-making within the school (Hughes, 1970; Barry and Tye, 1972) and, more recently, action research studies in the processes of change and innovation (Richardson, 1973 and 1974). In addition, there has been a substantial amount of writing by heads themselves (Allen 1968; Halsall, 1970), in which they describe how they have dealt with the new demands being made on them.

Indeed, it is now clear that the kind of significant change in fundamental thinking about the head's role (the absence of which I noted in my paper) has now taken place. One train of thought has been concerned to minimise the positional authority of the head within the school by advocating some form of participatory committee control. Indeed, committee structures within large schools are commonplace and have grown up from sheer necessity: but they do not, from the studies and experience available, necessarily diminish the "pivotal" role of the head. On the contrary, they strengthen it (Musgrove 1971). Another train of thought has been perhaps more far-reaching in that it is concerned with the integration of the school with the community it serves. This has led, especially in primary schools, to an acceptance of the case for bringing parents into touch with the school's life and work; and in secondary schools, to the launching of community service schemes and work experience projects, to the school advancing beyond its usual boundaries. Furthermore, as a result of some forms of secondary reorganisation (for example, those involving "Middle Schools") and the coming of "linked courses", schools relate to the outside world not only through the head, but through teachers necessarily concerned with curricular planning extending beyond the school walls.

As I pointed out in my paper there was, at that time, the beginnings of an awareness of the complexity of the educational setting within which the head worked: this awareness has increased with the coming of new forms of examination and assessment, with such innovations as team-teaching and counselling, and with the introduction into schools of a wide range of audio-visual and other aids. Between the head in his study and the teachers in their classrooms, laboratories, studios and workshops there are areas of cooperative planning and decision-making in which his role is that of catalyst rather than that of leader. Nevertheless, in moments of crisis and in major confrontations with political or other pressure groups, the positional authority of the head becomes of critical significance. This is because his responsibility to his local authority and its expectations of his role have not substantially changed. There has not yet taken place in schools the *formal* redistribution of responsibility and powers which, in colleges of education and further education, has resulted from the rewriting of articles of government and the setting up of academic boards and councils.

I have argued that the prevailing industrial philosophy of the mid-nineteenth century had a major part in shaping the "headmaster tradition" at that time. It is again from industry—in the shape of modern theories of management—that ideas, including some as shocking as those that disturbed the unreformed endowed schools, are entering the minds of those responsible both for the school system and for individual schools. The trend in this direction has been met and reinforced by concern for the efficient use of resources at Department of Education and Science level and at local authority level. As a result, a "managerial" dimension in the concept of the head's role has now become part of established opinion. But debate is fierce and likely to be prolonged as to the nature of this new dimension. A first and inevitable step has been to draw on the experience of management teaching developed in industry, the armed forces and other branches of the public service. There are, of course, obvious limitations in this approach: schools and educational institutions generally do not fit into the patterns of product or service providing agencies; their purposes or "objectives" can only, save in a very limited sense, be assessed within wide social and occupational contexts; furthermore, schools exist within an environment of central and local government institutions which cannot be equated with that of the industrial world. Nevertheless, there are elements in common: the urgent need is to define these and also those aspects of educational institutions which merit their own distinctive forms of study and analysis.

The influence of industrial thinking in the mid-nineteenth century resulted in a redefinition of the role of the head in an entrepreneurial society. Trade unionism and "industrial relations" played no part in this process. In the second half of the twentieth century a major task in educational administration and in the management of schools, colleges and universities is to come to terms with this other side of the industrial world. The urgency of this task has been underlined by the entry of the National Union of Teachers, the Association of Teachers in Technical Institutions and the National Association of Schoolmasters into the Trades Union Congress and the increasing exasperation being felt by teachers in difficult schools with their conditions of work. There are signs of an emerging conviction among at least some groups of teachers that the duties they are assigned by heads acting on behalf of local education authorities should be matters not only for informal negotiation but also for collective bargaining. Action with regard to school meals supervision some years ago, and more recently in respect of over-large classes, has already tended to place heads in situations of a kind they have not hitherto experienced. The present emphasis on the managerial role of the head does not take into account the incipient "industrial relations" dimension of his task. Yet it is in this area, rendered still more sensitive by the mobilisation of parent and pupil interest groups, that the future distribution of decision-making in schools will be determined.

NOTES

1 Although much of this paper might apply, with slight variations, to the office of the headmistress in girls' schools and, with much greater variations, to the office of headteacher in the superseded elementary school, attention in this study is limited to the main body of tradition evoked by the term "Headmaster".

2 Its relevance until recent days is suggested by the literature of school-mastering in the present century, from Walpole's *Mr. Perrin and Mr. Trail* through Bernard Henderson's *Schoolmasters All; or Thirty Years Hard* and H. S. Shelton's *Thoughts of a Schoolmaster* to *Chalk in my Hair* by "Balaam".

3 This aspect of the headmaster's role probably derives from Thring, who declared that "as long as the Headmaster knows each boy, he is a Headmaster; the moment he does not, the man who does is so far Headmaster."

4 In Scotland, according to H. M. Knox (1953), as the range of subjects studied in secondary schools grew during the nineteenth century, there was a "tendency for the virtually independent heads of the separate departments to form a council of masters, sometimes presided over by each in turn, to manage the internal affairs of the school in republican fashion".

5 In some cases the new governing bodies set up by the Endowed Schools Commissioners signally failed to show the zeal expected of them and resorted to "farming" their schools to the headmaster. That is, they made over to him the income of the trust and let him keep whatever fees he could obtain. In return he shouldered all financial responsibility for the running of the school (Royal Commission on Secondary Education, (1895), Vol. I, pp. 45–6). This system persisted in remote rural grammar schools until the early years of the present century.

6 A notable case occurred at Grantham School in 1899, when a retiring headmaster dismissed his three assistants at short notice and his successor told them, a few days before a new term began, that he had appointed his own men and did not wish to re-engage them. (*The Journal of Education*, 1899).That this was not an isolated instance is borne out by the evidence of one of the witnesses before the Royal Commission on Secondary Education (1895), who stated that "when you dismiss the headmaster you dismiss every man in the school". Questioned further, he maintained that "unless the new headmaster

cares to take them on, they must all go". These statements were accepted without challenge (Royal Commission on Secondary Education (1895), Vol. IV, Minutes of Evidence No. 13, 223).

7 The Act provided that, in an endowed school, "any master in the school, by whomsoever appointed, and whether appointed before or after the passing of this Act, shall be deemed to be in the employment of the governing body for the time being of the school".

8 This was stressed with particular insistence in the Prefatory Memorandum to the *Regulations for Secondary Schools* (Board of Education, 1905). "Experience proves that in a school of the Secondary type full efficiency can be secured and the best teaching and organisational power attracted, only where the Head Master or Head Mistress is entrusted with a large amount of responsibility for and control over teaching, organisation and discipline. In particular the appointment and dismissal of Assistant Staff is a matter in which a voice ought to be secured to the Head Master. In the majority of Secondary Schools of the highest grade the appointment and dismissal of the Staff is entirely in his hands, subject to the obligation to report his action to the Governors and his liability to dismissal for improper exercise of his powers. In other cases he exercises these powers subject to the approval of the Governors. In any case, it is important that he should have formally secured to him the right to be consulted by the Governing Body and to submit his proposals to the Governors and have them fully considered, both as regards staff appointments and on all points relating to the conduct of the school as an educational organisation."

9 Save by W. O. Lester Smith (1950), who has tentatively suggested that teachers of experience should be able to follow courses designed to illuminate in a liberal way problems of educational organisation and administration. He envisages that "such courses should serve education much as the Staff College serves the Army as a preparation for leadership".

REFERENCES

ALLEN, B. (ed.) (1968) *Headship in the 1970s*, Blackwell.

BARRY, C. H. and TYE, F. (1972) *Running a School*, Maurice Temple Smith.

BOARD OF EDUCATION (1905) *Regulations for Secondary Schools*, Cmnd. 2492, p. xv. Endowed Schools (Masters) Act (1908) Section I (1) and (3).

HALSALL, E. (1970) *Becoming Comprehensive*, Pergamon.

HANSARD (1869) House of Commons, Third Series, Vol. CXCIV, 18 Feb. 1869, Cols. 1364–5.

HUGHES, M. G. (1970) *Secondary School Administration: A Management Approach*, Pergamon.

Journal of Education (1886) "Schoolmastering as a Profession" (author unnamed), Jan. 1886, p. 21.

Journal of Education (Sept. 1899), pp. 549 ff.

KNOX, H. M. (1953) *Two Hundred and Fifty Years of Scottish Education, 1696–1946*, p. 40.

MUSGROVE, F. (1971) *Patterns of Power and Authority in English Education*, Methuen.

NORWOOD, C. and HOPE, A. H. (1909) *The Higher Education of Boys in England*, p. 213.

PUBLIC SCHOOLS COMMISSION (1864) *Report*, Vol. I, p. 4.

RICHARDSON, E. (1973) *The Teacher, the School and the Task of Management*, Heinemann.

RICHARDSON, E. (1974) *Inside a Curriculum Project: A Case Study in the Process of Curriculum Change*, Methuen.

ROYAL COMMISSION ON SECONDARY EDUCATION (1895) *Report*.

SCHOOLS INQUIRY COMMISSION (1868) *Report*.

SMITH, W. O. LESTER (1950) *The Teacher and the Community*, Studies in Education No. 3, Evans Bros. for the University of London Institute of Education, pp. 13–15.

4.2 The Professional-as-Administrator: The Case of the Secondary School Head[1]

Meredydd G. Hughes

In summing up his extensive studies of scientists in research establishments, Abrahamson (1967) observed that "to most administrators, professionals are a major source of frustration". Professionals prize their autonomy and are not readily amenable to hierarchical control, preferring a "group of equals" pattern (Wardwell, 1955) .The organisational loyalty of professionals is also suspect, their prior commitment being to their specialised work activity and to their links, both formal and informal, with fellow workers outside their particular organisation (Reissman, 1949; Kornhauser, 1963; Blau and Scott, 1963; Cotgrove and Box, 1970).

A technique commonly used in seeking to resolve, or at least to diminish, the almost inevitable conflict which results when professional and organisational perspectives differ is to appoint professionals or ex-professionals as administrators of professionally staffed organisations (Etzioni, 1964). The professional-as-administrator, it is argued, is uniquely capable of achieving accommodation between the organisation's emphasis on superordinate control and the professional's desire for colleague control (Barber, 1963). Inevitably, as in all "boundary" roles, there is some degree of role strain for the professional-as-administrator: "professional norms stressing autonomous integrity for practitioners still make a claim upon him, which he considers legitimate, but so does the organisation's need for control" (Abrahamson, 1967, p. 83). Such positions often have a considerable prestige, however, and it has been noted that, though there is some tendency among professionals to disparage administrative roles, the expression of such sentiments does not normally inhibit the acceptance of administrative responsibilities when the opportunity is presented (Goss, 1962; Barber, 1963).

It may be claimed that the professional-as-administrator construct has relevance to many positions in the administration of education (Taylor, 1964; Browning, 1972; David, 1973). The present article reports selected aspects of recent research (Hughes, 1972a), in which the construct was applied to the role of the secondary school head. The secondary school

Source: Research Report (1973) *Educational Administration Bulletin*, Vol. 2, No. 1, pp. 11–23.

head is the *chief executive* of a professionally staffed organisation, and may also be regarded as the *leading professional* of that organisation.

In the study, 72 heads from a stratified random sample of maintained secondary schools ranging in size from under 400 pupils (6 modern schools) to over 1,600 pupils (5 comprehensive schools), and 123 members of staff, similarly selected, responded to items relevant to two role models of headship: the head as Chief Executive (the CE role model) and the head as Leading Professional (the LP role model). The heads were asked to indicate, on a five-point scale, their self-expectations, i.e. the behaviour they regarded as desirable in the context of their school, and also their perception of their actual behaviour; because of unease expressed during a pilot study, staff were asked only for their expectations for the head's role.

Avoiding technicalities as far as possible, it is proposed in the following *firstly* to indicate some of the inter-relationships which were found within the CE role model, demonstrating in particular the articulation of what may be called the internal and external sectors; *secondly* to identify two independent parameters within the LP role model; and *finally* to explore the inter-penetration of the two structures, with a view to facilitating the emergence of a more unified role model of secondary school headship.

THE CE ROLE MODEL

Nearly all executives, according to Chester Barnard (1938, p. 215), do a considerable amount of non-executive work, which is sometimes more valuable than the executive work which they do. Nevertheless, "executive work is not that *of* the organisation but the specialised work of *maintaining* the organisation in operation" (author's italics). Accepting Barnard's dictum that the executive functions relate to the work, within and outside the organisation, which is essential to its vitality and endurance, we differentiate between an internal and an external sector of the role model: the chief executive is concerned both with what happens within the organisation and with the relation of the organisation to the wider system of which it is a part. An elementary application of systems analysis then suggests the hypothesis that the two aspects are inter-related: "environmental influences are not sources of error variance but are integrally related to the functioning of a social system" (Katz and Kahn, 1966, p. 27). Before stating the proposition in more concrete terms it is desirable to consider the two sectors of the role model more specifically.

The internal aspect is broadly dealt with in the provision of the Ministry of Education's Model Articles of Government (AM 25, 26.1.45) that "... the Headmaster shall control the internal organisation, management and discipline of the school, shall exercise supervision ..." etc. Within this general framework, statements were included in the internal sector of the role model relating to two types of executive function which may be regarded as complementary: (a) the division and allocation of work (including the clarification of staff responsibilities and delegation of responsibilities by the head); (b) the co-ordination and control of organisational activity (including staff supervision, an insistence on deadlines and a general emphasis on efficient procedures). A correlation analysis of responses to individual items, taken in pairs, was performed at each of three levels of response (i.e. heads' expectations, heads' reported behaviour and staff expectations) using the English Electric 4-50 Computer at Cardiff University College, and significant positive correlations were obtained involving each of the items. From this it may be concluded that the internal sector of the CE role model, as constructed, can be regarded as a configurative whole, in which the parts are consistent, and mutually inter-related.

Items in the external sector were chosen to explore the head's relationship as Chief Executive to institutional authority in the guise of the school's governing body and the local education authority.[2] Topics considered were the head's freedom to invite visitors to the school without reference to outside authority, his access as normal practice to his chairman of governors, and the effectiveness of his involvement, if any, in the appointment of members of staff. Again an underlying common factor emerged in the statistical analysis which, at each of the three levels of response, may be interpreted as being related to the status and autonomy granted to the head by external authority.

We are now in a position to state and consider a problem of some interest concerning the inter-relation of environmental influences and the functioning of a school. Is there a relationship in terms of expectations and in terms of behaviour, between the standing and autonomy of the head in relation to external authority and the internal governance of the school? Such a relationship is frequently claimed or implied in the professional literature. Lewis, for instance, in a Headmasters Association publication (1967), states that "the privilege of making his own appointments contributes significantly to the head's status, on which the standing and effectiveness of the school so much depends". Baron (1956, p. 13 [see 4.1, p. 292] has noted that essentially the same point was made in the Board of Education (1905) Prefatory Memorandum to the *Regulations for Secondary Schools*, which states that:

Experience proves that in a school of the Secondary type full efficiency can be secured and the best teaching and organisational power attracted, only where the Head Master or Head Mistress is entrusted with a large amount of responsibility ... In particular the appointment and dismissal of Assistant Staff is a matter in which a voice ought to be secured to the Head Master.

The issue also exercised the Public School Commission (1970) when considering the possible absorption of the direct grant schools into the state system. Arising from such statements, the hypothesis is advanced that there will be at least *some* significant correlations between responses relating to the internal and external sectors of the CE role model. Refraining from predicting the direction of the relationships, we use the more stringent two-tail tests of statistical significance.

The correlational analysis amply confirmed the hypothesis. Both in terms of expectations and behaviour, the head whose position is less recognised by external authority takes less initiative in defining staff responsibilities and delegates less readily. He is less likely to supervise staff closely, insist on deadlines or emphasise efficiency. A person who feels that his authority is limited or uncertain, i.e. that he is "under-powered", to use Musgrove's phrase (1971), in relation to his responsibilities is naturally on the defensive. He is understandably reluctant to risk taking positive measures in the deployment or supervision of staff or to share with others the little authority which he has. On the other hand, the head whose position in relation to external authority is assured is more likely both to take initiatives himself in executive matters and to delegate effectively to members of staff.

The findings reported above provide grounds for formulating a general proposition in the following terms: *the occupant of an executive position, who is granted little authority and recognition by his superiors, tends to behave in relation to his subordinates in a cautious and defensive manner, which exposes him to as little risk as possible.* Conversely, the executive who is granted an appreciable measure of autonomy and recognition by his superiors is more likely, in his relations with subordinates, both to adopt a positive approach himself and to encourage others to become involved in the executive functions.

It is relevant to note that the above proposition receives support from studies in the very different cultural milieu of the United States. Thus Seeman (1960) found that school executives in Ohio whose status was precarious or ambiguous adopted a conservative type of leadership behaviour, which he interpreted in terms of "inauthenticity". On the other hand, leaders who rated themselves as high in status "described their leadership not only as high in authority and responsibility, but also in delegation". Seeman concluded that "leadership behaviour and ideology are, in significant part, functions of status considerations which stem from the community and culture surrounding the given organisation". Carlson (1965) found a similar relationship between the status of school superintendents and their encouragement of curriculum innovation in the schools under their control. Also noteworthy is the finding of Gross and Herriott (1965) that the executive professional leadership provided by elementary school principals is positively and significantly related to the perception by the principals of the professional behaviour of their administrative superiors, including the extent to which the higher administrators involve the principal in the appointment of his teachers.

Returning to implications from the present study, conducted within the educational system of England and Wales, the evidence suggests that it is unrealistic for governing bodies and local education authorities to expect the heads of their educational institutes to adopt a positive and dynamic approach to managerial responsibilities and staff involvement unless they are prepared, at the same time, to grant a generous measure of institutional autonomy. In a wider setting our findings, and the American studies which have been cited, have relevance to the centralisation-versus-devolution issue which invariably looms large in international seminars on educational administration and is a major concern of UNESCO and OECD in their studies of educational planning and the management of innovation (Lyons, 1970; Dalin, 1973). It may well be that professional initiative and the exercise of discretion cannot properly be expected from school executives who are regarded, and who regard themselves as the powerless minions of a centralised and powerful bureaucracy.

THE LP ROLE MODEL

Considerations of space make it necessary to report on this section more briefly in the present paper. The formulation of items was based on a review of the professional literature and on the writer's personal experience as a secondary school head, with some revision as a result of a pilot study.

A correlational analysis of the responses, taken in pairs, to the items finally chosen, revealed two distinct factors in the concept of the head as leading professional. Firstly, there is what may be called a *traditional* (or local) dimension, which is significantly related to high scores on the head's regular teaching and his pastoral relationship to, and personal involvement with, both staff and pupils. These aspects have been discussed on a number of occasions (Baron, 1956; Westwood, 1966; Rée, 1968; Cohen, 1970a and 1970b; Bernbaum, 1970; Bates, 1971).

Secondly there is an *innovating* (or cosmopolitan) dimension, which is indicative of an openness to external professional influences. Significant positive correlations at each of the three levels of response were found among the responses under the following headings:

the head's readiness to take the initiative in getting staff to try out new ideas and media;
the head's involvement in educational activities outside his own school, e.g. the meetings of professional bodies;
the importance attached to the head finding time for personal study.

The data showed clearly that the heads who expected (and were expected by staff) to be professionally active outside their school, expected (and were expected by staff) to give positive encouragement to innovation within their schools, a result confirmed in terms of the heads' reported behaviour responses. The conclusion which may be drawn, i.e. that there is an "innovative" dimension which provides a link between the in-school and out-of-school aspects of the head as leading professional, provides a new element in the discussion of the head as educational innovator (Hoyle, 1968; Hoyle, 1969; Tucker, 1970).[3]

An interesting finding in the study was that the traditional and innovating aspects are largely independent of each other, rather than antithetical aspects of the head's role, i.e. the two dimensions may be regarded as orthogonal. A typology of heads may thus be based on the following diagram:

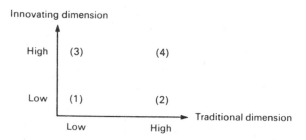

The four categories may be labelled as follows:

1   *The abdicator*—below average in personal teaching and pastoral emphasis and in openness to external professional influences.
2   *The traditionalist*—above average in personal teaching and pastoral emphasis but below average in openness to external professional influences.
3   *The innovator*—below average in personal teaching and pastoral emphasis but above average in openness to external professional influences.
4   *The extended professional*—above average in personal teaching and pastoral emphasis and in openness to external professional influences.

The "abdicator" type in its most extreme form is probably non-existent, but the other three types were easily recognisable in the research. A correlation of responses with the size of school showed some tendency for the small-school head to be a "traditionalist" and for the large-scale school head to be an "innovator", but there were numerous instances of heads, irrespective of the size of school, who placed a high emphasis on both aspects.

Large-school heads in the latter category might properly be called "*over*-extended professionals" (Hughes, 1972b). Several of them admitted, during interview, that they sought to live up to expectations of personal involvement with pupils which they themselves recognised to be unrealistic, e.g. "one should try to know all pupils, however large the school may be, though it is impossible in a large school".[4] Similarly Bernbaum (1970) found large-school heads reluctant to relinquish traditional human-relations aspects of their work, a result confirmed by Cohen (1970) and by Bates (1971). It is a matter for concern that there are still far too many heads who carry too great a responsibility for their school's success on their own shoulders (Benn and Simon, 1970; Conway, 1970).

THE INTER-PENETRATION OF THE ROLE MODELS

The incidental comments of heads of staff, during interview, provided cumulative evidence that the executive and professional aspects of the head's role, though analytically distinct, are closely inter-related. Organisational considerations were frequently mentioned, for instance, in favour of the proposition that the head "should do some regular teaching":

I believe that discipline is helped by the head teaching (head).

It gives an opportunity of being around the school without obviously snooping (head).

The head should teach one of the tough forms occasionally to know what we are up against (staff).

This is what keeps the Old Man in touch with reality (staff).

Similarly the reservations sometimes expressed by heads and staff of larger schools were often linked to organisational considerations:

I have always felt it important to have a foot in the classroom, regarding myself as still a teacher, but now I am not so sure. I still *do* teach, but I have become very doubtful about it, feeling that there is an element of escapism in getting away to the classroom. Am I justified? Ought I not to be more accessible and be about the school more? (head).

The previous head taught too much and was not available to staff as much as was desirable (staff).

After all, his *main* job is to run the school (staff).

The above remarks serve to illustrate the fact that a crude formulation of the professional-organisational dilemma in terms of the polar extremities of a single continuum would be singularly naive. The relationship between responses within the two role models may properly be expected to be much more complex, and this proved in fact to be so. When an inter-model correlational analysis was performed, nearly half of the item pairs yielded no significant relationship, while the rest provided one cluster of negative significant correlations and another cluster of positive significant correlations. We consider these in turn.

(a) The negative correlations

These were confined almost entirely to one area, revealing a conflict between "traditional" elements of the LP role model and aspects of the CE role model. In particular, there was a significant negative relationship between responses favourable to the head's personal involvement with individual pupils (pastoral care of pupils, knowing pupils by name, personally writing reports on pupils, etc.) and responses indicative of an emphasis on executive functions (the delegation of routine matters, stressing efficient procedures, etc.). A subsidiary analysis confirmed that the size of school was a significant intervening variable, a fact illustrated by the contrast between some of the comments on pastoral care in the small-school and large-school contexts:

Small school
The pastoral care of pupils is the most important function of the head (head).

This is central—I kill myself over this (head).

Know pupils by name? Yes, certainly; this is a school, not a factory (head).

Large school
I can only expect to deal with the outstandingly difficult cases (head).

The head should not let himself get bogged down with this (i.e. with pastoral care) (staff).

This school is too big for any normal person to know all the pupils, and I plan accordingly (head).

The head cannot possibly handle all the personal problems. He has to rely on others (staff).

The severe difficulties experienced by the large-school heads seeking to conform to the traditional stereotype have already been noted. There is evidence, however, that a change of emphasis is occurring both in the schools and in the professional literature (Holden, 1969; Hughes, 1971).

As a consequence, the counselling function is no longer regarded as an essential part of the head's role, but is able to develop an independent institutional existence with a distinctive professional expertise and ideology (Halmos, 1965). The head is no less "concerned" than formerly, but his professional care is increasingly expressed in the planning and maintenance of a comprehensive system of counselling and guidance, involving house tutors or year tutors, counsellors and careers staff, rather than in attempting personally to give an all-round one-man service (Halmos, 1970).

(b) The positive correlations

LP role model responses indicative of an "innovative" emphasis correlated significantly and positively with responses within the CE role model. Thus the head who reports taking the initiative in getting staff to try out new ideas tends to rate himself highly on sorting out staff responsibilities, supervising staff, insisting on deadlines and emphasising efficiency. Members of staff who expect the head to encourage innovation are more tolerant than other staff of his insistence on deadlines, and are more likely to approve of his being much in evidence about the school. The head's professional leadership is seen, by heads and staff, to have organisational implications.

The innovating head, it appears, relies partly on exerting influence on staff colleagues as a fellow professional; equally, however, he accepts his position as chief executive, and uses the organisational controls which are available to him to get things moving. Professional and executive considerations re-inforce each other as complementary aspects of a coherent and unified strategy.

The seeming paradox is also evident in the positive correlations, significant at each of the three levels of response, which link the personal guidance of inexperienced staff by the head (an aspect of his professional role) and the head's close supervision of staff (an aspect of his executive role). It seems that the fact that the chief executive of the organisation regards himself, and is regarded by the professional staff, as one of them, makes it unrealistic to seek to distinguish with any precision between his guidance of staff in the interest of their personal development and their supervision in the interests of the organisation.

Though the relevant literature is sparse, two references may be cited which support the above interpretation. Scott (1965) found that social workers who perceived their supervisors as "professionally oriented" were less hostile to routine supervision than those who had little regard for the professional competence of their supervisors. Baumgartel (1957) reported that in a research organisation staffed by highly qualified professionals, a leadership style which involved high interaction with subordinates was preferred to a more remote relationship requiring little interaction or involvement. While these accounts provide useful pointers, there is considerable scope for further study of the leadership of professionally staffed organisations.

In the research, which is only partially reported in the present article, the relevance of the LP–CE construct was further explored in relation to three areas of potential difficulty for heads: namely, the head's social interaction with staff, the school's relationship with parents, and the issue of pupil and staff participation. Though it is not practicable to report these aspects here, it may be stated that the findings provide further confirmation of the importance of the distinction drawn between a "traditional" and an "innovating" aspect of the head's professionalism. It is already clear from the inter-model correlational analysis reported above that the "traditional" emphasis is potentially in conflict with the basic features of the chief executive role, whereas an "innovating" emphasis is more easily reconciled with the head's managerial responsibilities.

Though they are useful as analytical and heuristic devices, it has to be recognised that our role models are but abstractions, which only partially reflect the reality. In seeking to develop a more unified role model it is therefore salutary to recall that many heads to some extent, and some heads to a great extent, succeed in simultaneously activating and integrating two contrasting and potentially conflicting aspects of their total role. For the head of a small school in a stable environment, this may not be too difficult, but it may be concluded from the research reported above that when these conditions do not apply a change of emphasis within the head's concept of his professionalism (and within staff concepts of the head's professionalism) may be necessary for some heads if the total role is to be successfully enacted without excessive strain.

In a specific context it has been shown that the professional-as-administrator fulfils his mediating role to a large extent by providing the kind of supervision of professional staff, and the kind of organisational leadership in responding to external change, which is acceptable to professionals. Other aspects of his professionalism may be inappropriate and even counter-productive.

Much therefore depends on the interpretation given by the professional-as-administrator to his professional role. If his professionalism is restricted and modelled on traditional stereotypes, his best endeavours could well exacerbate the problems of a large and complex organisation, subject to pressures from within and without. If the emphasis is on his leadership and encouragement of colleagues in their joint efforts, his contribution could be invaluable in enabling the combined expertise of a professional staff to be mobilised for the achievement of agreed organisational objectives.

NOTES

1 The study was grant-aided by the Nuffield Foundation under their Small Grants Scheme, and their support is gratefully acknowledged. Field work included over 300 structured interviews with heads and staff of maintained and non-maintained secondary schools, chairmen of governors and local education officers in South Wales and South-West England, arranged through the good offices of Professor William Taylor, Bristol University School of Education, and Professor Andrew Taylor, Department of Education, University College, Cardiff. Professor Paul Halmos, Department of Sociology, University College, Cardiff, supervised the study.

2 In order to keep the model as simple as possible, it was decided to refrain from considering the subtle relationship of the school to institutional authority at the national level, which is largely mediated through the activities of HM Inspectorate. Relations with parents, both individually and on a group basis, were dealt with in the study, but are not reported in the present article.

3 A parallel discussion by Hoyle (1972) of the teacher's professionalism, in which he distinguishes between a *restricted* and an *extended* professionalism, is also of interest. The "restricted" professional concentrates his attention, to the exclusion of all else, on his work in the classroom and his relationship with his pupils. The "extended" professional is also a good classroom practitioner, but is in addition "aware of the wider dimensions of his task, keeps himself profesionally informed, seeks to apply theory to practice and is willing to work out solutions to professional problems with his colleagues".

4 Controlling the size of school, the expectations of heads to try to know pupils by name correlated positively and significantly with the age of the head. A similar result obtained for staff expectations of the head's behaviour.

REFERENCES

ABRAHAMSON, M. (1967) *The Professional in the Organisation,* Rand McNally.

BARBER, B. (1963) "Some problems in the sociology of the professions", *Daedelus* No. 92, pp. 669–88.

BARNARD, C. I. (1938) *The Functions of the Executive,* Harvard University Press.

BARON, G. (1952) *The Secondary Schoolmaster, 1895–1914,* Ph.D. Thesis, University of London.

BARON, G. (1956) "Some aspects of the 'Headmaster tradition' ", University of Leeds Institute of Education, Researches and Studies, No. 14, pp. 7–16.

BATES, A. W. (1971) *The Administration of Comprehensive Schools,* Ph.D. Thesis, University of London.

BAUMGARTEL, H. (1957) "Leadership style as a variable in research administration", *Administrative Science Quarterly*, Vol. 2, pp. 344–60.

BENN, C. and SIMON, B. (1970) *Half Way There: Report on the British Comprehensive School Reforms*, McGraw Hill.

BERNBAUM, G. (1970) *The role of the headmaster: final report*, a mimeographed report to the Social Science Research Council.

BLAU, P. M. and SCOTT, W. R. (1963) *Formal Organisations*, Routledge.

BOARD OF EDUCATION (1905) *Regulations for Secondary Schools*, Cmnd. 2492, p. xv.

BROWNING, P. "Some changes in LEA administration", *London Educational Review*, Vol. 1, No. 3, pp. 4–12.

CARLSON, R. O. (1965) *Adoption of Educational Innovations*, Centre for the Advanced Study of Educational Administration, University of Oregon.

COHEN, L. (1970a) *Conceptions of Headteachers Concerning their Role*, Ph.D. Thesis, University of Keele.

COHEN, L. (1970b) "School size and headteachers bureaucratic role conceptions", *Educational Review*, Vol. 23, pp. 50–58.

CONWAY, E. S. (1970) *Going comprehensive: a study of the administration of comprehensive schools*, Harrap.

COTGROVE, S. and BOX, S. (1970) *Science, Industry and Society*, Allen and Unwin.

DALIN, P. (ed.) (1973) *Strategies for Innovation in Education*, CERI, OECD.

DAVID, M. E. (1973) "Approaches to Organisational Change in LEAs", *Educational Administration Bulletin*, Vol. 1, No. 2, pp. 24–33.

ETZIONI, A. (1964) *Modern Organisations*, Prentice Hall.

GOSS, M. E. W. (1962) "Administration and the physician", *American Journal of Public Health*, Vol. 52, pp. 183–91.

GROSS, N. and HERRIOTT, R. E. (1965) *Staff Leadership in Public Schools*, Wiley.

HALMOS, P. (1965) *The Faith of the Counsellor*, Constable.

HALMOS, P. (1970) *The Personal Service Society*, Constable.

HOLDEN, A. (1969) *Teachers as Counsellors*, Constable.

HOYLE, E. (1969) "How does the curriculum change? Systems and strategies", *Journal of Curriculum Studies*, Nov. 1969.

HOYLE, E. (1972) "Educational innovation and the role of the teacher", *Forum*, Vol. 14, pp. 42–4.

HOYLES, E. (1968) "The Head as innovator", in Allen, B. (ed.) *Headship in the 1970s*, Blackwell.

HUGHES, M. G. (1972a) *The Role of the Secondary School Head*, University of Wales Ph.D. Thesis, University College, Cardiff.

HUGHES, M. G. (1972b) "School headship in transition", *London Educational Review*, Vol. 1, No. 3, pp. 34–42. Also in *Headmasters Association Review*, Dec. 1972.

HUGHES, P. M. (1971) *Guidance and Counselling in Schools: A Response to Change*, Pergamon.

KATZ, D. and KAHN, R. L. (1966) *The Social Psychology of Organisations*, Wiley.

KORNHAUSER, W. (1963) *Scientists in Industry: Conflict and Accommodation*, University of California Press.

LEWIS, C. H. (1967) *The Head of a School*, Headmasters Association.

LYONS, R. F. (ed.) (1970) *Administrative Aspects of Educational Planning*, IIEP, UNESCO, Paris, 1970.

MUSGROVE, F. (1971) *Patterns of Power and Authority in English Education*, Methuen.

PUBLIC SCHOOLS COMMISSION (1970) *Second Report*, Vol. 1: "Report on Independent Day Schools and Direct Grant Grammar Schools", HMSO.

RÉE, H. (1968) "The changed role of the Head", in Allen B. (ed.) *Headship in the 1970s*, Blackwell.

REISSMAN, L. (1949) "A study of role conceptions in bureaucracy", *Social Forces*, Vol. 27, pp. 305–10.

SCOTT, W. R. (1965) "Reactions to supervision in a heterogeneous professional organisation", *Administrative Science Quarterly*, Vol. 10, pp. 65–81.

SEEMAN, M. (1960) *Social Status and Leadership: The Case of the School Executive*, Bureau of Educational Research and Service, Ohio State University.

TAYLOR, W. (1964) "The training college principal", *Sociological Review*, Vol. 12, pp. 185–201.

TUCKER, M. (1970) "Organisational change: the process of unstreaming", in Hughes, M. G. (ed.) *Secondary School Administration: A Management Approach*, Pergamon.

WARDWELL, W. I. (1955) "Social integration, bureaucratization and the professions", *Social Forces*, Vol. 33, pp. 356–9.

WESTWOOD, L. J. (1966) "Re-assessing the role of the head", *Education for Teaching*, Vol. 71, pp. 65–74.

L

4.3 Professionality, Professionalism and Control in Teaching

Eric Hoyle

ABSTRACT

Professor Hoyle discusses the word "profession" as it is used of teaching, draws a distinction between a teacher's "professionality' and his "professionalism", and identifies the need for teachers to respond to the demands of an "extended" as against a "limited" professionality.

The concept *profession* has given sociologists considerable difficulty as a logical category. For over sixty years efforts have been made to specify the criteria which differentiate a profession from other occupations. Initially the approach was to establish a model of the basic constituents of a profession and thence to dichotomize occupations as professions/non-professions. More recently this dichotomy has given way to a continuum with an "ideal type" profession at one pole and with occupations being located on the continuum according to their approximation to the ideal type. On such a continuum teaching is usually placed some way short of the ideal type and is sometimes classified as a semi-profession. (The interested reader is referred to valuable discussions of these criteria by Hickson and Thomas, 1969, and by Millerson, 1964.) For the purpose of the present argument it is sufficient to note that any list of criteria will inevitably include a reference to professional control and practitioner's autonomy. The consideration of profession as a logical category has now given way to the recognition that as a concept it is perhaps less logical than ideological. Hughes (1958) drew attention to the *symbolic* functions of the term and wrote: "the term 'profession' is a symbol for a desired conception of one's work and, hence, of one's self". For him the term related to the individual's identity and was not seen as being a wholly self-interested concept. A rather more critical view is often taken by economists; for example, Lees (1966) claims that the idea of a profession "to an economist schooled in the theory of competitive market seems at first blush suspiciously like mumbo jumbo". When one considers the ideological use to which the term is put, which often gives greater

---

Source: *London Educational Review* (Summer 1974), Vol. 3, No. 2, pp. 13–19.

emphasis to rights rather than responsibilities, there is a temptation to treat the term as little more than part of the rhetoric of an occupation which is seeking to improve its status, salary and conditions. This is usually referred to as the process of *professionalization*. In this paper a crude distinction can be made between the service interest and the self-interest components of the concept of a profession by using the term *professionalism* to refer to those strategies and rhetorics employed by members of an occupation in seeking to improve status, salary and conditions (see Vollmer and Mills, 1966) and the term *professionality* to refer to the knowledge, skills and procedures employed by teachers in the process of teaching. In everyday speech the distinction is not, of course, observed. One can refer to the "sheer professionalism" of a teacher when one is referring to that teacher's professionality as defined above.

In the quite extensive literature on professions two themes recur: the autonomy of the practitioner and the control of the organized profession over the service which it collectively offers. What follows is concerned mainly with the first. Almost invariably the criteria of autonomy and control are constituents of the "ideal type" profession. The implications have been discussed extensively in relation to a number of professions including teaching (see Lortie, 1969). They are always live issues, and the excuse for re-examining them is that changes which are at present occurring within education reveal new facets of these persistent problems.

The teacher has often been thought of as autonomous, independent and omnicompetent. It is true that teachers have been subject to the surveillance of Her Majesty's Inspector, but visits are irregular and inspections rare. However, teachers work within a formal organization—the school—and in the secondary school omnicompetence has been to some extent modified by a degree of specialization and hence differentiation. And in all schools the activities of individual teachers require a degree of co-ordination. Organization thus imposes constraints on autonomy, and a degree of control is implicit in the system. Early sociological studies of schools as organizations and of teaching as a profession tended to emphasize the bureaucratic nature of schools and to contrast this (usually unfavourably) with a professional model of organization. Uniformity, routine, rules and authority based upon office were contrasted with an emphasis on client-centredness, professional goals, flexible rules and authority based upon personal knowledge. More recently sociologists of education have pointed out that although schools do have some properties of bureaucracy to some degree, e.g. hierarchy and specialization, they also have professional elements.

Generally speaking the British school has been characterized by a mixture of control and autonomy. The head, with authority vested in him by the articles of government and enforced by his hierarchical status, has been in a position to exert considerable control over school goals and administrative structure, but he has had only limited control over the teacher's classroom activities. Conversely, although the teacher has enjoyed this relatively high degree of autonomy within the classroom, he has hitherto had a somewhat limited influence on school goals or administration and little opportunity to control the broader context within which he performs his professional activities. In short, his autonomy operates within the constraints of a structure which is not of his own creating. This pattern is now changing in a way which raises a new set of questions related to autonomy, control and teacher's professionality.

These changes have two distinct origins which, although convergent, are best considered separately. One arises from changes in curriculum, pedagogy and the organization of teaching and learning, the other from broad socio-political trends in society at large. The educational changes include: interdisciplinary inquiry, discovery learning, collaborative teaching, flexible timetabling, heterogeneous grouping, continuous assessment, open-plan architecture and closer school–community relations. Some implications of these trends which are particularly relevant to the present argument have been pointed out in two highly perceptive articles by Bernstein (1967 and 1971). Briefly the point is that a characteristic common to current trends in education is the increasing permeability of boundaries—between school subjects, ability groups, the roles of teachers and between school and non-school. Particularly relevant is the fact that teachers are moving from their independent classroom roles to a greater interdependence, and that in the more open school structures roles have to be *made*.

The second source of change, the socio-political, is well summarized in that now somewhat threadbare term *participation*, the belief that those who are affected by decisions should play a part in making them. After student power and pupil power, there has emerged, rather later on the scene, teacher power. This issue has rapidly moved up the list of topics debated at union conferences. Two models can be identified: the *industrial model*, which sees an inevitable conflict between workers (teachers) and management (head, governors) and takes the protection of the teacher as its dominant theme; and the *professional model*, which is no less concened with increasing the power of teachers to control their working situation, but sees the problem as one of transforming hierarchical power to collegial power in the school. Although a hard and fast distinction cannot be drawn, the educational trends outlined broadly to *collaborative teaching* and the socio-political trends to *collaborative decisionmaking*. These can be considered separately.

The term *collaborative teaching* is used here to cover a variety of situations in which teachers collaborate in determining syllabuses, methods and materials. The greatest degree of collaboration occurs, of course, in the various forms of team teaching. In order to examine the implications of the principle of collaborative teaching, the following comments will be restricted to working teams of teachers—although they also apply to a greater or lesser degree to all forms of professional collaboration. The nature of the integration between members of a team vary. Some teams may be highly specialized and hierarchical; others may have a lower degree of specialization and be less highly structured. The patterns of the collaborative relations in teaching teams have not been systematically studied in spite of a set of very valuable proposals for research put forward ten years ago by Lortie (1964), which have not been pursued. Lortie noted that two major patterns of relations might evolve: the *vertical-hierarchical* and the *horizontal-collegial*. In the hierarchical team the distribution of power could lead to a greater control being maintained over the work of some teachers—as compared with the situation of the independent class teacher—with a consequent standardization, routinization and limitation on professional choice by teachers low in the hierarchy. But perhaps what is more significant in relation to the present discussion are the implications of the collegial form. Lortie points out that a collegial team would have some of the qualities of all small groups, i.e. shared understandings, common expectations, group norms defining appropriate levels of work, and informal leadership which perhaps varies according to task. The point here is that the teacher loses his classroom autonomy and hence control over his immediate teaching activities but gains *at least the opportunity* of controlling the broader teaching context.

It is this opportunity to control the broader context of teaching, one level higher as it were, which is of interest in the moves towards greater collegiality in school policy-making. This process is still a considerable way short of full collegiality, where professionals govern their activities through democratic processes. There have been some experiments—the Countesthorpe "moot", for example—but the movement has so far been modest. For example, the National Union of Teachers' (1973) recommendations press for greater consultation in the short term as a step towards the achievement of teachers' participation in the long term, whilst the National Association of Schoolmasters (1972) advocates the creation of academic boards, at least in larger schools, with the head as the *ex officio* chairman. Again one is not concerned with the forms and degrees of collegiality, but with the implications of the principle that teachers should have an increasing opportunity to participate in collective decision-making with regard to school goals and organization. In so far as these decisions were taken in the past with little consultation, the teacher's scope has increased, but again control has to be achieved in collaboration with others.

Collaborative teaching and collaborative decision-making both involve a loss in teachers' autonomy but increased potentiality for teacher control. In a system of collaborative teaching the teacher loses his isolation from colleagues and enters into a functional interdependence in which the very act of teaching comes under the scrutiny of colleagues. Not only this, but if he is to play his part in controlling his work situation, the teacher is expected to contribute his ideas on educational objectives, teaching methods, appropriate materials and so forth to professional discussions. Collegial authority at the school level is also based upon the assumption that teachers will present their ideas on educational goals and means; and if the situation is to be avoided whereby control is exercised by those who are simply the most vociferous, then it follows that there is a premium upon informed professional debate. Thus both collaborative teaching and collaborative decision-making are predicted upon an informed professionality. Whether these implications of such professionality are either feasible or desirable is the problem which faces the profession.

The core professional act of the teacher lies in his transaction with pupils. Traditional notions of a profession emphasize that practice is informed by a body of theory and research. The theory–practice relation in education is a perennial problem. For whatever reasons, teachers tend to be atheoretical at the level of their day-to-day teaching, yet their work takes place in a context which is shaped by educational theory. For example, trends towards a greater openness outlined at the beginning of this paper have a theoretical rationale. Thus greater professional control would appear to require a more extended form of professionality, a professionality which is not limited to classroom skills alone but embraces a wider range of knowledge and skill. For the sake of discussion we can hypothesize two models of professionality: *restricted* and *extended*

Table 1. Restricted and extended models of professionality

Restricted professionality	Extended professionality
Skills derived from experience	Skills derived from a mediation between experience and theory
Perspective limited to the immediate in time and place	Perspective embracing the broader social context of education
Classroom events perceived in isolation	Classroom events perceived in relation to school policies and goals
Introspective with regard to methods	Methods compared with those of colleagues and with reports of practice
Value placed on autonomy	Value placed on professional collaboration
Limited involvement in non-teaching professional activities	High involvement in non-teaching professional activities (especially teachers' centres, subject associations, research)
Infrequent reading of professional literature	Regular reading of professional literature
Involvement in in-service work limited and confined to practical courses	Involvement in in-service work considerable and includes courses of a theoretical nature
Teaching seen as an intuitive activity	Teaching seen as a rational activity

(shown in table 1). It should be emphasized that these have no empirical support. They are heuristic models only.

In an increasingly open school situation where formal structures are being broken down and teachers are free to create–and re-create–their own orders, there would appear to be a case for teachers extending their professionality by acquiring a wider range of knowledge and skills which would enable them to contribute to policy and planning. However, a number of difficulties are obvious.

First, there is the problem of time. Time is the commodity in shortest supply in teaching. The problem perhaps has two aspects: actual time and perceived time. There is undoubtedly a sheer lack of actual time to undertake the collaborative activities which are necessary for the exercise of collegial authority at the level of teaching or policy-making. With careful planning, some time can be made available in the secondary school, but the problem is most acute in the primary school. The solution to this problem is partly political, in the sense that increased time for these activities depends upon more resources, in short more teachers, and partly professional in that the profession must judge whether any additional resources should be used for this purpose or for some other, such as the reduction of class size. But time is perceived to be available by teachers only if the worthwhileness of collaborative activity is accepted. Here too, then, time is a matter for professional consideration.

A second major problem turns upon the implications of extended professionality for teachers' satisfaction. It is reasonable to infer from a range of studies that, generally speaking, teachers obtain their job satisfaction from their classroom activities (Lortie, 1969, and Jackson, 1968). They value their autonomy and their relations with their pupils, and have relatively little interest in educational theory or research. The question which thus arises is whether, in addition to the satisfaction derived from the core activity, teachers can come to derive additional satisfaction from being involved in problem-solving activities and from a greater control over their work situation. Another question is whether teachers who are now entering the profession will feel comfortable in a situation in which "problems of boundary, continuity, order and ambivalence will arise" (Bernstein, 1967). These are ultimately empirical questions, which could be answered only through research that monitored teachers' response to a changing situation.

A third problem relates to the nature of professionality in teaching. The earlier pattern of school organization was based upon a structure which constrained teachers but at the same time allowed them a degree of classroom autonomy and freedom to develop a high degree of restricted professionality in relation to their core professional activity. Emerging models of open schools undermine this autonomy but permit the development of teacher control over the broader context of teaching and encourage extended professionality. The basic questions turn upon whether restricted and extended professionality represent divergent orientations, or whether the latter is an extension of the former. In this respect the model lacks clarity, since the components of restricted professionality may be variously read as excluding an extended orientation or as potentially capable of extension. This is again a most important empirical question. In my own experience, teachers' response to the model generally indicates a belief that extended professionality is almost inevitably achieved at the cost of effective restricted professionality at the classroom level. Extended professionality is associated with a career orientation rather than with expertise where it ultimately matters—in the teaching situation itself. This has been, of course, a long-standing question in one form or another, but the recent trends in education, predicted as they are—or so this paper has argued—upon an extended professionality, raise the problem in an even more acute form. It is again an important empirical question, but beyond this it remains a policy question. The issue throws into relief an important paradox: if teachers wish to resist the trends towards greater openness and hence limit uncertain situations, they need to have greater control over their work situation. But a greater control over their work situation implies an increased degree of collaboration and collegiality, which is itself a component of the extended professionality which is being resisted.

REFERENCES

BERNSTEIN, B. (1967) "Open schools, open society?" *New Society*, **10** p. 259.

BERNSTEIN, B. (1971) "On the classification and framing of educational knowledge", in Young, M. F. D. (ed.) *Knowledge and Control*, Collier Macmillan.

HICKSON, D. J. and THOMAS, M. W. (1969) "Professionalization in Britain: a preliminary measurement", *Sociology*, **3**, no. 1, pp. 37–53.

HUGHES, E. C. (1958) *Men and Their Work*, Free Press.

JACKSON, P. (1968) *Life in Classrooms*, Holt, Rinehart and Winston.

LEES, D. S. (1966) *The Economic Consequences of the Professions*, Institute of Economic Affairs.

LORTIE, D. C. (1964) "The teacher and team teaching: suggestions for long-range research", in Shaplin, J. T. and Olds H. F. (eds.) *Team Teaching*, Harper.

LORTIE, D. C. (1969) "The balance of control and autonomy in elementary school teaching", in Etzioni, A. (ed.) *The Semi-professions and their Organizations*, Free Press.

MILLERSON, G. (1964) *The Qualifying Associations*, Routledge.

NATIONAL ASSOCIATION OF SCHOOLMASTERS (1972) *Management, Organization and Discipline*.

NATIONAL UNION OF TEACHERS (1973) *Teacher Participation*, a statement of recommendations made to the Annual Conference, 1973.

VOLLMER, H. M. and MILLS, D. L. (1966) *Professionalization*, Prentice Hall.

4.4 Decision Making on the School Curriculum: A Conflict Model[1]

John Eggleston

ABSTRACT

The paper is concerned with curriculum decision making in the school and the attempts to apply a sociological analysis to this important area. Its focus is on the "micro" rather than on the "macro" decision making process, i.e. within the school rather than within the educational system, though the significance of macro decisions is recognized throughout the paper.

Commencing with a discussion of the role that may be played by the study of decision making in curriculum content and method, the paper goes on to suggest some of the orientations that influence such decisions. Six such areas are identified. In the light of these areas four ideological variables are hypothesized. These are finally brought together as components of a model of the autonomy and interrelationship of educational personnel.

For many years the preoccupation of sociologists with selective processes in school systems gave rise to a situation in which the content and methodology of the curriculum in the schools were largely ignored—even though the differentiation of pupils was often seen to be achieved through differential curricula. More recently the growing interest in the organization of the school and the roles of its personnel has brought sociological study nearer to a consideration of the curriculum by alerting it to the way in which curriculum can incorporate an expression of the structure and values of the organization and the roles and relationships of its teachers and pupils.[2]

In recent years the situation has changed rapidly. A number of sociologists have presented papers which review the areas in which a sociological perspective may be applied to the study of what is taught and how it is taught in schools.[3] These studies identify the curriculum as an important instrument, if not the most important instrument, in the socialization and selection undertaken by the school and in the establishment and maintenance of societal power and authority structures. Bernstein

---

Source: *Sociology* (Sept. 1973), 7, pp. 377–94.

(1971) has recently reminded us that "how a society selects, classifies, distributes, transmits and evaluates the educational knowledge it considers to be public reflects both the distribution of power and the principles of social control".

Sociologists have already undertaken a considerable body of work on the typology and classification of curricula[4] and a large body of curriculum case studies of considerable interest to sociologists has now been amassed.[5] Such studies have explored the ways in which curricula come to be regarded as acceptable and appropriate (legitimate) how through the status of their content or form they may affect the status of those who teach or study them, how they carry both rewards and penalties and are also reinforced by rewards and penalties, and how similar curricula may carry different meanings for different categories of pupils and teachers. One of the greatest areas of sociologicial interest, however, lies in the extent and nature of curriculum change.

There is widespread interest in curriculum change in most educational systems. This is not surprising; there is a degree of inevitability about curriculum change at a time of technological, ideological and social change. If education is to fulfil its most basic task of preparing the young to take or to modify adult roles it has to respond to the changing patterns of adult occupational, domestic and leisure activity. Mathematics has to change in an era of mechanical computation, science has to respond to an age of electronics and language training must take cognisance of the new requirements and techniques of communication.

Yet this rather simplistic socialization model offering in effect, a "stimulus/response" type of analysis, though relevant, is insufficient to explain current events in curriculum development. Both in Britain and N. America there are now many "curriculum development" projects both in traditional and new school subjects as well as in many "integrated" areas where educators are making a bid to break away from the "other directedness" that has characterized the content of the curriculum and to replace it with a structure in which the teachers and administrators endeavour to make the decisions on what is taught as well as on how it is taught. Kerr (1967) has outlined a model that is basic to this bid to establish control within the system (though by no means necessarily within the individual classroom). In its simplest form it involves the definition of curriculum objectives, the determination of relevant content and teaching strategies to implement them and the establishment of "feed-back" evaluative instruments to ascertain the extent to which the objectives are achieved and suggest appropriate modifications to the process.

Like the "socialization" model this is manifestly an oversimplification —though a captivating one—for many educators. Kerr himself is clearly conscious of the limitations imposed by the multitude of variables that must impinge upon this process of curriculum change—variables that are at most only partially subject to the control of the educator. These range from the nature and definition of "social" knowledge and its relevant communication media through to the extensive range of social factors that influence the value systems and motivations of teachers, parents, administrators and students. Decisions on teaching strategies and on evaluation are inevitably modified by these cultural factors, so too is the fundamental determination of objectives. Indeed the most striking demonstration of the existence of cultural factors is to be seen in the degree of conflict associated with curriculum decision making; often in marked contrast to the "consensus" expectations of many curriculum theorists as a brief period spent in any school staff room will confirm. An important case study of the way in which these and other variables influenced the acceptance by schools of the ideas and materials of a Schools Council curriculum development project has recently been completed by Shipman (1972). A more general discussion of curriculum variables has been outlined by Shipman in a recent Open University Course Unit (E 283, Units 4 and 5).

The influence of cultural factors is to be seen in all existing devices designed to bring about curriculum development. Yet it is unlikely that they can ever entirely diminish the efforts now being made by educators to influence the course of events. The enthusiasm for planned curriculum change has indeed introduced the possibility of a new and significant variable—that of planning itself. Though curriculum planning as a concept is not new almost all past applications have been small scale and localized—usually confined to the school of a progressive pioneer—and even here they have seldom been characterized by rigorous objectivity.[6] In the contemporary situation the operational area for curriculum planning may be large in scale—perhaps no less than an entire educational system.

The new movement towards curriculum engineering has generated a wide following in many parts of the educational system. Perhaps inevitably, many of the participants are characterized by a euphoric enthusiasm but there is also a significant growth of objective, critical appraisal of the movement from philosophical, psychological and sociological viewpoints. Some of this work may be seen in the pages of the *Journal of Curriculum Studies* (Taylor, Morris and Kerr, 1969–). It is in this publication that Hoyle (1969; see also Hoyle, 1970) has presented a valuable review of sociological work relevant to the structural and normative aspects of curriculum change. Here Hoyle attempts to apply concepts from the study of social change to the analysis of curriculum change and ranges from a consideration of general socio-economic factors and evolutionary trends to localized systems of influence and school organizational patterns. He offers a basic examination of interaction processes in which the whole spectrum of organizations within and around an educational system are incorporated and gives attention to the process of specific acts of curriculum innovation and diffusion with particular reference to the influence of the organizational climate in which it is attempted. Overall, Hoyle gives a picture in which curriculum decision making can be seen to take place against a backcloth of controlling factors—by no means all of which are in the consciousness of those taking the decisions.

Yet in the short period since Hoyle's work was written there have been important changes. Firstly there has been a continued increase in the numbers of persons aspiring to initiate new or modified curricula. Secondly, but arising from this, is that the still substantial groups of educators who wish to continue to engage in existing or traditional curricula find themselves required to make a more conscious decision to do so, which may even have to be justified publicly (as, for example, in the *Black Papers*[7]). In consequence decisions about curriculum content and method have come to take a more conspicuous and regular place in the educational system and the long existing but usually latent conflict situation between "traditional" and "progressive" views on education has become focused on the curriculum and in so doing is becoming both manifest and institutionalized.

It is the interaction between the two and the ensuing curriculum decisions, rather than the wide social context of curriculum change, that this paper attempts to examine, though the structural and normative context of society and its education system cannot be ignored in this examination.

It is possible to begin by identifying some areas of curriculum decision wherein this conflict may be most clearly seen. It is suggested that seven such areas may be delineated (the list is not exhaustive). They are:

1   The definition of what counts as curriculum knowledge—what is suitable for inclusion and what is unsuitable? Which areas of approved knowledge are regarded as being of high status and of low status?
2   The selection and organization of knowledge, the use of specialist disciplines and fields of experience or understanding with varying degrees of "identity"—and their employment separately or in integrated programmes.
3   The structuring of knowledge—how much shall be taught, in what order and in what relationship?
4   The presentation of knowledge—how shall it be taught, by which teachers using what "educational technology"—in what "mode" shall it be taught—shall it be presented to individuals, groups or classes?
5   The distribution of knowledge—to whom shall it be taught—at what stage and in what institutions? Shall it be universally available—even obligatory—or available only to a chosen élite?
6   The assessment of knowledge—how shall its acquisition be judged and by whom? Who shall be allowed to demonstrate their acquisition?
7   The corollaries of knowledge—the nature of the organizational values and maintenance and control functions that the curriculum is

required to carry and the extent to which, reciprocally, organization reflects the answers to the preceding questions.

All these areas not only require manifest decisions in all educational systems but also are likely to display the conflict between "traditional" and "progressive" members of the system. But at this stage the terms "traditional" and "progressive" that have previously been used to identify the polarities in curriculum decision making (terms that are widely used in curriculum literature) appear to be inadequate to describe the complex processes of interaction that are well known to all who take part in such decisions.

Here it becomes necessary to examine the fundamental ideological issues of which curriculum decision making is but a part. The role of ideology in educational change has recently been considered in an important study by Vaughan and Archer (1971). Though concerned with a historical period the study has great relevance for contemporary analysts. The work is based on a theory of change brought about by the interaction of dominant and assertive groups and examines the means whereby educational goals are implemented.

Thus ideology is not only a component of successful domination and assertion, but also defines the means by which educational goals can be implemented. Therefore it not only functions as a source of legitimation for domination and assertion, but also as a wider educational philosophy for the dominant and assertive group. Bearing these points in mind, the ideology adopted by either type of group can be said to serve three distinct purposes—those of legitimation, negation and specification. While each of these may not be stressed to the same degree, they must be consistently related to one another within a given educational ideology.

As has been seen, both the dominant and assertive groups must seek to legitimate their position to their followers as well as to a wider audience. This involves an appeal to certain principles consonant with the interests the group represents, but not derived automatically from them. Secondly, the same principles must be extended to constitute a negation of the sources of legitimation advanced by other groups. With an assertive group this happens immediately, since the claims of domination must be undermined before challenge is possible. It is because of this that assertive groups in their earliest stages may concentrate almost exclusively upon negation, that is upon unmasking or condemning the interests concealed by the ideology of the dominant group. However, a group whose domination has been unopposed over a long period may only begin to develop this negative function in proportion to the attacks launched at it. This is why the typical response of a well-established dominant group to new assertion is an immediate reformulation of its ideology, intended to strengthen its source of legitimation by extending it to negate the claims of other groups. Thirdly, a specification of the blueprint to be implemented within educational establishments, their goals, curricula and intake, must be derived from the same ideological principles [pp. 31–32].

In an attempt to explore decision making within a contemporary school situation, the ideological conflict identified by Vaughan and Archer presents a useful prelude. Its contemporary relevance to the emergence of the *Black Papers* is at once evident. It may be built upon by attempting to identify some of the "ideological variables" that may be seen to spring from the ideologies of the "dominant" and "assertive" groups that will be familiar to all who work in present day schools. (It must be emphasized however, that the identification and exploration of the ideological variables that follow must go beyond the analysis of Vaughan and Archer. Their work concerned an historical period when education was relatively unintegrated with other social institutions and the areas of conflict took place in a markedly less systematic and structured context. An analysis of contemporary decisions in terms of dominance and assertion would involve considerable oversimplification.)

It is possible to hypothesize at least four "ideological variables" that, in a manner somewhat similar to the Parsonian "pattern variables", each indicate two theoretically exclusive alternatives. Though it is not suggested that one or the other must be chosen by an individual before he can make curriculum decisions it may be claimed that the variables represent some of the basic dilemmas that are faced by the educator in his orientation to the curriculum. (In practice most educators achieve a compromise position somewhere on the continua that link the polarities.)

The four ideological variables of curriculum decisions may perhaps be set out as:[8]

1   Traditional/futuristic orientations
2   Determined/innovatory orientations
3   Commitment based/contract based orientations
4   Consequential/causal orientations.[9]

A brief description of these variables follows; it is important to remember at all times that these are models and are used as aids to classification and analysis. In the simplified "pure" forms in which they are presented they do not occur and perhaps cannot occur in real life.

1   TRADITIONAL ORIENTATION/FUTURISTIC ORIENTATION
On the traditional side of the dichotomy would appear orientations favouring the retention of long established curriculum patterns. Such attitudes may embrace compulsory training in some subjects of the curriculum and pre-determined norms of achievement in the various sub-

jects of a largely unchanging kind. They would tend to embrace beliefs that the knowledge, skills and values learned by previous generations have a continuing and major validity in the socialization of the young; that the curriculum possesses a "mystique" into which the young are initiated and that, when received by those who are chosen to receive it, it will be of continuing relevance throughout their adult lives, even though the "ultimate truths" may not be revealed until later in life, if at all. Such curriculum may be claimed to have "stood the test of time". It is scarcely necessary to illustrate this orientation by quotations; it is characterized by many contributions to the *Black Papers*. The recently established National Council for Educational Standards has been formed to advocate such an orientation to the curriculum, and in a publication closely associated with the organization one of its sponsors (Dyson, 1972) states:

> In place of rich and tried styles of human and social living, we have a restless quest for novelty as an end in itself. Great ideals, great schools and institutions, are recklessly bulldozed, before there is anything clear or coherent to put in their place. Or worse, they are replaced by structures attuned to their individual creators or to the guessed needs of the moment ("social relevance"), and made wholly subservient to fashion and whim. The most basic insight of all civilization is violated—that freedom, happiness, fulfilment exist only in a framework of law and structure, and in a continuing and fruitful tension between present and past . . .
>
> By the same token, structure is the essence of all reputable and efficient institutions, which cannot be always and restlessly in change. A school exists to pass on numeracy and literacy, civilized manners and morals, skills and achievements; how can it do this if its purpose is challenged or lost? [pp. 126–7]

Conversely the futuristic orientation will tend to be hostile to traditional curricula and favourable to new curricula that are believed to be "relevant" to the expected (different) social conditions in which the young are to be adults. It supports curricula based on "discovery" or "problem solving approaches" that embody the view that the future needs of the young will be better served by a developed capacity for "adaptability" and "inventiveness" than by remembered knowledge, values and skills. It tends to favour a curriculum that encourages the individuality of the child rather than emphasize his uniformities and embrace a view of a personalized and individual development and a partnership between teacher and students. Curriculum content is seen to be individually achieved rather than collectively ascribed.

Control mediated through these relationships rather than through the ritualistic devices of the traditional orientation is favoured. Most of the planned curriculum developments currently being reported fall into the futuristic frame of reference. Simply, the distinction between the traditional and futuristic orientations may often be seen as one between "culture taking" and "culture making". It is sometimes expressed as one between learning and understanding; certainly most futuristic curricula emphasize individual understanding rather more strongly than learning. There are close links between this dichotomy and the Durkheimian concepts of societies based on mechanistic and organic solidarity; the one based on a structure of established and relatively unchanging roles, to which the individual is ascribed; the other on a dynamic structure of individually achieved roles. Bernstein, in a well known paper, has already drawn attention to the relationship between the "open school" and the organic society.

2   DETERMINED/INNOVATORY ORIENTATIONS

The determined/innovatory orientations are closely linked with the preceding pair, but relate to decisions on organizational arrangements rather than to functional aspirations. On the determined side of the dichotomy are attitudes favouring a curriculum comprising separate elements falling into place in "coherent" and "rational" forms with traditional subject divisions and contents, usually involving sharply defined hierarchies of subject. Some subjects will be seen to contain high status knowledge, others the converse. The curriculum tends to comprise subject components each being legitimated by the nature of its "discipline" or its identifiable area of knowledge or even a "logical grammar" (Hurst, 1969).

The behaviour and status of both staff and pupils would tend to be dominated by subject specialization and by their ability to perform within the specialist subject. It involves a view of the nature and accessibility of societal knowledge that tends to be both structured and hierarchical. Thus Bantock (1964) an important exponent of the view, sees cultural activity as divisible not only into different forms—"élite" and "mass"—but also that the different forms should be available to different categories of children. To quote Dyson (1972) again:

> We also have to accept that any activity in a society, from that of ruling it and upholding its laws and customs downwards, is a specialist and expert function, which the greater majority of men have never been, and will never be, fitted to perform [p. 130].

Here we can begin to see the major importance of the determined curriculum as an instrument of social selection and social control, a theme developed in several of the various contributions to *Knowledge and Control* (Young, 1971).

The determined orientation can also be defined in terms of the concept of boundary maintenance as applied by Bernstein (1971) in that the contents of the separate subjects would be marked off from each other by strong classification, being in close relationship to one another. Similarly the teaching method would be marked by strong "framing" where both teachers and pupils have few, if any, options in the communication process.

The innovatory side of the dichotomy involves support for the "flexible school"; there is likely to be support for curricula that are "integrated" rather than subject based, integration being determined as much by the needs of the individual pupils as by the "logical grammar" of the subject. In general there is support for flexible school conditions that may be set up in an attempt to achieve objectives such as maximum opportunity for the development of individual pupils and students or to allow for special considerations for their social background and other personal variables. It is essentially a "child centred" rather than a "subject centred" education.

The traditional pattern of uniform written examinations appropriate to determined curricula are much less appropriate to the individualized and incompletely unpredictable outcomes of innovating curricula and they can be seen to present difficult if not insoluble problems if the imprimatur of the examination boards is still required. Innovatory curricula may be distinguished into two forms, *structured* and *opportunist*. The structured form may be seen in the planned innovatory strategies that characterize the work of many teachers involved in organized programmes to develop innovating curricula in national and local projects usually with local education authority support. Conversely the opportunist form, however carefully considered, is likely to be of unplanned and unpredictable nature; spontaneity of child and teacher are terms frequently used by its advocates. The Goldsmiths Curriculum Laboratory work has many of the characteristics of the oportunist form and, as Musgrove (1968) has observed, this may also embody important anti-authoritarian elements.

The following example from a recent advertisement in a journal of educational technology is an extreme but not wholly exceptional example of "opportunism":

You're all hanging up your coats at school and in comes Donnie with a cast on his arm. Everybody has to see it and touch it and write on it. "How long do you have to wear it, Donnie?" "Miss Sanders, what makes bones?" "How can you break your arm swimming?" "Will it grow back, Miss Sanders?" This is the teachable moment. It's the rare moment when you really want to learn. But your curiosity sure isn't satisfied by seeing just the cast. You want to see inside. Somebody goes to the film library and brings back a film selection on bones. You put it in the projector and—wow—a great movie.

This way Miss Sanders can teach you all kinds of things—more things than anyone would expect her to know—at the exact moment when you want to learn them. And it's alive, the way you're used to seeing it. [Information on an educational film company follows.]

It is important to separate opportunist innovatory behaviour from the organized and predictable progressivism which characterizes many "progressive" educationalists. Such behaviours have their own structured characters. Opportunism is essentially manifest by a curriuculum that is not fully institutionalized. The existence of the opportunist orientation is manifest by the occurrence of new and not fully institutionalized patterns of curriculum decisions. To use Bernstein's terms again, it is likely to be characterized by both weak classification of content and weak framing of pedagogy. Any "brand" of opportunism is likely to be a transient form in that it becomes institutionalized if it is regarded as successful. And indeed, any form of innovatory curriculum is likely to become, in time, determined through the development of text books and materials packages (particularly those regarded as "teacher proof"), examinations and "specialists."

3   COMMITMENT BASED/CONTRACT BASED ORIENTATIONS

Orientations favouring a commitment basis are likely to see the curriculum as a "total experience" wherein the student is not only involved in a straightforward learning experience but also in a necessary and unavoidable internalization of the official values of the school or college. Curriculum is seen to represent an ideal value system that embodies that which is appropriate or desirable for the adult society. For the students, working through the curriculum is not only a learning situation, it is usually designed also as an initiating commitment to an approved societal value system. An important element of the commitment based orientation is that no part of the curriculum is seen to be legitimately available to the student without the value commitment. Thus the student who renounces the official value orientations of the university may be seen to have no place there and is denied access to any part of its curriculum; the working class school child has to be converted to not only the knowledge content of the curriculum but also the values of the middle class school if there is to be "any point in his education" and he may well be discouraged from staying if his conversion is incomplete. The reward system of the school is of course fully incorporated into the curriculum.

The contract based orientation involves attitudes that see participation in the curriculum as a contractual arrangement in which students and teachers negotiate arrangements that are limited in their consequences and are usually for some specific rather than general purpose (to pass an examination, to learn a language, etc.). Contractual relationships are more commonly found in community colleges and further education establishments where "client involvement" has characteristically required direct negotiation between the institution and its students. Elsewhere, notably in universities, it is a position held more commonly by students than by their teachers.[10] An interesting recent development is an attempt to organize programmes of teaching that specifically exclude moral commitment even though they deal with "moral issues". A ready example arises in the Schools Council/Nuffield Humanities Teaching Project where, in the examination of controversial issues such as war, protest, authority and the like the teacher is explicitly required to encourage pupils to form their own views on these issues rather than to "receive" those of the teacher or of the school.

In society generally, contractual relationships usually occur between individuals or between organized groups in a structured context. It may be argued that to talk of contractual relationships between individualized students and teachers who form the core of the organization of the school is misleading. Whilst this is to ignore the considerable autonomy of teachers and the increasing extent to which it is exercised, (which will be discussed later) it has nevertheless considerable validity. Yet the demand for a "real" contractual relationship is clearly to be seen in a number of current moves—most notably in the free school and the "deschooling" movement in Europe and the US. In the context of higher education a specifically contractual set of negotiations has been urged in a joint statement by the National Union of Students and the National Council for Civil Liberties (Times Educational Supplement, 1970).

4. CONSEQUENTIAL ORIENTATION/CAUSAL ORIENTATION[11]

The consequential orientation is likely to view the curriculum as a by-product of other social factors including the normative and social structure (notably the class and occupational structure) and technological, economic and ideological change. It may support the view that little can be changed by education and that the programmes of social and knowledge engineering envisaged by a number of curriculum developers cannot be undertaken by educational strategies if, indeed, they can be undertaken at all.[12] The long term predictability of genetic if not cultural endowment is unchallenged and may be supported by statements as basic and apparently incontrovertible as "that's life" or "he was born that way". Another version of the consequential orientation, expressed in Young's introduction to *Knowledge and Control* (1971) is that the curriculum has no option but to support the social system and reinforce its control arrangements: that a curriculum that did not would rapidly become vulnerable.

The causal orientation is likely to view education, at least to some extent, as a determining factor in social behaviour and social organization. Thus social consequences may be expected to spring from the introduction of Educational Priority programmes designed to meet needs of "deprived" students; social as well as technological consequences may be expected from the introduction of a development programme such as Project Technology. The roles of teachers and students are seen to allow open prospects of achievement and development, they and their consequences can be "self-generated". Evidence such as that published by Douglas (1964) or Rosenthal and Jacobsen (1968) that suggests a high responsiveness of children to cultural environmental change is likely to be used enthusiastically.

At this stage it may be useful to state again what has been implicit throughout this discussion and, indeed, any discussion of ideological variables—that they are models or "ideal types". Reality is likely to involve elements of all variables and compromise between polarities, and as Merton (1968) reminds us, innovation is commonly likely to mean "the rejection of institutional practices but the retention of cultural goals". No curriculum totally ignores the contributions of inspired opportunism. No subject oriented curriculum completely eliminates child centred work even if it is largely relegated to hobby periods. And it must also be recognized that important and established positions cut across the dichotomies. Thus "cultural education" may require highly traditional behaviours yet an associated emphasis on individual expressive work may be seen as of equal importance, and some statements of position have an almost sphinx like inscrutability and unclarifiability such as, for example, Marshall's (1968) plea for a curriculum to produce "men and women who have poetry in their souls".

It is now suggested that the four paired variables may be put together as components of a model built around the idea of *autonomy* of curriculum decisions. In its simplest form the model would have two extreme identities that may be seen to have a degree of correspondence with Vaughan and Archer's ideological models of *domination* and *assertion*;

(i) Where there is no autonomy in curriculum decision making; where the personnel of the educational system have no significant areas of decision or discretion and are merely agents of a dominant ideology.
(ii) Where curriculum decisions may be wholly autonomous; where personnel are free to asert their own arrangements without hindrance by a dominant ideology.

Both forms are of course highly hypothetical. Nonetheless it is suggested that the educational systems in Britain are tending to shift from a position nearer (i) to a position nearer (ii). It is further suggested that this has been associated with a shift from a consensus of orientation towards the curriculum that has been predominantly associated with those on the left hand side of each of the four pairs of variables, viz.

1 Traditional orientation
2 Determined orientation
3 Commitment based orientation
4 Consequential orientation.

It is suggested that we may now see these orientations as falling within a "dominant" ideology; certainly they have been seen to serve the purposes of legitimation negation and specification indicated by Vaughan and Archer. The reciprocal movement from such a consensus of orientation has been associated with the four right hand variables, viz.

1 Futuristic orientation
2 Innovatory orientation
3 Contract based orientation
4 Causal orientation

It is suggested that we may now see these orientations as falling within an "assertive" ideology. The emergence of both groups has led to the development, even the institutionalization, of conflict over curriculum decisions. In practice this conflict, often associated with linked political conflict, has provided opportunities to move from a relatively prescribed non-autonomous curriculum to a relatively non-prescribed autonomous curriculum.

The institutionalization of conflict and the ensuing move towards autonomous decision making is charted, in many systems, by changed foci of curriculum decision making. In many school systems the period from the introduction of compulsory schooling through to the opening years of the twentieth century was marked by centralization of decisions about the curriculum. These tended to take place at a societal level whereby, as Halls (1971) has indicated, the dominant political and ecclesiastical élites determined the curriculum in conformity with the existing norms and values of society.

The educational system of England and Wales provides an interesting case study. In the period from the first introduction of legislation for compulsory schooling in 1870 through to the opening years of the 20th century the central decisions about curriculum tended to take place at a societal level whereby the dominant groups ensured that the structure norms and values of the society would be reinforced and not disturbed either by the elementary schools or by the public—"independent"— schools. A number of control mechanisms were available for the purpose —notably "payment by results" whereby teachers were rewarded for curriculum conformity and penalized for deviance—a system operated, in part through a team of central government inspectors. The constraints on the School Boards (later to give way to L.E.A.s) were clearly demonstrated by the 1899 "Cockerton" judgement when the London School Board was surcharged for its "establishment" of higher grade elementary schooling.

The relative decline of political, ecclesiastical and general cultural consensus by the end of the 19th century, amongst other consequences, facilitated a localization of decision making wherein the making of decisions on curriculum were, in part, delegated to the new local education

authorities who were more readily able to achieve a measure of consensus in their smaller areas. These included the development of
arrangements for primary and secondary curricula, the selection of pupils
to receive them and the development of important sectors of tertiary
education including teacher training and the technical colleges. Substantial areas of consensus to a dominant ideology still persisted, however,
for example, the relative unanimity of view on secondary schooling and
its curriculum that existed until the late 1940s is well recorded. Yet the
range of local variation that developed despite strong central influence
from the Board, later Ministry of Education, was unmistakable. Interestingly this can be seen clearly in the changing style of Ministry of
Education publications, for example, the various editions of the *Handbook of Suggestions for Teachers* first published under Morant's leadership in 1904 and regularly revised. The Prefatory Notes to this volume
contain, with increasing emphasis, versions of the following statement:

> The only uniformity of practice that the Board of Education desire
> to see in the teaching of Public Elementary Schools is that each
> teacher shall think for himself, and work out for himself such
> methods of teaching as may use his powers to the best advantage
> and be best suited to the particular needs and conditions of the
> school.

But in the 1950s a further decline in the dominant consensus occurred,
particularly in the field of secondary education. Here new political concern over the distribution of opportunity was matched by new economic
concerns for the "maximization of talent" and new sociological evidence
suggesting the existence of previously uncharted areas of social inequality
both with the educational system as a whole and with individual schools
and colleges. An important consequence of this was a move to a still
greater degree of curriculum autonomy; schools and their teachers
achieved a considerable extension in the range of decisions and dis-
cretions open to them, often on the argument that they might respond
more sensitively to the social and economic needs of their pupils. An
example of the way in which this took place in the secondary modern
schools, which served some 70 per cent of the school population up to the
mid 60s, has been well documented by Taylor (1963). He shows the
range of curriculum and examination developments that were initiated in
the schools in the 1950s. Many of them, notably the arrangements for
pupils entering examinations, were in direct conflict with the views of the
Local Education Authorities and the Central Government but were made
possible at least in part by the further development of the assertive
orientations to the curriculum. More recently the development of community schools in which the curriculum may require "community legitimacy" may, in practice, further enhance school autonomy. The point is
clearly made by Poster (1971): "recognition by the school of its place in

the community will have its effect on the curriculum where social relevance is desirable and on the responsibility and participation not only of parents and pupils but also the wider public".

But perhaps the best example of the development of autonomy within the system following the institutionalization of conflict is the development of the comprehensive school programmes in England and Wales. The administrative memoranda of both Labour and Conservative governments, (Circular 10/65 and Circular 10/70 respectively) both had the net effect of offering a far greater degree of autonomy to the education system on the matter of secondary school provision and curriculum than was ever available in the "consensus" decade that followed the 1944 Education Act. What is more the autonomy offered by Circular 10/70 is in some areas probably greater than that offered by Circular 10/65. Circular 10/65 offered a range of six patterns of comprehensive/secondary school organization; within three years, and with the aid of new legislation making it possible to modify the age of entry to secondary education from the original mandatory age of 11, the approved range of patterns had widened to a figure nearer 60 than 6. Indeed it could be argued that every local scheme of comprehensive schooling and its curriculum was, in some ways, unique. Yet Circular 10/70 has effectively extended local and professional autonomy still further in that it allows the possibility of approval of not only comprehensive school arrangements but also non-comprehensive ones as well. And it is in the area of curriculum not only in the new secondary schools but also in the primary schools that feed them that the consequences of such autonomy are most clearly to be seen.[13]

The development of curriculum decision making, under conditions of comprehensive education, may well mark the opening up of a further focal area of curriculum decision making—that by students or pupils in the school system. The very shifts in organizational and personal relationships that have been reviewed have moved the clients almost imperceptibly to a central place in many of the key decisions in curriculum. Open choice systems, problem solving approaches where the problems and solutions are pupil determined, voluntary "staying on", all lead to situations in which the school pupil may attain a considerable level of autonomy in the determination of his curriculum; his definition of the situation becomes of considerably greater importance.

The widespread employment of school counsellors may also be seen as a further move in this direction in that the counsellor can mobilize the curriculum choices of the pupil body and implement them in the organization of the school and educational system. (Though, as Cicourel and Kitsuse (1963) remind us, there is a likelihood that this may be more apparent than real.) There is of course an important link here with change in the university wherein students have already achieved some notable advances in their participation in curriculum decision making. Yet it is possible that pupils in the upper forms in a number of comprehensive secondary schools have already attained a level of curriculum decision making that may still elude most university students. And the embryonic "deschooling" movement, to which reference has already been made, with its "non-institutionalized" schools without walls contains the possibility of substantial further increments of curriculum determinations by "the clients" of the system. The publications of two leading U.K. bodies for the promotion of curriculum change (The Schools Council and Goldsmiths Curriculum Laboratory) both emphasize the role of pupils as decision makers and teachers as "enablers".[14] Thus the Goldsmiths literature speaks of the aim to "build collaboratively a kind of schooling that is based on sensitivity, suppleness and equality of esteem for persons and to invent an education based on collaboration, flexibility, making and openness to experience of people and things" (Goldsmith's Curriculum Laboratory, undated). (This is not to say that the ideology of both bodies is similar; as Musgrave has pointed out, the ideology of the Goldsmiths Laboratory is distinctly more anti-authoritarian than the more pragmatic approach of the Schools Council.) Some of the likely consequences for the roles of both teachers and students of changes in decision making have already been explored by Eggleston (1969) in an article in which the possibility of further convergence of role between teachers and students has been suggested.

The tentative model that has been discussed may now be brought together in a diagrammatic summary (Figure 1).

The diagram, in particular, serves to clarify two important features of the suggested model. Firstly, it indicates that it is not a simple shift from dominant to assertive or from social to client curriculum determination that has been suggested, rather one in which the societal (élite) determination has been joined by the local authorities, by the staffs of schools and colleges and most recently by the organized and unorganized clients of the system. It is this move associated with the institutionalization of the conflicting dominant and assertive ideologies in curriculum decision making that, it is suggested, gives rise to a greater degree of autonomy and destructuring in curriculum decision. But the second important clarification afforded by the diagram is that at no time is either an entirely non-autonomous situation or a fully autonomous curriculum decision situation portrayed. As has been suggested earlier, neither condition is feasible; at no stage have the personnel of educational systems been totally deprived of curriculum autonomy and at no forseeable future stage are they likely to be free of external constraint—indeed some of the economic and technological constraints imposed through financial and occupational demands on the system may well be intensified. But whilst this may deflect the diagonal cut off line of the diagram it appears unlikely to invalidate the model itself. A final comment on the diagram concerns the link between curriculum autonomy and conflict (and v.v.). Though it is suggested that the move towards autonomy springs in part

Figure 1

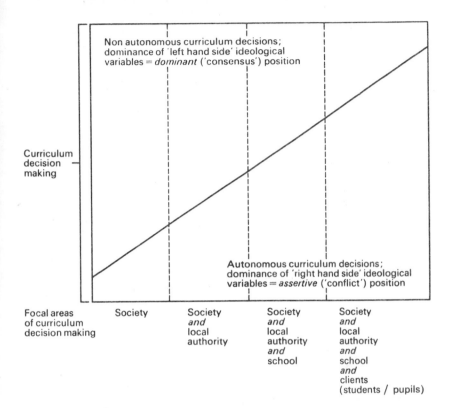

Direction of change ⟶

Curriculum
decision
making

Non autonomous curriculum decisions;
dominance of 'left hand side' ideological
variables = *dominant* ('consensus') position

Autonomous curriculum decisions;
dominance of 'right hand side' ideological
variables = *assertive* ('conflict') position

Focal areas of curriculum decision making	Society	Society *and* local authority	Society *and* local authority *and* school	Society *and* local authority *and* school *and* clients (students / pupils)

from the institutionalization of conflict between dominant and assertive ideologies it is not part of the argument that the existence of an autonomous area is necessarily characterized by manifest conflict once it has come to exist. (Though, in the long run, a degree of conflict is likely to be necessary in order to retain autonomy.)

CONCLUSION

In this paper a very limited exercise has been attempted—the identification and analysis of some of the conflicting ideological positions that are at work when curriculum decisions are being made and the ways in which changes in these positions appear to have led to curriculum change. Only passing reference has been made to the wider social implications of their decisions—a fuller discussion of these implications is to be found in M.F.D. Young's *Knowledge and Control*, which considers, amongst others, the view that the child's perception of the curriculum, like that of the teachers, is in part determined by his social background which leads him to respond and "construct reality" in certain ways. The links between the curriculum and the other systems of the school—examinations, reward/punishment, discipline, stratification, staffing and administration require a fuller discussion than is possible in a short paper and are considered in detail in the author's book *The Sociology of the School Curriculum* (Eggleston 1975).

NOTES

1 A substantially developed version of a paper originally presented to Working Group 9 (Education and Cultural Planning), World Congress of Sociology, Bulgaria, 1970. The author gratefully acknowledges the helpful comments of colleagues and students, notably of Marion Jordan and John Piper, on earlier versions.

2 See, for example, Dreeben (1969), Young (1971) and Davies (1970a).

3 Such papers include Musgrove (1968), Musgrave (1971) and (1972).

4 Bernstein (1971), Musgrave (1971), Hopper (1967), Turner (1964) and Davies (1970b).

5 A valuable series of such studies is that commenced by the Centre for Educational Research and Innovation attached to the Organisation for Economic Co-operation and Development, Paris. A particularly interesting paper is that of Bernbaum, G., who reports on Innovation at Countesthorpe College, Leicestershire. A further wide range of such studies is to be found in the publications of the Schools Council, London and other organizations promoting curriculum developments in Britain and America. A useful collection of excerpts from Schools Council publications is available in Schools Council (1967).

6 For an account of the "progressive movement" see Stewart (1967) and (1968).

7 Dyson (1969), Cox and Dyson (1970). *The Black Papers* are, of course, matched by opposed ideological messages, for example Rubinstein and Stoneman (1970).

8 No attempt is being made here to suggest that these variables would form part of any general attitude scales: they are chosen *ad hoc* as the most suitable formulation for the study. However, once this reservation has been made, it is fair to point out that the first two pairs have much in common with Eysenck's conservative-radical continuum and Oliver's idealist-naturalist continuum respectively. Furthermore, the third pair is closely akin to Parsons' universalistic-particularistic dichotomy, though much narrower since they are intended to apply specifically only to the particular situation under

scrutiny. The last pair, in some ways derivative from the other three, is listed separately here as likely to be fruitful in the analysis of specifically curriculum orientations.

9 An obvious further pair may be societally/individualist oriented but, although widespread, this is not an ideological variable that can in practice be demonstrated to have a clear influence on the behaviour of individuals in their curriculum decisions.

10 In the D.E.S. research study of the sociology of the youth service in England and Wales, directed by the writer, it is notable that a marked divergence may be seen between the commitment orientations of the providing bodies and the contractual orientations of the clients. See also Trow and Halsey (1969).

11 In this attitudinal variable the writer has been able to use part of the formulation of McGee (1967).

12 For a useful discussion of evidence to support this view, see Hurd and Johnson (1967).

13 See, for example, Halsall (1970), Makins (1971) and Mason (1965). Mason, writing of comprehensive reorganisation and the ensuing end of the 11+ examination, says: "it has resulted in an explosion of creative activity in all subjects, innumerable experiments, a ferment of discussion and a search to understand the true nature and needs of the primary school child".

14 Representative publications are, respectively, Schools Council (1969) and James (1968).

REFERENCES

BANTOCK, G. H. (1964) *Freedom and Authority in Education*, Faber.

BERNSTEIN, B. B. (1967) "Open School, Open Society", *New Society*, 14 Sept. 1967.

BERNSTEIN, B. B. (1971) "On the Classification and Framing of Educational Knowledge", in Young, M. D. F. (ed.) *Knowledge and Control*, Collier Macmillan.

CICOUREL, A. V. and KITSUSE, J. I. (1963) *The Educational Decision Makers*, Bobbs-Merrill.

COX, C. and DYSON, A. E. (1970) *The Crisis in Education: Black Paper Two*, Critical Quarterly Society.

DAVIES, D. (1970a) *Knowledge, Education and Power*, paper presented to the British Sociological Association Annual Conference.

DAVIES, D. I. (1970b) "The Management of Knowledge, a Critique of the Use of Typologies in Educational Sociology", *Sociology* 4.1.

DOUGLAS, J. W. B. (1964) *The Home and the School*, MacGibbon and Kee.

DREEBEN, R. (1969) *On What Is Learned in School*, Addison-Wesley.

DYSON, A. E. (1969) *Fight for Education: A Black Paper*, Critical Quarterly Society.

DYSON, A. E. (1972) "The Structures we Need", in Boyson R. (ed.) *Education: Threatened Standards,* Churchill.

EGGLESTON, S. J. (1969) "Convergences in the Roles of Personnel in Differentiated Educational Organisations", in Mathieson, D. I. (ed.) (1970) *Education and Sociology,* Mouton.

EGGLESTON, S. J. (1975) *The Sociology of the School Curriculum,* Routledge and Kegan Paul.

GOLDSMITHS CURRICULUM LABORATORY (undated) *New Roles for the Learner,* Goldsmiths College, p. 4.

HALLS, W. D. (1971) "Elites and the Content of Education", *Pedagogica Europaea,* vi, pp. 197–205.

HALSALL, E. (1970) *Inside the Comprehensive School,* Pergamon.

HOPPER, E. (1967) "A Typology for the Classification of Educational Systems", *Sociology* 2.1.

HOYLE, E. (1969) "How Does the Curriculum Change?" *Journal of Curriculum Studies,* 1, 2 and 3.

HOYLE, E. (1970) "Planned Organizational Change", *Research in Education,* **3**.

HURD, G. E. and JOHNSON, T. F. (1967) "Education and Development", *Sociological Review,* 15.1.

HURST, P. in Peters, R. (ed.) (1969) *The Concept of Education,* Allen and Unwin, p. 53.

JAMES, C. (1968) *Young Lives at Stake,* Collins.

KERR, J. F. (1967) *The Problem of Curriculum Reform,* Leicester University Press.

McGEE, R. (1967) "Education and Social Change", in Hansen, D. A. and Gerstl, J. E. (eds.) *On Education: Sociological Perspectives,* Wiley.

MAKINS, V. (1971) "Countesthorpe: First Year Report", *Times Educational Supplement,* 25 June 1971.

MARSHALL, S. (1968) *Adventures in Creative Education,* Pergamon.

MASON, S. C. (1965) "The Leicestershire Plan", in McLure, S. (ed.) *Comprehensive Planning,* Councils and Education Press.

MERTON, R. K. (1968) *Social Theory and Social Structure,* Free Press.

MUSGRAVE, P. W. (1971) "Towards a Sociology of the Curriculum", *Pedagogica Europaea,* vi, pp. 37–49.

MUSGRAVE, P. W. (1972) "Social Factors Affecting the Curriculum", in Hughes, P. W. (ed.) *The Teacher's Role in Curriculum Design,* Angus and Robertson.

MUSGROVE, F. (1968) "The Contribution of Sociology to the Study of the Curriculum", in Kerr, J. F. (ed.) *Changing the Curriculum,* University of London Press.

OPEN UNIVERSITY, THE (1972) E283 *The Curriculum: Context, Design and Development,* Units 4 and 5, *Perspectives on the Curriculum,* The Open University Press.

POSTER, C. (1971) *The School and the Community,* Macmillan.

Rosenthal, P. and Jacobson, L. (1968) *Pygmalion in the Classroom*, Holt, Rinehart and Winston.

Rubinstein, D. and Stoneman, C. (eds.) (1970) *Education for Democracy*, Penguin.

Schools Council (1967) *The New Curriculum*, HMSO.

Schools Council (1969) *Society and the Young School Leaver*, HMSO.

Shipman, M. D. (1972) *Curriculum Innovation—a Case Study of a Curriculum Development Project*, Routledge and Kegan Paul.

Stewart, W. A. C. (1967 and 1968) *The Educational Innovators, Parts 1 and 2*, Macmillan.

Taylor, W. (1963) *The Secondary Modern School*, Faber.

Taylor, P. H., Morris, G. and Kerr, J. F. (eds.) (1969–   ), *Journal of Curriculum Studies*, Collins.

Times Educational Supplement (1970) 23 Oct. 1970.

Trow, M. and Halsey, A. H. (1969) "British Academics and the Professorship", *Sociology*, **3**, p. 3.

Turner, R. H. (1964) *The Social Context of Ambition*, Chandler.

Vaughan, M. and Archer, M. S. (1971) *Social Conflict and Educational Change in England and France 1789–1898*, Cambridge University Press.

Young, M. D. F. (1971) "Curricula as Socially Organized Knowledge", in Young, M. D. F. (ed.) *Knowledge and Control*, Collier-Macmillan.

4.5 The School as a Social System

B. Sugarman

It is surprising that the analysis of the school as a social system has attracted so little attention from scholars, especially since the sociology of education and organization theory are two of the most highly developed areas of the social sciences today. In spite of a distinguished early start by Waller (1938), some more recent theoretical attempts of a more limited nature,[1] and some interesting sociological analyses of particular types of schools,[2] we are very far from having a systematic general model for the analysis of the school (of any type) as a social system. It is the aim of this article to make a contribution towards the development of such a model.

1 FUNCTIONAL PROBLEMS AND SUB-SYSTEMS

Boundary, Inputs, Outputs[3]

We now begin to look at the school as a unit in its own right. As such we may conceive of a *boundary* dividing the school from the environment or the larger social system. This boundary may be a physical one, like the high wall or fence round a borstal. More often it takes the purely symbolic form of notices to outside visitors and rules restricting pupils from wandering abroad during school time. The notices to visitors may be welcoming or forbidding or they may merely announce the name of the school. The point is that a boundary is marked and, having crossed it into the school, one enters the jurisdiction of the school.

The boundary should not be seen simply as a spatial or territorial one. It is rather a matter of "social space". Pupils who are on a field trip or an organized school holiday are considered to be still under school jurisdiction and expected to obey teachers who are held responsible by the general public for their conduct. The same children on holiday with their parents are considered beyond the boundary of the school. Consensus often breaks down about the intermediate situations, such as the time when pupils are travelling between school and home. Schools often try to

---

Source: *Moral Education* (1969) Vol. 1, No. 2, Pergamon Press, pp. 15–32.

control pupils' behaviour during this time but these efforts are not always very effective, partly because pupils and parents do not always accept that the school has the right, but more because of practical difficulties of enforcement. Grammar schools have often tried to control pupils' activities during their evenings and weekends, even though pupils lived at home, by forbidding them to take part-time jobs or join voluntary organizations. The heads of these schools defined their pupils' leisure time as falling, to some extent, within the boundary of the school.

The boundary is not only a way of defining how far the long arm of the school reaches out beyond the territory of the school grounds or beyond school hours; it also enables us to conceptualize the degree of control which the school attempts to exercise over what pupils may bring *into* the school with them. School rules regulate the kind of clothes the pupils may wear; forbid the importation or consumption by pupils of tobacco or other drugs, pornography, pets and many other possessions which the pupils may legitimately keep at home.

The notion of a boundary further enables us to conceptualize the flow of inputs and outputs between the school and the larger society. Into the school, across the boundary flow various *inputs*, notably three kinds: resources (money and supplies), personnel (pupils and teachers) and expectations or demands concerning how the school will run and what it will achieve. The demands that matter are those imposed by the "controlling agency" of the school. In the case of independent schools this agency is the same as the governing body; in state schools it is the local education authority. The controlling agency may be conceived as located at the boundary, where it acts in several ways: it collects resources from outside sources and channels them into the school; it recruits staff and pupils, in some cases selecting from an excess of applicants and in others beating the bushes for suitable personnel; and it responds to pressures from public and pressure groups concerning what should be expected of the school and formulates its own policy of legitimate expectations, taking the former into account as much as it feels necessary.

The *outputs* of the schools flow out across the boundary to the larger society. They consist of all the changes which the school has produced; all the learning of skills, knowledge, attitude and behaviour, as well as the analogous changes in staff, especially in the form of professional development. These outputs are, in theory, open to comparison with the expectations handed down by the controlling agency which has the power in law to dismiss staff who fail to meet its standards, to withold funds or to close down the school in the event of their extreme displeasure.

There is very little similarity in the position of the school governors between the independent and state-maintained schools. In the former case they represent an important power in their own right, as well as the channel for pressures emanating from Whitehall and the market-place. In the latter case, that of the maintained schools, the governors have precious little power and do not even function as the main channel for outside pressures, which most often go straight to the head. The autonomous local school board found in the USA is not in this position, though they have to fear the reaction of local voters who elect them. The private trust which controls many independent schools is likewise less hamstrung. Though independent of government control, it is inevitably constrained by the views of the parents on whom it is financially dependent for fees and the old boys for gifts and legacies.

The governing body exists at the boundary and by its behaviour determines in part the nature of the boundary itself. This body may operate to protect the school from pressure groups and opinionated members of the public, or it may side with them and demand full responses to complaints and demands. The governors of an independent school may secure a great increase in the autonomy for their school by cultivating more diverse and plentiful sources of funds, or by improving the image of the school so that recruitment of both pupils and staff is facilitated. In these sorts of ways the governing body can influence the boundary relations between the school and the larger society.

Equally important from the head's point of view is his relationship with the board itself and the degree of autonomy permitted to him in running the internal affairs of the school. Schools in England appear to enjoy a degree of autonomy in this respect considerably greater than those in most other countries. They are very much freer from governmental interference than the schools of France or the Soviet bloc of countries, and also more free from the interference of organized parents' groups than the schools of the USA. On the other hand, the power of the organized teachers' organizations is relatively great in England, which imposes restraint on the freedom of action of heads and governors.

The expectations of the independent school's governing body or the maintained school's local education authority may have direct implications for the internal structure of the school. If they merely defined the goals and objectives of the school, the relative weight to be laid on the different kinds of output, this in itself might be taken to imply a preference for certain forms of structure rather than others. But they might go beyond this in their expectations to include definite policies as to the structure of the school itself, so defining not only objectives but the organizational means to be taken. For example, they may be resolutely decided *not only* that they may expect a large emphasis on moral education in the school *but also* that they expect this to be implemented by means of the traditional boarding-school house system.

The effectiveness of the school in producing its outputs is affected by the inputs available to it, including the kind of backgrounds from which pupils come, the quality of teachers and the generosity with which resources are provided, which will affect pupil-teacher ratios. In addition to these input factors, though, it is likely that some ways of organizing a school are more or less effective than others in terms of producing specific outputs.

Internal organization

Certain organizational approaches may be precluded in schools with certain input conditions, but across the broad range of variation organization may be regarded as independent of input conditions. That is, a wide range of organizational alternatives exists in any school and which combination is adopted will affect both the school's effectiveness in terms of producing its outputs and the kinds of operational problems which are met in running it.

Within each school there is generally an *established structure* or blueprint, which describes the allocation of duties and responsibilities among staff.

A major part of the blueprint comprises the formal structure of academic work. This includes a scheme for dividing the total body of pupils into "manageable" teaching groups, a timetable for dividing up the day into assigned activities and the assignment of teachers to particular subjects and groups of pupils. A further part of the blueprint may be a pastoral system, assigning to specific teachers a responsibility for the general welfare of particular pupils. There are also likely to be further parts covering extra-curricular activities, competitive sports and schemes for co-opting certain pupils into the formal authority system.

Each school has a chief executive or head, appointed by its governing body. One of his main responsibilities is to ensure the operation of the official structures established in the school and to make such modifications to them as seem to him necessary, subject to the approval of the governing body.

The head who takes over an established school inherits the official structures set up by his predecessors, of course, and his scope for modifying them is limited by what he can persuade the established staff (and perhaps even the pupils) to accept.

Again we find a big difference in the power of the heads of independent and maintained schools. The newly-appointed head of an independent school is likely to be confronted by a long-established group of senior staff, especially house-masters, who are well-connected with members of the governing body and well-known to parents who are sending (or planning to send) their children to a particular man's house at a particular school. Quite apart from any matter of legal tenure, these staff are close to being irremovable and they are a powerful and conservative obstacle to the reforming head. The head of a maintained school is likely to have a higher rate of staff turnover, hence a smaller core of established senior staff. On the other hand, he may have difficulty in recruiting qualified staff and therefore be constrained against squeezing out senior staff who oppose his policies. Provided that he can engage the support of a significant part of his staff, there are extremely few policies that the head of a maintained school cannot put into effect. With some policies, such as starting a school council or introducing a prefect system, the support of senior pupils is also necessary for success. Even without securing this

M

support there is nothing to stop the head of a maintained school from going ahead with his innovations—nothing except good sense.

Any discussion of the official structures is likely to involve either justifying them or justifying proposed changes by reference to their alleged contributions to the effectiveness of the school in relation to certain outputs. However, it need not take this utilitarian form but may proceed along other lines, for example: "X has been an established tradition in this school since 1769", or "St Jeremy's, which we all know is a very renowned school, has Y and it would look good if we had it too", or "the parents are always very impressed when the school has a Z, so we should have one".

Staff and pupils enter a school with some preconceptions of their roles, which are then modified by their experiences in the school. They find that certain ways of behaviour are established as normative among their peers. There is a process of informal socialization which affects both new pupils and the less experienced teachers and bends their preconceived notions in the direction of those established among their peers. Older teachers would be an exception to this. Younger teachers and especially those straight from their training are very susceptible to the influence of the established staff and the general atmosphere of the common room. This implies a great weight of conservatism or tradition on the school. Big changes within a relatively short space of time are not generally possible, except when the head can ruthlessly purge and replace his staff and uses very great tactical skill and guile. Even the head who is starting a new school is constrained to some extent by the preconceptions of the staff and pupils whom he recruits. So unless he can afford to be very choosy, he will find it hard to set up in his school structures and procedures that deviate widely from those which are conventionally accepted as normal in the educational world.

In the course of day-to-day events neither the behaviour of pupils nor that of teachers will conform perfectly to that laid down in the official blueprint. The strains of responding to situations that were not foreseen in the plan and the strains of reconciling previous habits with new expectations will lead to the innovation of new practices, some of them not anticipated, others forbidden.

"Social control" refers to the provisions made within the school for detecting deviance and imposing sanctions, as well as (to a lesser extent) noting excellent performance and rewarding it. Since the teaching staff have been trained, tested and screened at length before appointment it can be assumed that they can be trusted to conform to a far higher degree than can pupils. Hence the investment of time and other resources spent by staff in checking upon pupils is vastly greater than that spent by the head and senior staff in checking up on other staff. It should not be forgotten though that, at some level, social control is done to the staff as well as being done by them.

Staff are sometimes assisted in matters of pupil discipline by some specially appointed pupils in the role of "prefects" or "monitors" and this work is often supervized by a senior member of staff appointed to this job of chief disciplinarian by the head, who remains ultimately responsible. The head is thus spared the odium of being the dispenser of special punishments (whether canings, detentions, or talkings-to) and he can be used as the ultimate deterrent with which to threaten rebellious pupils, all the more fearsome for being rarely used. In some tough areas of New York the policeman on patrol regularly calls into the schools on his beat to see whether his help is needed in controlling trouble.

"Corrective action" in response to deviance by pupils may take different forms. A private reprimand may suffice or a general warning to all may be necessary as well. Suspension or even expulsion (if the culprit is above the legal minimum age) may take place for a severe offence, while a lesser one will merely put the offender in the head's "bad books". Certain kinds of deviance indicate, to the head who is willing to see it, a shortcoming in the official structures. This may lead to corrective action on the system level, removing the *causes* of the deviant behaviour.

Pupils whose conduct is revealed as praiseworthy will be praised and rewarded in various ways—with privileges, prizes, good testimonials, positions of privilege and so forth. But approval and disapproval expressed by teachers remains the most pervasive of all rewards in the school. The effectiveness of the system of social control is crucial to the smooth functioning of the school and the form which this control takes is likely to have a significant effect on the attitudes to authority developed by pupils.

Another set of mechanisms exists within the school whose funtion is to build up the *motivations* of members so that they will strive to conform to the official norms. These mechanisms also function to remove psychological obstacles to conformity which may exist, a function which can be called '*tension management*'. The difference between these mechanisms and those that we called social control lies in the fact that social controls come into play after the event, whereas the mechanism of motivation and tension management operate beforehand. One is the cure, the other is the attempt at prevention. However, in practice the distinction is not such a clear one. Given the existence of rewards and penalties which are well-known (including approval and disapproval) people will to some extent anticipate them and act so as to earn rewards and avoid penalties. The anticipation of social controls is in effect building up motivation and tending to override tensions that might lead to deviance. However, there are some mechanisms which clearly fall into the category of motivation and tension management but not that of social control. For example, where the school provides the opportunity for pupils who are experiencing psychological problems to talk to someone who is sympathetic and helpful, this would count as tension management rather than social control.

Those mechanisms of social control and motivation which support the official norms of the school are not the only ones operating within those boundaries. Pupils in general, and certain categories of pupils in particular, may develop their own social system in which roles and norms are defined in ways that differ significantly from those officially approved: they may elaborate these roles and norms in ways extending far beyond the definitions, though not necessarily in conflict with them, and they may have their own system of social controls operating mainly in informal (but powerful) ways. Teachers in general and certain categories of them in particular may do exactly the same. In such cases one has a three-way confrontation between the officially prescribed structures, the deviant social system operating among pupils and that of the teachers—though not necessarily including *all* pupils or *all* teachers. In later sections we shall be concerned with ways in which the guardians of the official structure attempt to come to terms with the potential powers of the pupil social system.

There is no aspect of the school whose functioning is not affected by the efficiency of *communication*, since this is a fundamental element in all social relationships. In a complex organization, such as the school, the problem is not just to get A and B to talk clearly and listen carefully to each other. It is more complex than this. The head must be able to get messages to all staff and pupils, or to any particular set of them, such that they are accurately received and understood; he must be able to get accurate feedback on how well staff and pupils are complying with the expectations of the official blueprint; staff must have access to him with information on the difficulties involved in attempting to fulfil certain expectations; there must be ready interchange of information among staff, especially pertaining to the behaviour and unfolding personalities of pupils; the latter themselves must be able to get adequate information as to what is expected of them, what choices are open to them and what are the probable consequences of non-compliance; equally pupils must have access to staff when they have grievances or personal problems.

On the other hand, it is possible for the communication system to be overloaded with messages, with the result that production of outputs is hampered. In most schools, though, there are formal rules prescribing who may communicate with whom, when and in what manner. In other words, communication is restricted to "proper channels" with a consequent loss of information.

Every school will have rules indicating categories of prohibited and prescribed conduct, though there will be much variation between schools in the actual content, extensiveness, explicitness and formality of the rules. They play an important part in relation to pattern maintenance.

In addition to the school-wide rules each teacher will add his or her own rules for each of the classes they teach. This personal element is greatest in the earlier years of the primary schools where each class may have only one teacher, and it declines as pupils progress up the school. Gradually pupils are exposed to a more and more impersonal system of rules and are more likely to come to see rules as existing independently of the particular individuals who enforce them.

In the school one can, in principle, discern some allocation pattern of rewards and punishments, whether or not anyone consciously intends it to be so. This may or may not relate closely to officially stated policies as expressed in school brochures or in headmasters' speeches about what the school stands for and what it will not stand for.

This analysis implies, firstly, making some kind of catalogue of the various rewards that are utilized: such as school reports, prizes, "points", praise from teachers, testimonials, privileges and so forth. Having defined the rewards, one then has to see who gets them: whether it is, for example, the outstanding scholars, the star sportsmen, or the most morally educated pupils, or some other group. What kind of excellence is most highly rewarded in each school? We might hypothesize that the more heavily any particular line of excellence is rewarded, the more intensely it will be pursued by members of that school, other things being equal.

However, it should be appreciated that the school where certain awards are made annually or termly with great ceremony is probably rewarding this area of behaviour less effectively than the school where less dramatic rewards and reinforcements are given weekly or daily by staff who show by their examples that they are truly committed to that set of values.

There is a second aspect of reward systems in schools that must also be considered. This involves looking beyond the question of what kind of achievement is most highly rewarded to establish to what extent any *one* kind of excellence monopolizes the rewards allocated in the school. In other words, we are concerned with the degree of pluralism or multi-dimensionality in the reward system of schools. The more uni-dimensional is the reward system of a school, the more pupils it tends to exclude from a feeling of success; and hence the less favourable will be the aggregate of pupils' attitudes to school, with obvious implications for social control. That, at least, is the hypothesis.

The social control system of the school, based on positive and negative sanctions (rewards and deprivations) operates in different ways in different sectors of the school. In the area of academic work sanctions operate automatically and independently of the school, in so far as pupils will have to compete for future social positions in merit-based competition. If they do not conform, they are likely to fail their exams. We are assuming here that teachers know better than pupils what is required to pass the exams and that their demands on pupils correspond closely to those requirements.

In so far as pupils are indifferent to future success, are aiming at success in fields not governed by scholastic entry criteria, or have privileged entry to desired future positions, these sanctions will not apply. These are all typical situations, of course. For most pupils their chances

349

in the labour market are predetermined by their performance in school, and the extent to which they are aware of this, the problem of social control within the school is simplified. It is simplified because the reward system internal to the school is supplemented by a vastly greater universe of anticipated rewards in the occupational system. To a great extent this accounts for the greater success of middle-class pupils in adjusting to the demands of the school compared to working-class pupils (though it is also due, of course, to the differential socialization experiences of these two groups of pupils). This also suggests why we would expect far fewer problems of social control within schools in totalitarian societies, where the monolithic labour market is so highly controlled by the state, than we find in schools in the West. Thirdly, one would predict on the basis of this principle that pupils who expect to work in their own family businesses will be worse risks from the point of view of school disciplines than pupils of similar social class who expect to seek jobs in the open labour market.

In other sectors of school life where rules exist and pupils' conformity is expected the sanctions are multiple and less obvious. To the extent that those who play the dominant roles in these areas (e.g. house-masters, prefects) are liked and respected by pupils, the latter will tend to emulate them and their standards. The sanction involved is partly the pupils' desire for approval from the admired superior and partly his "identification" with the other.

Even aside from the above, the existence of a hierarchy of privileged and status-bearing positions open to pupils serves as an incentive. Promotion to monitor, house prefect, head-boy, etc., presumably depends upon the pupil's convincing the appropriate superiors that he conforms to a satisfactory degree to the norms and expectations of the school. For pupils who lack any "identification" with school authority figures that would by itself motivate them to conform to these standards, the desire for the prestige and privileges accruing to a prefect may provide a sufficient incentive.

A pupil's reputation with his teachers and head can have important consequences for his future career, constituting a further set of sanctions. The testimonials as to character which they write for him may play an important part in affecting his chances of getting desirable jobs or places in college. In such assessments of character for prospective employers and others, having held a position of responsibility carries some considerable weight and so also does the manner in which he is judged to have discharged it. None of this applies to pupils who plan to work in unskilled casual labour, or the family business, or in certain highly individualistic and achievement-oriented fields (e.g. clothes designing, composing music). With all others, however, it gives the teacher a considerable power over his pupils which is none the less effective if it is unstated on the teacher's side and sub-conscious on that of the pupil.

2 ATTAINMENTS AND OUTPUTS

As a result of the activities of staff and pupils in the framework of the official structure, various *attainments* can ensue in the form of learning increments. Usually attention is focused on the attainment of pupils as a result of their participation in the school to the exclusion of that of the teachers. This is in accordance with the ideology that teachers go to school to teach others and that pupils go to school to learn from others. On reflection, however, it will be clear that pupils learn not only from teachers but also from each other, and that teachers gain from their involvement in school, at the very least in "experience".

When we refer to attainment we are referring to something which the objective observer coming into the school from outside may measure. Those attainments which the school is officially dedicated to cultivating (its "goals") will be defined differently from school to school, of course. Exactly how they are defined and how they are officially measured will in themselves affect the strivings and attainments of pupils in the school. The system of rewards and social control will be geared to these definitions. And both pupils and teachers will be spurred to direct their energies towards those attainments which are emphasized, praised, and concretely rewarded in their particular schools.

The distinction between attainments or outputs as measured by the objective observer and those chosen for measurement by the school itself in its own terms is an important one. Any school is likely to be unaware of many of the impacts which it has upon its pupils. Equally it is likely to exaggerate its effect on those individual qualities which it is most anxious to influence. Moreover we must look at the effect on pupils and their teachers of the attempt by the school to measure those aspects which it does attempt to measure, or which are measured by external assessment procedures such as university examining boards or independent testing agencies. Other things being equal, it would seem, the more attention is called to a certain area of attainment by the school's attempts to measure it, and the more susceptible such an area is to precise measurements, the more will the efforts of the pupils and teachers tend to be transferred to these areas from others—both efforts towards genuine learning and efforts to simulate it.

Looking at pupil attainment in the objective sense, we may make a broad distinction between "cognitive learning attainments" and "moral learning attainments".

To define these two categories in a way that is precise, mutually exclusive and theoretically serviceable is not easy. One way would be to differentiate between cognitive learning and the learning of value-preferences (or moral education). Conceptually this is clear but in every concrete social situation both are inextricably bound up together. Moreover one is interested in outcomes of a more complex kind which would fit in neither category, outcomes such as "social skills", "rationality", "autonomy". Another approach would be to differentiate between learning that is relevant mainly to one's future vocational roles and that which is mainly relevant to one's personal growth and private life. This dichotomy could never be mutually exclusive, though, for many learning attainments would perforce belong on *both* sides, for example, conscientiousness, role-playing skills, or knowledge.

Another approach would be to make a dichotomy between formal academic learning oriented to formal examinations and all other kinds of learning which take place in school. These categories would at least be mutually exclusive and they correspond roughly to two sides of the formal structure of the school. "Formal academic learning" is a narrower category than "cognitive-learning" and it corresponds more closely with "classroom learning". Most formal academic learning takes place in the classroom (aside from private study) rather than some other part of the school structure and much of what takes place in the classroom is formal academic learning, though this is far from exhausting all the important learning that occurs in the classroom. The residual category is wide and so enables us to include in it quite properly not only the learning of value orientations, but also the development of personality resources, role-playing skills and also the learning of cognitive data in informal situations. Thus we can very broadly differentiate between two distinct areas of learning or outputs from the school and we can associate with them (very broadly) two sides of the school's official structure: the formal structure of academic learning on the one side and the other aspects of the formal structure (including the pastoral system, organized sports, extra-curricular activities and so forth) on the other side.

One large and highly significant difference between these two areas of attainment is that cognitive learning attainments can be measured quite easily and, in practice, are subjected to routine measurement in the school, whereas moral learning attainment (at present) cannot and is not. One consequence of this is that the success of the school and of the individual pupils, as judged by people outside the school, including parents, politicians and potential employers, will be based very largely on measurements of cognitive learning. The absence of recognized and objective measures of moral attainment means that the school which wishes to lay heavy emphasis on this side of the educational process will be greatly handicapped because, unlike the academically oriented school, it cannot demonstrate to the outside world that it is attaining the results it claims. For the purposes of the internal operation of the school, the personal judgements of teachers on pupils' progress in the area of moral attainment may be perfectly satisfactory, but a problem arises when the school must give an account of itself to its controlling agency and to other interested groups in outside society. It also arises when individual pupils ask for some certificate of their attainment which will be recognized in the job market. Public examining boards can certify levels of academic attainment but not (at present) moral ones. Here the pupil has only the testimonial of his teachers—and the weight accorded to this will most often depend mainly on the prestige of the school, which is based usually on quite irrelevant considerations, such as the date of its foundation, its sporting prowess and social class of intake.

In analyzing the social organization of any school, including both the official structure as well as the patterned deviations that may have arisen from it, we may look at the question of how each of these features contributes to, fails to contribute to, or undermines each of these two areas of attainment—academic and moral. Thus we can try to link each of the social roles which we find in a school to one or both of these outputs-attainments: the roles of subject-teacher, head of department or director of studies all belong mainly to the area of cognitive learning, and the roles of housemaster, form-teacher, tutor and counsellor may contribute to the area of moral education. Note that any teacher can (and usually does) play roles of both kinds. Note also that there is no explicit term to designate the role of the subject-teacher as moral educator, which every one of them is—even if he does not occupy an officially pastoral role. We refer here to the informal but powerful effects of the human interaction between every teacher and his pupils.

There will be considerable overlap. The moral education area especially depends upon the activities of many other teachers who do not occupy specialized roles with respect to moral education—which is another way of saying that every teacher, whether he likes it or not, is a moral educator. Nor must we completely forget the non-teaching staff of the school with whom pupils may come into contact such as dinner supervisors, caretakers, matron, secretary. Although none of these roles is normally defined to include a responsibility for moral education they may in fact, depending upon the individual in question, be quite important in this respect. There are reports of pupils who were quite alienated from the teaching staff of the school forming close attachments to members of the non-teaching staff who became in effect the pupils' counsellors and confidants.

Some aspects of the formal structure of the school clearly relate mainly to cognitive learning or to moral education. The academic timetable and curriculum blueprints, for example, clearly pertain to the academic side and any formal arrangement made for pastoral care, such as the house system or a counselling system, pertain to the moral education side. But this is not to say that the formal structure of academic learning will not have implications for moral education, for example in so far as it dictates the nature of work, the composition of work groups and the criteria of achievement and reward. Moral education is involved in what may appear to be strictly academic learning on several distinct levels: firstly, the personal relationship between subject teacher and pupil, which will communicate to the pupil the attitude of the teacher towards him and hence his self-concept, his image of the social order and how he fits into it; secondly, the structure of the working situation in the classroom with its rules permitting or forbidding competition or co-operation among

353

pupils, and its rewards for different kinds of performance; and thirdly, the macro-structure of formal cognitive learning throughout the school, which groups pupils in different ways for their lessons, making homogeneous or heterogeneous working groups, either changing the individual pupil's workmates many times during the day or not, and affecting in various ways the integration of his experiences in different lessons and sections of the school day.

Other facets of the school organization have grown up for various historical reasons not specifically connected with either cognitive or moral learning systems. Organized games, prefect systems, house systems, school assemblies, extra-curricular activities, school councils, are some of the notable examples. We shall look at these kinds of institutions also and try to specify the implications that each of them has for social control, motivation and tension management, and moral education.

3 OFFICIAL STRUCTURES AND THEIR IMPLICATIONS

We turn now to look at a number of common features of the official structures of schools, which we believe may be generally useful in the analysis of the individual or types of schools. The value of studying particular cases is to help us to answer some general questions such as the following:

1 What variability exists in the structural arrangements through which the functional requirements of the school (social control, tension management and production of learning attainments or outputs) are fulfilled in different schools?

2 How effective, in terms of producing the different outputs, are these different alternative arrangements?
   What constraints do the different structures put upon each other? What are the limits of compatibility? How does the presence of one particular structural variant in one area of a school limit the range of structure that may operate in other areas?

We look first at two parts of the official structure of the school that are each manifestly related to specific functional sub-systems.

Academic learning: its formal organization[4]

The formal structure of academic learning includes: a system for the differentiation of pupils into teaching groups, a system for differentiating teachers and allocating them to teaching groups; a scheme for dividing the teaching time and linking specific teachers with specific groups of pupils at specific times of the day and in specific places. Theoretically there are a vast range of alternative ways of organizing the academic work of a school along these dimensions, though in practice there are conventions which tend to be followed by heads and school administrators, ignoring many of the theoretical possibilities.

The limiting case of a school with the simplest possible formal structure for academic learning is that of the one-teacher, one-room school. This is assuming that all pupils in this school are taught together as a group. But this is in practice unlikely since the school intake covers a wide range of age and ability. As soon as the one teacher begins to differentiate systematically among these pupils, some formal organization of the academic work has begun.

Within the one-teacher school and within the one-teacher classroom pupils may be differentiated by the teacher. Pupil differentiation in this kind of setting tends to be under the control of the individual teacher and not highly formalized. On the level of the whole school, when there is more than one teacher and they work singly rather than in "teams" the division of pupils into teaching groups and the differentiation of teachers' roles has a formal basis.

Pupils might be grouped on the basis of their attainment, either overall or in certain subjects. In a school that was run exclusively on this basis the pupils would advance from one class to the next whenever they passed the appropriate promotion test. Instead of differentiating pupils on the basis of what they have learned, one can do this on the basis of what they have studied. On this basis all those who have completed the work designated for class one are ready to move to class two. This principle of "curricular age" may be combined with one of attainment so that rather than making the poor achievers in class 1B repeat another year in 1B while their age mates proceed to 2B, they may be moved to 2C.

The principle of curricular age comes quite close in practice to the system of differentiating pupils by seniority in the school. Curricular specialization gives another basis for dividing and grouping pupils in their academic learning. The curriculum branches at certain points into alternative subjects, of which a pupil can do one only, whether by choice or designation.

The formal structure of pupil role differentiation is likely to have certain effects on the patterning of pupil–pupil relationships. Formal role differentiation among pupils will affect the stability or fluidity of teaching groups in the school, that is the extent to which pupils change their classmates from one lesson to another in the course of their typical day. And that may affect such variables as the proportion of social isolates among pupils, the solidarity of cliques and classes, the polarization of cliques and classes in terms of attitude to school and other variables.[5]

Role differentiation among teachers has several dimensions. One concerns the degree of specialization; another concerns the basis of specialization; the third concerns the extent to which teachers work individually or in teaching teams. The form of role differentiation found among teachers, especially on the individual–team dimension will influence the development of teacher–teacher relationships.

The formal structuring of role differentiation among teachers is also likely to affect the pupil–teacher relationships in so far as it affects the number of different teachers to whom each pupil is exposed during the course of a typical day or week. The more teachers a pupil sees and the shorter time he spends with them, other things being equal, the less likely it is that a diffuse and personal relationship rather than a specific and narrow one will develop between them.

The pastoral structure

This may be defined as the complex of formally-prescribed role relationships within a school in which one party (often but not always a teacher) is made responsible for watching the general welfare of another and for taking action to foster it. The system encompasses, for example, the roles of counsellor, tutor, housemaster and others. Schools will vary greatly in the extent to which the work of moral education is embodied in a formalized role system of this kind.

Having defined two parts of the official structure that may be found in any school, we may consider the relative level of investment in them. Some objective measures of a school's relative investment in academic and moral education might include a comparison of the relative salaries of staff with formal pastoral responsibilities and those without, on similar levels of qualifications and seniority; their teaching loads; the amount of office space, secretarial help and other facilities made available to them; their relative influence when policy discussions involve conflict of interest between the two goals.

Organized games and extra-curricular activities

Both extra-curricular activities and organized games involve an extension of the role of the pupil from that of passive recipient of information and attitudes emanating from the teacher in formal lessons in the classroom. On the whole they have more relevance to moral education than academic learning, and more to social control than to either.

It is likely that pupil-controlled groups, whether formal or informal, tend to be subversive of the official norms and values of the school because they have their own, which will seldom correspond closely to those of the school and are often concerned with advancing the collective interests of pupils, supported by their own systems of social control and rewards. By creating groups that offer somewhat comparable satisfactions to pupils, teachers may hope to bring their pupils more under their own control in so far as teachers have ultimate control of these substitute groups. At any rate, this seems to have been the thinking behind the introduction of organized games and extra-curricular activities into schools both in Britain and the USA (Bamford, 1967, pp. 78–9 and Waller, 1938, p. 112). Since that time, they have been copied very widely, often without much awareness of the original intentions of the innovators, but sociologically these connections may still be postulated.

The postulated relevance of organized games to the problem of maintaining social control within the school is not just a matter of keeping pupils busily occupied in playing and training (under supervision); nor is it just a matter of tiring them out in this way so that they will be less troublesome. Both factors are important and can be subsumed under tension management but there is more to it than this. Organized games involve a reward system in which those pupils who are selected for the team enjoy a great amount of fame among their fellow pupils, plus various concrete privileges. The point is that it is in the power of the school staff to remove any pupil from the team, and hence to deprive him of his fame and privileges. Players who flout school rules or who set what their teachers consider a bad example to other pupils may be punished in this way, and the threat of this may be quite sufficient to keep them in line. In this way teachers can ensure that those pupils who occupy positions of high prestige in the pupils' own social system are a "good example" to the rest of the school. (Waller, 1938, pp. 116–17).

To some extent the same analysis can be applied to other organized groups in the school (such as extra-curricular clubs). Also important is the opportunity these groups present for a more personal teacher-pupil relationship to develop, decreasing the probability of rebellious conduct on the pupil's part. Then again, the existence of these groups with their diverse activities represents an extension and pluralization of the school's official reward system. Participation and success in one of these areas of organized activity will be rewarded with prestige—at least within the group itself and often beyond. To the extent that this implies that the school offers gratification to a wider proportion of pupils it is likely to increase the degree of their commitment to school and the influence of the school over them.

From the point of view of moral education, participation in these organized groups, where they involve social contexts different from the traditional classroom, will give pupils the experience of operating in a wider range of social situations and will extend their social skills[6] and understanding of social situations. In addition, it will give them certain experiences which are important for moral education in rather special ways. In the case of organized games, two aspects of this experience seem to be important: firstly, the contest is conducted within a framework of rules, respect for which is expected to override the desire to win the contest; and secondly, the success of a team depends on members co-ordinating their efforts, accepting the authority of their captain or leader and sometimes subordinating the desire for personal glory to the interests of the whole team.

Prefect system

There are various ways in which selected pupils can be officially co-opted into the authority system of the school, by being vested with the right and duty to watch over the conduct of their fellow pupils and issue sanctions (usually negative) when deemed appropriate. The best-known version of this is probably the prefect system, originally developed in the British independent boarding schools (Lambert, 1969, pp. 31–43).

The prefect system works in so far as it prevents solidarity developing among pupils as a separate group and succeeds in making them identify as individuals with the school as a corporate body. In the perfectly functioning prefect system the prefects are the natural leaders to whom pupils look. This depends in part on staff making sure that those senior boys who possess the individual attributes which tend to give prestige among pupils (such as sporting prowess) are made prefects, which in turn implies that they are willing to accept the position and its duties.

Those schools which operate the most successful prefect system are those which have been doing it for a long time. Thus each new generation of pupils sees a body of prefects who possess both institutionally given prestige and prestige based on their individual qualities and no prominent senior pupil who repudiates the official norms of the school or the legitimacy of the prefect system. If there are such dissident individuals, at least they do not lead a dissident *group*. Once established in schools with highly selective recruitment, a prefect system generates a tradition which makes its continuance far easier than its initial establishment was.

School councils
Another approach to the strategy of co-opting pupils into the authority structure involves the creation of a representative school council, which discusses pupils' grievances and suggestions pertaining to changes to school rules and policies, formulates suggestions and presents them officially to the head. The fundamental difference between this system and the prefect system is that the school council allows pupils to participate in the *making* of policy, while the prefect system allows them to participate in administering a given policy.

The prefect system can be seen primarily as a means to better impose social control on the pupils. It can also be claimed to teach those pupils who occupy such positions to see things from the perspective of those in authority and to teach them the responsibilities that go with the exercise of authority. Thus it would have some implications for moral education too. The function of the school council, as defined here, is less that of social control than of tension management and integration, serving as a channel for the expression of grievances and perhaps leading to remedial action. On the one hand, it enables the head and his staff to be better informed on the climate of opinion among pupils and, on the other hand, it gives pupils a means of expressing and debating their grievances.

Whereas the role of prefect provides experience and perhaps training in the social skills of leadership or management of people, the role of school council representative is more involved with the democratic processes of discussion, persuasion and compromise. The individual prefect has the power to impose various sanctions on individual pupils, within the discretion allowed him by the rules; the council representative has no power as an individual but may participate in changing school rules—perhaps abolishing the role of the prefect—if a majority of the council are in agreement and if the head and staff are disposed to take heed of the council in this area.

The attitude of the head and governors to the council is crucial. The school council can function as a mechanism for integration and tension management, providing feedback on grievances and leading to corrective action aimed at the causes of the discontent. Equally, it can function as a private debating society for a small number of pupils who co-operate with the head in maintaining the pretence of consultation and representation in return for various privileges and implied promises of preferment, serving purely as an agency of social control.

4 SOME OTHER IMPORTANT ASPECTS OF SCHOOL STRUCTURE

All of the patterned features of the school so far discussed may be regarded as distinct role-complexes defined in the official structure and demarcating activities that take place at definite and distinct times and places. Subject-teachers and pupils enact their roles at the times and in the places prescribed in the timetable; at other times the roles within the pastoral system are enacted; at other times those concerned with extra-curricular activities, and so forth. We shall now isolate for analysis some other features of the social patterns associated with the school, this time taking for the unit of analysis not different role-complexes but several aspects of social relationships in the school at large. We shall look briefly at cohesiveness, ritual, ceremony and authority relations in the school.

Cohesiveness, ritual and authority

To what extent can the school be viewed as a cohesive unit? The degree of its cohesiveness is a fundamental factor in determining the effectiveness with which pattern maintenance in the school is achieved and also in determining the impact of the school upon the values and attitudes of those who go through it, both pupils and staff.

Cohesiveness is a difficult concept to define but for our purposes here we will regard cohesiveness as the property of a group in which the members feel themselves to be closely bound together, with a strong loyalty to each other, to the group and to the norms and values which exist among them as a group. This is the kind of property one associates with a well-run sports team, military squad and friendship group. Note that the examples which come most readily to mind are small groups in which the members have a common activity. Within the school, cohesiveness will often be a property of cliques of pupils, of classrooms, the staffroom, extra-curricular groups, sports teams and so forth. The question here, however, refers to the school as a whole.

A primary school at assembly, with all present singing enthusiastically together or listening attentively to the head, clearly represents a high degree of cohesiveness. Similarly, a whole school out on the sports field cheering for the school team represents this. Note, however, that both our examples refer to occasions that are quite shortlived in the life of the school where they happen. After the assembly or the sports level, they all return to their separate classes and lessons. Then the level of apparent cohesiveness drops sharply, as there is no visible focus for it and it remains at best a latent property of the school, ready to be called forth by some appropriate event.

If our aim is to compare the levels of cohesiveness in different schools, it will not do, therefore, to observe one school while at assembly, another during playtime and a third during lessons. If we observe them at similar times, though, it is meaningful to compare them in cohesiveness. Schools will vary in the amount of enthusiastic participation in assembly, in the enthusiasm of support for school teams, in the willingness to exert voluntary effort on behalf of the school, in the amount of effort they make to conform to the rules and norms of the school (relative to the amount of effort they make to conform to other norms of other groups to which they belong), or the amount of pride they feel in their membership of the school.

Ritual and ceremony both play important parts in the social system of the school, especially in relation to cohesiveness. "Ritual" refers to certain forms of social behaviour which are highly stereotyped and hence are highly predictable from the social situation. That is to say that these actions which we call ritual do not indicate anything about the individuals concerned or their personal attitudes to each other, they merely indicate the formal relationship existing between them and the formal definition of the social situation in question (Bernstein, Elvin and Peters, 1966). Between teachers and pupils in the the school, especially in certain types of school, ritual plays an important part in defining, reinforcing and stabilizing teacher-pupil relations in the officially approved form. (Waller, 1938, p. 128).

That is to say, the function performed by such rituals as the teacher insisting that pupils stand when he enters the classroom is to symbolize and impress upon all concerned the status difference between teachers and pupils as well as the formality of their relationships. The wearing of academic gowns by teachers makes the same point again. Since many rituals in the school serve to underline status differences between teachers and pupils, it might seem that the effect of rituals would be to diminish rather than increase cohesiveness. This, I suggest, is not so though the situation is complex and a little paradoxical.

Rituals of the sort mentioned have the effect of emphasizing the similarity among pupils in their social position, at the same time as they emphasize their distinction from teachers. Cohesiveness among the pupils as a large peer group is thus enhanced—but is this at the expense of the cohesiveness of the school as a whole (both pupils and staff)?

There are or were schools (examples spring more readily from the past than the present) which appeared to achieve a certain kind of cohesion on the basis of a highly ritualized system. The old-fashioned elementary school, sometimes in quite tough areas, which operated a ritualized, regimented but smoothly-operating regime represents one answer to this problem. This smoothly running system does not depend on similarity of background and attitudes between pupils and teachers. It depends upon a highly ritualized system of routines regulating behaviour. These can be readily understood and learned by all pupils. Their very repetitiveness gives them a compelling force, which makes conformity relatively easy—especially given the oversight of the strict but predicatable teacher/drill sergeant. In describing the system this way my purpose is not to sneer at or derogate it but merely to provide a vivid image of the kind of system to which I am referring. I think it is not at all unreasonable to suppose that many pupils in such schools felt a measure of pride and identification with the school, if not pleasure in their particpation.

"Ceremony" refers to a special class of rituals in which a relatively large number of participants are involved and their attention centred on a common object or activity. The principal examples would be the school assembly (including the religious service) and the school gathered to cheer their representative team in contest. Note that we have already cited these two events as examples of the school in a state of high cohesiveness. Less common examples would include the initiation rite organized by the senior pupils outside the official school structure and the so called "pep rallies" found in American high schools, which serve the function of deliberately whipping up enthusiasm among the school and its teams for a forthcoming game (Waller, 1938, pp. 13, 120, 122–5). The distinguishing feature of ceremony, which differentiates it from ordinary rituals, is its ability to generate strong emotional responses from the participants. The staging of the ceremony in itself has a dramatic power, based on the effect of the massed bodies, the music, the lighting, the focusing of all eyes on one object, frequently a symbol of the group which is solemnly paraded into place (flag, mascots, and so forth).

Whereas the effect of ritual in general appeared to be ambivalent, on the one hand increasing cohesion, but, on the other hand, emphasizing divisions within the body, ceremony appears to have a more unequivocal effect in increasing cohesiveness in the group as a whole.

The functions of both ritual and ceremony lie in the area of pattern maintenance. Ritual in general reinforces the officially prescribed pattern of social relations on a *habit* level. It reinforces these definitions, not explicitly by spelling out the rights, duties and expectations, but by the opposite approach of creating unreflecting habits through sheer repetition and drill. Ceremony operates on a more affective or emotional level, tending to create *sentiments* of identification with the group as a whole and a feeling of loyalty to it.

In the US high school the most important ceremonies are the graduation and prize-giving and the inter-school sports matches. In English

schools there is the daily assembly, though this is not as highly ceremoni-
alized as the assemblies for the end of term and other special occasions.
The inter-school sports match takes place within a competitive context
which casts the team as the champions of the whole school, who appear
in great numbers to cheer them on; it is helped by the dramatic staging,
with music, chanting, cheer leaders, and so forth, to produce a very powerful effect. Powerful though it is, however, it tends to unify the members
of the school in terms of a set of values unrelated to the official academic
or moral objectives of the school. The assembly or graduation ceremony
though it may be less powerful, does permit the head to articulate the
official values and ideology of the school.

The emotional power of the inter-school contest derives to an important extent from the conflict or competition in which "the school" is a
competitor. This is a situation analogous to that of warfare on the
national level or a strike on the level of industrial relations. In all of these
situations cohesiveness is increased for the group which finds itself
involved as a major party to a conflict, in which gains or losses will accrue
to all individual members more or less equally. The school assembly,
graduation ceremony or speech day lacks the emotive power which the
conflict situation bestows. On the other hand, these occasions do give the
platform to the head, who has a relatively suggestible audience to hear
him articulate the official values and ideology of the school.

It should be noted that ceremonies will not necessarily involve the
whole school as a unit. They may also involve smaller units, such as
the house or the year group; they may involve smaller units still, such as
the form or tutor group, extra-curricular clubs or fraternities. It is likely,
however, that school authorities will discourage or forbid ceremonies by
smaller units within the school if they seem to reach a level of intensity
that may threaten their members' loyalty to the larger school collectivity.

Compared with the family, the authority patterns of the school are far
more formal and impersonal. Whereas in the family the child associates
authority with two particular people (its parents), in the school authority
is vested in a much larger number of adults, whose social position is
formally designated and formally defined. In the school authority is thus
associated with a certain *social position* rather than being with certain
persons[7]. The ritualization of teacher–pupil relations in the school helps
to underline this distinction up to a point. There are, however, two
distinct types of positional authority and the distinction is a crucial one.
One is based upon custom and tradition; the other is based upon a formal
body of rules and regulations. In practice, of course, these two principles
overlap; many schools fall in between and combine both principles.

Individual schools will vary greatly in the way they combine these two
principles of authority. In schools which are most highly ritualized, rules
will be implicit and a customary or traditional authority system implied.
At the other extreme are schools where rules are explicitly stated and
where reasons are often given for having these rules. At one end of this

scale teachers are likely to justify their authority by claims of "I'm the teacher and I say so", or "that's the way we do things in this school", and at the other end by reference to the formal rules and the justifications attached to them.

Though the amount of emphasis placed upon ritual in the school may vary greatly from school to school, it is not suggested that any school could be entirely without ritual. Even in a school with the most highly rationalized authority system it is unlikely, if it is not too new and a tolerably well-functioning school, that is operating without a good deal of custom and ritual. The test of a rationalized authority system is what happens on the rather rare occasions when someone questions one of the rules. They are told that the rule was formulated in the approved or legitimate fashion and, on pressing further, they will be told how it is necessitated by one or more of the generally agreed values of the system, such as the requirements of safety, getting pupils through exams, smooth administration, etc.

In general, however, the authority system of the school tends to be rational-legal in character and training its pupils to operate in terms of such an authority system is one of the most important outputs which the school produces for the larger society. For in a highly industrialized society most adult positions in the economic and political system involve this kind of positional authority rather than the personal kind which the child learns in its early years in the family. Thus the school functions as an agency of transition between the family and the occupational and citizenship sectors of society (Drebeen, 1968). The transition is a graduated one, from the relatively personal relationship between the infant teacher and her class who see her virtually the whole day, to the academic secondary school teacher who sees a different class each lesson. Between these two extremes there is a considerable range in the impersonality of the authority patterns and in the degree of their rationalization.

CONCLUSION

This analysis of the school is put forward in the hope that it provides a more satisfactory framework than any other yet available for the study of the school as a system of patterned social relationships. The usefulness of such a comprehensive framework should be twofold; to enable case studies of individual schools to be made mutually comparable and to make possible the integration of studies that deal with limited aspects of the school. Obviously the analysis of the school as a social system must precede any discussion of the effects of the school on those who pass through it.

NOTES
1 Brim (1958), Hoyle (1965), Bidwell (1965), Wheeler (1966) and Griffiths (1964).

2 Among the more valuable studies of specific types of schools are: Blyth (1965), Inner London Education Authority (1967), Coleman (1961), Fichter (1958). Finally, the English independent school, privileged as in all other respects, has commanded the most attention: Bamford (1967), Kalton (1967), Lambert *et al.* (1969), Wilson (1962).
3 Two important sources for the discussion of "source systems" and general "open systems" are Parsons (1965) and Katz and Kahn (1966).
4 The field of school administration has its own extensive literature. See, for example, Pope Franklin (1967).
5 Bany and Johnson (1964), Hargreaves (1967) and Lacey (1966).
6 Kohlberg (1966) has shown that moral development is related to the child's social experience.
7 For the distinction between "personal" and "positional" authority see Bernstein (1969).

REFERENCES

BAMFORD, T. W. (1967) *The Rise of the Public School*, Nelson.

BANY, M. A. and JOHNSON, L. V. (1964) *Classroom Group Behavior*, Macmillan.

BERNSTEIN, B. (1969) "A Socio-linguistic Approach to Socialization", in Gumperz, J. and Hynes, D. (eds.) *Directions in Socio-linguistics*, Holt, Rinehart and Winston.

BERNSTEIN, B., ELVIN, H. L. and PETERS, R. S. (1966) "Ritual in Education ', *Philosophical Transactions of the Royal Society of London*, B., Vol. 251, pp. 429–36.

BIDWELL, C. E. (1965) "The School as a Formal Organization", in March, J. G. (ed.) *Handbook of Organizations*, Rand-McNally.

BLYTH, W. A. L. (1965) *English Primary Education: A Sociological Description*, 2 Vols., Routledge and Kegan Paul.

BRIM, O. G., Jnr. (1958) *Sociology and the Field of Education*, Russell Sage Foundation.

COLEMAN, J. S. (1961) *The Adolescent Society*, Free Press.

DREBEEN, R. (1968) *On What is Learned in School*, Addison-Wesley.

FICHTER, J. H. (1958) *Parochial School*, University of Notre Dame Press.

GRIFFITHS, D. (ed.) (1964) *Behavioral Science and Educational Administration*, National Society for the Study of Education, 63rd Yearbook.

HARGREAVES, D. H. (1967) *Social Relations in a Secondary School*, Routledge and Kegan Paul.

HOYLE, E. (1965) "Organizational Analysis in Education", *Educational Research* VII, p. 97, Nov. 1965.

INNER LONDON EDUCATION AUTHORITY (1967) *London Comprehensive Schools, 1966*, I.L.E.A.

KALTON, G. (1966) *The Public Schools: A Factual Survey*, Longman.

KATZ, D. and KAHN, R. L. (1966) *The Social Psychology of Organizations*, Wiley.

KOHLBERG, L. (1966) "Moral Education in the Schools: A Development View", *The School Review*, LXXIV, Spring 1966, p. 16.

LACEY, C. (1966) "Some Sociological Concomitants of Academic Streaming in a Grammar School", *British Journal of Sociology*, XVII, Sept. 1966, pp. 245–62.

LAMBERT, R. *et al.* (1969) *New Wine in Old Bottles?* Occasional Papers in Social Administration, No. 28, Bell.

PARSONS, T. (1965) in Parsons, T., Skils, E., Naegele, K. D. and Pitts, J. R. (eds.) *Theories of Society*, Free Press, pp. 36–41.

POPE, FRANKLIN, M. (1967) *School Organization: Theory and Practice*, Rand-McNally.

SUGARMAN, B. (1968) "The School and Moral Education", *Journal of Curriculum Studies*, I, Nov. 1968, pp. 47–67.

WALLER, W. (1938) *The Sociology of Teaching*, Wiley.

WHELLER, S. "The Structure of Formally Organized Socialization Settings", in Brim, O. G., Jnr. and Wheeler, S. *Socialization after Childhood: Two Essays*, Wiley.

WILSON, J. (1962) *Public Schools and Private Practice*, Allen and Unwin.

365

4.6 Organizational Analysis in Education: An Empirical Study of a School

Joyce Oldham

INTRODUCTION

Are educational institutions different from other kinds of organizations? Consideration of this question was prompted by the growing interest in the concept of "management" as applied to education and an increasing awareness of the need for more attention to be given to the training of those who hold, or who are preparing for, positions of responsibility within the management of education. As a consequence, a number of programmes of study in "education management" are now available and their aims, in general terms, are to improve conceptualization and develop knowledge and skills in the areas of analysis and problem-solving, and to provide insights and experience in the use, limitations and applications of management techniques in the field of education.

There is, however, the danger of "education management" being perceived as some kind of panacea which has ready solutions for the most deep-seated and intractable problems. Some of those involved in education management programmes have been aware from the beginning of the need to be explicit about underlying values and assumptions and of the danger of transferring uncritically the "ideology of management" to spheres for which it was not originally intended. One serious drawback which is central to this dilemma and to the problem of teaching practitioners in education management is the lack of adequate conceptualization, theory and research related specifically to educational institutions.

Attention has been drawn to this deficiency by a number of writers in recent years, whose concern has been to advance the general theory of organizations or to seek to relate the sociological techniques of organizational analysis to the school. Studies have been carried out on various aspects of the internal organization of the school and on the school in its social setting, but many suffer from the lack of an adequate theoretical framework and from the serious methodological problems involved.

It was against this background that the decision was made to undertake an empirical study of a school in the process of change, using the Action frame of reference developed by Silverman. At the time of writing, the

Source: Commissioned for this volume by The Open University.

analysis of data is not yet complete but preliminary findings give some indication of the usefulness of this form of analysis and its limitations, and show the inadequacy of models of educational organizations which do not take into account the wider political context.

THE IMPORTANCE OF THEORETICALLY-BASED RESEARCH

Despite the early work of Waller (1932) which drew attention to the dilemma facing teachers, that the creation of a motivating environment conducive to learning runs counter to the bureaucratic requirements of the school organization, interest in the school as a formal organization is of comparatively recent origin. An important impetus both in America and in this country was produced by the needs of administrators faced with radical changes in the educational system, and extensive use has been made of material from other fields which seemed relevant.

Early studies in educational administration followed the pattern of similar studies of large organizations in government and industry: much of it was "management" oriented, viewing "human relations" through the eyes of the administrator, and was open to criticisms similar to those made of the early management writers—the exposition of general principles without reference to research findings, research unrelated to theory and consequently lacking in a sense of direction, and methodology not reported in detail (Chase and Guba 1955). Later work indicated a greater awareness of theory and what it can offer. A number of studies explored the contribution which sociology can make and there was an emergence of interest in those aspects of educational organizations which differentiate them from industrial organizations, in particular the nature of power, authority and decision-making relationships in organizations staffed by professionals (Campbell and Faber 1961).

The considerable volume of subsequent work relating to educational organizations has been derived from a number of different approaches and can be said to fall into three main groups: work which is prescriptive and anecdotal, based on practice; that which is based on theoretical discussion, without empirical verification; and partial studies, focusing research on a limited area. The most significant contributions are discussed, from different perspectives, by Davies (1973)[1] and Hoyle (1973).

Whilst much of this work develops valuable insights and adds to our cumulative knowledge of the field, what is particularly striking is the absence of empirical studies dealing specifically with the management of the school. Various reasons have been put forward to explain this: in particular, the "haziness and dissensus that characterize educational procedures and outcomes", perhaps providing "a further origin of resistance to institutional research designed to penetrate the relationships between values and procedures" (Davies, 1973), and "the problems of access in this sensitive area" (Hoyle, 1973). That policy-making and implementation in conditions of very considerable change *is* a sensitive area is beyond dispute. In the school which was the subject of the research the changes involved the combination of three former grammar schools into a single very large comprehensive school, adjustment to an intake of pupils representing the full ability range and drawn from a defined localized catchment area, the introduction of coeducation and the utilization of scattered buildings on a large campus site. Under these conditions, tribute must be paid to the assistance provided by the headmaster and staff over a considerable period of time. A very high degree of co-operation and interest was forthcoming from the majority of those approached; nevertheless, a few questioned the legitimacy of the study to the extent that they felt unable to participate in any way, whilst others expressed reservations to a more limited extent.

A further problem encountered in research of this kind is the selection of a theoretical viewpoint which is relevant to the analysis of educational organizations. This point was discussed by Hoyle (1969) when he expressed concern at the tendency to overemphasize the importance of general theories of administration and to neglect the potential contribution of theories directly concerned with the unique features of educational institutions. He returns to it later (Hoyle, 1973), in an important paper in which he reviews the study of schools as organizations and the potential theories and methodologies with which the researcher is confronted.

The seriousness of the problem is underlined by the tendency for the managerialist tradition to overlap into educational administration, as was the case earlier with organization theory. During the last decade there has emerged a wide range of literature attempting to apply concepts and techniques derived from a variety of sources to "education management", at the levels of the national education system, local education authority and specific institution. The "management of innovation" has been the subject of particular attention and much interest is now being displayed in the areas of objective setting, corporate strategy and resource utilization.[2]

It is, therefore, particularly important that the search for relevant theory is not undertaken in isolation from the purpose towards which the study is directed; whether this is to be from a sociological perspective in order to gain theoretical understanding, or whether a management perspective is adopted in order to contribute to the solution of some practical problem of immediate concern to the host organization. In the latter case it is particularly important that the underlying assumptions and values are made explicit and subjected to rigorous scrutiny.[3]

The problem of adequate conceptualization and theory is not confined to the study of educational organizations but is part of a more general dilemma in the development of organization theory and its relationship with the main stream of sociological theory.[4] The question whether or not organization theory can benefit from the application of a more strictly sociological perspective has been considered from different viewpoints by Mouzelis (1967) and Silverman (1970), both of whom are of the opinion that it can. Mouzelis sees the area of power and control and the political activity of organization members, in the context of the wider problems of power in modern societies, as a neglected area compared with value integration and consensus which, he considers, refers to complementary aspects of an organization; he calls for the development of a general theory able to account for both integrative and conflict aspects of social systems in the study of organizations and of sociology in general. Silverman, on the other hand, is critical of attempts to integrate within the framework of the systems approach the apparently isolated phenomena of early organizational studies and presents an alternative theoretical scheme and method of analysis based on a sociology of social action, contrasted with a sociology of social systems. He refers to the fundamental issue in the development of sociological theory, namely, the nature of social order, and considers the implications of a view of social reality that is "socially constructed, socially sustained and socially changed". In other words, man is seen as autonomous and society develops as a result of the interactions and interpretations of its members, rather than existing prior to and as a source of contraint upon them. The important implications of these conflicting theoretical arguments are outside the scope of this paper, but the case is well presented by Dawe (1970).

THE CHOICE OF MODEL

It was against this background that a choice of approach had to be made when the opportunity arose to undertake a study in organizational analysis in the context of comprehensive reorganization. The purpose of the study is to use a sociological perspective in order to develop theoretical understanding and the main focus is upon the school as an organization rather than upon educational issues as such—the case for and against comprehensive education has been amply argued elsewhere. It is not the intention to assess or evaluate the decisions reached or the progress made within the school in relation to its changing situation. The main concern is with the decisions which were made, the process by which they were made, which decisions were successfully implemented and which were not and how the whole process relates to the declared aims of individuals and groups both within the school and in the wider environment. The criteria used are those established by the participants themselves, although data from other sources[5] has been used for purposes of comparison.

In this situation a number of alternative models or starting points were considered. The possibility of carrying out a comparative study of a number of schools was rejected; the research was concentrated on one school and the selection of this approach was influenced by Hoyle (1965). Since the focus was to be upon reorganization, a short-term "snapshot" was considered to be of less value than a longer-term study and the research has developed to cover the five-year period from the inception of the new comprehensive school in 1969, including the "working out" of its previously "selected" intake, the planning and introduction of new courses and planning for the first sixth form to be drawn from its "unselected" intake.

The theoretical framework was adopted after spending time in the school, talking informally to members of staff, attending meetings and developing an awareness of some of the issues involved. An initial striking similarity was observed to the problems discovered by Burns and Stalker (1961) in their study of firms in the Scottish electronics industry [cf. 2.7, p. 148*ff*]. Their concern was with the way in which management systems changed in accordance with changes in the technical and commercial tasks of the firm; in their case to develop and market commercial products in the post-war years after a long period on standardized production for defence contracts—a transition from conditions of relative stability to those of considerable change. They contrast "mechanistic" and "organic" systems; the former, which can be effective in stable conditions, are characterized by the definition of functions together with the methods, responsibilities and powers appropriate to them, and by definite boundaries to the individual's area of commitment, while the latter are more suited to conditions of change: the individual is expected to be concerned with any task which appears and his commitment is extended to the success of the organization as a whole.

If one accepts that schools are "people-processing" organizations, it is not in any way to diminish the expressed concern of many individual teachers for their pupils to suggest that, as grammar schools, they were in the main aiming, and were so expected, to produce O and A level successes from a relatively standard (selected) pupil intake, using relatively standard procedures. For the comprehensive school, at any rate in theory, the nature of the product is by no means so clear, nor is the pupil intake so standardized. The comprehensive school is expected to cater for a wider range of abilities, motivation and aspirations, involving changes in structure and organization, type of course and teaching method (the technology) and has a "marketing" function for what it has to offer, to both pupils and parents, which was much less necessary for the grammar school. In these circumstances it would be reasonable to assume that similar problems might arise in devising appropriate management systems to those encountered in the industrial organizations studied by Burns and Stalker.

Within the open socio-technical system framework adopted by Burns and Stalker it is possible to consider the influence of technology and the demands of the environment and the authors place a great deal of emphasis on the way in which members of the organization interpret their situation and modify their behaviour accordingly. Nevertheless, their treatment of the interaction between the organization and the environment is limited and as an "adaptive" model seemed inadequate for the analysis of an educational organization. A further difficulty arises from the fact that for them the centre of interest is in management itself. Although they use the word in the sense of "directing, coordinating and controlling the operations of a working community" in which everybody can be involved at different times and in different ways, the extent of involvement must be problematic in any type of organization. In other words, the major orientation is that of "management" and the objections to this emphasis have already been discussed. The use of the open socio-technical system for the analysis of educational institutions, with a more sensitive conceptualization of goals, has been suggested by Davies (1973). However, like Hoyle, he is aware of the dangers of over generalization and lack of attention to the history of the organization, which he attributes to the "ahistoricity of the systems approaches in general and managerialist perspectives in particular".[6]

In view of these considerations it seemed clear that what was required was a method of empirical analysis which could be applied to educational organizations in order to direct more attention to such questions as what, if anything, differentiates them from other types of organization. The decision was therefore made to adopt the Action frame of reference developed by Silverman (1968 and 1970). Silverman is concerned with social action from the standpoint of the individual, the nature of meanings which he brings to a situation and the causes rather than the consequences of action. He does not claim that the Action approach, in itself, provides a theory of organizations, but he seeks to develop a method of analysis from which can be derived a series of related questions about the nature of social life in any organization. This analysis can be applied at micro level in terms of the orientations and behaviour of particular actors and at the macro level in terms of the pattern of relations that is established by their interaction.

Such a method of analysis would overcome the problem of a narrow focus on selected aspects of the organization of the school, which might preclude the exploration of other pertinent questions. It is able to deal with the history and environment of the organization as a source of meanings for the actor, meanings from which will arise his definitions of situations and subsequent courses of action, instead of a mechanical model of the "organization" adapting to change. Nor does the method of analysis require the selection of a series of hypotheses for testing; what is advocated by Silverman is the view of the research process put forward by Glaser and Strauss (1968), in which they urge the use of research *to generate theory from data,* instead of concentrating on the testing and verification of theories. As has been stated earlier, it seemed particularly inappropriate to superimpose categories derived from other sorts of organizations and likely to hinder the emergence of any features which might be distinctive to educational organizations. Therefore it was considered that the development of theory might best be served by using the research to generate "grounded" theory, based upon the categories used by the participants themselves to order their experience. Silverman

(1970) pp. 229–30 suggests that from this would emerge first "grounded substantive theory", which would seek to explain the nature of social relations in one particular setting and secondly "grounded formal theory", seeking to generalize about the recurrent characteristics of an aspect of social life by ever broadening the scope of the study.

METHODOLOGY

The method of analysis adopted was that suggested by Silverman (1970) p. 154—to look at six interrelated areas in sequence:

1 The nature of the role-system and pattern of interaction that has been built up in the organization, in particular the way in which it has developed historically and the extent to which it represents the shared values of all or some or none of the actors.

This involved an examination of the history and development of the three component grammar schools: each was concerned with standards of academic achievement and behaviour and with the individual well-being of their pupils, but there were clearly differences of emphasis which were reflected in the way in which the schools were organized and in the norms and expectations of the staff and pupils. Then followed consideration of the reorganization plan for the City and the way in which changes in the plan over a period of years affected the schools. Detailed information was obtained on the physical reorganization in terms of: the use of existing buildings; the arrangements made for staffing in the context of the reorganization plan; the organization of the new school; the academic and pastoral arrangements made for the new intake and for "phasing out" the selected intake and its effect on the pattern of interaction. The opinions of staff and others were sought on these aspects of the reorganization.

2 The nature of involvement of ideal-typical actors (e.g. moral, alienative, instrumental) and the characteristic hierarchy of ends which they pursue (work satisfaction, material rewards, security). The way in which these derive from their biographies outside the organizations (job history, family commitments, social background) and from their experience of the organization itself.

In this section information was sought on the norms and expectations of teachers in relation to what they considered to be the most important duty of a teacher, reasons for entering teaching, education and training, work experience, family and social background and outside interests.

3 The actors' present definitions of their situation within the organization and their expectations of the likely behaviour of others with particular reference to the strategic resources they perceive to be at

their own disposal and at the disposal of others (degree of coercive power or moral authority; belief in individual opportunity).

This section is concerned with workload, both teaching and other duties; perception of the aims of the school and the resources available; the climate of decision-making, authority and influence; opportunities to display personal initiative and for career advancement.

4   The typical actions of different actors and the meaning which they attach to their action.

The analysis is now directed towards the actions of particular individuals and groups and their involvement in different aspects of the work of the school, for example, in responding to or resisting the need for innovation.

5   The nature and source of the intended and unintended consequences of action, with special reference to its effects on the involvement of the various actors and on the institutionalization of expectations in the role-system within which they interact.

6   Changes in the involvement and ends of the actors and in the role-system, and their source both in the outcome of the interaction of the actors and in the changing stock of knowledge outside the organization (e.g. political or legal changes; the varied experiences and expectations of different generations).

In these sections the effects of actions and policies will be analysed, taking into account factors internal to the school and those which arise from the local and national context.

Data was collected by conventional means: the study of documents, observation, extensive interviews, questionnaires, attendance at meetings and public events. With the exception of two group discussions with sixth formers and occasional unplanned contact with children, the research has been entirely concerned with teaching and non-teaching staff, officials of the Education Authority, teacher organizations and other interested parties.

As the inquiry proceeded it became apparent that its scope must be extended to include environmental factors with much more emphasis than as a source of meaning and orientation for actors in terms of their personal biographies and experiences. It was necessary to consider the history and context of the schools, taking into account local and national political policies, pressure groups and power positions in a further interlocking network of relationships.

The analysis of data is proceeding within the framework described on two levels, namely, the pattern of relationships established by interaction at macro level and, at micro level, the orientations and behaviour of particular actors. It is central to Action analysis to regard the behaviour of participants within organizations as problematic, depending upon the way in which they interpret their situation, the way in which they interact with others, the nature of their expectations and the ends they seek to attain. This then poses the problem of "getting in" to the subjective world of the participants and seeking to establish the subjective meaning and orientation to action attached by actors to the situation in which they find themselves.[7]

The approach adopted with the present study is to analyse data on the basis of categories emerging from the comments of respondents; to look for the source of each opinion or action and the individuals or groups involved and to seek to relate this to common characteristics, and to analyse significant incidents identified as such by respondents.[8]

PROVISIONAL RESULTS

At the time of writing analysis of data is not yet complete but some broad indications have emerged, although their detailed implications require further examination.

The claim that emphasis on the meaningful nature of human interaction enables the Action frame of reference to cope with the content of social life in organizations at micro level (the orientation and behaviour of participants) and at macro level (the pattern of relationships that is established by their interaction), and that in this way it provides an alternative to the systems approach, is supported by the results to date. In particular, the open-ended nature of the method of analysis has enabled new developments to be incorporated as the work progressed and in fact has led to a more extensive study, in both scope and length, than had originally been envisaged.

Nevertheless, certain important dimensions require more explicit consideration. These are:

1   the significance of power factors *within* the organization—the question of the weighting and impact of social actions;
2   following the wider scope of the inquiry to which the Action approach led, the significance of the wider political context.

Three key questions concerning the analysis of organizations are selected by Silverman; they are the types of attachment to the role system of an organization, the nature and source of the strategies that are used in the pursuit of given ends and the pattern of interaction emerging from the recurrent behaviour of the actors. He suggests that the nature of the attachment to the role system is an emergent characteristic, shaped and reshaped by the orientations which actors bring to the situation and by their subsequent experience of the situation itself. When this subjective view is expressed in action one may speak of the use of tactics or strategy—the purposive nature of social action. The "rules of the game" represent the institutionalization of these subjective views, depending, *inter alia,* upon the already existing "world taken for granted" of the participants, the ends they pursue and the degree of attachment to the existing pattern that this implies, the strategies and resources they perceive to be available to them, the actions in which they engage and their ability to convince others of the legitimacy of these acts; apparently stable definitions of situations are always threatened, sometimes by "heroes, prophets or saviours" (in this case sometimes by "villains") but more frequently by meanings which emerge in the course of everyday interaction.

There is, of course, considerable common ground here with the work of Burns and Stalker (1961), who draw attention to the strains which occur during the process of change from a "mechanistic" to an "organic" form of organization, in which the main difference for the participant is in the extent of his commitment to the organization—a situation in which individual managers might experience unease and anxiety. In addition they identify other forms of commitment within the work organization; to a "political" structure, to a status/career structure, to friendship and other groups as well as to the work organization itself—and the resulting organizational dynamics.

The relevance of these questions in the school has been confirmed during the study in terms of the relationships between the previous and current experiences of the teachers concerned and their reactions to the changes required in the new situation and the strategies adopted by significant individuals and groups. The emergent nature both of the role system and attachment to it has become apparent in changes both in the formal organization of the school, in the pattern of interaction, both social and professional, in involvement or otherwise in changes in the academic and pastoral organization of the school and the legitimation of various courses of action by reference to approved value systems.

What has emerged as an area of crucial importance is the climate in which decision-making takes place, and power factors within the organization. These issues are not explicityly considered by Silverman, but both Mouzelis and Burns and Stalker refer to them from different points of view. Burns and Stalker see as the key variable the extent to which the man at the top can interpret the tasks facing the organization and adapt the working organization to elicit the required individual commitment. Their reference to his symbolic as well as overt authority, the pervasiveness of his authority and the complicated network of mutual expectations and responses which characterize his relationships with his subordinates, is particularly relevant to the role of the "man at the top" in a school. In the complex structure of a large school the emergence of the roles of the heads and deputies and heads of departments requires further consideration, with particular reference to their part in the formation of policy and its dissemination to the rest of the staff, and to the tensions which develop when attempts are made to change roles and role expectations legitimized by tradition.

Turning to the wider social context, it seems clear that the environment must be regarded as more than a source of meanings to organizational participants, more than the "stock of knowledge in the outside world", and that factors of power and ideology external to the school as an organization must be taken into account. During the course of the study there was a climate of political change at national level; following the issue of the Department of Education and Science Circular 10/65 by the then Labour Government, with the objective of ending selection at 11+ and of eliminating separation in secondary education, there has been both public controversy and policy change by successive governments on the subject of comprehensive education. Although this is clearly the outcome of the interaction of individuals in the context of a particular society, it cannot be divorced from the "differential control over resources, economic, political *and* symbolic, which participants bring to their interaction", (Goldthorpe 1973). At local level the concern was with the detailed implementation of the political decision to complete the reorganization of secondary education which had commenced some years earlier.[9] In addition there were local pressure groups seeking to influence decision-making at local authority level, besides arrangements for consultation with local teacher organizations and the newly constituted School Managers and Governors. Although it is difficult at this stage to reach firm conclusions on their effectiveness, all were concerned with such matters as parental choice, the definition of catchment areas and post 16 education, all of which have implications for the school in relation to, amongst other things, its size, its claim on resources and the career expectations of its members.[10]

EVALUATION OF MODEL

It emerges from the current study that the Action frame of reference has much to offer and is capable of further development as an approach to the study of organizations. The method of analysis is sufficiently flexible to enable consideration to be given to such factors as the weighting and impact of social action within the organization, and power and ideology external to the organization, which were not explicitly stated in the original paradigm but emerged as important issues as the work progressed. Nevertheless certain operational and methodological issues are raised. Problems of access, time and resources are common to all but the most limited research, irrespective of its theoretical perspective, as is the question of establishing the cut-off point—the limitation imposed on the scope of the study. These problems are, however, particularly pertinent in a study using this framework because of its emergent and continuous nature, and the need to be able to explore developments taking place simultaneously in different parts of the organization and in the wider society.

A more serious difficulty is that of understanding the subjective meaning by which individuals interpret their situations, since one cannot enter into the experience of another. This difficulty arises at two stages obtaining the basic information by interview, observation or the examination of records, with all the possibilities for inadvertent distortion that this entails, and the interpretation of the data itself. It is clear that further methodological development is required; the problems which arise are still the subject of debate amongst sociologists and the exploration by Goldthorpe (1973) of the issues involved is particularly useful. He questions, amongst other things, the extent to which the situation determines interaction, and this is especially relevant to this research. It is necessary to consider to what extent the "rules" by which interpretations of everyday interaction are made are significantly affected by, for example, professional socialization, and whether this is adequately dealt with as part of the personal biography of the actor.

CONCLUSIONS

The study was undertaken with two main purposes. The first was to examine empirically the claim that the Action frame of reference provides an alternative to the Systems approach to the analysis of organizations, and this is confirmed by results to date, notwithstanding certain operational and methodological difficulties.

The other purpose was to discover what features, if any, differentiate the school as an organization from other types of organization. The study indicates that the whole area of power distribution and its effect on decision-making has been neglected and that, certainly in the field of education, more attention should be paid to this aspect, both within the organization and in the wider society. It indicates the inadequacy of models of organizations not taking into account these wider issues.

It would be improper to generalize on the basis of one study, but it does demonstrate the need for further empirical and comparative studies using a consistent analytical framework, so that further theoretical development may take place.

NOTES

1 This was originally presented as a paper to the Annual Conference of the British Sociological Association in 1970. The reference given is that of the book in which the paper is included.

2 For example, the Society of Education Officers took as the theme for its summer meeting "Management and Management Training" and edited versions of the main papers were published as a supplement to *Education*, 19.7.74, opening with the statement that "Public Administration has been pushed inexorably towards doctrines of man-

N

agement efficiency, effectiveness and systematic administration" with the assumption that programmes, with costs and benefits, can be attributed "to the pursuit of values".

In another case, members of a local education department concluded that the department's "relationship to the education service is essentially managerial" and developed a matrix form of organization designed to facilitate its three main functions, namely, the development of policies and strategic planning, the implementation of policies, and the monitoring of the effect of policies and discovering consumers' needs (Mann 1973). At school level, a recent work examines in depth and detail the critical problems of change and expansion in secondary schools and focuses on the organization of a group of teachers into a "management structure" (Richardson 1973).

3 See Hanson (1972) and the summary of the paper by Professor P. B. Checkland in the Supplement (*Education Management*, 1974) to *Education*, 19.7.74. It would be unfortunate indeed if in education, with its diffuse goals, the result of the application of some management techniques was a situation in which the efforts of teachers were concentrated only on those things which can be seen to be measurable.

4 The main theoretical perspectives are introduced in the Open University Course DT352, Units 3–14.

5 The main studies which are being used for this purpose are those sponsored by the Department of Education and Science and carried out by staff of the National Foundation for Educational Research in England and Wales. The three-stage project covered *Comprehensive Education in England and Wales* by T. G. Monks (1968), *Comprehensive Education in Action*, edited by T. G. Monks (1970), and *A Critical Appraisal of Comprehensive Education* by J. M. Ross *et al* (1972). In addition reference is being made to *Half Way There* by C. Benn and B. Simon (1970).

6 The problems in the open systems approach are apparent in the very detailed research by Richardson (1973). The study draws from the work of Bion, Miller and Rice and is concerned with intergroup and interpersonal relationships in the management structure of a school. In particular, the "management orientation" raises the familiar problems of reifying "the institution" and from what standpoint "rationality" should be defined.

7 The theoretical and methodological questions raised are discussed in Cicourel (1964) and in Filmer *et al.* (1972). In the latter, Silverman develops his own position in a paper titled "Methodology and Meaning".

8 For further examination of the issues and problems involved see Glaser and Strauss (1968). There are similarities in the approaches adopted by Cicourel and Kitsuse (1963) and the critical incident

method is used by Revans and Baquer (1972) in the context of action research.

9 The development of comprehensive education in Sheffield has been taking place over a long period, following the decisions, in 1958 to establish its first comprehensive school, and in 1962 "to move as quickly as possible towards a comprehensive system of secondary education for the whole city with the ultimate aim of abolishing segregation at the age of 11 + ".

10 These wider issues have been raised from a number of different perspectives; for example, the complex and often subtle way in which the Department of Education and Science works in its political and economic context (Medlicott, 1974), the way in which the national policies of the Conservative and Labour parties on comprehensive education have been influenced by their respective ideologies (Bilski, 1973), the way in which curriculum decisions within the school reflect ideological positions (Eggleston, 1973 [see 4.4, p. 325]).

REFERENCES

BENN, C. and SIMON, B. (1970) *Half Way There*, McGraw-Hill.

BILSKI, R. (1973) "Ideology and the Comprehensive Schools", *Political Quarterly*, April/June 1973.

BURNS, T. and STALKER, G. M. (1961) *The Management of Innovation*, Tavistock.

CAMPBELL, R. F. and FABER, C. F. (1961) "Administrative Behaviour: Theory and Research", *Review of Educational Research*, Vol. 31.

CHASE, F. S. and GUBA, E. G. (1955) "Administrative Roles and Behaviour", *Review of Educational Research*, Vol. 25.

CICOUREL, A. V. (1964) *Method and Measurement in Sociology*, Free Press.

CICOUREL, A. V. and KITSUSE, J. (1963) *The Educational Decision-makers*, Bobbs-Merill.

DAVIES, B. (1973), "On the Contribution of Organisational Analysis to the Study of Educational Institutions", in Brown, R. (ed.) *Knowledge, Education and Cultural Change*, Tavistock.

DAWE, A. (1970) "The two Sociologies", *British Journal of Sociology*, Vol. 21, No. 2.

DOUGLAS, J. D. (ed.) (1971) *Understanding Everyday Life*, Routledge and Kegan Paul.

Education Management (1974), a supplement published with *Education*, 19 July 1974.

EGGLESTON, J. (1973) "Decision making on the School Curriculum; a conflict model", *Sociology*, Vol. 7, No. 3.

FILMER, P., PHILLIPSON, M., SILVERMAN, D. and WALSH, D. (eds.) (1972) *New Directions in Sociological Theory*, Collier-Macmillan.

GLASER, B. G. and STRAUSS, A. L. (1968) *The Discovery of Grounded Theory*, Weidenfeld and Nicolson.

GOLDTHORPE, J. H. (1973) "A Revolution in Sociology?" *Sociology*, Vol. 7, No. 3.

GREEN, G. (1974) "Politics, Local Government and the Community", *Local Government Studies*, June 1974.

HANSON, D. (1972) "Management Ideology in the Schools", *New Society*, 28 Sept. 1972.

HOYLE, E. (1965) "Organisational Analysis in the Field of Education", *Education Research Bulletin*, Vol. 7, No. 2.

HOYLE, E. (1969) "Organisation Theory and Educational Administration", in Baron, G. and Taylor, W. (eds.) *Educational Administration and the Social Sciences*, Atholone Press.

HOYLE, E. (1973) "The Study of Schools as Organisations", in Butcher, J. H. and Pont, H. B. (eds.) *Educational Research in Britain 3*, University of London Press.

MANN, J. (1973) "3D Management", *Municipal and Public Services Journal*, 12 Jan. 1973.

MANNING, P. K. (1971) "Talking and Becoming: a view of Organisational Socialisation", in Douglas, J. D. (ed.) *Understanding Everyday Life*, Routledge and Kegan Paul.

MEDLICOTT, P. (1974) "Education in Whitehall: How the D.E.S. Works", *New Society*, 22 August 1974.

MONKS, T. G. (1968) *Comprehensive Education in England and Wales*, National Foundation for Educational Research.

MONKS, T. G. (ed.) (1970) *Comprehensive Education in Action*, National Foundation for Educational Research.

MOUZELIS, N. P. (1967) *Organisation and Bureaucracy*, Routledge and Kegan Paul.

OPEN UNIVERSITY, THE (1974) DT352 *People and Organizations:* Units 3–6 *Structure and System: Basic Concepts and Theories;* Units 7–11 *Organizational Control: Interaction, Roles and Rules;* Units 12–14 *Knowledge and Information*, The Open University Press.

REVANS, R. W. and BAQUER, A. (1972) "*I thought they were supposed to be doing that*", The Hospital Centre.

RICHARDSON, E. (1973) *The Teacher, the School and the task of Management*, Heinemann.

ROSS, J. M., BUNTON, W. J., EVISON, P. and ROBERTSON, T. S. (1972) *A Critical Appraisal of Comprehensive Education*, National Foundation for Educational Research.

SILVERMAN, D. (1968) "Formal Organisations or Industrial Sociology: Towards a Social Action Analysis of Organisations", *Sociology*, 2.

SILVERMAN, D. (1970) *The Theory of Organisations*, 301.15, Heinemann.

WALLER, W. (1932) *The Sociology of Teaching*, Wiley.

4.7 Organization Development in Schools

Terry Newell

Literally billions of dollars have been spent over the past several years to design, test, package, and install an unprecedented number and variety of educational innovations in our Nation's classrooms. Additional sums have been spent to train school staffs, modernize the physical plant, and expand the range of educational services available to American school children. The time, money, and hope that have been invested in these efforts offer a striking example of America's belief in the importance of education to its future.

Whether these reform efforts have succeeded, and if they have, to what extent, are by no means settled questions. Educators and lay observers disagree about both the meaning and existence of evidence that reflects on what works and what doesn't in improving the education of children. One point on which they do agree, however, is that the *results* of the educational innovations in which billions were invested have not fully matched the *promises* with which such efforts were launched. While the gap between reality and expectation may not be causing a "crisis of confidence" in American education, as some have suggested, neither has it resulted in a sense of satisfaction that all is well.

There are undoubtedly many complex reasons for the failure of innovations to fulfill their promises. One such reason may well be that innovators have paid too much attention to isolated aspects of the innovation or the school—design of the innovation, for example, or training of teachers, scheduling, curriculums, media, to name a few—and too little attention to the school as an organization, composed of complex sets of interrelationships of people and nonhuman resources. In the view of an increasing number of educators, too often attempts have been made to implement innovations without realizing that certain interperonal, intergroup, or structural aspects of the school environment would simply not support the change.

Richard Schmuck and Matthew Miles (1972), two education researchers and advocates of this outlook, state the view succinctly: "Schools are primarily *organizations,* and many if not most efforts at

---

Source: *American Education* (Dec. 1973), Vol. 9.

educational reform have collapsed or have been absorbed without effect precisely because of the limited attention given to the organizational context in which reforms have been attempted." They point out that schools, as organizations, are characterized by a variety of individual and group behavior patterns which form the climate into which innovations are introduced. If this climate is marked by distrust, lack of commitment to the innovation, poor communication, intergroup conflict, unclear goals, ineffective decision-making, or similar behaviors, the chances for successful reform are considerably diminished, regardless of the quality of the innovation itself. The conscious or subconscious assumption by innovators that they can ignore these characteristics of the organizational environment yet still implement their reforms guarantees that their innovations will at best achieve but limited and temporary success.

Why the organizational context in which school reforms have been attempted has received so little attention is not entirely clear. Innovators in business and industry have been aware of the importance of this outlook for some time, and even though no one maintains that students should be "turned out" like automobiles or computers, proponents of an organizational approach to school reform do point to the fact that an educational system shares much in common with business and industry. Each is confronted with the problems posed by rapid change, growth in size and diversity, scarce resources, and the demands of consumers. Any organization faced with these problems must either adapt and grow or stagnate. And stagnation, taking the form of outmoded structures, rigidified procedures, disrupted communications, and stereotyped thinking, may ultimately lead to pronounced organizational ineffectiveness. Unfortunately, ineffective schools, unlike dying businesses, do not always fade from existence. Instead, they linger on to infect the lives of thousands of students to come, impeding learning and choking innovation. Schools need not, however, develop organizational hardening of the arteries.

How to achieve organizational health is, of course, the key question. One answer, suggested by such workers as Schmuck and Miles, is to be found in the relatively new field of organization development, more commonly referred to as "OD". Richard Beckhard, an early worker in OD theory and its application in business and industry and presently at MIT's Sloan School of Management, offers a useful definition in his work, *Organization Development: strategies and models:* "Organization development is an effort (1) *planned,* (2) *organization-wide,* and (3) *managed* from the *top,* to (4) increase *organizational effectiveness* and *health* through (5) *planned interventions* in the organization's "processes", using *behavioral-science* knowledge."

It is this last part of the definition which is most descriptive of OD, for it is in its use of the behavioral sciences that OD departs most drastically from more traditional organizational improvement efforts such as time and motion studies and management by objectives. OD rests on the assumption, born out of sociological and psychological research, that organizational health requires an organizational climate characterized by mutual trust, open communication, and participatory decision-making. Only in such a climate can an organization hope to enlist the full commitment and energies of its members in the pursuit of organizational goals. Beginning with the pioneering work of the National Training Laboratories, an expanding body of theory and technique now provides practical means to translate the discoveries of the behavioral sciences into improved human interaction.

The behavioral science techniques used in OD vary considerably, although all proceed from two common basic assumptions: first, that employees are human beings, not parts of an organizational machine to be manipulated in order to make the machine run efficiently. OD advocates maintain that this concern for people does not conflict with management's concern for production, and that only as both concerns are met simultaneously will an organization make the fullest use of its resources. Second, that the organizational health toward which the behavioral sciences are employed is more than the mere absence of organizational ill-health. OD specialists aim their techniques at the attainment of positive growth, achievement of the fullest potential of the organization. The "self-actualization" of the school, not just the treatment of its problems, is the ultimate goal.

Using the behavioral sciences to improve the organizational *climate*, however, is only a part of OD which seeks also to improve the *processes* by which an organization operates. OD advocates are convinced that how the members of a system diagnose their problems, prescribe remedies, and implement alternatives is basic to the successful solution of these problems and equally as important as what the problems are. To meet this concern with process, OD uses a wide variety of techniques to improve the skills of organizational members in conducting meetings, analyzing problems, making decisions, implementing solutions, and resolving interpersonal and intergroup conflict.

If improvement of the organizational climate and processes is essential to a successful OD effort, no less fundamental are the requirements for a planned, system-wide approach under the direction of top leadership. OD recognizes that organizational change is a highly complex undertaking which cannot be approached extemporaneously or in bits and pieces. Systematic, scientific problem-solving is considered essential. OD also recognizes that changes in organizational behavior are more fundamental and thus more threatening and likely to encounter resistance than are more surface changes such as the installation of new equipment. If top leadership, in the person of the superintendent, principal, and members of their immediate staffs, is not actively committed, it may quickly abandon the OD effort at the first sign of staff unrest or outside pressure.

Educational applications of the basic OD theory outlined above are being conducted in a wide variety of settings. Universities, State departments of education, and Federal Government agencies as well as local school systems are experimenting with OD. Their efforts are beginning to form a nationwide mosaic of OD resources. A small sample of the range of these activities may be seen in the work of researchers at the Center for the Advanced Study of Educational Administration (CASEA) at the University of Oregon. For the past six years, CASEA specialists have been engaged in a series of interventions aimed at subjecting OD theory to the reality of schools.

In August of 1967, almost the entire staff of a suburban Oregon junior high school, including the head cook and the head custodian, entered a six-day OD training session aimed at improving communication within the staff and at enhancing group problem-solving. During the first two days of the training, CASEA specialists focused on illustrating the importance of clear communication and collaborative behavior to effective school functioning. Exercises—the NASA trip-to-the-moon and the five-square puzzle, for instance—served as one training vehicle. In the latter exercise, five people sit around a table, each with a pile of puzzle pieces. No person has all the pieces to make a complete puzzle, the task of the exercise being to transfer pieces among the group until everyone has been able to complete a puzzle. The rules, however, prohibit talking or any form of gesturing, and no one may take a puzzle piece from anyone else; only giving of pieces to others is allowed. The exercise thus focuses attention on the importance of communication by demonstrating the frustrations that emerge when one is not able to communicate but is wholly dependent upon the observation and concern of others. Each exercise in the training session was followed by a discussion by the participants of what was learned and how this could be applied to improve school functioning.

The last four days of the training were devoted to the development of problem-solving and decision-making skills and their use on real school problems. The six-day training session was reinforced and extended in two follow-up sessions in December and February of the 1967–68 school year.

The results reported by CASEA from this application of OD to schools included a decrease in the teacher turnover rate; creation of a new vice-principalship aimed at facilitating change throughout the school; and an increase in the extent to which teachers saw the principal and themselves as able to make and apply better decisions, conduct more effective meetings, and facilitate more open communication. Of special significance, in terms of the goal of sustained self-renewal, were later reports of faculty-planned and conducted OD training and the spread of the new vice-principalship to other schools after withdrawal of the CASEA team.

In April of 1968, after seven months of discussion with staff from all professional levels in the Kent, Washington, school district, CASEA trainers began a series of OD interventions aimed at developing a self-sustaining cadre of organizational specialists. This careful, prolonged beginning paid off in June of 1969 when, despite a tight budget, the district agreed to provide a half-time coordinator and ten days released time for members of an intradistrict cadre of OD specialists. Volunteers for the cadre were then solicited, with applications coming in from all types of district personnel. The resulting team, containing teachers, counselors, curriculum and student specialists, principals, and an assistant superintendent, then entered a two-week workshop to develop its own OD capabilities and make plans for the coming school year.

The potential of OD to help assure the success of innovations appears to have been demonstrated by one of the many interventions conducted by the cadre. In a series of four brief sessions which took place between August and November of the 1969–70 school year, the OD cadre, assisted by CASEA trainers, worked with an elementary school staff trying to implement a new multiunit structure. Training emphasized communication and problem-solving in an attempt to head off the difficulties bound to arise as a result of such a major change. The effectiveness of this application of OD was evidenced by later reports from the teachers that the innovation was being successfully introduced and that the OD training seemed to have played a significant part.

By March of 1970, according to CASEA, the Kent OD cadre had fully taken over the planning and conducting of OD efforts in the district—a satisfying sign that planned organizational change can become an ongoing process without continued outside assistance. Of added significance in this respect is the recent report that the cadre is still operating despite the superintendent having departed, many of the cadre members having moved away or having been replaced and the district budget having been cut—events that have traditionally sounded the death rattle for innovations.

While these two examples represent but a small percentage of the types of OD activities in schools, they do serve to illustrate the outlines of a four-stage generic model of OD intervention. The first stage, usually called *"entry"*, involves initial contact between the educational system and OD specialists followed by detailed negotiation to establish the conditions that will govern the OD effort. Clear communication, openness, and trust are considered essential at this stage to assure mutual commitment to ends and mutual agreement on means. The second stage of the effort, *"diagnosis"*, consists of collecting extensive data from system members, analyzing organizational needs based on this data, and planning intervention activities to resolve the problems identified. Client system participants are the diagnosticians along with OD specialists at each step of this process. Most emphatically they are not merely survey respondents for whom a cure will be announced. This crucial point, OD advocates maintain, distinguishes OD from the typical school-consultant relationship that presently characterizes much of outside assistance.

Planned *"interventions"* represent the third stage of the generic model and may vary immensely in nature and purpose. Training activities may be conducted to improve communication, clarify organizational goals, alter systemic norms, resolve conflicts, and improve meeting, problem-solving, or decision-making skills. Intervention may also take the form of instituting structural changes in the organization, inviting outside consultants or trainers for assistance in solving specific problems of a technical nature, or training staff to form their own OD team, as in the CASEA approach in the Kent district. Continuous assessment and feedback are considered vital during the intervention to assure that OD goals are either being met or that strategies are being revised as necessary. The final stage of the model, *"withdrawal"*, sees the departure of the outside OD specialists and, if the effort has truly succeeded, the beginning of an internally operated system capacity for continuous self-renewal. The development of this capacity is perhaps the critical factor upon which the success of OD as a lasting reform strategy may ultimately rest.

It is appropriate here to note several dangers and misperceptions that OD must overcome if it is to fulfill its goal of facilitating organizational health. Perhaps the most serious threat to a fair test of the worth of OD is that it will join the already long list of educational fads that were touted as panaceas yet failed to deliver. The pattern is familiar: a new concept is proposed, a label is attached, a bandwagon begins to roll, an immediate "how to" prescription is demanded; the resulting "package" yields no improvement, the fad is discredited (to await "discovery" in another 20 to 30 years). This bandwagon behavior prevents the cautious and systematic development of theory and technique which alone can provide a solid basis upon which to judge the value of any innovation. To their credit, most of its advocates make a point of noting that OD is not a panacea, *the* educational wave of the future. Nor is it necessarily the only or entire way to facilitate organizational health. It is, instead, one way of improving the ability to find answers and to make these answers truly fulfill their promise.

A closely related problem OD faces is the misperception by many potential clients that OD is a packaged product, neatly assembled and ready for consumption the same way in every educational system. It is, instead, a body of theory and technique, by no means complete, which must be used carefully and differently according to the particular educational system and situation to which it is applied. OD advocates insist that it is not, nor should it ever be, a "teacher-proof" or "administrator-proof" prescriptive program of the type that many educators have come to expect from outside innovators.

While the more conscientious OD specialists are sensitive to the dangers of the "fad cycle" and the potential misperception of OD as a "package" and strive to counteract those trends, not all practitioners of OD in schools necessarily share this concern. As with other innovations, the formation of a group of OD "hucksters" bent on the hard sell is a distinct possibility. The problem has already confronted such conscientious groups as National Training Laboratories and may soon confront the OD-in-schools research community as a whole. Researchers may choose to ignore it, insisting that all their time must be devoted to their work, but they do so at the risk of having poorly trained practitioners give the field a bad name before it has even had the time fully to develop its theoretical foundation. Consumer education and professional ethics can be disregarded but the price paid may prove to be too high.

Another misperception of OD that threatens to retard its acceptance and development is the tendency of potential clients to confuse OD with sensitivity training. The result of this confusion is a false understanding of OD as an innovation that uses personality change and emotional encounters as its prime tools for change. This perception of OD quite understandably creates concern on the part of teachers and administrators who wonder if they will be forced to reveal innermost secrets or engage in highly charged interpersonal confrontations in the service of their schools. To counter this fear, OD practitioners note that the prime focus of OD is the improvement of groups, not individuals, and that encounter sessions of the Bob and Carol, Ted and Alice variety are by no means prerequisites to effective organizational change.

A final caution to potential OD clients is to avoid perceiving OD as a management tool to "adjust" individuals to the organization or spruce up the behavior of a recalcitrant school or department. OD seeks to move beyond enlisting organizational behaviors and structures and therefore demands a democratic not an authoritarian approach on the part of school system administrators. It cannot be "laid on".

Even if misperceptions such as these did not confront the developers and potential users of OD theory and technique, there would still be significant research and practical problems to be overcome to make OD applications effective in schools. Perhaps the most crucial research problem is the need to test and expand the framework of the OD generic model. Much remains to be learned about the entry, diagnosis, intervention, and withdrawal stages, and much that is already known experientially needs to be subjected to the rigors of experimental testing. Much current OD practice seems to rely on an intuitive sense as to what is called for in a given situation. To make OD as much science as art requires that confirmed hypotheses increasingly replace transmission of knowledge and skills by example and anecdote.

A significant aspect of this problem is the need for incontrovertible research evidence. The demand for accountability in education applies to researchers as well as to teachers and superintendents. Impressionistic evidence such as personal recollections and testimonials by satisfied clients will not be sufficient to convince potential users of OD in schools, nor should it be sufficient for OD specialists themselves.

What kind of evidence is needed? While laymen and some educators may insist on standardized test scores, OD practitioners, such as those at CASEA, contend that this is demanding too much, at least in the short run. They are convinced that the linkage between OD and improved student test scores is too indirect and rely instead on measures showing improved staff problem-solving, communication, use of resources, and assessment of progress towards goals. But while playing down the utility of test scores, they also caution against over-reliance on attitude surveys which are susceptible to "telling them what they want to hear" responses. Philip Runkel, a member of the CASEA team, argues for the necessity of using two or more independent measures for each of the variables in OD research as well as for the conduct of studies over long periods since educational change and its manifestations occur slowly. Whichever direction research takes, however, it is clear that OD specialists must find education equivalents for the profit and productivity variables used to measure the success of OD interventions in business and industry. This cannot be avoided if they are to gain the trust of educational managers who have been led astray by many past claims and who demand to be shown that OD does, in fact, lead to improvement in the learning of children.

Still another research problem confronting OD specialists is the need to develop alternative OD models that more realistically address the political confrontations with which school people are all too familiar. Change by consensus, upon which most current OD work is based, must be joined theoretically and practically to change through power and conflict. Related to this is the need to test OD theory in a wider range of school systems than has been the case thus far. The bulk of OD work in schools has been conducted in suburban, mostly white, mostly middle-class settings. It is essential to determine the validity of current OD theory in big-city, low-income, and minority settings and to provide the restructuring necessary to make it applicable in these situations. OD must also be applied to an increasing degree in university change efforts to determine its suitability at this level. Finally, OD interventions must more and more involve students as essential participants in change efforts.

Turning from research to practical problems confronting advocates of OD in schools, the most serious may well be the difficulty of raising funds at the local level to implement an OD effort. Considering the facts that fixed costs constitute approximately 80 to 90 per cent and sometimes more of most school budgets, and that taxpayers are not enamored of more innovations, it may be increasingly difficult in the years ahead to find available funds for use in OD. While some preliminary data indicate that the cost of OD in schools may be relatively low as far as innovations go, those interested in engaging in such an effort may well have to rely on the reallocation of existing resources or the argument that costs for OD represent "risk capital" which promises a heavy return at a later time.

Another practical problem is the need to tie OD to other innovative techniques or products being used in the schools. It is essential to remember that OD is a method of finding problem solutions; it does not assure that the solutions will be used or that they will work. For example, group consensus about the need to revise an existing curriculum does not necessarily assure that the revision will be instructionally and technically of high quality or that teachers will be more effective in using it than in using the old one. Similarly, a problem-solving exercise that results in the decision to improve system program monitoring will not indicate whether to use PERT (Program Evaluation and Review Technique), management by objectives, or some other planning tool. Nor will it give appropriate staff the skills necessary to establish the selected procedure in an effective way. OD as a process has its limits and must be married operationally to product-oriented measures such as PPBS (Program Planning-Budgeting Evaluation System), PERT, and operations research, to name a few.

Finally, for the field of OD to be fully useful on other than a small research basis, professionally competent OD specialists will have to be trained. While this may be done through the CASEA cadre approach, other methods either exist or can be devised. (In this latter respect, the Managers of Educational Change Fellowship program recently initiated by OE's National Center for the Improvement of Educational Systems is an example). It will also be necessary to create and expand networks of OD resources (people, places, materials, and the like) and make these known and available to OD clients.

Given the various assets and liabilities attached to the use of OD in schools, it is tempting to tote up a balance sheet on this new concept for change. This would, however, be deceptive and premature. While the emphasis on organizational norms, roles, and group dynamics as key variables in educational innovation is a highly significant step in the conceptualization of educational change, and while OD can offer some useful techniques now, considerable developmental work is needed to make this approach fully effective. This should not, however, in any way deter increased attention to one of the few change strategies which offers the potential of ending the cycle of frustration in educational reform. OD is aimed at achieving the continuous self-renewal of educational systems. To the extent that it succeeds, we may yet escape the observation of the French satirist Alphonse Karr, recently echoed for education by Seymour Sarason in *The Culture of the School and the Problem of Change:* "The more things change, the more they remain the same."

REFERENCES

BECKHARD, R. (1969) *Organization Development: Strategies and Models,* Addison-Wesley.

BENNIS, W. G. (1969) *Organization Development: Its Nature, Origins, and Prospects,* Addison-Wesley (part of six-volume Addison-Wesley series on OD).

BURKE, W. W. and HORNSTEIN, H. A. (1972) *The Social Technology of Organization Development,* NTL Learning Resources Corporation.

SCHMUCK, R. A. and MILES, M. B. (eds.) (1972) *Organization Development in Schools*, National Press Books.
Further Reading on Organization Development in Schools.
SCHMUCK, R. A., RUNKEL, P. J., SATUREN, S. L., MARTELL, R. T. and DERR, C. B. (1972) *Handbook of Organization Development in Schools*, National Press Books.
"Organizational Development in the Schools", *Education Technology*, Vol. 12, No. 10, Oct. 1972 (entire issue devoted to OD in schools).

4.8 The Management of Educational Change: Towards a Conceptual Framework

Ray Bolam

INTRODUCTION

The literature on innovation in general and on educational innovation in particular is already extensive and is growing rapidly. Some of this work dates back to the early fifties but most has been written since the mid-sixties. One American reviewer (Havelock, 1969) identified 4,000 studies and estimated that at least 1,000 more were being carried out each year. In fact these figures were certainly too low since his review included very little European work. Moreover, this literature "comes from many fields of enquiry, both within and outside of education, and covers a great range of topics. It is also characterised by a wide variety of publications, sources, research traditions and contributions to research knowledge" (Chin and Downey, 1973). Thus writers often adopt widely different theoretical perspectives and in consequence the reader is faced by a bewildering variety of models and theories and by frequent terminological and conceptual overlap and confusion.

It is, of course, beyond the scope of this paper to try to review this wider literature or to attempt any significant clarification of issues and theories arising from such diverse fields as knowledge diffusion and utilization, curriculum innovation, educational administration, organization theory, systems theory, the management of planned change, phenomenologocial sociology etc. My purposes are more modest: first, to provide an organizing framework for this wider literature as it relates to educational innovation; second, to provide a heuristic framework which may act as an aid to understanding some key problems, tasks and procedures associated with the management of change at several levels in the educational system; third, to suggest guidelines for practitioners engaged in the mangement of change.

In any innovation process we can usefully distinguish between four major factors: the change agent, the innovation, the user system and the process of innovation over time. These four factors are represented in Figure 1 as a two-dimensional conceptual framework. The various components in this framework are drawn from the literature on change.

Source: Commissioned for this volume by The Open University.

Havelock (1969) highlights some key factors in the knowledge diffusion process by asking the simple question: who (the change agent) says what (the innovation) to whom (the user system)? Hull *et al.*, (1973) also working within the knowledge diffusion tradition, distinguish between the antecedent, interactive and consequent stages. Several writers suggest the value of conceptualizing the user as a social system (e.g. Katz and Kahn, 1964; Fullan, 1972) and by using the same approach with the change agent and innovation, we can explore the systemic implications and consequences of an innovation as the three factors interact with, change and are changed by each other during the process of innovation over time. We also have to recognize that the way in which individual members of these three systems perceive their own system, the other two systems and the process over time, may crucially affect the fate of the innovation (Silverman, 1970; Open University, 1972a).

A model of this kind is bound to be over-simplified. Its prime purpose is to provide a framework which may be of help in focusing our thinking

Figure 1 A conceptual framework for the study of educational innovation

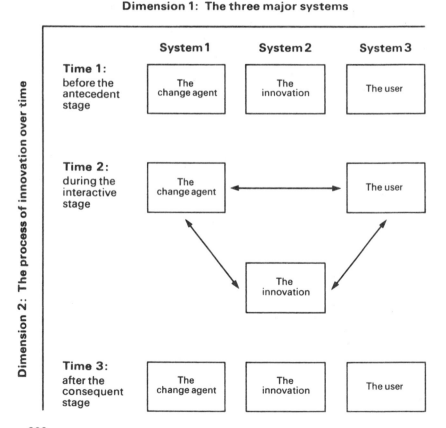

Dimension 1: The three major systems

	System 1	System 2	System 3
Time 1: before the antecedent stage	The change agent	The innovation	The user
Time 2: during the interactive stage	The change agent	The innovation	The user
Time 3: after the consequent stage	The change agent	The innovation	The user

Dimension 2: The process of innovation over time

about and understanding of the innovation process. In the following sections, the four factors are explored in greater detail and then the limitations and strengths of the conceptual framework are considered in relation to an actual, complex innovation.

DIMENSION 1   THE THREE MAJOR SYSTEMS

It is a fundamental assumption of this paper that most changes in education take place in an organizational context. Classrooms, schools, teachers' centres, colleges of education, universities, local education authorities, the Schools Council, the Department of Education and Science, etc., may all be thought of as organizations. Accordingly it should be helpful to look to organization theory as an aid to understanding what happens when these various educational organizations become involved in the process of educational innovation.

Although theorists from different disciplines have conceptualized organizations in a variety of ways, there now appears to be some consensus that, with the qualifications outlined below, general systems theory has much to offer as a means of ordering data from various social sciences, as a model of an organization and its environment and as a powerful heuristic device (Hoyle, 1969). Within this tradition the closed system approach has been criticized because it devalues the importance of external or contextual factors (Eggleston, 1969; Hall, 1972). The common characteristics of open systems include input, throughput, output, differentiation and equifinality (Katz and Kahn, 1964). The open systems approach has been criticized because it introduces more factors for consideration than any researcher or administrator can reasonably be expected to take into account. More fundamentally, it has been criticized because it ignores the motives of individuals (March and Simon, 1958). This has led to the formulation of an alternative approach—the action frame of reference—which argues that systems should not be reified; that they do not determine the behaviour of their members; and that only individuals, and not systems, can have needs and goals or take decisions. Writers in this tradition stress the need to look to the causes as well as the consequences of actions and advocate the use of qualitative research methods, like the analytic case-study, as a means of understanding the part played by individual perceptions, motives and actions in particular organizations (Silverman, 1970; Greenfield 1974 [see 2.1, p. 59]).

The view taken here is that the systems and action frames of reference can be treated as complementary (cf Cohen, 1968; Dawe, 1970). Hence three of the major factors in the innovation process—the change agent, the user and the innovation—have been conceptualized as open systems but particular account is taken of the way in which individuals and groups within those systems construct their own phenomenological worlds and thus affect all aspects of the organization, including its innovation activities.

(i) *The change agent system*

The change agent system is also often referred to in the literature as the change advocate, consultant or innovator and may be analysed in terms similar to that suggested below for the user system, although those dimensions will not always be relevant. The change agent may thus be, for example, an individual teacher, head or adviser, a teachers' centre, a local authority or a national government. It may be a part of the user system (e.g. the head of a school) or outside it (e.g. a project director working with a pilot school). Both its internal and external characteristics may influence and be changed by any particular innovation process. It will probably be perceived differently by the user and innovation systems according to its status, location and the change strategies it adopts.

Perhaps the most important basic characteristic of the change agent as far as innovations are concerned is its *authority relationship* with the user system. This authority may be based either upon administrative status, professional colleagueship, external consultancy, or a combination of the three. For example, in his administrative or inspectorial role a local education authority adviser has the power to assess teachers and schools on behalf of their employers, whereas in his professional advisory role he seeks to advise them as a respected professional colleague. This inevitably causes difficulties and effectively debars most advisers from carrying out the consultancy role described below (Bolam, Smith and Canter, 1975). Several writers have devised change agent role typologies (e.g. Jones, 1969; Hoyle, 1970). Havelock's 1969 linkage role typology distinguishes nine roles: conveyor, consultant, trainer, leader, innovator, defender, knowledge builder, practitioner and user. He recognizes that such roles rarely exist in their pure form and that in the real world any one linkage agent may play several roles simultaneously or sequentially. The typology is nonetheless useful in clarifying the way in which, for example, knowledge about innovations may be transmitted to teachers by various educationists. Thus we can analyse the "linkage" role played by colleagues, heads, local education authority advisers, teachers' centre wardens, etc.

The change agent system may have access to a number of innovation strategies. We may adopt Dalin's (1963) broad concept of strategy as "all available procedures and techniques used by individuals and groups at different levels of the educational system to reach desired objectives". Bennis, Benne and Chin (1969) offer the following well-known typology of innovation strategies:

(a) *Power/coercive* strategies depend upon access to political, legal, administrative and economic resources. Typically they involve the use of legal or administrative power. Governments, local education authorities, inspectors, headteachers and teachers all employ such strategies at some time or other.

(b) *Empirical/rational* strategies assume that men are reasonable and will respond best to rational explanation and demonstration. Typically they involve the use of education, training and publications to disseminate knowledge and research findings.

(c) *Normative/re-educative* strategies assume that effective innovation requires a change of attitudes, relationships, values and skills and, therefore, the activation of forces within the client system. They typically involve a consultant/change agent who works in cooperation with a client system and uses behavioural skills.

Although these categories are helpful for purposes of analysis, they are inevitably somewhat arbitrary and rarely exist in their pure form. For instance, innovations frequently require changes in both curriculum and organization and innovators frequently employ both power/coercive and empirical/rational strategies. At the national level, the major strategy used by governments to disseminate *policy* is probably a power/coercive or political/administrative one. In both centralized and decentralized systems, governments usually attempt to change their educational system's goals and structure by political/administrative means, but such policy directives are probably generally followed by empirical/rational strategies of information dissemination and training; latterly, empirical/rational strategies of research and development often precede policy directives. It seems likely that in most countries the problems of changing role relationships and attitudes have been underestimated when introducing, say, curriculum innovation and that, accordingly, normative/re-educative strategies have rarely been used. At the school level, a typical variant on the power/coercive strategy is one which Hoyle (1970) calls administrative and Dalin (1973) political/administrative. It involves, for instance, the use of various forms of incentive (Pincus, 1973; Becher, 1974).

In considering the *diffusion of knowledge* rather than policy, Havelock (1969) provides many insights into the workings of empirical/rational and normative/re-educative strategies. (Though his work is not, it should be emphasised, very relevant to an understanding of power/coercive strategies.) He seeks to explain the way knowledge diffuses through social systems by formulating four models of the knowledge diffusion and utilization process:

(a) The *social-interaction* model describes a process which is probably historically the earliest approach to knowledge diffusion. Essentially it involves the transmission of knowledge by individuals along informal networks of professional colleagues and friends. It is unsystematic and unplanned, though the original source of the knowledge (or innovation) may nowadays be research-based. Although it may be categorized as an empirical/rational process, it derives its strength from the well-documented fact that we are more likely to be influenced by people whose judgements and opinions we share or respect. In decentralized

395

systems this was, until fairly recently (i.e. until about 1960) in the UK), probably the principal way in which knowledge about innovations in curriculum and pedagogy diffused through the system.

(b) The *research, development and diffusion* (RD and D) model describes a process with several major stages: basic research; applied research; development and testing of prototypes; mass production and packaging; planned mass dissemination; receipt by the user. It is essentially an empirical rational strategy and has come to be widely adopted over the last fifteen to twenty years as the principal approach to curriculum development and innovation. In this context, we can point to the establishment of the various national organizations, e.g. the Schools Council in the UK, Research for Better Schools, Inc., in the USA and the National Council for Innovation in Education in Norway (CERI, 1973, Vol. 1). The RD and D approach has recently provoked increasing scepticism because of its apparent lack of success in bringing about change at the user level (see (iii) below).

(c) The *problem-solver* model is presented by Havelock as a single model but, arguably, consists of three quite distinct sub-models. The first, which we may call the *problem-solving user* model, is based upon empirical/rational assumptions. It describes a user, say a school, which employs a cyclic, problem-solving strategy: felt need; problem diagnosis; search and retrieval of resources, from within and without the school; fabrication of solution; application; evaluation; restart of cycle (cf Stufflebeam *et al.*, 1971). The second sub-model, which we may call the *task consultant* model, is also an empirical rational one, and describes the role of an outside change agent who seeks to help a school with a specific task, e.g. curriculum development. The third sub-model, which we may call the *process consultant* model, is based upon normative/re-educative assumptions and describes the role of a non-directive outside change agent who typically seeks to help a school with its decision-making and problem-solving procedures. Recent suggestions that in-service training should adopt a system-focused approach rather than withdrawing individuals for off-the-job training indicate that the problem-solver perspective is finding increasing support (Hoyle, 1973a). In the UK, consultancy approaches are only just beginning (e.g. Richardson, 1973), but in the USA organization development consultancy is being increasingly used (Schmuck and Miles, 1971), though not uncritically (Chesler and Lohman, 1971).

(d) The *linkage* model is Havelock's attempt to unify and integrate the three preceding models by emphasizing the need for linkage procedures and agencies which both offer resources to users and link them with more remote resource agencies. These resources could consist of curriculum materials from a central agency, consultancy, or information about other users with related experience or interests. In the UK the proposed professional centres provide an obvious example of a linkage agency (Hoyle, 1973a).

Finally, according to Havelock (1969), whatever strategy it adopts, the change agent may have access to several communication modes (e.g. written media, television, etc.), training techniques (e.g. survey feedback, micro-teaching, etc.) and feedback techniques (e.g. evaluative research, observation, etc.).

(ii) The innovation system

Key terms like "change" and "innovation" are often used in different senses in the literature. Following Hoyle (Open University, 1972b) it is, therefore, worth defining "change" as a generic term embracing a family of concepts (e.g. innovation, development, renewal, etc.). We can also distinguish between innovation as being an intentional and deliberate process and change, which can also include accidental or unintentional movements and shifts, though it must be conceded that this distinction is frequently not adhered to in the literature. A quotation from Edmund Burke (1796)—"to innovate is not to reform"—reminds us that there is nothing inherently good about any innovation. Following Esland (Open University, 1972a) therefore, it seems sensible to treat newness or goodness as characteristics which are likely to be perceived differently by the various people involved and, since these perceptions may have a crucial bearing upon the fate of an innovation, to ensure that they are adequately taken into account in studying any particular innovation process. This leads to a fourth preliminary consideration which relates to what I shall call the systemic nature of innovations. Innovations do not exist in any unchanging, objective sense: they are constantly being defined, changed and redefined as a result of experience and the differing perceptions of the people who handle them (cf Shipman et al., 1974). Even within a project team, fundamentally different notions of the "innovation" may coexist. Hence I am suggesting it may be helpful to define an innovation as an open system (cf, Open University, 1972c).

Innovations have been analysed along a number of sub-dimensions with two broad purposes in mind: first, simply as an analytic aid to understanding; second, as an attempt to explain why they succeed or fail. At the most basic level Havelock (1969) distinguishes between four *types of knowledge* from which innovations may be derived: basic knowledge, applied research and development knowledge; practice knowledge; and user feedback knowledge. Hull et. al., (1973) says that innovations come in three broad *forms*; information documents, training materials and an installable system. We can add to this that many of the innovations generated at the user level come up in the form of untested, and often vaguely formulated, ideas. An innovation is usually aimed at a particular *target* system (see (iii) below) but it is important to note that this may differ from the user system which actually takes it up. This may well explain some of the problems encountered by a user system. An innovation will also usually *focus* upon a particular aspect of the target user system; upon, for example, aims, values or perspectives; organization and administration; role relationships; curriculum, pedagogy and evaluation (see Hoyle, 1970; Dalin, 1973).

We now move to a consideration of those factors which appear to have a more direct bearing upon the success or otherwise of an innovation. Most of them are very subjective and are often referred to as perceived characteristics since they are likely to be judged differently both between *and* within the user, change agent and innovation systems. Perhaps the first question likely to be asked by members of a user system about an innovation would be to do with its *relevance*. Their answers would probably be dependent upon the extent to which they considered it to have some *relative advantage* over their current practice (Rogers and Shoemaker, 1971), upon its *competitive strength* as against other innovations or activities requiring scarce resources, and, finally, upon its *feasibility* within a particular organizational context.

The answers to all these questions may well turn upon considerations of the *magnitude* of any particular innovations (Hull *et al.*, 1973). This dimension would include several sub-dimensions: the *scale* of change involved, e.g. one teacher, a department, a school staff, all local education authority staff, etc.; the *degree* fundamental or superficial (see Open University, 1972; Bernstein, 1971); its *trialability/divisibility*, i.e. the extent to which it can be experimented with on a limited basis (Rogers and Shoemaker, 1971). All of these factors will have implications for the innovation's *communicability* which in turn will depend upon its *complexity*, i.e. the extent to which it is perceived as being difficult to understand and use, and its *observability*, i.e. the extent to which others can observe it in action or observe its results and ideas (Rogers and Shoemaker, 1971).

Next, we need to consider a group of *normative* factors. The perceived *compatability* of an innovation with existing values and practices in a user system is, according to Rogers and Shoemaker (1971) a crucial factor. An aspect which is rarely mentioned in the literature is *adaptability*. Research and development agencies understandably deplore the fact that their materials are adapted, but from the user's viewpoint this may be the chief strength of the innovation. The problem is to decide when an adaptation is so significantly different from the original that it ought not to bear the same name. Some innovations may be valued less for their own sake than for the opportunities which they create for the introduction of other, more highly valued innovations (Zaltman and Lin, 1971).

Finally, we come to some fundamentally important factors to do with the *costs and benefits* of an innovation. These can be either actual or perceived, material or non-material, and initial or continuing (Havelock, 1969). Material costs and benefits may relate to finance, output, time, space, personnel, training and equipment. Non-material costs and benefits may relate to organizational and administrative changes, decision-making procedures, psychological discontent or reward, working conditions, career opportunities, status and prestige. Any one or more of these costs and benefits may loom large for a particular innovation and may have a significant impact upon the other factors identified above and, ultimately, upon the fate of the innovation.

(iii) *The user system*

This is the system which is either inventing or adopting an innovation or is being aimed at by a change agent. Several other terms are commonly used in the literature, e.g. receiver, client, adopter, target and consumer. In education the user may be an individual teacher, a departmental team, a school, a local education authority or a national education system. In the past, there has been a tendency for work in the diffusion and adoption tradition to focus upon individuals to the neglect of groups and organizations. There is now general agreement that individuals in educational settings are rarely free to choose whether or not to adopt an innovation since they are constrained by the need to obtain the co-operation and support of professional colleagues, pupils, parents, administrators, etc. (Gross and Bernstein, 1971). It follows that schools, colleges, departments, etc., have to be viewed as open systems if the fate of an innovation is to be understood. There is also considerable agreement amongst writers from several countries (Hoyle, 1970; Fullan, 1972: Dalin, 1973) that the research, development and diffusion strategy of change has made very little impact upon the curricula and organization of schools: hence, attention is now increasingly being paid to the user system's view of the innovation process and its associated problems.

Individuals, whether they be teachers, pupils, parents, administrators, advisers, etc., are likely to respond differently to innovation, Guskin (1969) refers to enduring and difficult-to-change characteristics, like authoritarianism, and to less endurable and easier-to-change characteristics, like a sense of threat. He regards open-mindedness and the use of incentives as important factors but concludes that the most critical variable is the extent to which enduring personality characteristics are aroused by an innovation. "If they are highly activated then the new knowledge will be accepted if it is congruent with them, rejected if it is not. If they are not activated, then congruence to personality is only one of many variables influencing the decision" (pp. 4–39). A number of writers have tried to explain the way in which key individuals respond to innovations in educational settings (e.g. Carlson, 1964, on American school superintendents and Hughes, 1973, on British headmasters [see 4.2, pp. 301–306]). Hoyle (1974 [see 4.3, pp. 314–320]) hypothesizes two ideal-types of teacher—the restricted professional, who is mainly interested, for example, in children and classroom teaching, and the extended professional who is in addition also interested in, for example, attending courses of a theoretical kind and participating in decision-making. Although the typology has not been verified empirically, it does draw attention to the phenomenological world of the teacher as an important variable in the innovation process (cf Jackson, 1968). It seems unlikely, for example, that restricted professionals will respond favourably to the requests of central curriculum developers to adopt their complex technical terms and concepts or want to spend time participating in decision-making.

Significant characteristics of organizations have been summarized by Hall (1972) in terms of their functions and goals (both operative and official): their effectiveness; their general contextual environment (e.g. technological, legal, political, economic, demographic, ecological and social); their specific contextual environment (e.g. the people and organizations with which a school was in frequent contact); their structure (e.g. size, complexity, degree of formalization); their processes (e.g. power and conflict, leadership and decision-making, communications). In this context it is worth recalling Silverman's (1970) critique of the systems perspective: he argues that the way in which individual members of an organization perceive and react to its context, inputs, structure, processes and outputs will vary and that their views and behaviours may well affect both the organization itself and the fate of an innovation.

With specific reference to the key *internal* factors which affect innovations in educational organizations, a number of writers have commented on the problem of defining both goals and outputs (Miles, 1967; Hoyle, 1973b), though this has not deterred advocates of the application of management by objectives (cf Harries, 1974) or of planning, programming and budgeting systems (Eidell and Nagle, 1972) to schools. Several writers, too, have sought to identify the characteristics of innovative organizations in terms of such concepts as organic and mechanistic systems (Burns and Stalker, 1961 [cf. 2.7, p. 148*ff*], open and closed systems (Bernstein, 1971), organizational health Miles, 1965), organizational climate (Halpin, 1966) and knowledge dissemination and utilization in organizations (Havelock, 1969). All of these approaches have considerable heuristic and sensitizing value but they tend to be difficult to operationalize and, especially in a UK context, difficult to use, because of their central focus upon sensitive professional issues. Furthermore, they frequently tell us little either about the way in which particular people and interest groups see each other or about ongoing processes within, say, a school. For instance, they say little about the problems of curriculum development, innovation management or participation at the school level (see Bolam, 1974).

Two recent projects of the Organisation for Economic Co-operation and Development have highlighted many of the issues associated with the user system's perspective of educational innovation. The first was on the creativity of the school which was defined as "its capacity to adopt, adapt, generate or reject innovations" (Nisbet, 1973). This project built upon ideas similar to the problem-solving user concept (Havelock, 1969) in the context of practical international educational experiences. It summarized, and to some extent synthesized, certain key ideas concerning the major internal system variables and also identified some of the key external or *contextual variables*. For example, it stressed the importance of such constraint upon innovation as local education authority regulations, the examination system and the views of parents (cf Taylor *et al.*, 1974). It also pointed to the importance of an external support structure for the innovative school, e.g. teachers' centres, the inspectorate, in-service training, etc. The second OECD project has also focused on these external factors by stressing the importance of training educationists to manage the change process (Dalin, 1973).

DIMENSION 2: THE PROCESS OF INNOVATION OVER TIME

The second dimension of the conceptual framework is a time dimension. A number of writers have stressed the notion of innovation as a dynamic, social process which takes place over a period of time during which the innovation may be redefined and modified as a result of that social process (Gross and Bernstein 1971; Open University, 1972a). This dimension can be analysed in terms of three major stages: the antecedent, interactive and consequent stages (Hull *et al.*, 1973). Of course, these distinctions are somewhat arbitrary but they are useful for analytic purposes.

Time 1: Before: The antecedent stage

It is vital to have a clear understanding of the situation before the innovation process begins (Greiner, 1967; Gross and Bernstein, 1971). At this stage the three systems—change agent, innovation and user—may be said to exist separately, though each may have a relationship with, or opinion of, the other. The relationship between the change agent and user system may be of particular significance, especially if the former is a member (e.g. the head) of the latter (e.g. a school). The characteristics and relationships of the three systems at this stage may be analysed in terms of the dimensions outlined above.

Time 2: During: The interactive stage

During the innovation process the three systems may be said to be in interaction with each other. This period is both the most critical and the most complex as far as understanding the outcome of the innovation is concerned. The general aim should, therefore, be to identify and monitor what precisely happens during this stage (Stufflebeam *et al.*, 1971). The interaction probably begins during the dissemination or awareness stage and is certainly taking place during the trial and implementation stages (Guba and Clark, 1965). Key questions here relate to the change agent's strategies and communication modes and the user system's initial response to them and the innovation.

Time 3: After: The consequent stage

After the completion of the process, the three systems may be said to be separate again and some assessment can then be made of the impact of the interactive experience on all three systems, using the dimensions discussed above. They will almost certainly be different. For example, the teachers in the user system may have changed their teaching methods (though not necessarily as much as, or even in the same direction as, the change agent intended), their opinion of the change agent (who could be their head) and their opinion of the innovation materials. The change agent head may have learned some new techniques in the management of change and be more wary about introducing an innovation without careful planning (cf Gross and Bernstein, 1971). The innovation itself may have undergone some change and may subsequently be radically revised by, say, an external project team. The overriding consideration will probably be the impact upon the user system. It is likely that an evaluative research approach (Weiss, 1972) will provide the most satisfactory mode for handling the complexities and uncertainties of the innovation process, especially with respect to its unintended consequences.

The user system may respond in a variety of ways during both the interactive and consequent stages. First, it may reject the innovation for one or more reasons (Eicholz and Rogers, 1964). Since the worthwhileness or desirability of an innovation is not here being taken for granted, then rejection is not necessarily a cause for concern: on the contrary, it will be an inevitable and desirable fate for some innovations in a creative or problem-solving user system. Second, the user system may resist the innovation for one or more reasons (Watson, 1966) but here, too, this is not necessarily a bad thing: Havelock (1969) argues that "defenders" are essential for the creative or problem-solving system. An important variant on resistance is the "façade phenomenon" (Smith and Keith, 1971) in which those involved (e.g. teachers, heads and inspectors) unintentionally collude to present an image to each other and to the outside world which suggests that an innovation is working successfully although "objective" outsiders report otherwise. Third, the user system may adapt an innovation, usually to the dismay of the outside project team (Macdonald and Ruddock, 1971), though its adaptability may be its chief strength from the user's standpoint. Fourth, the innovation may be fully institutionalized as an integral part of the system (Guba and Clark, 1965). Fifth, an enthusiastic user system may become an advocate of an innovation. Finally, account has also to be taken of the terminal relationship between the change agent and the user system. This may range from cooperation to conflict (Hull et al., 1973).

APPLYING THE CONCEPTUAL FRAMEWORK
In essence, the framework generates four sets of questions about the change agent, innovation and user systems:

1   What are their significant characteristics with respect to any particular innovation process?

2   What were they like before the process began?
3   What happened when they interacted with each other during the process?
4   What were they like at the end of the process?

The ultimate purpose of the framework is to deepen our understanding of any educational innovation but, of course, it falls far short of that aim at present. Perhaps we may best explore its strengths and limitations by applying it to a complex innovation like the Teacher Induction Pilot Schemes (TIPS) project.

The problems of beginning or probationary teachers have been the focus of concern in the profession for some time past. In a recent White Paper (Department of Education and Science, 1972), the Government proposed some quite radical improvements in the procedures for inducting new entrants into the profession. The proposals can be summarized as follows: probationers to receive special help during their first year and to be released for not less than one fifth of their time for in-service training; their overall teaching timetable to be lightened; sufficient replacement teachers to be made available; the profession to play a full part in the induction process; teacher tutors to be appointed in each school and to be trained; professional centres to be established; regional coordinating committees to replace the present university-based area training organizations. As a result of these proposals two official, government-funded pilot schemes were set up in Liverpool and Northumberland and other local authorities were encouraged to set up their own unofficial experiments, in preparation for the introduction of a national scheme. The two official schemes and several unofficial schemes are being monitored on a national basis using the conceptual framework outlined above (Bolam, 1975).

The TIPS project is essentially concerned with the introduction of a massive and complex innovation which in itself consists of several sub-innovations. Each sub-innovation involves a different change agent and user system and each is implemented on a different time-scale. In Table 1 these parameters of the project are explored at four levels and twelve significant sub-innovations are identified. The identification of the significant sub-innovations and their associated change agents and user systems present very real practical and conceptual problems. First, the tasks or sub-innovations have to be identified and then so, too has the person with the responsibility for carrying them through. The system concept can then be used to handle any apparent arbitrariness or overlap. For example, although the LEA adviser is not administratively responsible for the scheme's logistics and finances, he is, of course, interested in them; this can be catered for by interviewing him about his views on the logistics and finance as a member of the administrator-change agent's specific contextual environment (Hall, 1972).

The next step is to relate the four broad questions listed at the begin-

Table 1. The TIPS project: major components

Level	No.	*1 The change system*	*2 The innovation system*	*3 The user system*
National	1	Minister + DES administrators	National scheme: finance and logistics	The national system: LEAs; professional associations; colleges; universities; polytechnics; etc.
	2	Minister + HMI	National scheme: professional aspects	The national system: LEAs; professional associations; colleges; universities; polytechnics; etc.
Local education authority	3	LEA administrator	Finance + logistics of the whole Induction Scheme in the LEA	The LEA: local politicians; administrators; professional associations; schools; colleges; etc.
	4	LEA adviser	Professional aspects of the whole Induction Scheme in the LEA	The LEA: professional associations; schools; colleges; etc.
Professional centre	5	Warden	Creation of a new role: professional centre warden	The professional centre and its catchment area
	6	Director of training course/ programme	Teacher tutor training programme	All teacher tutors in an LEA
	7	Director of induction course/ programme	Probationer induction courses outside school	All probationers in an LEA
School	8	Head	Probationer induction programme inside school: logistic aspects	All staff in a school

9	Teacher tutor	Creation of a new role: teacher tutor	All staff in a school
10	Teacher tutor	Probationer induction courses inside school: professional aspects	All probationers in a school
11	Teacher tutor	Professional induction of one probationer	One probationer
12	One probationer	Creation of a new role: beginning teacher	One probationer

ning of this section to each of the components of the overall innovation. Continuing with the previous example, we first have to study the LEA adviser and his colleagues as a change agent system, the previous induction procedures in the user system and the characteristics of the innovation (cf Department of Education and Science, 1972; Taylor and Dale, 1971; Bolam, 1973). Next the interactive stage has to be carefully monitored. Finally, the impact of the innovation process upon all three has to be evaluated. The analytic case-study method is particularly well-suited to this kind of evaluation, as are such instruments as questionnaires, structured interviews, observation schedules and content analysis of documents. The detailed questions and issues for consideration within each sub-innovation are derived from the fuller version of this conceptual framework as it has been developed for the TIPS project. The final task is to make an assessment of the overall outcome of the total, complex innovation in the light of the findings arising from these studies of the various sub-innovations.

CONCLUSION

This has necessarily been a brief and sketchy account of a tentative conceptual framework for the study of educational innovation. This two-dimensional framework distinguishes between the change agent, the innovation and the user. These three factors are defined as open systems, with internal and external characteristics which interact with, and are changed by, each other during the course of the innovation process. Each factor is analysed along a number of sub-dimensions with two views in mind: to aid description, analysis and understanding, and to attempt to explain why an innovation succeeds or fails. Fuller and more detailed versions of these sub-dimensions have been developed elsewhere. The overall framework has three main purposes: to provide an organizing framework for reviewing the growing literature on educational innovation; to help in understanding the problems, tasks and procedures associated with the management of change; and thus to offer some suggestions as a guide to action.

The conceptual framework's very obvious eclecticism and crudeness probably indicate how far we still are from being able to answer Bennis's (1969) plea for an adequate theory of changing. Although it is hardly comprehensive and is certainly over-simplified, we must also bear in mind the dangers of emulating "economic man" and tackling the impossible task of trying to base our actions on a complete understanding of all relevant information (Simon, 1957). The strengths and limitations of the framework are probably best explored empirically in studies like the one outlined above. In this way, the problems of operationalizing its various dimensions and sub-dimensions can be tackled and both their independence, or otherwise, as variables may be established. Some assessment can then be made of their relative importance in affecting the fate of a particular innovation. The framework is flexible enough to allow for various theoretical perspectives to be adopted within it. Its principal message is that all four factors are relevant to an understanding of the way in which changes do or do not take place. Both students and managers of change should, therefore, beware of either ignoring or underestimating the importance of any one of these factors.

REFERENCES

BECHER, R. A. (1974) *Incentive Systems for Teachers*, Working paper for the "Creativity of the School" Project, Centre for Educational Research and Innovation, C/CS/74,06.

BENNIS, W. G. (1969) "Theory and method in applying behavioural science to planned organisational change", in Bennis, W. G., Benne, K. D. and Chin, R. *The Planning of Change*, Holt Rinehart and Winston (2nd edition).

BENNIS, W. G., BENNE, K. D. and CHIN, R. (1969) *The Planning of Change*, Holt Rinehart and Winston.

BERNSTEIN, B. (1971) "On the classification and framing of knowledge", in Young, M. F. D. *Knowledge and Control*, Collier-Macmillan.

BOLAM, R. (1973) *Induction Programmes for Probationary Teachers*, University of Bristol School of Education.

BOLAM, R. (1974) *Teachers as Innovators*, Organisation for Economic Co-operation and Development, DAS/EID/74,53.

BOLAM, R. (1975) "The Teacher Induction Pilot Schemes (TIPS) Project", *London Educational Review*, **4**, 1.

BOLAM, R., SMITH, G. and CANTER, H. (1975) *The L.E.A. Adviser and Educational Innovation*, University of Bristol School of Education.

BURKE, E. (1796) "A Letter to a Noble Lord".

BURNS, T. and STALKER, J. (1961) *The Management of Innovation*, Tavistock.

CARLSON, R. O. (1964) "School superintendents and the adoption of modern maths: a social structure profile", in Miles, M. B. (ed.) *Innovation in Education*, Bureau of Publications, Teachers College, Columbia University.

CERI (Centre for Educational Research and Innovation) (1973) *Case Studies in Educational Innovation*, Vol. 1, Organisation for Economic Co-operation and Development.

CHESLER, M. and LOHMAN, J. (1971) "Changing schools through student advocacy", in Schmuck, R. and Miles M. (eds.) *Organisation Development in Schools*, National Press Books.

CHIN, R. and DOWNEY, L. (1973) "Changing change: innovating a discipline", in Travers, R. M. W. *Second Handbook of Research on Teaching*, Rand McNally and Co.

COHEN, P. S. (1968) *Modern Social Theory*, Heinemann.

DALIN, P. (1973) *Case Studies in Educational Innovation: Strategies for Innovation in Education*, Organisation for Economic Co-operation and Development.

DALIN, P. (1974) *International Management Training for Educational Change (I.M.T.E.C.)*, paper given at the Third International Intervisitation Programme on Educational Administration, London.

DAWE, A. (1970) "The two sociologies', *British Journal of Sociology*, **21**, 2, pp. 207–18.

DEPARTMENT OF EDUCATION AND SCIENCE (1972) *Education: a Framework for Expansion*, HMSO.

EGGLESTON, J. (1969) "The social context of administration", in Baron, G. and Taylor, W. *Educational Administration and the Social Sciences*, Athlone Press.

EICHOLZ, G. and ROGERS, E. M. (1964) "Resistance to the adoption of audiovisual aids by elementary school teachers: contrasts and similarities to agriculture innovation", in Miles, M. (ed.) *Innovation in Education:* pp. 299–316, Teachers College, Columbia.

EIDELL, T. L. and NAGLE, J. M. (1972) *SPECS: School Planning, Evaluation and Communication System: Second Progress Report*, University of Oregon Centre for the Advanced Study of Educational Administration.

FULLAN, M. (1972) "Overview of the innovative process and the user", *Interchange*, **3**, 2–3, pp. 1–46.

GREENFIELD, T. B. (1974) *Theory in the Study of Organisations and Administrative Structures: a New Perspective*, paper read at the International Intervisitation Programme for Educational Administrators in Bristol.

GREINER, L. E. (1967) "Antecedents of planned organisational change", *Journal of Applied Behavioural Science*, **3**, 1, pp. 51–85.

GROSS, N., GIACQUINTA, J. B. and BERNSTEIN, M. (1971) *Implementing Organisational Innovations*, Harper and Row.

GUBA, E. and CLARK, D. L. (1965) "An examination of potential change roles in education", National Education Association Committee for Study of Instruction Symposium "Innovation in Planning School Curricula", Airielhouse, Virginia, 2–4 Oct. 1965, quoted in *Strategies for Educational Change Newsletter No. 2*, Ohio State University, Oct. 1965.

GUSKIN, A. (1969) "The individual", in Havelock, R. G. *Planning for Innovation*, University of Michigan Institute for Social Research.

HALL, R. H. (1972) *Organisations: Structure and Process*, Prentice Hall.

HALPIN, A. W. (1966) *Theory and Research in Educational Administration*, Macmillan.

HARRIES, T. W. (1974) "M.B.O.: a rational approach and a comparative frameworks approach", *Educational Administration Bulletin*, *3*, 1, pp. 42–50.

HAVELOCK, R. G. (1969) *Planning for Innovation Through Dissemination and Utilization of Knowledge*, Centre for Research on Utilization of Scientific Knowledge, Institute for Social Research.

HOYLE, E. (1969) "Organisational theory and educational administration", in Baron, G. and Taylor, W. *Educational Administration and the Social Sciences*, Athlone Press.

HOYLE, E. (1970) "Planned organizational change in education", *Research in Education 3*.

HOYLE, E. (1973a) "Strategies of curriculum change", in Watkins, R. (ed.) *In-Service Training: Structure and Content*, Ward Lock.

HOYLE, E. (1973b) "The study of schools as organisations", in Butcher, H. J. and Pont, H. (eds.) *Educational Research in Britain III*, University of London Press.

HOYLE, E. (1974) "Professionality, professionalism and control in teaching", *London Educational Review*, **3** (2).

HUGHES, M. G. (1973) "The professional-as-administrator: the case of the secondary school head", *Educational Administration Bulletin*, **2**, 1, pp. 11–23.

HULL, W. L., KESTER, R. J. and MARTIN, W. B. (1973) *A Conceptual Framework for the Diffusion of Innovations in Vocational and Technical Education*, The Center for Vocational and Technical Education, Ohio State University.

JACKSON, P. W. (1968) *Life in Classrooms*, Holt Rinehart and Winston.

JONES, G. N. (1969) *Planned Organisational Change*, Routledge and Kegan Paul.

KATZ, D. and KAHN, R. L. (1964) *The Social Psychology of Organisations*, Wiley.

MACDONALD, B. and RUDDOCK, J. (1971) "Curriculum research and development projects: barriers to success", *British Journal of Educational Psychology*, **41**, 2.

MARCH, J. G. and SIMON, H. A. (1958) *Organisations*, Wiley.

MILES, M. B. (1965) "Planned change and organisational health: figure and ground", in Carlson, R. O. (ed.) *Change Processes in the Public*

Schools, University of Oregon, Center for the Advanced Study of Educational Administration.

MILES, M. B. (1967) "Some properties of schools as social systems", in Watson, G. *Change in School Systems*, National Training Laboratories, National Education Association.

NISBET, J. (1973) *Strengthening the Creativity of the School*, working paper for the "Creativity of the School" Project, CERI/CD(73)7. Organisation for Economic Co-operation and Development.

OPEN UNIVERSITY, THE (1972a) E282 *School and Society*, Unit 12 *Innovation in the School*, The Open University Press.

OPEN UNIVERSITY, THE (1972b) E283 *The Curriculum: Context, Design and Development*, Unit 13 *Facing the Difficulties*, The Open University Press.

OPEN UNIVERSITY, THE (1972c) E283 *The Curriculum: Context, Design and Development*, Unit 14 *Perspectives on Innovation*, Section 4 *Geography 14–18: A Framework for Development*, The Open University Press (modified version of a paper by John Reynolds, Research Assistant, Schools Council 14–18 Project).

PINCUS, J. (1973) "Incentives for innovation in the public schools", *Review of Educational Research*, **44**, 1, pp. 113–43.

RICHARDSON, E. (1973) *The Teacher, the School and the Task of Management*, Heinemann Educational.

ROGERS, E. M. and SHOEMAKER, F. F. (1971) *Communication of Innovations: A Cross-Cultural Approach*, Collier-Macmillan.

SCHMUCK, R. A. and MILES, M. (1971) *Organization Development in Schools*, National Press Books.

SHIPMAN, M. D., BOLAM, D. and JENKINS, D. (1974) *Inside a Curriculum Project*, Methen.

SILVERMAN, D. (1970) *The Theory of Organisations*, Heinemann.

SIMON, H. A. (1957) *Administrative Behaviour*, Macmillan.

SMITH, L. and KEITH, P. (1971) *Anatomy of Educational Innovation: An Organizational Analysis of an Elementary School*, Wiley.

STUFFLEBEAM, D. *et al.* (1971) *Educational Evaluation and Decision Making*, F. E. Peacock.

TAYLOR, P. H., REID, W. A., HOLLEY, J. B. and EXON, G. (1974) *Purpose, Power and Constraint in the Primary School Curriculum*, Macmillan Educational.

TAYLOR, J. K. and DALE, I. R. (1971) *A Survey of Teachers in Their First Year of Service*, University of Bristol School of Education Research Unit.

WATSON, G. (1966) "Resistance to change", in Watson, G. (ed.), *Concepts for Social Change*, Cooperative Project for Educational Development Series, Volume 1, National Training Laboratories.

WEISS, C. H. (1972) *Evaluation Research—Methods for Assessing Program Effectiveness*, Methods of Social Science Series, Prentice Hall.

ZALTMAN, G. and LIN, N. (1971) "On the nature of innovations", *American Behavioural Scientist*, **14**, pp. 651–73.

O

INDEX

Index

Ability grouping, research and, 90; relationship to pupil subcultures, 93, 94; mixed, 101

Action research, 91; application to educational organizations, 366, 371, 376; frame of reference and organizational theory, 393; and human interaction at micro- and macro-levels, 374–5; and alternative to system approach, 377

Action schema, classification of components, 23–4, 25, 31; "action", 23, 27; "outcome", 23–4; "action/outcome relationships", 24, 27; independent variables, 24, 27; integration of additional information, 30

Actions and outcomes, distinction between real-world and institutional, 26; and decision making process, 26

Administration, changing nature, 5–6, 7–8; demise of its mystique, 6–7; responsibility for decisions, 9; influence of management, 12; and substantive activities of organizations, 14–15; measures degrees of success, 15; common bureaucratic pattern, 16, 17, 109–11; accomplishment of desired objectives, 17; and pursuit of leisure, 18; process in decision making, 28, 29, 30; need for a focus in dealing with problems, 47; movement to "dis-establish" existing systems, 53–4; claims for scientific and professional sta-

tus, 60; under patriarchal authority, 111–12; under estate system, 112; under patrimonial rule, 113, definition of, 133, 134; as an open sub-system, 136

Administration, academic, 8–10

Administration, academic (US), becomes more centralized and authoritarian, 37, 42–3; student /faculty distrust, 39–40; use of decision making process, 41; high level joint selection committees, 42, 43; rotation of administratators, 42; role of information technology expert, 43

Administration, educational, distinguished from general, 3, 14, 15–18; a model for other organizations, 14, 18; general and informal functions, 15; joins the "cult of efficiency", 15; imprecise evaluation of success, 15–16; and education for leisure, 16–18; formulation of goals, 17; and the intrinsically valuable, 18; education for its professional management, 18–19, 60–1, 127; provision of optimum conditions for intellectual life, 19; concept as a professional and social science, 60–2; phenomenological view, 62; basis of ideological conflict, 62; movement towards international study, 76; development of a new more sophisticated approach, 86, 89–90; compared with organizational

413

tenance of order, 116; notion of "reference groups", 120–1; of office and of expertise, 121; of headmasters (teachers' evaluation), 207; and behaviour to subordinates, 304; "personal" and "positional", 364n7

Autonomy, central dimension of schools, 88, 94, 103; applied to teachers, 315, see also Decision making

Bacon, Sir Francis, 50–1

Barnard, Chester, 61; systems theory of organizations, 73–4; notion of "states of tension", 74; and managerial loyalty, 150; and executive functions, 302

Baron, G., legacy of "headmaster tradition", 285, 287–99, 303

Beckhard, Richard, definition of OD, 382

Behavioural theories, and human aspects of organizational life, 7, 69, 89, 239, 249; and changing nature of administrative decision, 7–8; and industrialization, 50, 52; and leadership, 161, 195; "appropriateness" for certain roles, 202; nomothetic dimension within organizations, 202, 203; value of "models", 256; and management in education, 285; divorce between opportunist-innovatory and organized progressivism, 330; and OD, 382, 383ff

Belasco, J. S. and Alutto, J. A., and job satisfaction, 159, 220ff

Bennis, W. G., "Future of the Social Sciences", 18, 19n3

Bernstein, B., implications of new trends in education, 316, 319, 321–2; relationship between

"open school" and the organic society, 328; and opportunist orientated curricula, 330

Black Papers, 324, 326, 327, 338n7

Blake, R., two approaches to executive leadership, 189, 195

Blau, P. M. and Scott, W. R., (quoted), on sources of professional control, 123

Board of Education, 292; its officials, 293; and classroom and school independence, 293, 294; Regulations for Secondary Schools, 299n8, 303

Brown, R. G. S., (quoted), "search activity" in decision making, 29–30

Budgetary systems, development of sophisticated methods, 7; and contents of management, 12

Bureaucracy, substitute of experience for mystique, 6–7; pattern of administration, 16; (US) need for "existentialist executives", 47; systems analysts and, 66; power outside organizations, 73; (US) and school counselling, 101–2; North American operationalization concept, 103; a form of legal authority, 109–10, 119; multiplication in all power structures, 111; and industrialism, 150–1; defects of committee system, 156; and school executives, 305

Burnham, Peter S., role theory and educational administration, 159, 201–15

Burnham's Theory, 11

Burns, Tom, survival of irrelevant systems, 57; industrial legacy, 285

Business, and management infor-

flicting views, 63–6; systems analysis, 66; redirection of training of administrators, 76–7; measuring of term "organization", 116; concept of role, 201, 202; and educational innovation, 393

Organizations, 7, 14, 16; input and output models, 17, 49; present day crisis, 46, 47, 52; total inclusion of workers, 48–9; need for new concepts, 53, 54; move towards non-hierarchical and client orientated, 53–4; assumed reality, 59, 66, 74–5; individual adaptation to universal forms, 60, 62, 63; phenomenological view, 62–3, 65, 67, 69, 72, 76; natural system and human invention view of their reality, 63–5; expressions of diverse human ideologies, 72, 74, 75; access to power, 75; institutional school of analysis, 77, 201; three-dimensional behaviour interaction (nomothetic, idiographic, group-climate intention), 89; definitions, 118–19, 133–4; informal interaction characteristics, 119–20; achievement of objectives by coercion, 189; idiographic dimension, 202; relevance of trust, 229–30, 383; executive span of control, 243; areas of conflict, 253, 256; seen as collective human beings, 253–4; individual personifications, 254, 258; nature of vested interest, 255, 258; concept of membership, 255–7, 259; personal and interpersonal psychology, 262; status ordering and conflict, 268; educational and industrial similarities, 382; require-

ments for a healthy climate, 383; various conceptualizations, 393; summary of significant characteristics, 400

Organizations, educational, environmental and human inputs, 220; importance of member satisfaction, 220, 228, 230; value of continuance of service, 223, 228; and younger group of teachers, 230; need for management strategy, 230; differentiated from industrial, 367, 371; application of theoretical and empirical studies, 367; methodology, 372

Organizations, industrial (formal), interaction with individual structures, 233, 236–7; basic properties, 236ff, 249; essential rationality, 236, 242; creation of a logically-ordered world, 237–9; importance of scientific management, 238–9; traditional assumptions concerning, 239–44, 246; task (work) specialization, 240–1, 243, 246; hierarchical structure, 241–2, 246; technically competent leadership, 242; effect of competitive situations, 242–3; unity of direction, 243, 250n13; impact on individuals, 244–7; employment of the mentally retarded, 245–6; inter-subordinate hostility, 247–8; management/employee interactive behaviour, 248; value of departmental differentiation, 276

Organizations initiating change, 132ff; mechanism, 134; systems theory, 134–6; major impulses (from the outside, insiders, the supra-system), 137–40; changing the adminis-

345, 352, 356–7; the head as chief executive, 345; effecting new policies, 345–6; staff/pupil role conceptions, 346; weight of tradition and conservatism, 346; concept of social control, 346–7, 349–50, 351; appointment of prefects and monitors, 346–7, 350, 357–9; maintenance of discipline, 346–7; corrective action in response to deviance, 347, 357; rewards and penalties, 347, 349–50, 351, 357–8; tension management, 347–8, 357, 358, 359; power of pupil social system, 348, 356, 358; efficiency of communication, 348; rules of conduct, 348–9, 360, 362–3; hierarchical and status bearing positions, 350, 354, 357; forms of learning (cognitive, academic, moral), 351–4, 354–6; organized games, 352, 354, 356–7, 360, 361, 362; basis of outside assessments, 352, 353; non-teaching staff, 353; house systems, 354; school assemblies, 354, 361–2; pupil controlled groups, 354–9; concept of cohesiveness, 359–62; ritual and ceremony, 360–1, 363; inter-school contests, 361–2; two types of positional authority, 362–3

Schools Inquiry Commission (1868), 289, 291

Scotland, 288, 298n4

Simon, H. A., 61; (quoted), on organizations, 236–7; and span-of-control principle, 244

Silverman, D., contributions to organizational theories, 366, 368, 369, 371–2, 374–5; "Methodology and Meaning", 378n7; and systems perspective, 400

Smith, Adam, 148, 149

Social reality, alternative systems of interpretation (natural and human invention), 63–6, 69; philosophical bases, 64, 66–7; role of social sciences, 64, 67–9, 80; method of understanding, 64, 69–70; theory, 64, 68–9, 70–2; research, 64, 70–2, 77; methodology 64, 68, 70–2, 77; society, 64, 72–4; organizations, 64, 65, 72–4, 75; organizational pathologies, 65, 74–5; prescriptions for curing ills, 65, 74–5; phenomenonological perspectives, 66–7, 67–8, 69; Kantian influence, 66–7; functional analysis, 69; battle for conflicting interpretations, 72–3; in schools, 77; Silverman's theories, 359

Social science, scientists, and organizations, 60–1; and educational administration, 61–2, 89–90, 215; and a planned school change, 91; and an ultimate social reality, 64, 68–9; quantophrenia, 71–2; (us) and role theory, 201, 215

Social workers, school, 100, 309

Sociology, sociologists, academic image of man, 48; influence of phenomenology, 62; and organizational analysis, 86, 266; and the school, 86–7, 315, 321, 322, 338n5, 342, 366; discovering theory from data, 87; of education, 89–90; consultancy role, 91; concept of authority, 103; use of term "charisma", 115

Socrates, 50–1

Spain, and management activity, 11–12

Spencer, Herbert, 46